REASON, EXPERIENCE AND THE MORAL LIFE:

Ethical Absolutism and Relativism in Kant and Dewey

Benjamin S. Llamzon

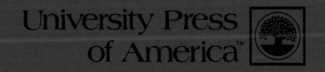

University Press of America™

REASON, EXPERIENCE AND THE MORAL LIFE:

Ethical Absolutism and Relativism in Kant and Dewey

Benjamin S. Llamzon

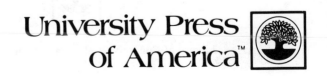

University Press of America™

Copyright © 1978 by

University Press of America™

division of

R.F. Publishing, Inc.

4710 Auth Place, S.E., Washington, D.C. 20023

ISBN: 0-8191-0534-1

Library of Congress Catalog Card Number: 78-58444

REASON, EXPERIENCE AND THE MORAL LIFE
(Ethical Absolutism and Relativism in Kant and Dewey)

By Benjamin S. Llamzon

"We cannot too much or too often repeat our warning against this lax and even mean habit of thought which seeks for its principle among empirical motives and laws; for human reason in its weariness is glad to rest on this pillow, and in a dream of sweet illusions (in which, instead of Juno, it embraces a cloud) it substitutes for morality a bastard, patched up from limbs of various derivation, which looks like anything one chooses to see in it; only not like virtue to one who has once beheld her in her true form. To behold virtue in her proper form is nothing else but to contemplate morality stripped of all admixture of sensible things." Kant, *Fundamental Principles of the Metaphysic of Morals.*

"The notion that valuations do not exist in empirical fact, and that therefore value considerations have to be imported from a source outside experience is one of the most curious beliefs the mind of man has ever entertained." Dewey, *Theory of Valuation.*

TABLE OF CONTENTS

Preface, I-IV

Part I: KANT

1. Background: Kant's Life and Theory of Knowledge, 1-16.
The Problem, 3-9; Space and Time, 9-11; Understanding, 11-14; Reason, 14-16; Key to Abbreviations, 17.

2. Fundamental Principles of Morals, 18-43.
Point of Departure, 19-22; The Categorical Imperative, 22-24; Questions on Inconsistency, 24-25; Back to Basis for Morals, 25-26; Toward the Moral Ought, 26-33; Two Aspects of Will, 33-36; Holy and Virtuous Wills, 36-37; Heteronomous Moral Theories, 37-39; Man the Inhabitant of Two Worlds, 39-42; Freedom Not Contradictory, 42-43.

3. Kant's Ethics: A Closer Look, 44-85.
The fact of Moral Constraint, 45-49; Characteristics of Moral Constraint, 49-52; The Moral Imperative as Categorical, 52-68; Universalizability: The Moral Norm, 69-70; Duty, 70-73; The Four Examples, 73-79; Respect, 79-85.

4. Implications, 86-100.
A Kingdom of Ends, 86-88; Virtue and Immortality, 88-90; Happiness and the Existence of God, 91-98; Conclusion, 99-100.

Part II: DEWEY

1. A Dramatization, 101-108.

2. Philosophical Reconstruction, 109-125.
Romance, Poetry and Symbols, 109-111; "Higher" and "Lower" Knowledges and Classes, 111-112; Separation of Metaphysics, 113-120; The Advent of Science, 120-126; Key to abbreviations, 126.

3. Instrumentalism, 127-140.
Setting, 127-128; Instrumentalism, 128-140.

4. Meliorism, 141-162.
A Philosophical Landmark, 141-143; Recourse to Science, 143-145; Ethics and Satisfaction, 146-147; Ends-in-view, 147-151; Means-Ends-Continuum, 151-155; Religion, 155-162.

5. Theory of the Moral Life, 163-205.
Against Kant, 163-165; Counter-Considerations, 165-168; Moral Theory as Centered on Ends, 168-179; Moral Claims, 179-182; Approbation: The Standard and Virtue, 182-187; Unity of Virtues, 187-189; Moral Judgements, 189-195; The Moral Self, 195-204; Summary, 204-205.

Concluding Remarks, 206-230.
Acknowledgements; Key to Abbreviations, 231.

Notes, 232-240.

Index, 241- 250.

PREFACE

It is puzzling, at first to come across Immanuel Kant and John Dewey both laying claims to having accomplished the Copernican revolution in philosophy. Their thoughts seem poles apart. They seem, to use an earlier expression, different in kind, not merely in degree. In ethics, which is my concern in this book, Kant reared a theory from pure reason alone, with experience and all its empirical load firmly (if not always neatly) excised away. Dewey, on the other hand, intermingled ethical considerations with all of his philosophy which was a veritable *organiza-tion* of sheer experience from its matrix to all its various peripheries. What two viewpoints can be more obviously antithetical? Yet, the fact that both can lay claim finally to the accomplishment of the same historical feat in the long chronicle of philosophy warns against any quick conclusions about their radical differences.

This piece of philosophical curiosity started me on the way, some years back, to writing this book. It occured to me that the two might just possibly be the very philosophers who could bring off an ethics course in college. I was looking for materials to show ethical absolutism and relativism at their best and purest forms. For I had slowly become convinced then, as I am still now, that a substantial course in ethics should dig deep and long into the perennial issues of absolutism and relativism. This is said, of course, against the temporal inexorabilities which hem in all the aims of education within a university, namely, the alloted time for each course (one semester in my case.) No one can take in all or even half the number of philosophers one would like to within that span of time and still do a respectable job of teaching. Severe editing has to be done. That was clear. The issues I preferred to spend the time on were likewise clear. And the more I myself pursued the ethical doctrines of Kant and Dewey, the more I became convinced that they were exactly the two philosophical models who suited my purpose.

Kant knew Aristotle and went beyond him. He was also an expert in typically English theories in ethics. The nice things he wrote about their affinity to virtue through sentiment, amidst his diatribes against those who base ethics on other empirical content, shows he always had a "fellow-feeling" for them. Lastly, he was familiar with Scriptures. The ethical absolutism he rears from all these is formidable indeed.

On the other side, it is my belief that Dewey represents ethical relativism (or experiential ethics) at its best. From the ancients to the mediaevals it had always been a philosophical dogma that experience is shot through and through with contingency; that from purely changeable being and truths of fact it is impossible to draw truths universal, necessary, eternal, etc. How then do you hold pure experience in your two hands, as it were, and declare that this is all there is to reality, at the same time that you seriously philosophize that ongoing material into a stable and enduring ethical theory? The feat seemed impossible. It was Dewey's genius to have seen that the instrumental nature of thought as crystallized in science was the breakthrough philosophy had so long needed to recover

I

its credibility. From science as the paragon of human knowledge he was able to fashion what I consider a relativistic ethics that stands as a great turning point in the history of philosophy, as he himself claims.

Thus both Kant and Dewey claim to have effected Copernican revolutions through their philosophical systems (if that is the word for Dewey) and of course Dewey was thoroughly familiar with Kant. The ethical dialectic between the two is a very natural one as I hope to show in the following pages. Perhaps the point should also get across that while the two are admittedly at an irreconcilable distance from one another in their ethical theories and philosophical outlooks, still on a closer look they came quite near each other after all.

If at the end of the two parts of this book the student comes out somewhat perplexed at the paradoxical distance and closeness of Kantian absolutism and Deweyite relativism, that is precisely the condition of mind I aim at so as to move him toward his own conclusions, and hopefully, toward an ethical synthesis no matter how inchoate. To serve this aim, I have offered my own concluding remarks as possible guides toward a "wholing" ethics that at once accepts absolutes *and* leaves them *really open* as to experiential content and conclusions. By *really open* I mean not just lip-service pretensions that are merely adopted to make immoveable dogmas look respectable. In that section, I suggest that what Kant emphasizes (the act itself and motive) and what Dewey focused on (the self and consequences) be all three *wholed* continuously with one's personal situation when actually making a moral decision. Anyone alive knows the difference between merely speculating on moral conclusions and actually making a decision which affects one's existence in depth and permanently. One answers to nothing in the former---it is mere game playing. In the latter one demands judgements to live by in some sort of bearable and durable peace. Even those who have never read St. Augustine will agree, presumably, that qualified, not absolute peace is all that we can have while alive. And to enrich the mind with some of the materials necessary and useful for coming to terms, to a settlement, with one's self---this I consider an essential part of the role of an ethics teacher.

Everything I have labored for and written in this book, therefore, was done with only one objective in mind: to make the materials on Kant's and Dewey's ethics, as well as my own thoughts on them, clear and interesting to students. No, that is not quite accurate---to *my* students. "Students" is an abstraction. For many semesters I have used the materials now compressed in this book. The students whose interest I wanted to catch and whose intellects I wanted to stimulate were actual individuals. Many times they have gladdened me, sometimes they have annoyed me. But always their faces were in my imagination and memory, as I think any reader of these pages will see.

It is against this pedagogical intent that I would like this book measured. Does it in fact serve to open up the student's consciousness to the possibility that there might be ethical absolutes as Kant claims? Does it prepare and spur the students' curiosity to read Kant and Dewey directly in the paperbacks referred to (which the professor can easily order from the respective publishers) instead of frightening them away by formidable sounding titles in a foreign tongue available only to profes-

II

sionals in specialized libraries? Does it ignite the natural dialectic of the mind as it presents what I consider the strongest opposition and position against Kant, namely, Dewey's advocacy of science and reflective experience as constituting the core of all ethics? And in the end, gripped by this tension between pure reason and experience, between ethical absolutism and relativism, is the student pressured into fashioning the beginnings of his moral framework and principles, something he can work at and improve for the rest of his life? If the book helps toward this objective, all other considerations are for me peripheral. Were this not so, failure of nerve would have gotten the better of this manuscript. It would have shared the fate of some excellent works I know from teacherly hands and minds better than mine. Exaggerated fastidiousness over endless scholarly minutiae finally aborted their projects. All because concern had been distracted away from the classroom which had been their life-giving locus in the first place and all along.

A glance at the chapter headings should point up this pedagogical objective. I cannot forget an August morning when a student boarded a bus and sat beside me memorizing a sheet of definitions as we sped along lovely Lake Shore Drive in Chicago. I found out she was preparing for a test after a week of Whitehead's *Process and Reality*---and with only three more weeks to go on that book! The distress in her voice and the glazed look in her eyes as most of us blinked from the dazzling reflection of the sun on the lake waters told the whole story. I do not believe one can plunge a sophomore student *in medias res* in Kant's ethics, or even Dewey's, and bring it off successfully. One would be forever interrupting lectures to go back and explain prior conceptual structures and premises. Consequently, I have decided to make haste slowly by easing the student into each philosopher's center of thought, chapter by chapter. The beginning chapter of each part gives an overall view of the grounds, as it were, with a deep pool at the center. Next comes an invitation to dip one's toes in the waters and slowly wade in. After that plunges into by then familiar waters. The same key concepts are usually treated from chapter to chapter, but with increasing details of depth and extensiveness. In philosophical awakening, at any rate, it seems that the natural motion of the mind is still from simplicity to complexity---a method better, in any case, than the glazed-eye producing shock of instant complexity.

While I wrote most of this book in my home in Evanston, Illinois, I am putting the final touches here in Rome, Italy, where I am presently on a teaching stint for two semesters. I do not have with me the resources I had back home. I have also had to make a major personal adjustment. Consequently, I well realize how portions of the manuscript can still stand yet another round of revisions and improvements. However, another consideration here in Rome has become decisive. The University Press of America publishes by photocopying the manuscript as submitted, and only while I am in Rome do I have the opportunity of personally overseeing the typesetting of my pages under favorable terms. Everything points to *now* as the appointed time to bring this work to an end and move it out to daylight. I take this risk then happily on the basis of the objective I explained above. Out of the interplay between *la forza del destino* and the many wills involved in the publication of this book, may the result redound to the profit of my student readers.

III

My own personal inclination and temperament go against giving merely *general* thanks to those who have helped me along the way in the production of this book. However, the imperatives of interpersonal delicacy provide no other alternative. Much of their help was in the form of encouragement, supportive friendship and the boosting of a fluctuating morale (which is really just a synonym for the birth pangs of a book). I shall therefore make the briefest mention possible.

In Chicago: Dr. Thomas Wren; Sr. Louise French, B.V.M.; Dr. and Mrs. Gerald Kreyche; Fathers David Hassel, S.J. and Walter Krolikowski, S.J.; Dr. John Reed; Dr. Mary Schaldenbrand; David and Sandy Horn.

In Cuernavaca, Mexico: the Staff at CIDOC; the Sisters at the Guest House of the Carmelite Convent.

In Rome: Sr. Rita Stalzer; Dr. John Nicholson; John and Kay Felice; Noëllvie Rice; Beverley Bishop; Carlo Cancrini; Ernesto Cimbalo; Ornella Faina; Stefano Gamboni; Giuseppe De Masi.

At Loyola, I thank the University for a semester's leave to work on this project; Dr. Ronald Walker, College Dean, for readily granting generous secretarial help through Mrs. Merle Lufen; Dr. Kenneth Thompson, Jr., Philosophy Chairman, for a teaching schedule which enabled me to face a blank sheet on the typewriter with diminished dread. Finally, I thank James Lyons, editor, for patiently moving back the deadline for me time and again. It goes without saying that all errors and shortcomings that may be in this book are to be attributed only to me.

Benjamin S. Llamzon
Professor, Philosophy
Loyola University of Chicago
Rome, Italy
Easter, 1978

1

BACKGROUND

Immanuel Kant (1724-1804) was born, went to school, taught and died in the East Prussian town of Königsberg, Germany. His family was Pietist, a kind of Protestantism which generally stressed ethics more than dogmatic theological doctrines, and which laid great store on individual conscience. From the time of his infancy an indelible impression was made upon Kant's sensitive consciousness by the exemplary life of "duty" his mother led amidst a materially poor life. On the other hand, he also experienced, during his early schooling, Protestantism at its worst: the sort that deemed external acts of piety worth more than undemonstrative sincerity.[1]

As may be expected of a man who stayed most of his life in the very same place where he was born, Kant engaged for the most part in reading, thinking and lecturing. Later, he wrote philosophy books. He was fifty-seven by the time his first *Critique* was published, and only one of his books ever became "controversial." His unexciting and routine life earned him what someone has called "the greyness of his popular reputation."[2] As L.W. Beck puts it:"Most people who know nothing else of Kant do know that the housewives of Königsberg used to set their clocks by the regular afternoon walk he took, and that his life was said to pass like the most regular of verbs."[3] Yet, one need only read Kant to see for himself what a rich and exciting experience it must have been both for his students and those people of Königsberg he met to have had the opportunity to chat with him on those afternoon walks.

Though the fact is not always noted, we know that in his earlier works Kant followed the British moralists on the matter of founding morality on "feeling."[4] And in a page designed to offset the popular caricatures of Kant as an intellectual machine devoid of spontaneity and heart, H.J. Paton shows how Kant used to be known as *"der schöene Magister."* It is said that he was so good at cards that he gave them up because his partners were too slow for him: also, that he was as fond of ladies as they were of him. Though he ate only one meal a day, it was usually with guests. To his dying day before his attending physician, he was the embodiment of humaneness and courtesy. Yet, as Paton writes:"And when in later middle age, he had been appointed to a full professorship, the wiseacres could still shake their heads and say that he was too much of a dilettante to be much good at philosophy."[5]

Some of Kant's writings we should at least know the titles of are: *Critique of Pure Reason* (1781 first edition *A*, and second edition *B*, 1787); *Prolegomena to Any Future Metaphysics*, (1783); *Fundamental Principles of the Metaphysic of Morals*, (1785); *Critique of Practical Reason*, (1788); *Critique of* Judgement, (1790); *Religion Within the Limits of Reason Alone*, (1793).

Notice how the *Fundamental Principles of the Metaphysic of Morals* and his second critique on Practical Reason (i.e.morals) were published four and six years after his first work which had dealt with Theoretical Reason. Since the problems he raised and tried to solve in his ethical writings arose directly out of the system of knowledge he had presented in his first critique, we cannot hope to understand his theory of morals without in some way getting at least a general idea of his theory of knowledge. Many technical expressions which he does not pause to explain in his later works have to be learned either from that first critique or its shorter version, *Prolegomena to Any Future Metaphysics*. Without some knowledge of these technical terms we could not make much sense out of Kant's ethical writings. However, a scholarly mastery of their meanings is not really necessary to appreciate the points Kant makes as he applies those terms in his ethics. This is why some summary of his theory of knowledge is usually found in any book which sets forth his moral theory. What follows is yet one more of such summaries based on Kant's own synopsis.

One of the stories (apocryphal or not) told of the young Kant was that he supported himself by playing billiards.[6] However that may be, Kant himself tells us he read and greatly admired the writings of the Scottish philosopher, David Hume, (1711-76).[7] Now Hume had used billiard balls to illustrate his theory of causality.[8] In his early years, Kant also had studied the rationalism of W. Leibniz (1646-1716) and C. Wolff (1679-1754) with their constant stress on the *necessary* character of truth, a necessity that seemed to be from within the mind itself. There is nothing necessary, they pointed out, about the many fleeting sense impressions which beset us from every side. On the other hand, even these rationalists themselves in effect admitted an empirical grounding of truths when they provided for "empirical" branches whenever they outlined their divisions of human knowledge. Obviously then, empirical knowledge could not be dismissed in favor of exclusively truths from within the mind. Truth was rather an interplay between rationalism and empiricism.

Furthermore, Kant followed his mentor Christian Crusius in taking Newtonian Physics[9] as a decisively successful instance of genuine knowledge, one based on the method of *analysis* instead of mathematical *synthesis*[10] (as mathematics was understood before Kant, v.g. in Galileo who held that experiments serve only to verify and illustrate previously worked out mathematical truths). Newtonian concepts are formulated from sense experiences instead of from ideal objects (these latter being the starting points of rationalistic philosophy and pure mathematics then). It is one thing to start with definitions and then through sheer mental analysis rigorously *deduce* one consequence after another from that initial idea until one has progressed to a whole "system," as one finds rationalists like Descartes, Spinoza, Leibniz, *et al.* doing. Kant calls this the "progressive" method. It is another thing to concede the empirical starting points of knowledge, *and then construct* analytically and formulate general laws of nature from sense observations and experiments, as Newton and his followers had done in natural science. Or, like Kant, to uncover step by step the ultimate ground which makes the synthetic proposition at hand possible.[11] Clearly, generalization and necessity as well as empirical observations entered into the Newtonian account of nature, and indeed into mathematics, as Kant discovered.[12]

The Problem

Aristotle observed long ago that philosophy starts with wonder. And it was Kant's wonder at this precise point which gave rise eventually to his whole system of philosophy. He wondered how it was that Newtonian knowledge was at all possible. If Newton started with sense impressions which are obviously manifold and disorganized, how did he end up, after analysis, in rule-determined accounts of sense data? The problem is simply that no generalization seemed possible out of mere sensations. Sensations are manifold and amorphous. How is it possible for the mind, from such empirical and disconnected beginnings, to terminate in an orderly and coherent account of nature such as one finds in Newton's Physics?[13] What relations or conditions obtain between the world around us, as it appears to us through sensation (phenomena), and our minds which obviously are able to organize and formulate these phenomena into Laws of Nature? If not everything valid in knowledge can be attributed to mind on the one hand, nor on the other hand everything attributed to the mere sense manifold (as empiricists would have us do), what then are the limits of each claim as both finally merge into a coherently organized system of knowledge? This was the tremendous problem which Kant sums up in his now famous question: "How is a synthetic a priori proposition possible?"[14] In brief, Newton's laws of nature were synthetic a priori propositions. How were they possible? What theory of knowledge can successfully account for and justify those propositions in a coherently worked out system of thought? Obviously, this is a theoretical question. Instead of doing or producing anything, one simply wishes to understand something already there and effectively functioning (scl. Newtonian Physics). One wishes to understand as precisely as possible the intricate workings and products of the human mind which brought forth Newton's Physics.

The terms "synthetic" and "analytic" may be a bit confusing. By way of clarification, let us quickly note that when we said mathematics (especially as conceived before Kant) employs the "synthetic"[15] while the experimental sciences with their pivot on sense observations employed the

3

"analytic" method, we were talking precisely of that, the analytic *method* (or what Kant sometimes called the "regressive" method) as distinguished from *propositions. Methods* of inquiry terminate in *propositions.* Thus when applied to propositions, the meanings of the terms "synthetic" and "analytic" are reversed from their methodical meanings.[16] We *synthesize* any proposition which originates from sense observations. Newton's laws of motion are synthetic or "expansive" in this sense. So are statements like, "I am typing now;" "You are there infront of me wearing a maroon sweater," etc. In a word, propositions are synthetic whose predicates are not logically included in the concept of the subject but grasped directly through sense perception. No necessity is found in the connection here between subject and predicate, v.g. I and my typing. By contrast, we "analyze" propositions when we draw a predicate out of our very concept of a subject term in an "explicative" way. By merely thinking out the meaning of the subject, we conclude that a certain predicate *necessarily* belongs to it.[17] It is an analytic proposition, for instance, to say, "The whole is greater than anyone of its parts;" or, "all bodies are extended;" or, "a spirit is not in any place," etc. Another way of putting it is to say the analytic or regressive method moves from the conditioned to the conditions. The "progressive" and "synthetic" *method* (*not* propositions) move from conditions to what they do condition.[18] Hence "experience is nothing but a continued synthesis of perceptions."[19] We can schematize these contrasting terms thus:

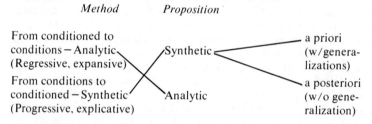

Method	*Proposition*

From conditioned to conditions — Analytic (Regressive, expansive) ⟶ Synthetic ⟶ a priori (w/generalizations)

From conditions to conditioned — Synthetic (Progressive, explicative) ⟶ Analytic ⟶ a posteriori (w/o generalization)

The terms *a priori* and *a posteriori* usually refer to the movement of one's reasoning from cause to effect and effect to cause respectively. Thus it is an a priori sort of reasoning if I conclude that whenever it rains something is wet; or, if from my knowledge of our tried and tested friendship I conclude that you could not possibly have been the one who sneakily harvested my vegetable garden in the night even though the footprints seem to fit yours. In brief, a priori propositions are deduced from ideas as their starting points independently of sense observations. They are deduced by analyzing the meaning necessarily contained in ideas which are then brought forth into propositions. Thus *analytic* and *a priori* coincide as a description of a proposition rooted internally in the mind itself. On the other hand, the terms *synthetic* and *a posteriori* refer to propositions rooted externally in the sense manifold. Hence too there are two kind of synthetic propositions, namely, *synthetic a priori*, meaning one that contains a necessary or general piece of knowledge about the sense data it is saying something about; or *synthetic a posteriori* in which there is no such necessity or generality, but merely a report about a purely

4

contingent and immediate perception at hand, v.g. I am typing now.

From this we can see how Newton's laws in Physics, as indeed all laws in the empirical sciences, are classed as *synthetic a priori* propositions. In our readings in Kant we will also see that mathematical and ethical propositions are classed in the same way. However, statements without generalizations and which are contingent merely on sense data are *synthetic a posteriori*. Thus we have three kinds of propositions which we will find Kant mentioning: analytic a priori, synthetic a priori and synthetic a posteriori. It should be clear that *analytic a posteriori* cannot constitute a fourth type of proposition since it is a contradiction in terms.

To repeat, Kant's question was: how are synthetic a priori propositions such as are found in Newton's scientific propositions possible? How are we to conceive the structure of human consciousness vis-a-vis the sensible world so that we can understand how from a mass of sense data, scientific analysis is able to tabulate them according to cause-effect rules and generalizations? (Note that analytic and synthetic a posteriori propositions do not pose the same problem since they merely state either meanings only or immediate sensations).[20]

To understand how Kant set about answering this question, we should recall how Kant knew Hume's philosophical works. Hume had raised the issue of whether the cause-effect relationship which we so readily attribute to objects we perceive around us are really *objective*, i.e. real. For instance, does the motion of one billiard ball hitting a second ball really *cause* the motion of this second ball? We take it for granted that it does. But *does* it? What exactly do we mean by "cause" anyway?

There seem to be only two ways of handling this question. Either one holds that by simply thinking about something (anything) one is able to draw forth ideas of its forthcoming effects; or else, one has to concede that not by mere analysis of ideas but rather by sense perception are we able to perceive the cause-effect relationship between things. But now Hume maintained that in neither one of these two ways can we really *see* the objective cause-effect relationship. Certainly, by simply thinking about something, we could never tell what it will effect or produce. Then secondly, when we do watch things around us we still find out that we really never do perceive the cause-effect connection between them. We only perceive discrete, individual things in the world, separate and loose from one another, somehow *succeeding* one another in certain cases with regularity. We then proceed to call this regular succession between certain things *causes* and their *effects*. We say of the billiard ball, for instance, that one ball *caused* the motion (effect) of the other ball. Yet all we really see are two individual separate balls with a successive motion from one to the other. We *see* nothing else. We certainly do not see visually *motion* flowing from one to the other connecting, as it were, the two billiard balls, do we? Even at the moment of impact the two balls remain loose and discrete from one another. The same seems true of anything else we talk of as cause and effect. All we see are things regularly succeeding one another, and when after analysis through various rules of elimination and discovery (the English philosopher John Stuart Mill, for instance, drew up a list of such rules) we are able to hold up two things as precisely the ones which succeed one another *regularly*, we call the first the *cause* of the latter.

Think for instance of your attempt to pinpoint what your car trouble is. You test the various mechanical systems and their sequences. You keep eliminating those that work until you get to where the sequence fails. You fix this up. The whole series of sequences function once again. Without further ado we think of that part as what *caused* the trouble. Our minds gravitate naturally to the ideas of cause and effect in such situations. Yet this tendency to associate things in cause-effect relationship is merely subjective to the mind, according to Hume. In the objective world only the *succession*, not the connection of things, appears to us. Why the mind then so readily makes this a cause-effect predication, Hume seemed unable to explain except to say that the mind does have this "gravamen" or tendency to so characterize phenomena which regularly succeed one another. Since science revolves on the cause-effect ideas in the formulation of its laws, we can see how Hume's question readily merged in Kant's mind with his problem on the possibility of synthetic a priori proposition.

> *Hume started chiefly from a single but important concept in metaphysics, namely, that of the connection between cause and effect (including its derivatives force and action, and so on). He challenged reason which pretends to have given birth to this concept of herself, to answer him by what right she thinks anything can be so constituted that if that thing be posited, something else also must necessarily be posited; for this is the meaning of the concept of cause. He demonstrated irrefutably that it was perfectly impossible for reason to think a priori and by means of concepts such a combination, for it implies necessity. We cannot at all see why, in consequence of the existence of one thing, another must necessarily exist, or how the concept of such a combination can arise a priori.[21]*

If we ask why this concept of cause and effect which involves necessity cannot arise a posteriori, then we will find Kant telling us over and over that nothing can arise of necessity a posteriori in relation to our knowledge, since sense experiences merely make us aware that this or that *is* so, not that they must *necessarily* be so. Yet strangely enough, this latter is precisely what we do assert whenever we posit one thing as the cause of a certain effect.

Moreover, the idea of two worlds, one visible before us, and the other invisible, beyond sense appearances, mysterious and ever eluding our thought, had always fascinated Kant. We have already mentioned his youthful impression of his mother as one who lived her life according to duty. It is also said that as a young, starving graduate student, Kant nevertheless saved enough money so as finally to fulfill his ambition of buying the whole set of books on psychic phenomena written by the Swedish philosopher and mystic, Emmanuel Swedenborg, (1688-1722) who was making news in those days. When Kant came to write his doctoral dissertation, he entitled his work, "Dissertation on the Form and Principles of the Sensible World." He also wrote *Dreams of a Spirit Seer* to counter Swedenborg's pretensions to knowledge about details of a life beyond the one we sensibly experience. In all his subsequent writings, this distinction between the world as it appears to us (phenomena) and the world as it is in itself (nuomena; *ding-an-sich*) played a central and unchanging role. At times the two sides of this distinction are referred to by various terms but they refer to the same basic opposition: phenomena-nuomena,[23] sensible-intelligible,[24] appearances-things-in-themselves.[25] The first half of these pairs mean the world of sense, the second half reality-in-itself beyond the appearances. Kant's point was that our knowledge is limited merely to the sensible world. All metaphysical claims to know reality beyond sense experience are to be rejected.[26] Kant calls such claims to knowledge of what actually constitutes metasensible reality the theory of transcendental realism, and his whole "critical" philosophy is a continuous argument against this sort of dogmatic and naive (thus uncritical) position. Finally, we should mention, no matter how briefly, Kant's admiration for Rousseau with this latter's optimistic view of pre-societal man.[28] Said Kant, "There was a time when I despised the masses...Rousseau has set me right...I learn to honor man."[29]

Someone is bound to ask at this point whether Kant is contradicting himself when he tells us we cannot know anything as it really is in itself beyond the appearances, since he is obviously talking about it and apparently knows quite a bit about it after all. He tells us, for instance, that it is the other side of appearances, that it is unknowable to us, and later in his ethical writings, as we shall see, that it has its own mode of causality quite diverse from that of the phenomenal world, etc. This is a serious question. Kant and his commentators have struggled with it especially as it comes up in his moral theory.

In reply Kant would ask us to reflect on what it means to say that all we know are appearances before us. Is not any appearance the appearance *of* something that is appearing?[30] We cannot help but think of appearance as precisely the appearance of something, can we? Even though our knowledge is restricted to the limit of sense appearances, our thought transcends those appearances through the idea *of* something that is appearing, does it not? True, we do not have any *positive* knowledge of what that reality-in-itself is constituted of, but our thought is at least able to point towards it. We have, in other words, a limit-idea (*grenzbegriffe*) *of* something-in-itself beyond the appearances. Kant writes:

> *Reason by all its a priori principles never teaches us anything more than objects of possible experience. But this limitation does not prevent reason from leading us to the objective boundary of experience, namely, to the relation to something which is not itself an object of experience, but is the ground of all experience. Reason does not, however teach us anything concerning the thing in itself; it only instructs us as regards its own complete and highest use in the field of possible experience.[31]*

In brief, Kant would say he would be contradicting himself only if he claimed positive *constitutive* knowledge of the nuomenal world (what it is in itself) as some metaphysicians, psychics, media, spirit seers and mystic visionarie sometimes do. As it is, Kant in only pointing *negatively* at the other side of the limit, namely, to the nuomenal world, all the time *regulating* his thought to its only valid area of knowledge, namely, the sensible world. All the time he forbids it to stray beyond this limit over into the world of nuomena, of things-in-themselves devoid of any sensa. In any case, if thought does stray into its own pure domain away from sense data, then it should be effectively aware that it has so strayed. It can then be aware that no matter how high-flying metaphysical conclusions it may reach, it can never take that last all-crucial step of saying, "Therefore, this is the way it really is in the nuomenal world." We can now understand the import of Kant's famous statement in the first *Critique* that "concepts without percepts are empty."[32] Let us turn now to the other half of that statement, namely, "Percepts without concepts are blind."

Percepts are sense impressions, sensuous intuitions. We have said more than once that sensations by themselves are chaotic, disorganized, amorphous. It is sheer multiplicity. Kant learned from Hume [33] that this external world is one in which everything stands loose from every other thing else. We perceive no connection at all between them. Now knowledge can certainly have no part in such an amorphous mass of sense data. For the intrinsic mark of knowledge is *unification*. The many are always subsumed into one (unified) in any piece of knowledge we claim to have. Even when we give up in a moment of exasperation and say the world around is nothing but a "buzzin' bloomin' confusion" it is quite clear that we have unified disorganized impressions under the leading ideas of "buzzing," "blooming," and "confusion." Each one of these ideas has one definite meaning which can be applied to any number of impressions we recognize as falling within the meaning of the idea. If we may use a bit of Kantian paradox along the lines of the unknowable nuomena, we can say that of sheer multiplicity by itself we cannot have any idea! Before such sheer multiplcity we would be speechless because we would be thoughtless.

In fact, however, we do think and we do have patterned sense impressions vis-a-vis this mass of sense manifold. Even in extreme situations we can still sense an enormous object blacking the sun out, or swarms of nits forcing me to flee the woods or beach in summer. And so we ask: how is this possible? The traditional answer would have rejected Hume's version of absolute looseness in things. It would have rejected the idea that the sensible world by itself is simply an amorphous, atomic mass. As Plato and Aristotle taught, there were "forms" in things, whether participated by them from another world, or intrinsic to them without further relationship to some other world. As composed of "forms" things were intelligible in themselves. The forms served as the unifying factor for "matter" (the principle of indeterminacy and thus of multiplicity). Material objects were said to make an impact or impression upon the mind which then through the complicated process of "abstraction" now reproduced within itself in an immaterial "intentional" way the formed object before it. It is a whole theory of knowledge, well-developed, with many complex and intricate accounts of various processes of consciousness, starting from the sense impact to the various modes of abstraction. But the final picture is one of mind being affected by external reality and reproducing in its immaterial own way the forms of things out there.

If one belonged to the rationalistic or idealistic schools of philosophy which held the theory of innate ideas and denied the originating impact from the outside with regard to those ideas, then the priority of knowledge was given to those innate ideas vis-a-vis the empirical elements of sensation; and vice versa, if one belonged to the empirical school. In actual fact, as we have already mentioned, neither school had really drawn the strict limits of genuine knowledge, since their accounts overlapped the two sources of knowledge (i.e. ideas and sense impressions) even as they granted priority to one over the other.

It was this ancient and age-long problem of giving a sound account of knowledge that Kant took on in what has come to be called his "Copernican revolution." Far from being passive or isolated from sensa, Kant pointed out, the human mind *contributes* something to the world as we know it. To get some idea of this Kantian account of knowledge, let us go step by step into the various functions of consciousness, bearing in mind that our interest here is not a specialized in-depth mastery of Kant's epistemology (theory of knowledge) but merely a background sketch, sufficient and necessary for us to understand his theory of morals. We will discuss in succession the forms of sensibility (space and time), and imagination; the categories of the Understanding, and finally the role of Reason.

Space and Time

In the first sections of the *Prolegomena to Any Future Metaphysics*[34] and the *Critique of Pure Reason*,[35] Kant shows how space and time are subjective forms *we* ourselves *contribute* to our perceptions of all sense appearances. Space and time are not objective realities adhering in things and reproduced from the outside upon our consciousness inside. Kant shows how this is so in context of the question: "How is Pure Mathematics possible?" That is to say, given the existence of pure mathematics, how are we to understand the structure of consiousness so as to explain such mathematics?

He first points out that the intuition involved in pure mathematics has to be a priori since mathematical conclusions are universal, definite, conclusive and absolutely necessary. Their objects, therefore, cannot be given synthetically a posteriori since then no necessity could ever come from such purely contingent sense deliverances. Yet "intuition" means actual *sensuous perception* of an object in front of me. How then can intuition be a priori? This seems to be a contradiction in terms. Here it should be recalled that we do not actually perceive (intuit) things-in-themselves, but only appearances. And even if we did intuit things-in-themselves, this still would make no difference. For our intuition in either case would be a posteriori and as such could not give rise to the a priori intuition of mathematical objects. It seems clear then that pure mathematical intuition *anticipates* its object. Now this can only mean that not appearances (much less things-in-themselves) cause my perception, but rather my intuition of mathematical objects contain "nothing but the

9

form of sensibility, antedating in my mind all the actual impressions through which I am affected by objects."[36]

To find out what these a priori forms of my senses are by which I sense all actual representations made to me, I go to the two branches of mathematics, namely, geometry and arithmetic. There I find that, "geometry is based upon pure intuition of space. Arithmetic achieves its concept of number by the successive addition of units in time, and pure mechanics cannot attain its concept of motion without employing the representation of time."[37] Kant points out that whatever objects we locate externally in space, we so locate only on the basis of our own selves as reference points already in space. Whatever succession or contemporaneity we perceive in things we are able so to perceive only in relation to our own internal consciousness of ourselves as the other relative term of the measure. Hence space is the form of outer sense, time of inner sense.

At this point Kant goes on and presumes that what is true of a priori mathematical intuitions must also be true universally of all our sense perceptions, i.e. that all the material of sensation is subsumed into our subjective forms of space and time. He observes how prior to all our sense perceptions and intuitions we already know that all our objects therein will be *in* space and time. How else then explain this anticipated universality unless we hold that space and time are our own subjective forms of sensibility which *we contribute* to our own actual sensations.

> *Should any man venture to doubt that these are determinations adhering not to things in themselves, but to their relation to our sensibility, I should be glad to know how he can find it possible to know a priori how their intuition will be characterized before we have any acquaintance with them and before they are presented to us. Such, however, is the case with space and time. But this is quite comprehensible as soon as both count for nothing more than formal conditions of our sensibility, while the objects count merely as phenomena; for then the form of the phenomenon, that is, pure intuition, can by all means be represented as proceeding from ourselves, that is, a priori.[39]*

Here are two confirming examples which perhaps any one can try out for himself.

> *Triangles drawn from either side of the equator as the base line and covering both hemispheres are internally equal in every objective respect except space, yet the one cannot be put in place of the other, (that is, upon the opposite hemisphere).[40]*
> *As I stand in front of a mirror, my image is perfectly similar to me and every part of me, yet I cannot put such a hand as is seen in the glass in place of the original; for if this is a right hand, that in the glass is a left one. So with the ear, etc.[41]*

One could ask why from space and time as internal forms in mathematical objects Kant went on to say they were forms of *all* our sense objects. He, however, obviously believes he has already dealt with that question. Moreover, he would go back to the point that we know only sense

10

appearances, not things-in-themselves.[42] These latter as *other than* their appearances in space and time are, as we saw, grasped *at* only negatively by our intellects. Finally, we should note that space and time as forms of our sensuous intuition are precisely that, forms of sensibility. As such they are different from our intellectual ideas of space and time.[43]

Understanding

Kant defines nature as "the existence of things, so far as it is determined according to universal laws."[44] Lest the first words of the definition mislead us, he quickly points out that by "existence of things" he does not refer to nuomenal reality or things-in-themselves which we cannot know whether a priori or a posteriori. Not a priori, for by dissecting (analyzing) merely our concepts we obviously would get only to other concepts, not to things themselves. Not a posteriori, for "experience teaches us *what* exists and *how* it exists, but never that it must *necessarily* exist so and not otherwise. Experience therefore can never teach us the nature of things in themselves."[45]

To repeat, knowledge can never go beyond sense appearances. These appearances by themselves are haphazard, contingent, unstable and indeterminate. Anything that exists, as Hume had said, can be thought also to be not existing. Though the forms of sensibility (space and time) do give them the characteristics of being here and now, or there and then, they still are at that stage far from being the fairly organized and coherent account we have of things. And they are organized and coherent by the time we make pronouncements about them, discuss and question them with ever more refined precision. Everyone in the discussion *understands* what things we are talking about. Indeed we even have a scientific knowledge of things. This means we have knowledge of appearances as they are *ruled necessarily and determinately by laws*. Nature is rule-determined and rule-necessitated behaviour of appearances according to the cause-effect relationship.

Here is where Kant comes in with his question: "There is then in fact a pure science of nature, and the question arises, 'how is this possible?'"[46] By now we know what he means by this question, namely: are necessity, determinacy, indeed the whole notion of a coherently organized world of appearances really *out there* as an intrinsic characteristic inhering in things themselves? Or are all these instead "contributions of our mind?" By now too we know what his answer is. How could we know what intrinsic characteristics inhere in things themselves when it has been shown repeatedly that we do not have and cannot have knowledge of things themselves but only of their appearances? Sense appearances, even as shaped by our sensible forms of space and time, and organized by the schemata of the imagination, have certainly nothing *necessary* about them. By sense experience we can only know this or that particular event. No matter how often we experience a posteriori that this or that particular fish dies out of water, that would be all we could ever really say, namely, this or that fish died out of water; this or that particular frog responded to this experimental prod thus; this or that rat caught cancer through nicotine intake, etc. We could not possibly, through such a posteriori sense experience (an obvious redundancy) *alone* go beyond those particularizations. Yet, we *do* go beyond them in setting up our sciences. From them we rise to necessary scientific *laws*, v.g. that nicotine causes cancer. That is, it so causes not only in those experiments, not only in individual instances already observed, but *everywhere* it is so taken. This is the characteristic we always find whenever we rise to the level of scientific laws, namely, necessary knowledge of cause and effect in the world of appearances, or the *rule-determined behaviour* of things in nature.

If *necessity* is not from things, where is it from? We can already anticipate Kant's answer. It can only be *from the mind.* The mind's own nature and structure imposes such necessity upon the sense manifold presented to it by the imagination. And again we can anticipate Kant's next step, namely, to extrapolate this explanation for the possibility of scientific knowledge to the entire domain of human knowledge. Employing hylomorphic language, Kant talks of the sense world as the *matter*, and of our mental contribution to it to shape knowledge as *form.* Together as matter and form, the one from the outside and the other from the inside, so to speak, they constitute our human knowledge.

All this is still vague. Precisely what forms does the mind contribute to knowledge? To answer it is necessary to stress the irreducible difference between sense experience and thought. As Descartes pointed out, you see a piece of wax melt in heat and you *know* through *thought* that it is the same piece of wax every moment it is melting, even though your senses report differently. Or, as the same Descartes maintained, you cannot *exactly imagine* what a plane figure with precisely a thousand sides would look like, yet you obviously have a very precise *thought* about it--- else you couldn't be so positive you cannot imagine it. And this is really what you are saying when you assert that the "image" you have does not correspond exactly with the thought or idea you are trying to picture.

Thought thus, or *Understanding* is different from sensation. What then is the essential act of Understanding? If we could pinpoint that, we might be put on track of the nature and number of forms the mind contributes to organize the sense manifold. Now, Kant saw that the essential act of the Understanding is *Judgement.* We have as many forms of knowledge about things as we have judgements about them. A judgement, as Aristotle defined it long ago, is simply the act of saying something about something else. This seems to complicate the problem impossibly, since we seem to have countless ways of talking about and conceiving things. Consider, for instance, the almost countless fields of knowledge cited in a university catalogue. Consider the limitless fertility of the human mind in conceiving novel plots, dramas, poetic expressions, musical melodies, brilliant metaphors, etc. "O the mind, the mind has mountains, sheer cliffs never fathomed!" exclaimed the poet Gerard Manley Hopkins. How in the world then could one ever hope to categorize all these modalities of judgements?

Kant hit on a happy clue. Ever since Aristotle up to Kant's own days, logicians had shown that though there are indeed countless variations of judgements, their kinds or categories can be quite precisely shown to be twelve and only twelve! All statements we ever make can be shown to fall under one of those twelve categories. Consequently, Kant contended (he taught Logic practically all throughout his teaching career) there are also twelve categories in the human mind by which we formally organize all our sense perceptions into knowledge. We see how one structure of consciousness (consciousness-in-general)[47] with its one essential function of judging or understanding is to be found in us all. This Kant sometimes refers to as the "transcendeltal ego." Its general function is to *unify*, to organize the sense perceptions into knowledge. Knowledge is meaning. Meaning is unity, the unity of judgement. And this judgemental unity takes place according to one of the twelve forms or categories which are all a priori, i.e. innate in the mind. They are there prior to all experiences. They are in the mind independently of the senses. It is through them that we contribute necessity, or more precisely, that we are able to inform our sense experiences with necessity in the cases of synthetic a priori propositions. Here is an illustration.

> *As an easier example, we may take the following: When the sun shines on the stone, it grows warm. This judgement, however often I and others may have perceived it, is a mere judgement of perception and contains no necessity; perceptions are only usually conjoined in this manner. But if I say: the sun warms the stone, I add to the perception a concept of the understanding, namely, that of cause, which necessarily connects with the concept of sunshine that of heat, and the synthetical judgement becomes of necessity universally valid, namely, objective, and is converted from a perception into exper-ience.*[48]

To go further here and talk of the twelve categories themselves would take us far beyond the introductory and background nature of this chapter. Enough has been said to clarify Kant's dictum: "Without sensibility no object would be given us, without understanding, no object would be *thought*. Thoughts without content are empty, intuitions without concepts are blind."[49]

It remains for us here to note the gap between the sheer diversity of perceptions, even when subsumed under the forms of space and time, and the various twelve unities so neatly categorized in our understanding. How is this gap closed, so to speak, so as to have the various incoming perceptions sorted out for information by their proper and proportionate categories. For this another internal sense, namely, imagination with its own various "schemata" is needed. Needless to say, a question can be asked of Kant especially by one who is sceptical about things *out there* being merely and purely appearances without intrinsic forms themselves. How can imagination sort out the various sense deliverances for propor-tionate composition with their respective categories unless indeed there be something in the objects themselves, mere appearances though they be, which characterizes or forms them intrinsically? To say they are with the forms of space and time from our sensibility is not enough. For even with space and time there would not be enough diversity there for imagination to schematize them according to their various and proper categories.

However, our interest here is in understanding, not objecting to Kant. So we move on to the last function of the mind, namely, Reason.

Reason

We have seen that Understanding, with its twelve a priori categories, is irreducibly different from the senses. Kant now further distinguishes between Understanding and Reason.[50] Whereas Understanding with its twelve categories makes possible "nature" or the various generalizations we make of our sense perceptions, we find now that it is also possible for Understanding to cut itself off, so to speak, from any sense perception at all and then "brood," simply over the *logical* content of the categories themselves now empty of all sensa. When the mind functions in this way, Kant calls it Reason. It is this Reason, Kant maintains, which gives rise to Metaphysics, that is, to claims of knowledge beyond the sensible world.

> *The third question (first was the possibility of mathematics; second was the possibility of natural science) now proposed relates therefore as it were to the root and peculiarity of metaphysics, that is, the occupation of reason merely with itself and the supposed knowledge of objects arising immediately from this brooding over its own concepts, without requiring, or indeed being able to reach that knowledge through experience.[51]*

We should note the ambivalence in the word "metaphysics" in our reading of Kant. Sometimes he refers to metaphysics in the traditional sense which claims knowledge of realities beyond the sensible world- - -a position he rejects. Sometimes he means it in his own way: Reason brooding over its own empty concepts only in a *regulative*, not a *constitutive* function. He saw that while it is possible to set forth the strict limits of our knowledge, as he did, it is impossible simply to restrict the mind to those limits, or to prevent it from transcending the limit of the sensuous world. This is because the mind has a natural impulsion to understand everything in a systematic and total, not just a partial, view of things.[52]

> *That the human mind will ever give up metaphysical researches is as little to be expected as that we, to avoid inhaling impure air, should prefer to give up breathing altogether. There will, therefore, always be metaphysics in the world.[53]*

Every act of judgement is merely partial knowledge. The mind's natural impulsion is to total knowledge, and this takes the form of Reason brooding on its own sources: the categories by themselves alone and devoid of all sense content. This is an entirely subjective operation cut off from all the objective content of the sensible world. This has its own *regulative* uses for the mind when it tries to form for itself the complete and total picture of things. But it would be impossible to validate any

14

claim made on the *constitutive* character of this knowledge. That is to say, subjectively, to satisfy its own tendency towards completeness and totality of knowledge, Reason can use the knowledge it acquires from brooding over its own empty concepts to organize and regulate knowledge into a total picture. But it must be careful not to attribute any *objective* or *constitutive* reality to whatever ideas it acquires from such a brooding. To *transcend* its subjective limits and claim objective content for its Ideas about things-in-themselves would be an illusion.[54]

We can see why Kant calls the distinction between the empty Ideas of Reason and the concepts or Categories of the Understanding when conjoined with sense experiences in both day-to-day and scientific knowledges of "nature" "so important a point."[55] We can also see why in "experience" resulting from sensation, the role of the Understanding is called "analytic" and in metaphysics the role of Reason brooding over the empty Categories to give birth to the Ideas is called "dialectical." As Kant holds, it is the self-same Reason and no other that can and must "critique" itself, i.e. set its own limits of valid knowledge and come to recognize its own boundaries as the regulative, never the constitutive, use of its own ideas. Reason can conceive of how things-in-themselves (nuomena) as other than appearances might be, but these are only limit ideas.[56] On this Reason must be clear to itself.

Since Reason is dialectical, Kant falls back again on Logic to solve the obvious problem: how many Ideas of Reason are there? In a way this was like asking previously how many judgements there are in the Understanding, and what? Kant went back to those same Logic books of the categories and used the three forms of syllogism traditionally listed there, namely, the categorical (flat assertions, affirmations and negations); the hypothetical (If-Then); and the disjunctive (Either-Or). The first type gives rise to the Idea of "substance" and "soul"; the second to the Idea of "the world;" the third to the Idea of "God." Let us see briefly how this is so.

We can take Descartes' statement, "I think" as the most fundamental categorical judgement. Kant maintains that the "I" here is a product of non-instuitive awareness. Indeed even if this "I" had objective content through sensuous intuition, it would not be able to discern or observe any permanence in its successive acts of consciousness, just as Hume had observed. It follows that our concept of substance and related ideas such as the immortality of the soul, etc. as a perduring substrate of sense appearances is only an Idea of Pure Reason. As such it has no constitutive or objective value. To maintain otherwise would be to fall into the "paralogisms" (misled reasonings) on the soul.

Vis-a-vis the world, our Reason functions hypothetically thus: If the conditoned is given, the entire sum of conditions, and consequently the absolutely unconditioned is also given.[57] The conclusion follows because it is only the absolutely unconditioned that makes the conditions possible. What this whole procedure has forgotten, however, is Kant's repeated insistence that our knowledge of the world as "conditioned" is based merely on phenomena or appearances, and therefore they cannot be used as a basis for nuomenal conclusions about the Unconditioned ground of everything in "the world." The very phrase "the world" is only an Idea of Pure Reason, with its regulative use towards a total conception of things, but devoid of any constitutive validity. To maintain otherwise is to fall into the four antinomies (i.e. stalemate between thesis and anti-thesis) about the world, namely: (1) that the world has and has not a beginning in time and spatial limit; (2) that the world is and is not of composite or of simple parts; (3) that a free kind of causality must or must not supplement the determined laws of causality in nature or the world of appearances; (4) that an absolute being belongs and does not belong to the world either as part or as its cause.[58]

We will see that the major issue we will confront in our study of Kant's ethical writings is lodged in that third antinomy. There the possibility is raised of a free causality outside the world of appearances really existing and operating so as to have effects even in the phenomenal world. This is different from the first two antinomies (which were mathematical ones and treated of both conditions and conditioned as always homogeneous). In those both theses and anti-theses were false since they mistake the phenomenal character of the world as though it were a thing-in-itself. What we deal with in the third and fourth antinomies is nature in a *dynamic* view. Here Kant points out the possibility of heterogeneity of cause and effect. For the cause can always be more than its effect. Hence it is possible for both theses and antitheses to be both true since, according to Kant, they may refer to different orders respectively, namely, to the world of things-in-themselves (nuomenal) or to the world of appearances (phenomenal). For our purposes it is well to remember the third antinomy which in effect says that though everything in our empirically observable selves have determined causes, there is room for believing that these determined effects in the world of appearances have a basis in a causality purely intelligible and free in the nuomenal world.

Finally, we have seen how Reason brooding over the empty categories gives rise to the paralogisms of the soul and the antinomies of the world. We have also seen how the native bent of Reason always impels it towards a systematic completion of all its concepts.[59] The supreme point of unification Reason gives birth to is the idea of the most perfect being (*Ens Realissimum*), God, in whom all perfections are completely and totally summed up. Kant has an extended treatment which by now has become classic in philosophical theology, particularly his refutation of the Ontological Argument. For our purpose here, suffice it to say that since the concept is only logical from the pure categories, Kant contends that it is impossible to prove that "existence" which has a constitutive nuomenal content can ever be drawn from our mere conception of "God." Hence the Idea of God remains precisely that, the Ideal of Pure Reason, with only a regulative use for bringing our conception of things to its highest point of systematic completion.

This brief background has tried to single out those points in Kant's life and theory of knowledge which we will find pertinent to our study of his ethical writings. We are now in a position to look at his ethical theory.

As we do so, the main points we want to bring with us from this chapter are, first and foremost, Kant's division of the world visible to our senses (phenomena, appearances) from the invisible world of things-in-themselves (nuomena) known only in a negative way to our intellects; his insistence on our inability to make *constitutive* statements as regard the invisible, nuomenal intelligible world; the method of regressing, moving back from our sensible experiences to the fundamental structures or principles which make them possible; and finally the elements which constitute a synthetic a priori proposition, namely, material from the phenomenal world of our sensations, feelings, appetites, desires, inclinations, etc., and the organizing, universalizing forms contributed by the mind. We shall see how Kant locates the source of moral obligation in that nuomenal, invisible and incomprehensible world of "freedom" whose laws categorically govern and constrain what otherwise would be the unruly mob of our sensual desires. Those laws effect this constraint through synthetic a priori commands or imperatives. And it is the nature of this synthetic a priori as it operates not in Newtonian physics but this time in practical moral matters that will occupy Kant.

Key to abbreviations*

PAFM = *Prolegomena to Any Future Metaphysics*, With an Introduction by L. W. Beck, Indianapolis, 1950.

FPMM = *Fundamental Principles of the Metaphysic of Morals*, Translated by T. K. Abbott, Indianapolis, 1949.

CPR = *Critique of Practical Reason*, Translated by L. W. Beck, Indianapolis, 1956.

MPV = *The Metaphysical Principles of Virtue*, Translated by J. Ellington, Indianapolis, 1964.

MEJ = *The Metaphysical Elements of Justice*, Translated by J. Ladd, Indianapolis, 1965.

RWLRA = *Religion Within the Limits of Reason Alone*, Translated by T.M. Greene and H.H. Hudson, with "The Ethical Significance of Kant's Religion," by J. R. Silber, New York, 1960.

LoE = *Lectures on Ethics*, Translated by L. Infield, New York, 1963.

CPPR = *Critique of Pure Reason*, Translated by F.M. Müller, New York, 1961.

* All the above are in paperbacks.

2

FUNDAMENTAL PRINCIPLES
OF MORALS

Commentators often disagree as to the right sequence of ideas, and as to "what Kant really means" in his various ethical writings. They agree, however, that Kant's ethics *seems* inconsistent with his theory of knowledge at worst; at best, the many gaps one finds in his sequence of ideas seem to indicate the well-nigh impossible task of presenting an ethical theory as ultimately and thoroughly foundational as Kant claimed he had done, given the limits of knowledge he had prescribed.[1]

Once Kant had demarcated the line of valid human knowledge and once he had shown that we really have no *constitutive* knowledge of the intelligible world, he faced a seemingly endless tangle of problems in ethics.[2] He seemed almost afraid to confront them. He kept postponing the task. Even with just the sketchy background in the previous chapter, it should be possible to appreciate his dilemma. In ethics he faced the certain prospect of delving into the intelligible world and making whole sets of pronouncements about it, *after* he had devoted gruelling years of work writing stern strictures against precisely such an uncritical, naive and illegitimate "dogmatic slumber." Yet what was he to do? On the one hand, it was clear that he could not situate morality in the world of phenomena and nature. For there everything moved in rule-determined behaviour, mechanically---that is, one thing causes another. In nature, "heteronomy," as Kant called it, prevailed. To put morality in this phenomenal world would negate freedom which lies at the very heart of morality. If freedom is cancelled, morality becomes an illusion.

It will not do to say we only "appear" to be free. Even if we say we cannot but act *as if* we are free, we still either are or are not equivalently free. Nor will it do to say we cannot know ourselves to be *really* free, given the limits of knowledge prescribed by Kant himself. This line of thought would lead us to say that we either are not really moral beings (if we cannot ascertain the reality of freedom in us), or that we cannot *know* ourselves to be moral beings.[3] No one, least of all Kant, wants to say this of the awesome and very real presence of moral obligation in *all* men, even in the "most consummate villain" who recognizes this moral law within himself while he transgresses it.[4] No, moral obligation cannot be merely an appearance. It is real alright. The same holds for human freedom.

The problem was that Kant had held that we cannot really *know* anything beyond appearances. Yet he went on to write so much and so lengthily (when he finally got going) on morality and freedom and their implications, all of them in the noumenal world beyond appearances.[5] This was Kant's problem. And almost every difficulty his readers encounter can ultimately be traced back to his attempt to stay within the canons he set up in his critique of knowledge, at the same time that he seems forced to transgress them in order to get at the foundations of moral law. He was trying to have something both ways after he himself said it could not be done. The fact is he went ahead and did it anyway. Whether he brought it off, his readers must judge for themselves. What is certain is that the question provides continual excitement as one reads his ethical treatises.

We saw how Kant knew Hume. Now Hume had clearly dilineated the ethical *ought* as other than the *is.*[6] Failure to keep this simple yet radical distinction in mind dooms any ethical theory. Ethics deals exclusively with what men *ought* to do, not with what in *fact* they do. Men's actual actions are the subject matter of other disciplines, notably the empirical sciences. The ethical *ought,* on the other hand, is the proper subject matter for philosophical thought. To let anything empirical (the *is)* filter in to the *ought* as we speculate on it can only mislead *us.* To support Kant's contention, we can perhaps use the "happiness" theories of ethics as an illustration. Start from the empirical fact that all men seek happiness, as Aristotle did. Then the ethical question immediatley becomes *which sort of happiness* men really *ought* to seek, does it not? Morality is quickly assimilated into the concept of "happiness" instead of staying pure by itself. Had this latter obtained, then the question would have been whether men *ought* to seek happiness at all, especially if one holds that on this matter men are not free since such a search is natural to them. Clearly, if we are to do justice to the nature of the *ought,* we will have to hold it strictly apart from the empirical *is.*

Point of departure

The ground a philosopher has for trying to understand morals is simply the evident and common understanding men do in fact have of duty and of moral laws.[7] Our point of departure is the universal presence of moral obligation in all men. Is this a lapse right back into the *is?* No. For all we are saying is that we are studying something real, not a figment of the imagination; and that in our study of it we will be careful not to confuse the moral *ought* with our experience of nature and its various mechanical laws. For the *ought* is other than such experience. Moral duty bears "absolute necessity" within it, while nothing is absolutely necessary in our experiences.[8] Of course, in nature (i.e. rule-determined behaviour) we know that *if* a cause exists, its effect exists with it. But the very statement itself shows the hypothetical character of the situation.

Moral obligation thus is other than experience. From the outset it reveals itself as universal and absolutely necessary. There are no if's or but's, qualifications, provisos or conditions about the presence of moral obligation within us. The *ought* is in all of us, period. As such it is universal, bears absolute necessity. We are inescapably moral agents by the mere fact that we are human.

We note next that the moral ought is obviously a command, an imperative to act. This means that an action cannot be considered as precisely *the* effect of a command merely because it happens to conform to what was commanded. To be *the* effect of an imperative, an action has to be done precisely *for the sake of* the imperative. This is clear enough. Two boys may tell the same truth to their parents. If one merely blurts out the information, while the other gives it *out of* a conscientious decision that this is the right act he *ought* to do regardless of consequences, then we clearly separate the latter as an act that properly belongs to the domain of morals. Mere conformity with duty does not automatically invest an act with moral quality. The will to obey a moral command is precisely what constitutes a moral act.

The notion of *will* connects to that of the "good". This is so because, first of all, the will can will only what it sees as "good." Second, because morality is obviously about the "good," if it is to be about anything at all. Now we have already noted the universal and absolute character of moral duty. So we can perhaps arrange these various ideas thus. Our attempt to understand the *ought* is really an attempt to understand and explain its source, its ground or foundation. This source, we have seen, is the "will" whose nature is to move towards the good. We can also say that it is not just any good the moral will moves to, just as it is not simply any action at all that we call moral. The *moral will* which bears the characteristics of universality and absolute necessity within itself must also move towards the same kind of "good," namely, an *absolute good.* If morals are indeed beyond the pale of experience and the empirical world, where everything is contingent, then the good entailed in its concept must also be beyond anything contingent. It must be impossible to conceive that good as other than itself ever. It has to be "absolute good" the presence of which is necessary anytime anything is said to be moral. Reversely, its absence would make it impossible for anything to be called moral. In other words, it is good-in-itself. All moral goodness derives from it, while its own goodness derives from no other than itself. What could this be?

Whether we look to goods external to us or to goods internal to us we find that all *except one* are merely conditional goods. Power, fame, prosperity, etc. are clearly conditional goods. When we see them possessed by someone morally depraved or underserving, we cannot bring ourselves to approve of the situation, regardless of whether it is in our power to alter it or not. This shows that we judge happiness and the goods usually associated with it as inseparably related to a man's *moral worthiness* to possess those goods, does it not? The same is true of health, beauty, athletic agility, brilliance of intellect, etc. In a vicious or morally depraved person, far from being good, those pose the greatest evil, namely, danger to others. We need think only of an "evil genius" to see that this is so. The corruption of the best is the worst, it is said. None of all these goods thus can be considered good absolutely.

By elimination we come to the only unconditional good which is identically the moral good, namely, a good will. And if this is the object of the moral will, then this also is what man is commanded by duty to achieve within himself. In reality, we never meet a man who has achieved the absolutely good will in himself. Nevertheless, when we do meet with a truly *virtuous* person, even if he be in penniless misery, the good will in him would "still shine like a jewel in its own light."[9] Should someone insist that happiness, not this good will, is what man is destined to achieve for himself (as in fact many philosophers have maintained in all ages) Kant is quick to disagree. For nature, though stingy and "stepmotherly" towards man in other ways, endowed him, on an equal basis with other things in the universe, with the precise means to achieve his end, namely, *reason.* Yet, interestingly, the sheer cultivation of reason for its own sake begets not happiness, but all too often its opposite, namely, a disgust with reason itself. Zorba, the Greek, in the movie by that title, exemplified this point. Hence reason is merely a conditional good, relative only to that one absolute good which is the object of morality, namely, the good will. This is the same as saying that man's destiny is moral fulfillment. This in turn means acting *for the sake of duty* not merely in conformity with it. This in turn is the same as saying that man's end is *worthiness* to be happy, not necessarily *actual* happiness.

Here we should pause to note that all these conclusion have been drawn simply by reflecting with reason on the pure nature of the *ought,* once it has been freed from any admixture with the *is.* We could not have drawn these conclusions from the empirical world, says Kant, since we really are incapable of judging whether what we or others do are really done out of a pure motivation of duty. The hidden springs of human motivation are so complex and full of disguises (as we have learned from Freud) that it is well-nigh impossible even to be sure whether one simple action done purely for the sake of duty has ever taken place. Yet we do draw conclusions in morals. How? By clearly identifying the *ought* as other than the *is.*[9] As conclusions simply of reason itself, we can even hold that moral laws are true even of beings other than men, if such there be, who may likewise be gifted with reason. For we deal here, not with the physical world of experience, but beyond that with the metaphysical world of morals.

We can bring these points out by two contrasting examples. Take a "dealer" who charges everyone a fixed price so that "a child buys of him as well as any other."[10] He does this, however, so that his *business may prosper.* The "dear self" is the real motivation in what otherwise looks like an act of impartial justice to everybody. Clearly, this is not to be considered a *moral* act, even though it does conform to morals. By contrast, one who goes on living despite the crushing hardships at hand, solely because it is moral duty to maintain one's life, and not out of a natural impulsion to do so, is acting morally. The will to act solely from moral duty then is what constitutes morality, not the other impulses and sensual motivations which Kant calls "inclinations."

Inclinations must be held strictly apart from moral *duty*. This, according to Kant, is the same as saying that a moral act is done strictly out of *respect* for the moral law without any other motive filtering in whether from inclination, or even from the will itself. Again, the point is that neither the consequences of an action (as utilitarians maintain), nor anything else except action done simply and solely out of respect for the moral law constitutes a moral act.[11]

Some perplexing passages now call for an attempt to reconstruct Kant's sequence of ideas. We have seen that the essence of morality centers in the one unconditional good of the good will. For this to remain good-in-itself, it is clear that it cannot be determined by objects outside itself, whether these be objects of inclination or even of the will itself. For then it would become good derivatively from them. The will thus must be determined from within itself. Now, we can conceive of nothing else which can possibly do this except *respect for law*. What else can the will, which is pure pratical reason itself, use from within itself in order to make itself act? What else but commands, imperatives, in a word, *law?* Deprived of all other motivations, that one single motivation left to the will, namely, *respect for law*, is, nonetheless, all that is needed to generate moral action, i.e. action done for the sake of duty. All this shows how a moral act comes to be, how we should act.

The Categorical Imperative

But act what? Do what? *What* is the moral law? What does duty command? Kant pushes back and uncovers his all important supreme principle of morality, namely: "I am never to act otherwise than *so that I could also will that my maxim should become a universal law.*"[12] We have seen how the moral will must be "deprived" of anything external to it as a determinant of the moral act. Only respect for duty or moral law then could determine this will to action. When next we ask *what* that law is, we can see that it is pure reason commanding itself to realize in its own self the one unconditional and intrinsic good-in-itself. Negatively, this good-in-itself would contrast with the good only for the "dear self" which would be only a conditional good, i.e. good *for me* for *my interest.* If then the good-in-itself cannot be identified with the good of only the "dear self" what else could it be but a good for *all the selves?* Kant's presentation is quite involuted at this point, but this way of unravelling it enables us to relate it to the concept of the good will as that by which everything else is conditionally made good but which itself is unconditionally good, i.e. the source of goodness for everybody. What the categorical imperative would have us do is realize the good will in ourselves. This is done not by subsuming it to our "selfish" individual ends (v.g. the unbelievable situation where one decides to live morally so as to gain the social acclaim and veneration that usually goes with the reputation of sainthood), but by respecting it in its pure nature, i.e. not as narrowed down to any one individual, but rather as universal to all beings gifted with reason. Kant's sequence of thought is unclear here. It is debatable whether he has made his point. But his intent is clear: to back up to the necessarily universal character of moral law, step by step, starting from its universal presence in all men.

What is good for all, then, is the essence of the moral law, namely, the *universalizable*. This is so since the moral law comes out of the womb, so to speak, of pure reason itself. It has no extrinsic "bastardly" admixtures from the phenomenal world of inclinations and experiences. Now, something purely rational cannot really be such if it is rational only for a few, can it? A rational idea is rational, *de jure*, for anybody else to whom it is presented. Hence Kant could even go so far as to say the conclusions of morals are applicable not only for men, but for any other rational beings if such beings exist. It follows, on the other hand, that the act that would exempt one from the universal law would precisely be the immoral act. And since the universality is of reason, the immoral or the unlawful would be what goes against reason, namely, a contradiction. We should thus be able to show that the individual who exempts himself from the law is in effect contradicting himself. How is this so?

Kant takes up the notion of "maxims." Almost everyone functions according to individual subjective maxims, i.e. "subjective principles of action."[13] You have your own reasons for doing certain actions and not others, do you not? Now, clearly, not all subjective principles are moral. They must first be assessed, and Kant would assess them precisely against the norm of *universalizability:* Can you universalize the maxim on which you are about to act? If you can, then your maxim is moral. And if you act purely for its sake, i.e. out of respect for that moral law, then your action is moral. If, however, upon bringing up your maxim against universalizability, you conclude to a contradiction, then what you have is not the law but what goes against the law. Some examples might help here. For brevity, let us use what moralists consider already loaded and tautological terms like "shoplifliting," "adultery," etc., since presumably it is clear that the physical actions involved are what are being morally assessed.

Take shoplifting. If I am about to act on the maxim that shoplifting is alright, I should conscientiously ask myself whether that act can be *universalized.* That is, can I will that all men shoplift? The answer is clear. If all men shoplifted, no shops would be left! Without shops to lift from, there could be no sense to the term "shoplifters." The maxim thus as universalized is self-contradicting. Should I go ahead anyway and shoplift, it is clear that I do so only because I have agreed that not everybody is allowed the act. Yet what I deny others I allow myself. Does this make sense?

Or take adultery. Can I will that every married person violate the commitment to marital fidelity whenever he or she can do so? If indeed every married person lived by this "principle," marital commitment would be self-contradicting. It would be commitment that is not really commitment. If a person goes ahead anyway with an adulterous act, it is clear that this would not be because of the act's universalizability, but because it is seen as allowed to the doer while forbidden to others in similar situations. The individual has exempted himself from the universal, the moral law.

Or take Kant's example. Ought you to make false promises when in dire need? Can you universalize the maxim that one may make promises when in dire need, promises he does not intend to keep? If everyone in need were allowed this, then no one would ever accept promises from those in need. There would then be no promise makers because there would be no promise takers. If a person goes ahead anyway and makes false promises, clearly he does so not because of the universalizability of the action, but because he makes his act an exception to the universal rule.

Questions on Kant's Inconsistency

Two questions can be raised at this point. Is not Kant guilty of mixing empirical elements with his analysis of the *ought,* the very thing he keeps insisting should not be done? In addition, is not Kant being some sort of a utilitarian after all and thus contradicting himself when he says that his theory of morals is a metaphysics free from the error of making morals depend on the *effects* of an action? In reply, Kant points out that *empirically* there is no way we can be sure that a moral act even takes place at all. Indeed, a "cool observer" who has grown old and wise in the ways of human beings would doubt that men ever act purely for duty's sake without any trace of the "dear self." How then can this theory be charged with bringing in the empirical to the moral? To the contrary, this theory emphasized the irreducible difference between the *is* and the *ought,* so much so that nothing could ever alter or weaken a command of duty on the basis that men have been observed to act in the way duty commands.

> ...*whether this or that takes place is not at all the question; but that reason of itself, independent of all experience, ordains what ought to take place, that accordingly actions of which perhaps the world has hitherto never given an example, the feasibility even of which might be very much doubted by one who founds everything on experience, are nevertheless inflexibly commanded by reason; that for example, even though there might never yet have been a sincere friend, yet not a whit the less is pure sincerity in friendship required of every man, because prior to all experience, this duty is involved as duty in the idea of a reason determining the will by a priori principles.*[14]

The second question is much more complicated and there are those who claim that utilitarianism is indeed entailed in Kant's theory.[15] However, there certainly is a basis for holding that Kant himself would have rejected this linking of his moral theory to utilitarianism. True, he includes consequences in his *conception* of an action which is being assessed against the norm of universalizability. But it is the resulting contradiction of reason against its own dictate, not the consequences themselves, which decides the issue. In the examples used, for instance, it was not because there would be no more shops, nor marriages, nor promise takers, if the acts in question were allowed universally, that they were deemed immoral. Rather they were judged immoral because of the

24

contradiction they involved, namely, shoplifting-not-shoplifting; adultery-not-adultery; promising-not-promising.

To confirm Kant's point we can also note that a consequential theory of ethics is necessarily empirical , i.e. we would have to consult experience to find out what consequences actions do produce: the cries of the wounded, or the smiles of the satisfied. And Kant insists on keeping moral theory out of the empirical area. He notes how reason reverses itself, as it were, when it goes from purely speculative to a practical or moral function. Speculatively, we saw how reason's concepts are empty without sense perceptions. We see now that in functioning practically (i.e. morally) "it is just when the common understanding excludes all sensible springs from practical laws that its power of judgement begins to show itself to advantage."[16] Hence it is, says Kant, that all men consider themselves equally gifted and equally discerning when it comes to moral evaluations of action. This is also why moral debates always constitute the staple of party talk! Invariably, after the initial small talk and banters, social conversation tends to center on moral arguments.[17] Descartes, earlier, had noted how common sense is indeed evenly distributed among mankind. And Kant, following Rousseau's optimistic evaluation of human nature at its deepest springs, thinks that with an awareness of what he has shown here to be the moral imperative, human beings "are well able to distingiush in every case that occurs what is good, what bad, conformably to duty or inconsistent with it, if without in the least teaching them anything new, we only like Socrates direct their attention to the principle they themselves enjoy."[18]

If this is so, why then all this effort at grasping and clarifying this moral principle? Because there are those counterforces to reason within us, namely, our inclination (sensual feelings, desires, urges, appetites) which are forever trying to adulterate and overpower the purity of our will-to-duty. The result is a "natural dialectic" within a human person between will and inclination whenever immorality occurs. Without the reinforcement of a solid philosophical understanding of the nature of morals, reason can be "easily seduced" away from moral duty into the satisfaction of inclination.[19]

Back to the Basis for Morals:
Second Section

Kant cannot repeat too often that to base morals on empirical elements would automatically destroy its universality. Morality must be located in pure reason which alone, because of its a priori nature, can serve as the unconditioned source of the categorical imperative. This should caution us against deriving moral principles from examples, as we are often apt to do when bringing up children.[20] This puts the cart, as it were, before the horse. The example is not the measure of morality. Quite the reverse. Our understanding of the moral act is precisely what enables us to judge the morality embodied in the example. This holds true even of Christ. The Holy One of the Gospels, says Kant, must first be compared with the ideal of moral perfection in our reason before we can recognize Him as holy. "Why call ye Me (whom you see) good? None is good (the model of good) but God only (whom you do not see)."[21] Recall how mere conformity to duty is not enough to qualify an act as moral. Moral motivation is essential. Yet this motivation is hidden not only to any "cool observer" but even to the performer of the act himself. Where then did we get the concept of God as the supreme good? "Simply from the *idea* of moral perfection, which reason frames a priori and connects inseparably with the notion of a free will."[22]

That is a remarkable text. In effect it closes off any and all possible entries from the empirical world into the pure fount of morality, pure reason. There can be no relativization of reason itself whether to God (above, so to speak) or to the world of experience (below). The *ought* of pure reason stands as the supreme norm and principle of morality, self-contained, secure in itself. Reason judges everything else and is itself judged by none other than its own very law written in its own being, namely, that of rationality or non-contradiction. Already there is the hint here of the idea of "autonomy of pure reason" which will be developed later.

Failure to hold that morals can only have a priori foundations has given rise to mistaken moral theories based on experience, the will of God, or what have you. Such theories cannot but provide weak motives for being moral, for nothing can be a stronger motive for morality than the realization that reason itself is able, prior to all experience, to command itself and generate its own action solely from its will to duty. It is on this bedrock foundation that a life of morality should be built, not on youthful hero-worshipping examples. You could, for instance, bring children up on the example of patriotic and courageous Audie Murphy who comes home to a glorious reception of the Congressional Medal of Honor, ticker tape parades and the approving roars of a grateful nation. But this is a subversion of the right order of moral thinking. All too soon, as the child grows up, real life teaches him that many good and heroic acts pass by not only unnoticed and unrewarded but even ridiculed by the very people who were the beneficiaries of those acts. At this point the will to do good, having been built on a shaky base, is liable to come unstuck and crumble. Instead of a moral man we now find all too often a moral dissolute, badly disillusioned and ill-used enough to realize Leo Durocher's famous saying that nice guys finish last.

The child must be brought up on one and only one principle, namely, to do what is right precisely because it is right regardless of consequences. This is a solid base which can withstand all assaults from discouraging experiences. (I will only confess that, personally, I have found it well-nigh impossible to bring up children according to this Kantian mentality.)

Towards the Moral Ought

We must next follow the practical faculty of reason from the general rules of its determination to the point where the notion of duty

26

springs from it. We need to dig into that all significant word *ought* which expresses duty.

To begin, we note that *ought* has various uses. We thus need to sort out its precise meaning when used in the moral context. Kant differentiates the various imperatives into three general kinds thus:

IMPERATIVE
(OUGHT)

Categorical = towards good-in-itself (morality: law binding on all rational beings.

Hypothetical

Assertoric / Pragmatic = prudential counsels towards happiness; scl. "since you want to be happy, do such and such." Condition is asserted.

Technical = concerns means to be chosen for solving a problematic situation. If you want to get this, do such and such. Condition is mentioned hypothetically, not asserted.

We start with the hypothetical imperatives which we must separate decisively from the unconditional and categorical imperative of moral duty. First there is the technical imperative. Every man knows that *if* he really wants something, he must go after it. He must use the means which effectively achieves his end. If I really want a college degree, I must do college work. Here the *ought* clearly depends on the hypothesis or condition of my really wanting something. We are talking here of a want not necessarily lodged in my nature and which I am free to dismiss at any time. Once my wanting along this line stops, the *ought* automatically becomes inoperative. In really effective volitions it is easy to see that by mere analysis of the idea of wanting the end one also comes to the idea of wanting the means necessary to attain that end. "Whoever wills the end wills also the means."[25] "For in willing an object as my effect there is already the causality of myself as an acting cause."[26] I cannot, in our example, conceive myself as really wanting a college degree without including in that very idea my wanting to do college work. "For it is one and the same thing to conceive something as an effect which I can produce in a certain way, and to conceive myself as acting in this way."[27]

Next we have the assertoric/pragmatic imperative of happiness. Since it is in the nature of every man to desire happiness, the imperative here takes the form of an assertion:"Since you in fact desire to be happy, you ought to do this or that."[28] The question is: since happiness is unlike the arbitrary ends which are the objects of technical imperatives on the one hand, and since on the other hand it is also unlike the categorical imperative which is directed to the production of a good will (whereas happiness is the satisfaction of our inclinations), what kind of imperative

27

could the imperative of happiness be? Clearly, it is midway between the two. Kant calls it assertoric, assertorial or prudential. It is not like the imperatives of technical skill where the ends are arbitrarily chosen but once chosen are clearly known. "Unfortunately, the notion of happiness is so indefinite that although everyone wishes to attain it, yet he never can say definitely and consistently what it is that he really wishes and wills."[29] Why is this so? Because the idea of what would really make one happy requires a *total* conception of an object that will be good for the person concerned *at all times.* This would include all of one's future existence, and only an infinite mind could possibly know such an object. Since exeperiences can be only of the past or the present and cannot extend to the future, it is clearly impossible to get a total conception of "all future circumstances."[30] Hence a universal prescription for happiness is impossible. If people do coincide in their objects of happiness, it is more like the proverbial yawn that becomes contagious in a crowd.[31] We see then how happiness, though a natural end of man, cannot generate more than a hypothetical imperative with regard to the means of attaining it. It is an end whose meaning lies in the means for its attainment, namely, pleasurable satisfaction of our wants and sensual inclinations. Kant calls the kind of imperative happiness generates only a "prudential" imperative because its command is really a counsel or advice formed out of experience as to what means *probably* (never certainly) would conduce to make us happy *if* we achieved it. Those then are the two hypothetical imperatives. Neither one is unconditional.

When we come to the moral imperative, we find it based, not on experience but beyond all experience, in the realm of pure reason itself. Our task then is not that of showing that categorical imperatives are actually in operation. For how could we point to any one act and be certain that it is a moral act seeing that men's motivations are so impenetrably complex and full of ruses and self-deception? Our task is rather to get to the conditions which enable the categorical imperative to be present in rational beings like men.

Yet soon after sayng this, Kant launches into egregious leaps of thought which leave his readers befuddled. We are told suddenly that explaining the categorical imperative is a very "profound," "special," and "laborious" study,[32] because it deals with a *synthetic a priori* proposition. Indeed we have already explained how he labored in his first *Critique* to explain precisely this sort of proposition . We can anticipate his thought here and explain how the categorical imperative is said to be a synthetic a priori proposition when all along he has been careful to hold it apart from the sensible empirical world. The point is that the moral command is issued as a universal law towards the sense manifold of the pathological inclinations. Of themselves these inclinations would be an unruly mob of disorganized desires and appetites. In a being without such pathological counterforces, pure reason would of itself do what is moral. If would be a "holy" will where a moral command would be superfluous. But in human beings there is this moral *ought* which links the universal laws of pure reason to the synthetic world of sensual inclinations.

Kant now proceeds to explain how the moral imperative as categorical differs from hypothetical imperatives. In the former we need not

conceive any conditions first to conceive its content. All that is commanded here is that one's subjective maxims, simply and without conditions,
conform to the universalizability demand of the moral law. We therefore
get the first formula for the categorical imperative, namely, *"Act only on
that maxim whereby thou canst at the same time will that it should become a
universal law."*[33] Here we have a clear instance of pure reason contributing
its law towards the organization of the sense world, an instance therefore
of reason making possible, now in a different realm, "rule-determined
behaviour." If we recall, that was precisely Kant's definition of "nature."
Hence he quickly follows through with a second way of stating the
categorical imperative: *"Act as if the maxim of thy action were to become
by thy will a universal law of nature."*[34] With this we come to the four
examples which illustrate the universalizability norm in operation.

First, a person contemplating suicide cannot universalize the act he
contemplates without contradicting the "special nature" which precisely
impels every man towards improvement, not abandonment, of life in
times of crisis. Second, should a man make false promises in distress? We
have already discussed this and shown that it would be self-contradicting.
The law would "annihlate itself."[35] Third, ought a person pass his life
away in lazy enjoyment without developing his talents? Here we can
have an act that can be universalized without annihlating or contradicting
itself apparently. Yet, though the concept may not be self-contradictory,
the *willing* of it would be. For "the system of nature" has implanted in all
men an instinct to develop their individual talents. To will that all men *not*
develop their talents would contradict this will precisely to develop one's
talents. Fourth, we have the case of the successful self-made man who
now refuses to lift a finger in behalf of others still struggling to make a life
for themselves. Now this quasi Ayn Randian mentality by itself would
probably not disrupt the "system of nature." It does not seem to be
self-contradicting either. Still, we would in fact contradict ourselves if we
willed it, says Kant, because as a universal rule "many cases might occur in
which one would have need of the love and symphaty of others and in
which, by such a law of nature, sprung of his own will, he would deprive
himself of all hope of the aid he desires."[36]

We can make three observation about these examples. First, the first
two examples fall under the category of what Kant calls "perfect duties"
in which there is no exception or playroom for choosing. The lattèr two
examples are instances of "imperfect duty" with room for choosing when
and in what circumstances duty may be performed. More on this later.
Secondly, Wolff, a commentator on this work who thinks all four
examples fail to uphold Kant's point makes an interesting observation
about the last example.

> *Suppose an individual adopts it as his policy never to set for himself an
> end whose achievement appears to require the cooperation of others
> and to foreswear any ends he has adopted as soon as it turns out that
> such cooperation is needed. Under these circumstances he could
> consistently will that his maxim of selfishness should be a universal
> law of nature, for he could be certain a priori that he would never find
> himself willing an end which in the ancient world was espoused by*

such Stoic philosophers as Epictetus, as perfectly consonant with the Categorical Imperative in both its first and second formulations. Thus we see that of the four original examples, only the example of false promising can be shown to be a valid application of the Categorical Imperative and then only after suitable alterations and reinterpretations.[37]

Thirdly, we see that the norm of universalizability is now taken to be operating as well on the level of the "will." Earlier, we had talked only of internal contradictions, i.e. we cannot even conceive those actions without falling into contradiction. The expression "system of nature" here can probably be assimilated into this non-contradictory interpretation of "universalizability." After all, the rule-determined behaviour idea of nature the mind contributes is obviously controlled by the principle of contradiction. Now we find, however, that this non-contradiction is not the only test of universalizability. The other test is that the act be universally "willable" morally. In the example, Kant says there is a will for help and sympathy from others in all of us, and this no one should contradict by willing that things be otherwise.

Now it may be that the two tests are reducibly one. Internal contradiction is, in a sense, the same thing as contradiction of the will since it is impossible to will what is contradictory. Wolff, for instance, thinks it follows from this that, according to Kant, we really cannot will an immoral act which by definition is contradictory.[38] Obviously, to avoid confusion, we need to stress here the distinction between *physical* and *moral* will acts. I can, of course, will an act that is conceptually, in the moral sphere, self-contradicting. Here the "I can" refers to the physical power to do the act, i.e. will it. The point here is that we are talking of *moral permissibility.* Can you *morally?* No. Furthermore, when Kant talks of a "natural will" implanted in all men, I think we can make sense out of that puzzling expression if we remember that for him *will* is simply pure reason in its pratical role. Hence it is governed by the principle of non-contradiction.[39]

If we have understood Kant's insistence on this principle of universality in morals, we should also see that an immoral action is always one which seeks to make itself an exception to the universal law, something to keep in mind in retort to the objection from Wolff we noted above. "In my own case," the immoral man says to himself in effect, "this act is allowed" but not in all the rest.

However, Kant should not be made to look silly on this point. We should not say that an immoral man says that to himself *explicitly* each time he is about to act immorally. That would preposterous. What Kant means is that if we were to analyze the situations in which an immoral act takes place, this in effect would be what the attitude is. When we are immoral we "take the liberty of making an *exception* in our own favor or (just for this time only) in favor of our inclination."[40] Kant points out that the immoral man has thus changed the universality of the moral law into "mere generality."[41] However, we should not insist on the distinction between "generality" and "universality" since soon afterward,[42] those expressions are interchanged. The point is that morality is intrinsic to all

30

rational beings, while immorality is an assumption of being exempted from that universal condition.

Here we see how the categorical imperative has to be categorical, not hypothetical. This latter would make the will subordinate to some further good, and ultimately to some good-in-itself on which all other relative goods depend. For not everything can be "good for something" (means) without something being good-in-itself; else, we would be in a Heraclitean flux of everything being good for everything else without anything being good-in-itself. We can recall that Kant opened this work with the observation that reason must conceive something as good in itself and that this cannot be anything else but a good will. If the will then were to be subjected to a hypothetical imperative, the object of such an imperative would be some end or interest other than the good will itself. Of course the spring for such an interest or desire can be traced back to the will act.[43] But clearly in this instance, the will would be determined extrinsically, by an object outside the will. Now we know that reason is precisely unlike inclination in that reason is capable of self-determination, while an inclination must always be determined by an object other than itself. There is no higher tribunal for reason than reason itself. And will here, as we have seen, is nothing more than practical reason itself.

Pure practical reason then, as *the* moral faculty, must be self-determining in its motive. Morality cannot be subordinated to anything below (v.g. experience) or above (revelation or any "tutelary nature").[44] The moral will is not determined by "another" as happens when the will functions as a *spring*. Now to say the will as moral is self-determining is to say it is determined a priori, away from all empirical material ends. For the will to be determined a priori simply within itself is to be determined by its own reasons solely because they are rational. That is why Kant keeps repeating that moral imperatives hold for *all* rational beings. If now it be asked what the a priori will is determining itself to, the answer is: it is determining itself to being a good-in-itself completely. Through this thought we are led to the conclusion that "man and generally any rational being exists as an end in himself, *not merely as a means* to be arbitrarily used by this or that will (os another) but in all his actions, whether they concern himself or other rational beings, must be always regarded at the same time as an end."[45]

Frankly, there seems to be some circular reasoning here. It is argued that the rational will of man must be self-determining and thus categorical, not hypothetical. Yet it is also asserted that as self-determining the will cannot be hypothetical. At any rate, commentators agree that there seems to be a *tour de force* here. Kant's way of concluding to the categorical imperative is less than airtight, though he obviously thinks otherwise. He simply goes on as though he has definitely established that man is an end-in-himself and never a means only. He quickly spells out the third formulation of the categorical imperative: "*So act as to treat humanity, whether in thine own person or in that of any other, in every case as an end withal, never as a means only.* "[46] He then reviews his four previous examples and shows how from the third formulation they can be successfuly analyzed to show how in each case there is immorality involved because man is being reduced to a means *merely* in each case.

31

Why is suicide, for example, wrong? Because the suicide makes himself a "means to maintain a tolerable condition up to the end of life."[47] Kant notes that this is not the same as a case of amputating parts of the body for the sake of overall health, or exposure of life to danger in order to preserve it, etc.

In the second example we ask why making false promises when in dire need is immoral. The answer: "he whom I promise by such a promise to use for my own purposes cannot possibly assent to my mode of acting towards him, and therefore cannot himself contain the end of this action."[48] This calls for more remarks. For obviously men are always using one another. Students use their teachers to gain knowledge; teachers use their students to gain a living: a husband uses his wife and vice versa in dozens of ways, and so on. This is why it is impossible simply to forbid the use of human persons. What is forbidden is the use of person as *means merely*. In this example a man is shown to be used as a means merely when someone manipulates conditions so as to make a free decision on his part impossible. Ignorance makes it impossible for him to contain his act in himself as his own end. The absence of a man's action as an end-in-himself lies in that free decision precisely to enter into any action, situation or agreement with another person. If that free choice is made impossible by manipulation of circumstances, then one man has used the other as a means *merely*. This is immoral. But there is nothing immoral about two persons freely and knowingly entering into a relationship of mutually profitable action, provided, of course, the act they cooperate in is not against the norm of universalizability.

In the third example, Kant again concedes that the categorical imperative itself is not directly violated by men who choose the lazy and unfulfilled life. *Advancement* of humanity is involved in the very conception of man as an end-in-himself. Hence the chronically lazy person is in effect renouncing his own nature by choosing not to fulfill his talent. Needless to say, some will question this contention.

In the fourth example we again seem to run into some textual inconsistency. Here Kant talks of happiness as *the* natural end of all men, all the time that he maintains the good-in-itself, or in other words, the moral end as *the* end for man. The inconsistency disappears, however, if we remember that morality is the highest good and supreme end of man which he has to achieve rationally, while happiness is an end to which man is naturally *inclined*. The first is in the area of freedom, the second in that of "nature." With that we can go on to notice that the fourth, like the third example, concerns an imperfect duty. The reasoning too is similar. The concept of humanity, or man as an end-in-himself, involves the advancement of human happiness. This means the advancement not only of my own happiness but that also of all human beings. The man who would not help in the advancement of others, even when he can and the situation is right, is in effect renouncing his own nature.

In a striking footnote, Kant notes that his categorical imperative is clearly not the same as the golden rule, "Do unto others as you would others do unto you." We have only to say the words to see that the motivation here is self-centered. It is the individual's interest in being treated the same way which motivates him to act. The contrast to Kant's demand for universality and purity of motive when it comes to moral duty is evident. If one were to follow the golden rule literally, even the criminal could demand of the judge not to sentence him!

The third formulation then applies to every rational being without exception.[49] Its premises thus could not have been empirical or experiential. Only pure reason could have generated such an imperative. And since pure reason prescinds from individual experiences and empirical situations, its nature cannot but be the selfsame one as found in every rational being. Now since it is this reason, as will, which legislates the categorical imperative, we can see that "the will of every rational being is a universally legislative will."[50] What *your* pure practical reason (will) legislates for you is legislated for us all. Likewise, what *my* pure practical reason legislates for me is legislated for everyone else. This is a peculiar subjection of the will to its own legislation, the peculiarly autonomous way of morality.[51]

The Two Aspects of the Will

Kant has already conceded that the will can have an interest in moral law. But it is a unique interest, namely, *respect*. Now, however, we are told the will can have no interest whatever in the realm of morals.[52] A careful reading should give the answer. We find him distinguishing between the will as lawgiver (sovereign) and the will as a subject of its own legislation (member) of the kingdom of ends. It was the will as a subject of its own legislation that he referred to earlier when he pointed to respect for law as the only possible interest the will can have in moral duty. What he is saying here is that the will as the objective lawgiver (not the subject) cannot possibly act from any individual interest. For then it would have to be subjected to other laws to make sure those interest are moral. What could those "other laws" be when we have seen that the will is self-restricting and self-determining? The failure to see this nature of morality as a self-legislating will, and the belief that the source of moral law was always from something other than the will itself, says Kant, was what caused all other moral theories before his own to fail. They failed to see the unconditional nature of the moral will because they made the moral good always subordinate to some other good interest. They thus made the moral will conditional when in its ultimate root it is unconditional.

If we recall the hue and cry which attended President Ford's pardon of Richard Nixon, we can see how men instinctively, as it were, demand that the law apply *evenly* to every citizen, every member of a nation. From this we can see how the concept of "law" leads to the idea of a "kingdom of ends."[53] Kingdom here means "the union of different rational beings in a system of common laws." The point to be grasped here is that pure reason in every man commands acts consistent with rationality itself, not merely with this or that individual man's peculiarly individual subjective reasons. The moral command thus issues forth not just from the individual whose reason at the moment happens to be the one from which the command is in fact originating, but really from everyone's and anyone's *rational* consciousness. If my pure reason commands something that is really rational and consistent with its own rationality, it cannot but be consistent also with reason in you and in every one else. Otherwise we would have to admit that its claim to be rational was invalid.[54] A position really rational would be rational all along and for everyone even if for the moment its rationality may be opaque to a few or more for whatever reason. Though one could press this question on and on to a thicket of both theoretical and practical difficulties and objections, it should suffice for our purpose here to insist on the self-transparency of reason to itself. We have said that there is no other tribunal available to reason than its own self. This is saying the same thing. Kant talks of this universal characteristic of pure moral reason as something a priori from everything empirical. Hence valid moral commands, though they issue from individual persons (only individuals exist, after all) are really universal in content.

Hence it is that all rational beings are subordinated to the same system of laws, namely, those of pure reason. This common subjection to the same laws of reason makes of them all members of one and the same kingdom, of the same "system of laws." And since the essential law for all of them, as we have seen, is enuntiated as never treating one another as means *merely* but as ends-in-themselves, we can call this a kingdom of ends.

Each end-in-himself in this kingdom may be viewed from two aspects. As active lawgiver he is *sovereign* (i.e. he is not subject to any other legislature). As a *member* he is subject to this kingdom's laws. Now, if a rational being were without wants and inclinations (the counterforces to duty) it is clear that he would be simply sovereign.

The universalized maxims of his will would of their very nature be untainted with anything sensual. It would thus retain its purely rational and universal character. There would be no need to subject him to reason's command since he would do them naturally. Morality is nothing more than measuring all actions against legislations of the rational will, *the* norm which, because it is applied equally to all, makes a community or kingdom of ends possible. We thus find a fourth (though some deny it really is a different formulation) form of the categorical imperative:
"So to act that thy will could at the same time regard itself as giving in its maxims universal laws."[55]

We rational beings, therefore, give and receive laws unto ourselves. And this gives us "dignity." "Dignity" leads us back to the concept of "worth." Worth is either relative or absolute. Relative worth is called *value.* Goods derive their value from the ends to which they are aligned. They are thus replaceable among themselves with things of equivalent value. Value or price[56] is twofold: market value (v.g. skill, diligence) and fancy value (wit, lively imagination, humor, etc.). In contrast to all these replaceable, relative worths, we have *absolute worth,* and this is *dignity,* the invaluable worth of moral beings who are ends-in-themselves. We can schematize these divisions of worth thus:

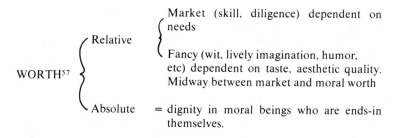

WORTH[57]

Relative
- Market (skill, diligence) dependent on needs
- Fancy (wit, lively imagination, humor, etc) dependent on taste, aesthetic quality. Midway between market and moral worth

Absolute = dignity in moral beings who are ends-in themselves.

Since rational beings as moral have intrinsic worth, the acts they do with the sole motive of respecting their natures as ends-in-themselves also have intrinsic worth or dignity. Keeping promises, for instance, is an act altogether different in nature from writing up jokes or TV scenarios about it for pay. If your script or play fails, the management can always substitute something else to fill up the slot and market demand is met. But what piece of art or nature can compensate for a moral act which failed to take place?[58] Nothing. It is forever and irretrivably lost. This is what is meant by dignity as "infinitely above all value." It is something *sacred.* It cannot be degraded to the level of comparison or competition.

What then decides the relative values of goods? Kant who, unlike Karl Marx, was not dealing in economics, replies simply: "Nothing has any worth except what the law assigns it."[59] Hence "if the law is the source of all values, it must itself be above value." Why? Because otherwise it would in giving itself a value reduce itself to an object. No, the law must have "unconditional and incomparable worth," that is to say, *dignity.* And the esteem that dignity properly evokes is *respect.*[60] Rational beings then as a source of all their own laws are autonomous. This autonomy constitutes their dignity.

We are explicitly told that the various formulations of the categorical imperative are reducibly one.[61] All are characterized by the same form of *universality,* and by the matter (that upon whom universality is imposed) of rational beings as ends-in-themselves ideally harmonized into a kingdom. The various formulations were given so as to bring the essential point about the foundation of morals "nearer to intuition."

We next meet with perplexing talk of a "will unconditionally good," a phrase he used at the very opening sentence of this book. The meaning seems to be as follows. The will as a member of the kingdom of ends is under the categorical imperative or moral duty. As such its goodness is conditional only; conditional on its acting not merely in conformity but strictly for the sake of duty. Dutiful action makes the will of a member good. But it is made good conditionally, that is, on condition that it obey the moral law. Yet since the moral command issues out of the selfsame will as *sovereign,* it really has no other determining object or condition. Seen from this aspect it can be considered as unconditionally good or good-in-itself. For if we were to derive the legislating will's goodness from another, we would be in an infinite regress. Consequently, we can see that as unconditionally good and the source of all laws, we have here a situation analogous to that of pure reason contributing its universal laws to sense data in order to constitute *nature.* Kant thus repeats the *nature* formula of the categorical imperative: *"Act on maxims which can at the same time have for their object themselves as universal laws of nature."*

Rational nature is distinguished "from the rest of nature by this, that it sets before itself an end."[62] The ends of irrational things (whatever they be) are set for them by nature. They cannot figure out ends for themselves. They are not rational. Rational beings, by contrast, can figure out and set forth ends for themselves. And they see that their rational nature itself is the source of laws which govern the ways in which the various ends they set up for themselves are to be *effected.* Hence an individual's own rational consciousness sees itself, as it were, as *the* end beyond all the other ends it sets up. He is an ultimate and basic end which cannot be referred to any further end without contradiction. He sees himself as the limit or norm against which the morality or immorality of the other ends to be set up is to be judged. In this way we conceive a rational being to be a negative limit to ends set up, i.e., he must never be relegated to the status of means only.

The individual who sees that he is subject to the moral law should also see that the law in a very real sense is dictated by none other than himself. For he is a rational being in exactly the same way as the actual enuntiator of the law, whoever this may happen to be at the moment. For "it is just this fitness of his maxims for universal legislation that distinguishes him as an end in himself."[63] In the *mundus intelligibilis* (intelligible world, nuomena) his dignity is equal to that of every one. We can thus perceive an analogy between the laws of efficient casuality in nature and the laws of morality in the kingdom of ends. Both are law-governed.[64] But nature is governed from *without.* (i.e. one thing causes another), while morality is governed from *within* (the will-act causes itself so to speak).

Kant seems to say since nature is *for man*[65] then ideally, if all men behaved morally, there would be an ideal unity and harmony between the kingdom of nature and of ends-in-themselves. However, such "expectation of happiness" is really beside the point. For the categorical imperative, as unconditional, binds with full force regardless of the failures of men and nature. Here again we see the dignity of man as one which does not depend on his physical conditions and wants. These are subject to the physical laws of nature. Rather, human dignity rests on man's sublime independence, as lawgiver, from the springs of interest or inclination, i.e. on his autonomy as a moral being. Even if the real union of the kingdoms of nature and ends came to pass under one actual sovereign so as to make membership in such a realm very desirable from many other motives, this would not really change the intrinsic worth of rational beings one bit. This worth is simply independent of such extrinsic benefits. They cannot in any way alter man's absolute worth by which alone he must be judged "even by the Supreme Being."[66]

The Natures of "Holy" and Virtuous Wills

A man's actions are to be judged morally permissible or not depending on whether they are consistent with the autonomous will in him. In a being of a perfectly holy will, action and law would be identical. Hence no obligation could arise in such a being. But in wills less than holy, obligation or duty goes with an autonomous will. Kant then goes on to show how one subject to duty is nevertheless sublime and bears dignity. It is not as subject to the law, but rather as legislator and giver of that same law to which he is subject that he has both sublimity and dignity- - -plus the fact that to be moral an act must be done not out of the unworthy emotion of fear or inclination, but out of *respect* for the law alone which confers moral worth on those actions. His words deserve to be pondered.

> *That the principle of autonomy in question is the sole principle of morals can be readily shown by mere analysis of the conception of morality. For by this analysis we find that its principle must be a categorical imperative, and that what this commands is neither more nor less than this very autonomy.*[67]

He explains that should one make morality heteronomous (i.e. dependent on some other object of the will) the result would be a hypothetical imperative commanding an action only *if* that object be wanted also. But the moral imperative commands without referring to any other motive. Hence it can only be autonomous, not heteronomous. The reasoning does seem to be circular, or perhaps just a simple assertion. We would do well to remember, however, that he has already-shown how hypothetical imperatives are restricted to the areas of prudence and skills (the world of inclinations) and that morals have no place in that world. Seen thus, perhaps the charge of circular reasoning is avoided. Whether, in addition, his contention that all this is brought out by mere analysis of the concept of a "moral will" is true is another matter. B.E.A. Liddell, a commentator, writes:

> *By analyzing the concepts of will and law we cannot prove that the will is subject to the moral law since subjection of the will to law is not part of the meaning of will. But we* can *prove by such an analysis of concepts that the categorical imperative is the essence of moral law.*[68]

Heteronomous Moral Theories

A classification of the various ways in which the principles of morality may be grounded may help at this point, especially the heteronomous ways. Heteronomous principles of morality can be drawn either from experience or, interestingly, even from reason. Those from experience may be either hedonistic or intuitive. Those from reason can be either idealistic or theological. The following schema summarizes these divisions.

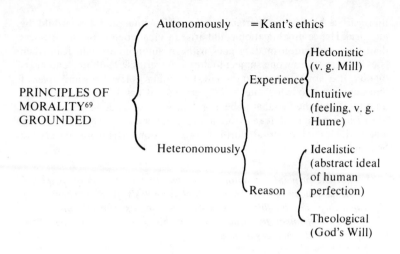

Against each of the heteronomous versions respectively Kant argues. Against hedonism we can say that good conduct and happiness do not always coincide. There is no intrinsic connection between the two. Why? Because the two belong to different realms as we have seen. Making one *good* and making one *happy* are by no means identical. Moreover, if we take pleasure and pain as the moral norms, we get into an ethics of self-interest. This is the destruction, not the defense nor construction of ethics. Even if the corrective of the "greatest happiness for the greatest number" be used, the result would still be an ethics of personal advantage and gain. This reduces ethics to mockery. It makes vice and virtue a matter of quantitative calculation. If one insists that John Stuart Mill advocated a *qualitative* ethics of pleasure and pain, Kant would reply that there still is that calculating element for the "dear self" in it. Even in the Aristotelian theory of virtue as the mean between excess and deficiency (courage, v.g. as the mean between the extremes of fanaticism and cowardice) what we have is still the right *amount* of courage to constitute virtue. This is something which even the prudent man cannot calculate beforehand, but must calibrate, as it were, in the situation itself. In such calculations the "dear self" must figure prominently. When I say seemingly unselfishly that I am after what will produce the greatest happiness for the greatest number, it is not as though I side disinterestedly with the greatest number after the count is taken. Rather, I am really partisan and side with a group on a given issue. I hope fervently that the count will be in our favor, albeit the hope is covered over by many psychic ruses and disguises even to my own consciousness. The fact that I abide with the majority *after* the count does not alter my real governing interest and internal disposition on the matter.

Next, experience as feeling cannot be the foundation of morality. The former is particular, the latter universal. Still, Kant feels sympathetic to this position more than others. Fot it seems to regard moral action as *beautiful* towards which it has an immediate feeling of attraction. This certainly seems preferable to having to go into long forced explanations in order to persuade even one's self that morality is something admirable.

Against the abstract ideal of "human perfection" we can say that is so empty of content that it tells us nothing. If someone commanded you to "Be perfect!" you would have no idea in the world what that required of you. Hence you could not act on it. A principle is supposed to generate action. Hence a vacuous principle like that is no principle at all.

Kant argues against God's Will as the source of morality first by declaring that God's will cannot be known to us. God is certainly not within the phenomenal world where alone for Kant genuine knowledge is restricted. If then we can have no knowledge of God's existence, much less do we have any knowledge of his will. If one answers that the will of God is made known to us by God, then we can reply that even in that supposition we would know first that it was God Himself commanding. This in turn we would know precisely by using our reason to sort out the evidences. Furthermore, even after we have established through reason that it is indeed God commanding us, this command still would not have any binding force unless reason *first* told us it is moral to obey God when he commands. As the source of morality then God's will cannot be prior to reason.

Man the Inhabitant of Two Worlds
(Freedom and Determinism)

In his final section Kant tries to bring the concepts of will, autonomy, morality, rationality and freedom in their proper order of sequence toward the conclusion that rational beings are free moral agents legislating their own moral law, each for all and all for each.

We start with the will as a kind of casuality: our choices produce effects. This is a casuality rooted in reason, not in the empirical world of experience or nature. Since the will is a cause, it too must contain laws. For regular succession (rule determined behavior) is involved in the concept of a *cause.* The will then as cause must have its own laws. However, since the will is a *rational* cause, and reason is other than the world of nature and appearances, the will's causality and laws must also be other than and independent of nature where all causality is heteronomous, i.e. one extrinsically determines another in rule-determined behavior/succession. Now to be free of extrinsic determination, to be independent of nature is precisely what we mean by freedom in a negative sense. If the will then is a cause but *not* a heteronomous cause, it can only be autonomous. Its laws cannot be from another, but rather from within itself. As a cause it must have its laws which determine it. As different from nature since it is reason (which is "even elevated above the understanding"[71]) those laws, unlike the laws of heteronomous nature, must be autonomous, i.e. from itself. The autonomous self-legislating nature of the will or practical reason is thus seen to be a conclusion from man's freedom or otherness from nature.

Kant notes that it makes no difference that we merely reason to our idea of freedom. True, his critique of knowledge forbids us to take that further step beyond the mere idea into the judgement that we *are* free. But it is enough that we cannot *but* have the idea that we are free. To act as if we are free is equivalently to be free. "Now I say that every being that cannot act except under the idea of freedom is just for that reason in a practical point of view really free, that is to say, all laws which are inseparably connected with freedom have the same force as if his will had been shown to be free in itself by a proof theoretically conclusive."[72] In brief, we presuppose freedom. That presupposition can withstand our inability to prove it *constitutively.*

It seems that Kant argues in a circle here. He argues to morality (self-imposed law) in man because he is free. Then he argues that man is free because he is moral, i.e. has self-imposed law, autonomy. Moreover, why should there be a necessary connection between the concept of a self-legislating agent and morality?

Why cannot self-legislating will be such without its "I ought" necessarily taking on the reality of moral obligation? In an all-perfect will (holy), for example, in which there is no counterforce to the will, the law would be exactly the agent's choice always and indefectibly.

What then makes us say that the autonomous will in man results in man being a moral being, the "I ought" in him becoming moral obligation?

Here we run into a lengthy discourse reminding us of the distinction between the perceptible world of phenomena and the unseen world of nuomena. We recall how we know there is something beyond sense-appearances. For appearances are always *of* something appearing. Kant contends that this is a distinction evident even to the ordinary man on the street who does not really believe that what he sees externally is what a person *really* is. Somehow, everyone believes there is an unseen world other than the image one displays to public perception. It's a pity, however, that no sooner do people get this sound insight than they immediately spoil it by proceeding to *imagine* it do be again another "self" in the order of sensible reality.[74] The fact is they came to know the presence of this unseen world only through their intellects, i.e. they *inferred* that there must be some reality other than the appearances actually contacted by their senses.

The correct procedure is simply to accept the two worlds, accept that a man is indeed a creature of two worlds, those of appearances and things-in-themselves. The two worlds are truly other to each other. Hence the laws of the two worlds are also correspondingly different. Now we have seen that the world of nature or appearances is governed heteronomously. What then should we say of the world other to this world and its laws? That there are laws in the intelligible world is clear. We make out conclusions not in just any haphazard way, but according to the right procedures of reason. Or, at any rate, we measure our actual reasoning against such *right* norms of reason. If then we inquire where such norms come, the answer is plainly that they come from reason itself. Hence our negative conception of freedom as otherness from nature's extrinsic causation. Positively, we conceive this freedom as self-determination, autonomous causality. Thus we come to see that man is a moral being because he is free, but his freedom is also *in* (makes effects) the world of appearances, i.e. his sensual inclinations.

Kant thinks that this way of reasoning avoids any vicious circle. We do not argue merely from freedom to morality and vice versa. Rather we argue to man's freedom first because we recognize in him the presence of both the phenomenal and nuomenal world, one different from the other. Once we have differentiated the two and held them apart, we at the same time recognize their mutual presences in a human person. We see their different sets of laws, and how the difference of Reason from Nature cannot be anything else but freedom or autonomy. Our basis for holding that man is free is our knowledge of him as a creature of two different worlds. In one he is free, in the other he is determined. Nor did we simply jump from freedom to morality. To repeat, a rational being can be free. But if such a being be without inclinations, those pathological counter-forces to reason, then execution of the categorical imperative, so to speak, is automatic and natural. Such a being would not have to choose whether to act out of pure duty or not.[75]

Now the same knowledge that tells us man is a creature of the nuomenal world of freedom also tells us that he is a creature of the phenomenal world of inclinations. As counterforces to morality the inclinations tend toward their own *individual* interest and happiness. This is in obvious contrast to the always universal dictates of reason. Clearly then, the pure will in man is not exactly all that pure, is it? It is always open to the pathological influences of the inclinations. This is what comes from being a citizen of two worlds. The "I ought" in man is not the same as his "I would" automatically, as it would be in a rational being without inclination.[76] In order to act according to the categorical imperative, man needs to over-rule all the interests of inclinations as they affect the will (the "bad will")[77] and impose upon them the pure motive of duty. This is to be a moral agent.

If, at this ultimate point of our moral study, we ask why we must obey our experience of moral obligation from the categorical imperative within us, Kant admits that here he has no further answers,[78] *We must because we must,* period. We see also how the universal rule imposed upon the riotous mob of our inclinations is a *synthetic a priori* proposition. And to repeat what we said at the beginning, everyone, without exception, experiences moral obligation.

> *There is no one, not even the most consummate villain, provided only that he is otherwise accustomed to the use of reason, who, when we set before him examples of honesty of purpose, of steadfastness in following good maxims, of sympathy and general benevolence (even combined with great sacrifices of advantages and comfort) does not wish that he might also possess these qualities. Only on account of his inclinations and impulses he cannot attain this in himself, but at the same time he wishes to be free from such inclinations which are burdensome to himself.[80]*

We soon meet the words "good will" and "bad will." The former is placed in the intelligible world. It is the good will which legislates. If it were ever found in a pure state without inclinations, it would obey the categorical imperative indefectibly. The human reality, however, is otherwise. The will in man is open to the sensible world of pathological influences.[81] Whenever it does go against the good will's "ought" it is "bad." In brief, the will can be considered either as a legislating sovereign, or as a member of the ethical kingdom. Under law the will is free *physically* to obey or not obey its own moral law. Later we will see this as the distinction between *wille* and *willkür*.

Kant now goes on to say that while

> ...all men attribute to themselves freedom of the will (since they judge their actions as something they ought or ought not to have done) it really is impossible to prove the reality of freedom since 'proof' if it is to be more than just fictitious must be located in the realm of experience or nature, and here everything takes place determinately, according to set laws. Thus freedom is merely 'an idea of reason.'[82]

In that precise sense freedom's "objective reality in itself is doubtful." Not that it can ever be shown to be false. Indeed freedom cannot be argued away,[83] because its narrow footpath "is the only one on which it is possible to make use of reason in our conduct." If we really "ought" to do certain actions, we obviously "can" do them. Thus if freedom cannot be argued away, it seems necessary at least to show that it is *not* a contradiction.

Freedom Not Contradictory

There is no contradiction because man is free from a point of view other than the one in which he is not free. Man does really experience himself and his actions as determined qua nature, but also as free qua effected by intelligence.[84] Qua intelligence, that is, through his will, he conceives himself as able to disregard and override his sense inclinations. About this will he knows nothing more than that within its own realm pure reason, independently of sensibility, gives the law. And men in fact consider their real and true selves to be most properly identified with this realm rather than that of their inclinations. For man's inclinational "self" could not prevail unless it were so allowed by his nuomenal "real" self.[84]

Kant insists that pure reason as practical borrows no motive from the world of understanding and its sense manifold. Instead it moves itself to action through its own rationality, that is, its own nature or law of universality. How it is possible thus for pure reason to be practical, that is, *free*, is a question no longer within our power to comprehend. This probes unduly far into the nuomenal world to which our knowledge is unable to extend. All we can know is that it is possible for pure reason to be practical, to act freely and that there is no contradiction here. If someone insists on an explanation, Kant again answers that explanations hold only on the level of nature where one thing can be explained by another. Nor is analogy possible. The two worlds, to repeat, are simply other to each other.[85]

This impossibility of explaining freedom is the same as the impossibility of explaining how man can act for the sake of moral law without any "interest" in it other than "respect," i.e. our understanding and recognizing the universality of the law itself as sufficient to constrain our actions. This is not to say reason has no power to "infuse a feeling of pleasure or satisfaction" in the fulfillment of duty. But to make this feeling the standard of morality or its motive would dilute the necessary purity of the moral act. Moral law is valid for us not because we have an interest in it. Quite the other way. It is valid for us, hence it interests us. Why is it valid for us? Because we know that our inclinational self must be subordinated to our rational/nuomenal self. Reason ought to be the prevailing human power because its universal scope transcends the limits of selfishness, and it should be evident that selfishness cannot be taken seriously as the norm for morality. Selfishness is basically disruptive. It could never be universally adopted as the moral norm. And it is foolish to hold that the aim of morals is the disruption of human existence.

We thus find ourselves between two extremes. One would locate the interest of the moral will in the sensible world where it will invariably lapse into heteronomy. The other would push for explanations beyond the well-founded autonomous morality and freedom of man - - - explanations that are impossible. Instead of these extremes, what we should do is draw out and develop from the valid concept of autonomous freedom the useful idea of men as belonging to a kingdom of ends.

Kant concludes by noting how Reason always seeks the unconditioned behind the conditions. Thus it seeks the absolute cause of the world when the world is seen as a series of conditions. Again, it seeks the necessity of moral law in its own world of freedom. Yet, when, true to its ever-unsatisfied and ever-probing nature, Reason seeks yet further for the explanation of freedom and its laws, it falters and flaps about helplessly with impotent wings. All the time, however, it understands its own probing tendency. Hence if it ever rested on an explanation or ground of morality other than itself, that would automatically spell the end of the moral law itself. For then heteronomy would take over. We can see then how the categorical imperative is ultimately "incomprehensible." All we can do, and all that can legitimately be expected of us with our human limitations is to comprehend its incomprehensibility.

3

KANTS ETHICS:
A CLOSER LOOK

However we may wish to define man, we would have to include in our definition at least two of the many components found in every human being, namely, reason and feeling. Put another way, we can say there are two human levels of consciousness: intellectual and sense (organic) consciousness. To each of these two kinds of consciousnesses there also correspond two tendencies toward their objects. Through our sense consciousness we grasp individual objects around us, and we experience the subsequent inclination or desire for these objects. Through our intellectual consiousness we grasp not only all the individual material objects grasped by sense consciousness, but we are also able to classify these individual objects into organized and ever ascending categories of larger and larger generality. In a word, through our intellect we understand things under the aspect of *universality*. We make one category or classification (one word, if you wish) stand for a whole set of individual objects sharing those same characteristics. Indeed, not only do we understand and classify things under universal categories, we can also organize them into dynamic relationships with one another. We can observe, understand and record how certain kinds of things act and interact with others producing this or that result. In a word, we can organize our knowledge of things not only into set static categories, but also into *dynamic* categories of causes and their respective effects.

We have seen how in Kant's theory of knowledge, he explains all these by distinguishing between sense consciousness (which includes the imagination) which knows all the many individual objects we do know (the manifold *appearances*/phenomena) and the *understanding* which organizes these appearances into categories under the aspect of nature, that is; the *rule-determined behaviour* of things: their cause and effect relationships. In addition, we have the obvious fact that we understand ourselves sensing; we understand ourselves understanding and organizing our knowledges in these precise ways. We even raise questions on the valid content and limit of what we can really *know*. This is *Reason* turning in on itself, as it were, and musing or "brooding," as Kant says, over itself, and producing the merely *regulative* or organizing (but contentless) ideas of God, the soul, and freedom.

We mention these points in Kant's theory of knowledge, no matter how briefly, only to point up the fundamental distinction he makes between sense and intellectual consciousness and between percepts, concepts and ideas. Sense consciousness by itself, whether as knowledge or tendency (appetite) raises no questions. It simply grasps its sensed objects here and now. It either inclines towards them or declines away from them, depending on whether these objects offer satisfaction or otherwise. Hence, left to themselves, without any further connection to a higher consciousness, sense inclinations are "blind." They naturally tend towards objects of satisfaction and away from objects of dissatisfaction.

In man, sense consciousness is actually conjoined to the higher consciousness of rationality,---that is, to *understanding*, with its categories and ideas of nature, and to *reason*, with its metaphysical brooding over itself and its own regulative ideas which we have just mentioned. The manifold objects of sense consciousness actively received and organized by the understanding is what Kant calls "experience." Experience thus comprises the empirical objects of sense consiousness. It is "synthetic." In addition, our experience of "nature" comprises the categories of understanding both statically and dynamically. The categories do not come from experience. They are a priori, that is, prior to and beyond the sense manifold. Kant calls our generalized experiences when distilled into laws or formulas (whether strictly scientific or merely homespun) *synthetic a priori* statements or propositions. This is the kind of proposition which will mainly concern us as we move from Kant's theory of knowledge to his investigation of the nature of morals.

In what follows I reorganize Kant's treatment of morality in a way that I deem better suited for classroom presentation, since Kant's treatment (as the student can find out by reading the FPMM) is not so suited, his protestations to the contrary notwithstanding. As his commentators have remarked, and as we saw in the preceding chapter, the sequence of ideas in his ethical writings leave much to be desired. Yet, despite this recasting, we need to stay as close to Kant's logic as possible. For despite complaints, no one who reads Kant's moral theory can fail to acknowledge its philosophical force, no matter how it has been ridiculed and parodied as unworkable in daily human living, as too Prussian, "out of this world," etc.

The Fact of Moral Constraint

Man then possesses both rational and sense consciousness (feelings). Now we may just as well get used to Kant's way of talking and call rational consciousness in this context *Reason*, and sense desires and appetites, *inclinations*. And, in our philosophizing on the nature of morality, we should start from the fact that Reason is obviously "higher" than inclination. Reason understands all the objects of inclination and more. Furthermore, it is a fact ("objective reality") that Reason actually intervenes and checks our inclinations. *How* often it does so intervene is not our question for now, but only *that* Reason does so intervene and "constrain" our inclinations. Not each and every inclination, surely, but *some*, indeed many of them. Again, which ones exactly is not our question just now. The point is simply that every adult person experiences *moral constraint*. Now someone may object that it is impossible to "verify" what universal constraint is. Does it mean, for instance, that every single adult human being must attest affirmatively to his experience of this moral constraint before the statement can be considered valid? If that is what is required, then we might as well do away with all generalizations, including the objector's explicit presupposition that really no generalization is possible. This latter is obviously a generalization itself, to which Kant and countless others would object, etc. No, we do make generalizations. Some, perhaps *many* of them, are valid. The only question therefore is whether this generalization, that every human being feels moral constraint, is a good generalization.

I say it is a good and valid generalization because (1) it has a sound basis; and (2) it can be confirmed by examples which everyone can recognize as illustrative of the reality of human living and experience. The sound basis here is simply that man is indeed composed of inclinations and Reason, and that Reason is higher than inclination. This is not to say that Reason always prevails over inclination. To be "higher" does not mean to be *always* prevalent. For obviously there are times when inclinations and feelings prevail over Reason. We should therefore state what precisely we mean by Reason being "higher" than inclination. We mean that Reason grasps all that inclinations grasp and *more*. It understands the whole domain and pattern of human knowledge and its limits, etc. It is thus within its power to prevail over inclinations on the grounds of its more extensive, intensive and comprehensive vision. "Reason" says Kant, "as the faculty of principles, determines the interest of all the powers of the mind and its own."[1] Now it is incredible that a higher power able to grasp more and prevail over a lower power never does so move to prevail. That would be like saying our minds do have the power to correct our erroneous sense impressions but *never* does so correct them even when it clearly perceives those erroneous sense impressions! That's preposterous. Hence we contend on sound grounds that Reason does so intervene to check inclinations sometimes, indeed many times, in *every* human being, though not every time.

What then of those times when inclinations prevail over Reason? Well, we certainly cannot say even then that inclinations grasp all that Reason grasps plus more in the way we have maintained that Reason does exactly that. Of course, we can make the word "higher" mean "whichever one prevails at the moment," but that is not our meaning here, even though it does serve to further the discussion. For now we are forced to ask: *ought* our inclinations prevail over our Reason? The question, to repeat, is not whether occasionally, or for the most part, or perhaps even always, inclinations do so prevail in this or that given individual. And it is worth noting that if we do hold that inclinations ought to prevail, whether only sometimes or always, it is still Reason which is still clearly stating this answer! Why? Because what is being stated is a *general* principle. As such it is beyond the power of the senses which can only grasp individual objects. In any case, the point is that all human beings do experience this constraint of Reason upon the inclinations, this "conflict" between the two tendencies in man. We are not talking of conflicting *inclinations*, such as the appetite of a dog for a piece of meat simultaneously present with fear of its master, as the animal moves apprehensively towards the morsel. Rather, we are talking of the *ideas* of good and evil intervening and attempting to constrain inclinations to the contrary. This is the "moral constraint" we are focusing on here as the starting point of our inquiry into the nature of morals.

Let us go on now to some of Kant's illustrations which are themselves classics of thought, and not infrequently of humor. Let us see if indeed they bear out his contention as to the universal experience of moral constraint/conflict, that is to say, the constraint of Reason on contrary inclinations. All this despite the fact that many philosophers (myself included) consider it misleading and even erroneous to talk of *pure* inclination or *pure* reason etc. in man who is in fact one essential composite of both, a spiritualized flesh and enfleshed spirit, as Gabriel Marcel puts it.

Kant takes the example of a man on his way to a brothel to satisfy his lustful inclination, protesting every step of the way that he just can't help it, that he just has to have his sexual urge gratified.

> *Ask him whether he would control his passion if, in front of the house where he had this opportunity, a gallows were erected on which he would be hanged immediately after gratifying his lust. We do not have to guess very long what his answer would be.[2]*

The example, while dealing precisely with free choice in man, is nevertheless still to the point, since, as we shall see, free choice and pure practical reason are one and the same thing in Kant. The example also points up the fact that we human beings do not plunge blindly forward in satisfying our inclinations. We subject ourselves at least to the prudential restraints of reason. True, prudence does not yet deal with moral good and evil, in Kant's mind, but it does move us closer to the point to be established, since moral constraint and freedom really go hand in hand.

Still speaking of the same man on his way to the brothel but who now hesitates over the prospect of being hanged afterwards, Kant remarks:

> *But ask him whether he thinks it would be possible for him to overcome his love of life, however great it may be, if his sovereign threatened him with the same sudden death unless he made a false deposition against an honorable man whom the ruler wished to destroy under a plausible pretext. Whether he would or not he perhaps will not venture to say; but that it would be possible for him he certainly would admit without hesitation. He judges, therefore, that he can do something because he knows that he ought, and he recognizes that he is free--a fact which, without the moral law, would have remained unknown to him.[3]*

The point in these two examples and others which could be cited along the same line is simply that the presence of Reason in man of necessity imposes a constraint on his inclinations.[4] This is simply another way of saying that Reason is the higher faculty which nature has given man to control and direct his inclinations. This rational direction can move along different lines. It can direct inclinations along the lines of prudential calculation, as in the case of Epicureans who sought the greatest amount of sensual satisfaction and happiness through sophisticated concepts, art and refined performances. Here the constraint is not yet that of morals. The direction of reason may even go so far as to direct a man to seek his pleasures and happiness in objects other and higher than his inclinations. It does not matter. Just as gold is gold, whether it comes from the mountains or from the rivers, says Kant, so too pleasure is pleasure whether it comes from objects of the mind or from the senses. As such pleasures are other than morality. The two have simply different objects. The constraint of Reason upon the inclinations is properly felt as a moral one only when it directs man to do an action because that is precisely his moral duty, regardless of the pleasure, pain or any other thing else that may result from the act. It is the experience of this specific constraint we seek to understand in a theory of morals. Kant contends that every human being experiences this peculiar function of reason, even as reason also moves along lines outside the area of moral duty.

> *Man is a being of needs, so far as he belongs to the world of sense, and to this extent his reason certainly has an inescapable responsibility from the side of his sensuous nature to attend to its interest and to form practical maxims with a view to the happiness of this and, where applicable, of a future life. But still he is not so completely an animal as to be indifferent to everything which reason says on its own and to use it merely as a tool for satisfying his needs as a sensuous being. That he has reason does not in the least raise him in worth above mere animality if reason only serves the purposes which, among animals, are taken care of by instinct; if this were so, reason would be only a specific way nature had made use of to equip man for the same purpose for which animals are qualified, without fitting him for any higher purpose. No doubt, as a result of this unique arrangement, he needs reason, to consider also what is in itself good or evil, which pure and sensuously disinterested reason alone can judge, and furthermore, to distinguish this estimation from a sensuous estimation and to make the former the supreme condition of good and evil.[5]*

There we have as good a text as any in Kant which definitely states that the end of man lies in the fulfillment of moral good or duty as defined by reason, the power nature has given him to achieve his end, just as in other beings nature has also given corresponding and suitable powers for the achievement of their respective ends.[6]

We need not pursue this point of moral constraint as universally experienced any further. Kant holds that *all* men, unless they have suffered chemical dissolution,[7] experience moral constraint. Either we agree with him or we do not. If we do not, we are in effect saying that not all men have a sense of right and wrong, a sense of moral compunction or conscience "whose voice makes even the boldest sinner tremble and forces him to hide himself from it." In sum, we would be saying that these men really have no reason, that peculiar human power of reflection and self-criticism. But a man without a rational faculty would be a contradiction. Hence we conclude that because of the presence in him of both Reason and inclinations at once, every human person experiences moral constraint, i.e., the demand of moral duty or obligation.

Characteristics of Moral Constraint

We note next how this constraint is (1) universal; (2) necessary; (3) rooted in Reason; (4) a command, an *ought*. Let us take these characteristics of moral constraint one at a time.

(1) *Moral Constraint as universal.* To sharpen this restatement of a previous point we can ask how there can conceivably be an exception to the experience of moral constraint in a rational being. One answer would be to think of a "holy will," a rational being without inclinations. For it is inclinations which are the counterforces to morality. A being with a holy will would therefore be wholly and completely attuned to doing whatever its reason sees as good. Now such a being is certainly not what we are concerned with here. Our focus is rather on a being capable of good and evil. Another answer would be that moral constraint is not experienced by a being made up simply of inclinations and devoid of all reason. Again, this is not the kind of being we are discussing here. No one would contend that a dog, for example, which wants and yet fears to move towards a piece of meat (for fear of his master) is experiencing "moral constraint." Not in the same way, at any rate, that a man as in the example above experiences it when asked either to lie against an innocent man or suffer death. Those are two entirely different situations. We are discussing human beings in whom both Reason and inclinations are found simultaneously, with Reason as the more comprehensive and therefore the higher, directing power. We need to linger on this point a little more.

Why should the less comprehensive direct the more comprehensive consciousness unless it be that somehow, the less is precisely taken to be really the more comprehensive on the matter at hand? Thus, we sometimes say with James, Pascal, et al., that we should follow our hearts more than our heads. But in support of Kant's point on the primacy of the rational, should we not note that the injunction to follow our hearts instead of our heads is, after all, a conclusion given final clearance by our "heads?" Thus there really is no higher tribunal than that of reason in us human beings, is there? The conclusions themselves of reason can only be judged right or wrong by no other than reason itself, is this not so? In a being therefore where inclinations and Reason are both present, Reason as the higher power communicates its vision to everything else in man that is not Reason specifically to his inclinations which often move along lines other than those pointed to by Reason. And when the issue is joined between Reason and inclination along the lines of good and evil, there arises the experience of moral conflict, moral constraint.

Perhaps too we can express the point of moral obligation as universally experienced in this way. A priori, we can say that every man, simply because he is a composite of Reason and inclinations, undergoes the thrust of Reason into the realm of his feelings, sensual desires, and/or inclinations. A posteriori, we can see from the literature men have written and the testimony they have given (whether orally or by their behaviour) that they do experience moral conflict, moral compunction, the moral sense of having acted rightly even though the results may have brought pain and unhappiness or vice versa.

> *Nonetheless every vicious man has a concept of virtue in himself, he has the understanding to recognize what is evil, and is not dead to moral feeling. No one is such an unmitigated blackguard that he might not at least wish to be good.*[8]

Such then is the basis for saying with Kant that universality is intrinsic to the very notion of moral duty or obligation. It is present in every man because he is a man.

(2) *Moral Constraint is necessary.* By this we mean that moral constraint is not something tacked on to man from the outside, as it were. It is not like a suntan, nor a contagious disease, nor even fear of punishment from another. Rather the constraint of morality is from the "inside." It flows out of the very nature of man himself precisely as a composite of Reason, will and inclinations. Everybody understands and makes the valid distinction between long-ranged interest arising from a comprehensive vision of things, and immediate short-ranged reactions of interest to objects thrust at one's consciousness in an instant. I deliberately enter into the long-term process of a doctoral education so I may be a professor someday, whereas I react impulsively to the idea of taking a break from my books to join the beer-bash tonight. Since Reason follows its comprehensive grasp of things, its interest seems obviously longer-ranged than that of sensual inclinations and desires which only relate to objects in their relatively narrower environment. Hence conflict between the two is inevitable. Of course, we do not and cannot know beforehand which of the two in any given situation will prevail. But there is no doubt that Reason will seek to impose its comprehensive idea on the shorter-ranged reactions of inclinations. Thus conflict is inevitable, with no appeal possible beyond the tribunal of that selfsame Reason. Now this is itself the moral constraint intrinsic to human nature.

We should be careful to note, however, that the relation between Reason and inclinations is not one of essential opposition. As Kant noted, there are natural inclinations which mesh in nicely with the commands of duty. But the point is that there will always be other times when the two are opposed. In either case, what is necessary and sufficient for duty to be fulfilled is that the act be done in obedience to the dictate of Reason alone.

> *On the other-hand, it is a duty to maintain one's life; and, in addition, everyone has also a direct inclination to do so. But on this account the*

often anxious care which most men take for it has no intrinsic worth, and their maxim has no moral import. On the other hand, if adversity and hopeless sorrow have completely taken away the relish for life, if the unfortunate one, strong in mind, indignant at his fate rather than desponding or dejected, wishes for death, and yet preserves his life without loving it---not from inclination or fear, but from duty---then his maxim has moral worth.[9]

Clearly, one can act against the rational constraint upon the inclinations. But one cannot do so with moral impugnity. If one disobeys the dictates of Reason upon the inclinations, one cannot escape the condemnatory judgement of that same reflective Reason within. To repeat, this impossibility of escaping moral constraint *before* the act, and the corresponding moral judgement within a man *after* the act, is what is meant by pointing to moral constraint as "necessary," something that comes forth from one's nature as human.

(3) *Moral Constraint as rooted in Reason.* There is no need to belabor this point further. It merely sums up what was said in the preceding paragraphs.

(4) *The Moral Constraint as an Ought, a Command.* This point can be brought out by asking: how else can Reason be conceived to constrain any other human faculty except by a *command*? Reason is obviously not a physical force able to ram its insights through by various forms of corporal subjugation. As Plato noted in the *Republic,* physical might is after all not identical with moral right. An unjust act perpetrated through physical superiority arouses in us a sense of moral outrage. It is not right, we say. It *ought not* to be. On the other hand, a just act, even when accompanied by physical unpleasantnesses, evokes our rational approval. It ought to have been done. To quote one of Kant's lighter examples:

> *When someone who delights in annoying and vexing peace-loving folk receives at last a right good beating, it is certainly an ill, but everyone approves of it and considers it as good in itself even if nothing further results from it; nay, even he who gets the beating must acknowledge, in his reason, that justice has been done to him, because he sees the proportion between welfare and welldoing, which reason inevitably holds before him, here put into practice.[10]*

In a negative form then, the constraint of reason is experienced by us as a command not to do an action: we *ought not* to do it, even though physically we can do it. In its affirmative form, moral constraint is experienced by us as a command to do an action: we *ought* to do it, even though we are physically free not to do it. To obey reason's constraint thus is to do one's moral duty, to do what one *ought* to do, and this necessarily wins reason's approval. To go against Reason's constraint by doing what one ought not to do or vice versa, is to fail in one's moral duty. This necessarily begets that selfsame Reason's condemnation. Reason, in other words, as self-reflective consciousness, cannot but see whether it has prevailed or failed vis-a-vis inclinations. We see then how the essence of moral constraint lies in Reason's command to do what we *ought* to do,

51

regardless of what inclinations or other considerations may set up as opposing interests. And this brings us to the heart of Kant's ethics: the analysis of that moral *ought* as a categorical imperative unique in itself and apart from the various imperatives of exerience.

The Moral Imperative as Categorical

We have just shown how no man is exempt from the experience of moral constraint (though obviously people differ at times as to which precise action the constraint bears on---an entirely different question) so long as the two powers of Reason and inclinations are combined in his being. The larger vision of Reason as to good and evil necessarily interposes itself upon the movement of inclinations towards their objects and of course vice versa.

Now, Kant agreed with a point the British philosopher, David Hume, made earlier, namely: nothing in the sensible, empirical world is universal or necessary. Obviously, there are only individual objects (this, that, etc.) in the world, including our own experiences which are merely individual events taking place in one situation after another. Nothing is necessary about them since, as Hume observed, there is absolutely no contradiction involved in thinking of anything that happens to exist now as also not-existing. Truths of fact or experience are contingent, not necessary. They are breakable at any instant. You may, for instance, be actually sitting down and reading this book at this instant. The next moment you may not be doing so. There are a thousand other conceivable alternative situations. You could simply close the book and stand up. Kant takes this lack of necessity and universality among empirical events as making them objects of *synthetic a posteriori* propositions. "You there are sitting down" is a synthetic a posteriori proposition. It is through and through contingent, non-necessary and non-universal. There is nothing a priori about it, that is, nothing necessary nor universal about it. As we are attempting to explain right now, necessity and universality must come from something before and outside of, not from, sheer experience itself.

We saw how in his speculative theory of knowledge Kant took necessity and universality as sourced in the mind, in the intelligible, not the sensible, world. We can thus make three conclusions at this point. One, because the moral constraint present in every human being is there universally and necessarily, moral constraint is sourced in the intelligible world of reason, not in the phenomenal sensible world. Two, the universality and necessity of moral constraint as imposed upon the sensual appetites and desires make the moral constraint or command, (the *ought* statement), into what Kant calls a *synthetic a priori* proposition. Three, there is a clear demarcation between the two worlds of nuomenal/intelligible world of morality and the phenomenal/sensible world of sensual gratification, desires and men's actual experiences. A word on each of these three points.

First, necessity and universality are intrinsic only to reason. For the contradictory of anything in the world of experience is conceivable and thus possible. Nothing then in the world of "bare facts" is either intrinsic or necessary. But a sound statement of reason cannot by rights be contradicted. It is in this sense necessary. A sound rational conclusion is precisely such because its contradictory has been by supposition carefully considered and found unsound. Again we are pointing here to the ultimately reflective nature of reason by which it is itself its own judge as to what is sound and/or unsound. Any other norm or standard appealed to must be judged and assessed by reason, while beyond reason there is no appeal. However, reason cannot judge what is sound or unsound arbitrarily against its own insights without itself being condemned by itself. Reason's sound conclusions therefore cannot by rights be otherwise conceived. They are thus necessary. Being necessary they are also universal. The implications of all this on Kant's theory of morals will soon become evident. Here it will suffice to reiterate the point that since necessity and universality are of the very nature of moral constraint, it follows that there is an a priori element in moral constraint whose root cannot possibly be in experience or the sensible world (where everything is contingent as we have seen). That root can be only in reason where alone universality and necessity originate.

The second point that moral constraint takes the form of a synthetic a priori statement we can deal with briefly as it is an idea which we will meet many times. Hopefully, it will become clearer with each meeting. Take any moral *ought* proposition or command, for instance, "Do not cheat honest customers." The moral constraint or imperative is obviously there because of some human inclination to cheat honest customers and thus achieve the material gratifications of such cheating. Here we have elements in the phenomenal world of the senses being subsumed under a universal and necessary command of reason. Let this suffice for now. A synthetic a priori proposition is one that sums up events in the phenomenal world under the aspect of universality, and this we find in every *ought* which comes from our moral reason. How this comes about is precisely what Kant is at pains to understand and what we are attempting to unfold.

The third point, that there is a clear demarcation between the intelligible world of reason and that of the sensible/phenomenal world of inclinations is a cardinal point in Kant's ethics. Indeed we can say that Kant almost holds to an *opposition* between them, although, as we mentioned, he shows how at times we in fact perform actions which are praiseworthy out of inclinations. Obviously, if there never were any opposition between them, "constraint" would be meaningless. To repeat, this is not to say there is *always* opposition between Reason and inclination. But it is interesting that in Kant's thought, even when inclination and moral reason happen to go hand in hand, he still insists on demarcating the dividing line between the two. He insists that the moral motivation must come purely from practical reason or the will, not from the inclinations in any way whatever. With these observations made, we can go on to the nature of the moral constraint as an *ought*, a command, an imperative.

We use the word *ought* in a variety of ways, each way having its corresponding meaning. Some examples: "Be civil and charming at that cocktail party!" "Take the exam!" "To produce Polynesian spareribs, do thus and so!" "Do not obstruct justice!" etc., etc. These are commands, imperatives. They *can* all have *ought* as their main verb. And a close inspection of those sentences will show that most of them are conditional imperatives with two parts. There is the condition or protasis (the "if" part) followed by a statement of the result or consequence (apodosis), the "then" part, should the condition be fulfilled.

We might as well come clean at this point and admit that some philosophers who differ from Kant hold that all imperatives are reducibly conditional or hypothetical, no matter how categorical they apper to be at first. You can always insert and explicitate a condition which is there implicitly in every imperative, it is claimed. Thus in every one of the examples above, you can make explicit the hidden hypothesis or condition. In the first example, the condition would be "if you want to be invited back to cocktail parties, be civil and charming," etc. Obviously, if you don't give a care about such invitations and such parties, all the force of the imperative evaporates. The same is true about the steps required to produce those spareribs. If you don't really go for all those exotic Polynesian flavors, strict adherence to the recipe becomes meaningless. In the last example, however, we have a case of morals. Here Kant stoutly maintains that there simply are no conditions attached to such imperatives. In other words, we can divide imperatives into moral imperatives which are *without* conditions, and into non-moral imperatives which are all *with* conditions. In the former we have categorical imperatives, hypothetical ones in the latter. The former belongs to the intelligible world of morals, the latter to the realm of empirical objects, the sensible world. Kant then further subdivides the hypothetical imperatives into technical imperatives which command adoption of certain means *if* one chooses or wills a certain end; and prudential imperatives, which command adoption of certain means (dictated by rational calculation) and certain goods meant to realize happiness in the way each individual seeks to be happy. We have seen the schematic divisions of the various imperatives in the previous chapter, namely, the categorical and the two kinds of hypothetical imperatives, namely the Prudential and Technical.

Since the categorical imperative is our main object of investigation here, we will move toward it starting from the hypothetical imperatives. There is first of all the technical imperative---perhaps the most common usage we have of the word "ought." We all know how we have to go after something we really want. Of course, the option is always there of ceasing to want something. In this case the imperative, the "ought" lets us go, as it were, releases us. If, for instance, I want a college degree, I must use the means which effectively achieves this end, namely, pass college courses. The *ought* here clearly is conditioned by my really wanting a college degree. This end I am always free not to want anymore. Should I stop wanting this end (i.e., the degree) all imperatives requiring me to take college courses automatically cease. The imperative has a bite on me, so to speak, only as long as I continue to want the end. Kant contends that mere analysis of the whole situation will show that anyone effectively wanting an end also wants its means. "For in willing an object as my effect, there is already thought the causality of myself as an acting cause."[11] It is clear that this kind of imperative is not what we are concerned about in our attempt to understand moral obligation since there is no way in which I can decide no longer to be subject to moral obligation---any more than I can will away the fact that I happen to be a man. I am stuck, so to speak, with my humanity which would paradoxically assert its reality in a very intense way even in an act of doing away with itself, as for instance, in an act of suicide. Being stuck with my humanity, I am also stuck with what we have called moral constraint, since I am necessarily a creature of both Reason and inclinations. Technical imperatives then cannot be the kind of imperatives involved in moral duty.

The next kind of imperative which bears on happiness is more complicated. Kant never stops discoursing on how it definitely has to be distinguished from the imperative of morality. Many moral theories before him, thinks Kant, went awry precisely because somehow they were misled by the ambiguity in the classic phrase "the good life." Morals are about the good life, alright. But this is definitely not identical with the "happy life."[12] This is because the good which morality is all about is an unconditional good, a good-in-itself, which is located in the intelligible, nuomenal world. Whereas happiness involves the gratification of our desires, sensual and otherwise. Gratification of desire is simply foreign to the conception of moral duty as such. For moral duty is universal and necessary, whereas gratification of desire is obviously as multiple and individual as there are individual agents each craving gratification in his own particular way.

Pass out slips of paper to each one in class with the words "Happiness is a _____," to be filled out individually. See how the slips of paper come back with indeed different objects of happiness filled in by different individuals. The fact that many, perhaps the majority, honestly equate money with happiness, far from denying Kant's contention, in fact reinforces it. For money is necessarily a *means*. You cannot eat, drink, or make love to money, though you usually can do all these by means of it. How, therefore, various individuals would spend their money would be the real point. What object of happiness or gratification would each one convert money into? When that is asked, we find that people do indeed differ from individual to individual. One goes for a house, another invests for the children's education, another one takes a world tour, while still another heads straight for Las Vegas, hoping that money will beget money. One starts a business, another one devotes full time to the pursuit of a professional degree, while yet another one goes off to the Virgin Islands to write that novel he has always wanted to write, especially when it's winter time in the northlands. For a few with relatively simple wants, happiness can be just the proverbial warm puppy! And so on. Kant's point is that we must hold happiness and morality strictly apart. Morals belong to the nuomenal/intelligible world. Happiness belongs to the sensual, empirical world of gratified desires and inclinations. Morals are universal and necessary. Happiness has neither universality nor necessity in the same way. The objects of happiness are as many and varied as there are individuals each with his own peculiar cravings, and ever shifts from period to period in life's various stages.

Where one places his happiness is a question of the particular feeling of pleasure or displeasure in each man, and even of the difference in needs occasioned by changes of feelings in one and the same man...for the determinant of the faculty of desire is based on the feeling of

*pleasure or displeasure, which can never be assumed to be univer-
sally directed to the same object.*[13]

But is not happiness something universal in that everyone, as
Aristotle noted, in fact desires happiness? Yes, Kant agrees, and therefore
strictly speaking we cannot even have an imperative or a command to
desire happiness, since we already naturally desire it.[14] The imperative of
happiness really concerns the *means* necessary in any given case to achieve
happiness, rather than the end itself of happiness the desire for which has
already been imprinted in us by nature. It is useless thus to command us
to seek some thing we already naturally seek. Hence the form of the
imperative of happiness is conditional in a way different from the
technical imperatives where the ends are freely chosen on the basis of
existing skills and abilities. With happiness, the imperative takes this
form: "*Since* you want to be happy, then do such and such." The such and
such differs from one individual to another.

But why this sheerly individualistic nature of happiness? Aside from
the practically infinite variety of ways in which inclinations mix and
predominate from individual to individual, Kant gives a deeper reason.
No one can really know for sure what exactly will make him happy.

*Unfortunately the notion of happiness is so indefinite that although
every man wishes to attain it, yet he never can say definitely and
consistently what it is that he really wishes and wills.*[15]

Why? Because the idea of what would really make you happy
necessarily requires a *total* conception of an object that will be good for
you at *all times*. This would include *all* your future existence. Only an
infinite mind could possibly know such an object considering how often
people end up shedding tears over answered prayers over which they were
ecstatic earlier. Happiness, in other words, really all comes down to
consulting our own experiences and calculating with the best prudential
judgement we have as to what *probably* would make us happy.

The difficulty is obvious. Experience can only be of the past or of the
present. It cannot extend to all the future, as Kant contends it must,[16] if it
is really to be such a clear and definite object that can rise to the level of
universality. If people do coincide in their choice of happiness objects, it is
more in the nature of a contagious yawn than a real universal.[17] Hence
happiness can never get out of the realm of hypothetical imperatives. It is
an end whose meaning lies in the *means* of its attainment, namely, the
pleasurable satisfaction of our wants and sensual inclinations, as our
prudential judgement dictates at the moment and for the time being.
Since Kant treats of this distinction between morality and happiness so
lengthily and almost everywhere in his ethical writings, we should at least
reproduce some of these texts. They separate the imperatives of happiness
from technical imperatives on one side, and from moral imperatives from
the other. Happiness is situated midway between the two, as the special
realm of prudential (assertive) calculation and counsel/advice. This
middle realm of happiness then is controlled not by technical imperatives
nor by categorical ones, but by prudential (assertoric) ones. In a rather

lengthy section (pp. 17-39 of the *Critique of Pure Practical Reason*)[18], for instance, we read how pleasurable satisfaction, even should it come from reason itself and not from sensual gratification, would still have to be held apart from and outside the realm of morality.

As the man who wants money to spend does not care whether the gold in it was mined in the mountains or washed from the sand, provided it is accepted everywhere as having the same value, so also no man asks, when he is concerned only with the agreeableness of life, whether the ideas are from the sense or from the understanding; he asks only how much and how great is the pleasure which they will afford him over the longest time.[19]

To be happy is necessarily the desire of every rational but finite being, and thus it is an unavoidable determinant of its faculty of desire. Contentment with our existence is not, as it were, an inborn possession or a bliss, which would presuppose a consciousness of our self-sufficiency; it is rather a problem imposed upon us by our own finite nature as a being of needs.[20]

Where one places his happiness is a question of the particular feeling of pleasure or displeasure in each man, and even of the differences in needs occasioned by changes of feeling in one and the same man..but the practical precepts based on the feeling of pleasure and displeasure, which can never be assumed to be universally directed to the same objects.[21]

And, finally, we have this example which we quote rather lengthily to highlight Kant's consistent distinction between prudence (happiness) and morality (duty).

Suppose that an acquaintance whom you otherwise liked were to attempt to justify himself before you for having borne false witness by appealing to what he regarded as the holy duty of consulting his own happiness and then by recounting all the advantages he had gained thereby, pointing out the prudence he had shown in securing himself against detection, even by yourself, to whom alone he now reveals the secret only in order that he may be able at any time to deny it. And suppose that he then affirmed, in all seriousness, that he had thereby fulfilled a true human duty---you would either laugh in his face or shrink from him in disgust, even though you would not have the least grounds for objecting to such measures if a man regulated his principles solely with a view to his own advantage. Or suppose someone recommends to you as steward a man to whom you could blindly trust your affairs and, in order to inspire you with confidence, further extols him as a prudent man who has a masterly understanding of his own interest and is so indefatigably active that he misses no opportunity to further it; furthermore, lest you should be afraid of finding a vulgar selfishness in him, he praises the good taste with which he lives, not seeking his pleasure in making money or in coarse wantonness, but in the increase of his knowledge, in instructive conversation with a select circle, and even in relieving the needy. But, he adds, he is not particular as to the means (which, of course, derive their value only from the end), being as willing to use another's money and property as his own, provided only that he knows he can do so safely and without discovery. You would believe that the person making such a recommendation was either mocking you or had lost his mind. So distinct and sharp are the boundaries between morality and self-love that even the commonest eye cannot fail to distinguish whether a thing belongs to the one or the other.[22]

The principle of happiness can indeed give maxims, but never maxims which are competent to be laws of the will, even if universal happiness were made the object. For, since the knowledge of this rests on mere data of experience, as each judgement concerning it depends very much on the very changeable opinion of each person, it can give general but never universal rules; that is, the rules it gives will on the average be most often the right ones for this purpose, but they will not be rules which must always hold and necessarily.[23]

He who has lost at play may be vexed at himself and his imprudence; but when he is conscious of having cheated at play, even though he has won, he must despise himself as soon as he compares himself with the moral law. This must therefore be something else than the principle of one's own happiness. For to have to say to himself; "I am a worthless man, though I've filled my purse," he must have a different criterion of judgement than if he approves of himself and says, "I am a prudent man, for I've enriched my treasure."[24]

We come finally to the categorical imperative of moral duty. We will discuss this under the aspects of (1) the moral *ought* as other than what *is*: (2) the moral good as the good-in-itself; (3) the distinction of the moral good from the prudential good of happiness and the technical goods of things in a means-to-end context; (4) the moral good as the good intention (subjective) of the will towards a projected action; (5) the derivation of the categorical imperative of duty (objective) and/or moral law. From that point on, we will be led into a whole new section on the formulation of the categorical imperative and its application.

1. *The Moral Ought as other than the Is.* It seems fairly evident that what *ought* to be and what *is* are two different things. Yet, as David Hume, the Scottish philosopher had observed, people very easily and imperceptibly drift from one to the other in their conversations as though what *ought* to be and what *are* were one and the same thing. Common expressions like "That's too bad," or, "How awful!," or, "It's enough to make you throw up!," etc. really show that even the commonest man who perhaps never set foot in an ethics classroom really understands this clear demarcation of morality (what men *ought* to be) from what men *actually do* and *experience.* Kant never tires of repeating that duty, what men ought to do, cannot be discovered by investigation, no matter how extensive, deep and ingenious, into what men actually do or have done. This latter belongs to the realm of empirical experience. It is a fit subject matter for anthropology or the other psychological and social studies, but

58

not for ethics which centers on morals, on what men ought to do. Put another way, we can call this difference between the *ought* and the *is*, the *de facto* and the *de jure* distinction. There is no question but that Ferdinand Marcos, for example, is, as of this writing, the *de facto* President of the Philippines. But there are thousands of those who question whether he is also *de jure* (by right) President. One is not the other. Kant thinks this distinction so evident that it is amazing how anyone can fail to see it. Yet there are even today ethicians who teach this distinction and very soon proceed to their task as though they never knew it. We soon find them arguing for what men ought to do because their sociological researches and what-not show that this is in fact what men have always done (or not done, as the case may be) successfully, etc. Later on we will see how Dewey criticizes the American obsession for *success* as the moral criterion. But for now we are simply stressing how the *ought* really is other than the *is* even in a "successful" state of things. For one thing "success", like happiness, is an obscure concept. A successful result could backfire in many ways. For now we need not belabor this point further. We simply point out how carefully the realm of morals must be held strictly apart from the empirical and phenomenal world of men's actual experiences. The *ought* obviously belongs to and comes from a dimension of reality beyond that of the empirical world of experience and nature. What dimension of reality is that? None other, says Kant, than the intelligible/nuomenal world of reality-in-itself, not the world of appearances.

> The causality of such actions lies in him as an intelligence and in the laws of effects and actions which depend on the principles of an intelligible world, of which indeed he knows nothing more than that in it pure reason alone independent of sensibility gives the law; moreover, since it is only in that world, as an intelligence, that he is his proper self (being as man only the appearance of himself) those laws apply to him directly and categorically, so that the incitements of inclinations and appetites (in other words, the whole nature of the world of sense) cannot impair the laws of his volition as an intelligence.[25]

2. *The Moral Good as the Good-in-Itself.* When we talk of morals, or what ought to be, the essential content of our talk is that of "goodness," isn't it? Every time we say, "You ought to do this; you ought not to do that," the essential implication is that one act is *good* and the other not good (in this sense, evil). Now we have seen how ambiguity lurks in the misleading phrase the "good life." And since morality is about the good, indeed about the good life, there are those who immediately confuse one for the other.[26] Clearly then, we need to sort out and pin down just exactly what we refer to when we talk of the moral ought as referring to something good.

What things do we call good? Those which lead to good ends, which produce good results. But this only postpones the problem since we can press on and ask: what ends/results are good? Now later in Dewey, we will see that any end can itself become a means, and that an end is good as long as it is experienced as good. But Kant does not accept this kind of answer, where everything is reducibly a *means* without there being anything good-in-itself as the ground for characterizing means towards it as *good*. What then could that ground be, what that good-in-itself which enables means towards it to be derivatively characterized as good? At the beginning of his *Fundamental Principles for a Metaphysic of Morals*, Kant sorts his way out for an answer.

Can this ultimate good-in-itself we are seeking be any of the things in the world external to man? Are not such worldly external things or objects all *sub*human? Isn't it true that they possess less reality than man since they have obviously no intellect nor free will? Even those who insist that non-human things in the world are not sub-human (and they are few and odd) would certainly admit that these subhuman objects do not possess human perfections (if they do at all) on the same level as human persons. For we can judge beings only through their activities, and no activities on the subhuman level really rise to the same grade as that of a human person---hence the term "subhuman." Clearly, the good-in itself cannot be located among these subhuman realities. Man uses such objects as means for himself, as their end. Man, the higher being, can insert any of these objects into a context which he sets up through his own thought and imagination. He can keep or discard them as good or not-good, depending on whether they are judged intellectually as fit or not fit for the end result he thinks out, imagines and desires. True, a persistent objector can complicate this argument endlessly and somewhat frivolously along the line of subhuman objects possibly using human beings. But this is so far out of line with Kant's concept of a human person that we need not pursue the point further. Rather, we can simply say that all such subhuman beings and external worldly objects like money, possessions, etc. are obviously good only relatively. That is, in relation to man's use of them. This shows that we must look for the good-in-itself in the human person himself.

Could the good-in-itself then be possibly the interpersonal good of fame, popularity, power over the others, etc.? Here the difficulty of considering these things intrinsically good is that they not infrequently are found in persons who do not deserve them, thereby revealing again their relative nature as good. Not the good-in-itself therefore that we are looking for. And yet, it will not do either to point to the entire human person simply and say "that is the good-in-itself." For again we condemn people at times. We condemn them so severely that even their own deaths and punishments for what they have done evoke in us only a sense of justice. Conversely, we recognize and even praise the goodness in a man who has committed an outrageous deed if, after listening to him, we clearly see that he really meant well after all. We cannot thus find the good-in-itself we are seeking simply by pointing to human persons in their entirety. We need to be more specific. What, in a person, precisely makes him a good or a bad person? When exactly do we say this or that person is a good human being? Is it when he possesses great riches, fame, power, etc.? We have already seen that it is not so. Is it when he possesses great bodily beauty, athletic prowess, skills, etc.? Obviously not. These attributes make for a beautiful build, for a great athlete, etc., but not necessarily for a *good person*. It is this concept of a morally good person we are attempting to penetrate to get at our object of search, the good-in-itself. What then do we mean by stating that so and so is a good man? That he has a brilliant intellect? That he is witty? That he is a profound man of learning? The answer to each is negative. For it is notorious how evil geniuses in history were profound thinkers. In sum then, whether within man or outside man, we find only relative or qualified goods.

The only last thing we can find which makes anything really good is its derivation or birth, so to speak, from a "good will." A man's "good will," says Kant, is the only absolute good we can conceive, since its presence makes everything else good by derivation from it. At the same time its very concept cannot possibly bear the slightest hint of evil without ceasing to be itself. It is beside the point to object here that such a good will does not exist anywhere. We are talking of what good-in-itself it is within our power to *conceive*. Eliminate other goods which reveal themselves to be merely relatively good. We hold up the one and only thing we find it impossible to conceive in any other way but as good-in-itself through which others may derivatively be characterized as good. We can then pin down the content of our conception of the good-in-itself. As Kant puts it in his famous opening sentence in the *Fundamental Principles*:

> *Nothing can possibly be conceived in the world, or even out of it, which can be called good without qualification, except a good will.*

And then he goes on to explain.

> *A good will is good not because of what it performs or effects, not by its aptness for the attainment of some proposed end, but simply by virtue of the volition---that is, it is good in itself, and considered by itself is to be esteemed much higher than all that can be brought about by it in favor of any inclination, nay, even of the sum-total of all inclinations.*
> *Even if it should happen that, owing to the special disfavor of fortune, or the niggardly provision of a step-motherly nature, this will should wholly lack power to accomplish its purpose, if with its greatest efforts it should yet achieve nothing, and there should remain only the good will (not, to be sure, a mere wish, but the summoning of all means in our power) then, like a jewel, it would still shine by its own light, as a thing which has its whole value in itself. Its usefulness or fruitlessness can neither add to nor take away anything from this value.[27]*

Here we have the key idea in Kant's theory of ethics on which his whole doctrine depends. All talk of morality and the moral good finally refers to the good will. By this alone and ultimately, as he says in the quoted text, every man is deemed good or evil, irrespective of his abilities, gifts or accomplishments along other lines. Clearly then, if we are to understand the nature of morality, the *ought*, we have to pry as deeply as we can into the nature of this good-in-itself, the good will.

3. *The Moral Good as distinct from the Prudential and Technical Goods.* We saw earlier how pleasure or happiness is in Kant's mind a

matter quite other than that of moral duty. The good we seek when we go after pleasure is obviously not the good-in-itself or the good will which we have just seen to be the moral good. Of course it could happen that to some people, for instance the ancient Stoics, the pursuit of virtue itself is deemed as *the* only real pleasure. Then paradoxically even virtueproducing pain is deemed happiness. There was that Stoic who in the worst paroxysm of gout cried out, "Pain, however thou tormentst me, I will never admit that thou art anything bad."[28] But still this does not make happiness and the moral good one and the same thing. For if we think on it, the pleasures of virtuous people, qua precisely virtuous, are not those of vicious people, precisely qua vicious. Moral good, in other words, is prior to the pleasures of virtue and duty, and immoral disposition prior to the enjoyment of vicious pleasures.

> *In order to imagine the vicious person as tormented with mortification by the consciousness of his transgressions, they must presuppose that he is, in the core of his character, at least to a certain degree morally good, just as they have to think of the person who is delighted by the consciousness of doing dutiful acts as already virtuous. Therefore, the concept of morality and duty must precede all reference to this satisfaction and cannot be derived from it.[29]*

From this priority of the morally good will to objects of enjioyment, we can see how pleasure and happiness are "extrinsic" or "material" objects of the will. They determine the will only extrinsically. This is in diametrical contrast to the case of the moral will. This latter achieves in itself the absolute unqualified good whose achievement, in order precisely to be absolute, cannot be referred to any object outside or extrinsic to the will. For then the resulting good would automatically be a qualified good. It would then need further justification as to its moral goodness. Whether the objects of happiness and pleasure come from the "pathological" inclinations,[30] or from the higher faculties even of reason itself, the point is that these *material* objects, as extrinsically determining the will, cannot be identical with the ultimate nature of the moral will as good-in-itself, a good which can only be determined from within itself. For, to repeat, if it were determined by an object extrinsic to itself, as in the case of any pleasurable object serving as the motivation of the will act, it would by that very act produce only a qualified good still subject to the further and ultimate norm of moral goodness or not.

> *A man can return unread an instructive book which he cannot again obtain, in order not to miss the hunt; he can go away in the middle of a fine speech, in order not to be late for a meal; he can leave an intellectual conversation, which he otherwise enjoys, in order to take his place at the gambling table; he can even repulse a poor man whom it is usually a joy to aid, because he has only enough money in his pocket for a ticket to the theatre. If the determination of the will rests on the feelings of agreeableness or disagreeableness which he expects from any cause, it is all the same to him through what kind of notion he is affected...[31]*

The goods then of pleasure, enjoyments and happiness are not identical with the moral good. This does not mean, to repeat, that the moral good never *coincides* with happiness or pleasure. But if they ever do coincide, it would be just that, a coincidence. There would be no direct connection between their two different natures. Later, we shall see a further precision made on this relationship between moral worth and happiness. For now let us conclude this section with the reminder that the whole realm of happiness and enjoyment falls, in Kant's mind, to the area of prudence[32], of reason calculating as shrewdly as it can which objects would indeed produce satisfaction and contentment in one's case, given his temperament, circumstances in life, opportunities, resources, etc.

The other point of this section, namely, that the goods involved in a technical imperative context are not the moral good, need not detain us long. If, as we just saw, for the moral good to be absolute and unqualifiedly good it must have to well up, as it were, from within the will itself without any extrinsic motivation, it is clear that the context of technical imperatives, which is that of means derivatively good because of the end to which they are ordered, cannot possibly be the same as the moral good. If the determination of the will in matters of happiness and enjoyment are considered by Kant as extrinsic even when their objects are from the pleasures of the higher faculties themselves, we can see how the goods in question in means-to-end relationship are all of them extrinsic. Kant calls this extrinsic determination of the will by objects outside itself "heteronomy," meaning a law (*nomos*) other than (*heteros*) the will itself. By contrast, the case of the moral will determining itself from absolutely within itself without any extrinsic or material object is "autonomy," that is, a law (*nomos*) that is *self-determining* (*autos*). This is a purely formal determination effected by the pure form of the moral law which itself is generated from the will.

We see now why Kant sweeps all the extrinsic, material determining objects of the will into the realm of the hypothetical imperatives; how he holds the good will or moral good apart from all of them as *autonomous* and *categorical*. Though his explanation contains ideas somewhat ahead of us at this point, we are already in a position to grasp it.

> If the will seeks the law which is to determine it anywhere else *than in the fitness of its maxims to be universal laws of its own dictation, conequently if it goes out of itself and seeks this law in the character of any of its objects, there always results* heteronomy. *The will in that case does not give itself the law, but it is given by the object through its relation to the will. This relation, whether it rests on inclination or on conceptions of reason, only admits of hypothetical imperatives: I ought to do something because I wish for something else. On the contrary, the moral and therefore categorical imperative says, I ought to do so and so, even though I should not wish for anything else.*[33]

Kant then gives an example to illustrate his point:

> For example, the former says: I ought not to lie if I would retain my reputation; the latter says: I ought not to lie although it should not bring me the least discredit.[34]

4. *The Moral Good as the Good Intention (Subjective) of the Will Toward a Projected Action.* Should we automatically attribute moral credit to someone who happens to be doing an action in accordance with, or in conformity to, the moral law? Let us not complicate the discussion impossibly by asking "what moral law?" The question pressupposes that you and I for instance agree that giving money to the poor when one can afford it is usually a moral act. We say "usually" became unless we look deeper into the *motivation* behind the action, we cannot tell.

Take two politicians. Both have ample means. Both gladhand money to their needy constituents. Politician A's motive, however, is at base, no matter how layered over externally with legal safeguards, buying his constituents' votes Indeed, in a few individual cases where he gives out larger sums, he really means to pay blackmail to keep information damaging to him from surfacing. On the other hand, Politician B's motivation is genuinely altruistic, (Again let us not abort the discussion by expostulating that there are no such politicians.) What then makes us say that only Politician B's act is moral, while A's is not? Objectively, i.e., giving to the poor out of one's ample means, both acts are the same. Without having to state the obvious, we can see why Kant maintains that it is not sufficient to do an action merely in accordance with duty to produce a moral act. Motive is of the essence. The action done must be done precisely "out of duty", i.e., purely from a sense of duty. You ought to do what is moral purely, solely and exclusively, according to Kant, because it is the *moral* thing to do, period. Any other admixture or influence upon the act from the "outside" would taint the act and take it out of the sphere of morality. We have "heteronomy" where the determining object of the will is not the morality of the act itself, but some other object, usually the satisfaction of our inclinations or the "dear self."[35]

Kant's well-known example is that of the butcher who is steadfastly upright and honest with his customers so that "a child buys of him as well as any other."[36] The butcher's motivation which is the cultivation of as large a clientele as possible based on his reputation for honesty shows that his action "was done neither from duty nor from direct inclination, but merely with a selfish view." To sharpen his point of distinguishing duty from actions in accordance with duty but based on inclination or selfishness, Kant gives the following example:

> *On the other hand, it is a duty to maintain one's life; and in addition, everyone also has a direct inclination to do so. But on this account, the often anxious care which most men take for it has no intrinsic worth, and their maxim has no moral import. They preserve their life as duty requires, no doubt, but not because duty requires. On the other hand, if adversity and hopeless sorrow have completely taken away the relish for life, if the unfortunate one, strong in mind and indignant at his fate, rather than desponding or dejected, wished for death, and yet preserves his life without loving it---not from inclination or fear, but from duty---then his maxim has moral worth.[37]*

And a little further on, Kant again observes:

64

Now it is a wholly different thing to be truthful from duty, and to be so from apprehension of injurious consequences.[38]

Now Kant was the very first to admit that when it comes to moral motivation one can never know for sure whether the actions done by others or even by oneself were really done from duty or nerely in accordance with duty---so complex is the makeup of human motivation, and so difficult to sort out the "secret springs" of men's actions. Nevertheless, this does not invalidate the point that moral duty which is really present in every human person cannot be fulfilled except the action be done with precisely duty itself as the sole motivation. The fact that we cannot point out one instance with certainty in which an act was done purely from a motive of duty does not matter. What men actually do, let us repeat, is not what morals are all about. Morals are about what men *ought* to do. Even if there were not a single act in the world done from duty, that would not in the slightest tell against the point that men ought in moral acts to act solely from duty.

...yet whether this or that takes place is not at all the question; but that reason of itself, independent of all experience ordains what ought to take place.[39]

Kant felt this point in his moral theory to be so important that he points out how vastly superior it is as a moral doctrine for the upbringing of the young, to all other moral incentives which "romanticize" noble and good acts. His point, if indeed practicable, seems impregnable. He contends that it is offbase to try to instill virtue in the young by pointing to examples of moral heroes, men of noble deeds, etc. who achieved their fellow-men's esteem and acclaim. Or, the reverse: the example of crooks who were caught and "got what was coming to them." That, says Kant, would be moral pedagogy gone awry. Any reflective adult whose years of living has made him, as Kant would say, an acute observer of the human condition would see why. For a child then begins to equate moral goodness with success and acclaim, and immorality with the opposite results. When the scales of childhood fall off one's eyes and one begins to see more and more how often in real adult life "nice guys finish last" and the vicious, far from being punished in fact prosper---then the person's whole moral spirit is likely to evaporate.

As one wag puts it:

Whenever I see how profitable
Notoriety is, I begin
To believe that the wages of virtue
Are less than the wages of sin

and Kant:

In our times when men hope to have more effect on the mind through yielding, softhearted feelings or high-flying, puffed up pretensions, which wither instead of strengthening the heart, than through the dry

65

and earnest idea of duty which is more fitting to human imperfection and progress in goodness, attention to this method is more needed than ever.[40]

... in other words, simply the law of itself, which can be an object of respect, and hence a command.[41]

Such things would never happen, says Kant, in his theory where the stress is on the purity of motive in doing what one ought to do, stripped bare of any further consideration. To those who doubt that children can be brought up in such a highminded if dry sense of duty the assurance might help that there is already in the human makeup a positive disposition for the precise kind of moral pedagogy advocated here.

We should prove by observations which anyone can make, that this property of our minds, this receptivity to a pure moral interest and the moving force in the pure thought of virtue when properly commended to the human heart, is the strongest incentive to the good and indeed the only one when it is a question of continual and meticulous obedience to moral maxims.[42]

The point then is that moral duty in order to remain itself cannot suffer any admixture of any other motivation from whatever source, whether from our sensual inclinations, desires, interests, etc., or from considerations of advantages for the "dear self" no matter under what ruses or complex disguises and rationalizations these considerations may present themselves.[43]

5. *The Derivation of the Categorical Imperative.* It is clear now where the essence of Kantian morality lies. It is, negatively, outside anything empirical. It lies apart and away from the "pathological" world of our sensual desires and inclinations, away from all material objects. These determine the will (practical reason) only extrinsically. Under this negative aspect we should also exclude the will of God (God's law, Revelation, religion or whatever) as a possible source of moral duty. First, because philosophically in Kant's system we neither intuit God nor are we able to prove his existence. Much less then do we know His will or law. Even if we claimed we did see God or know His will, this still could not be the source nor fount of morality. For even then we would still have to fall back on our own bare reason to settle two issues for God's will to be morally binding. We would have to see that it is indeed a duty for us to obey God. Ought I obey God? Without this prior duty, no command of God would be seen as binding. And if this prior duty is seen to be binding, then it becomes clear that this cannot be from God's command again, or we would be in a circular argument. Clearly then, the source and fount of morality cannot be located in God.[44] Second, any claim laid on us under the rubric of God's will would obviously need sorting out and judging by reason itself. This is true even of the "Holy One" of the gospels.[45]

And so finally in our search for the source of morality, we are down to reason and reason alone deprived of all and every object which can possibly determine it from outside itself. Nothing below it, so to speak, in the sensible world of inclinations can qualify as the moral source. Nothing above it, as we have just seen in arguing against God's will as such a source, can qualify either since, to repeat, we have neither intuition nor philosophical knowledge of such a being. We are thus left with bare and pure reason issuing moral constraints and commands within outselves and to ourselves. And what could possibly be the determining object of reason within itself which enables it to produce the moral command?

> *Here then we see philosophy brought to a critical position, since it has to be firmly fixed, notwithstanding that it has nothing to support it in heaven or earth. Here it must show its purity as absolute director of its own laws, not the herald of those which are whispered to it by an implanted sense or who knows what tutelary nature. Although these may be better than nothing, yet they can never afford principles dictated by reason, which must have their source wholly a priori and thence their commanding authority, expecting everything from the supremacy of the law and the due respect for it, nothing from inclination, or else condemning the man to selfcontempt and inward abhorrence.[46]*

Nothing but pure reason itself, dictating to itself to *act* in a certain way (hence it is practical reason, or will) can be conceived by us as the principle of all morality.[47] That kind of rational object, intrinsic to reason's own nature and not outside it, can be nothing else than the command or dictate itself *informing* the will along the lines of formal causality. This Kant calls the moral "law." And we have seen that the very same practical reason or will must move itself to obedience to that "law" within itself exclusively *from duty*, in order for moral duty to be fulfilled. The whole reality of morals thus lies within the will, dictating the moral law from within itself and obeying it purely from within itself, namely, from an exclusive sense of duty. All the rest are secondary to this concept of the will as morally autonomous.

> *As I have deprived the will of every impulse which could arise to it from obedience to any law, there remains nothing but the universal conformity of its actions to law in general, which alone is to serve as a principle, that is, that I am never to act otherwise than so that I could also will that my maxim should become a universal law.[48]*

We are now at the core of Kant's moral doctrine. Our efforts from here on in will bear on attempting to unfold this notion of morality as man's self-legislating reason or will (autonomy) that is at once universal.

It might help to group together all the synonymous terms we have used up to now thus:

CATEGORICAL IM-
PERATIVE (Com-
mand; Ought; Duty;
Law; Moral Con-
straint)

= from AUTONO-
MOUS WILL (Pure
Practical Reason)

As commanding the *law* (determining itself objectively; generating the categorical imperative from within itself)

As *obeying* the law (determining itself *subjectively* purely from duty = respect)

Or, an even fuller schematic summary might go like this:

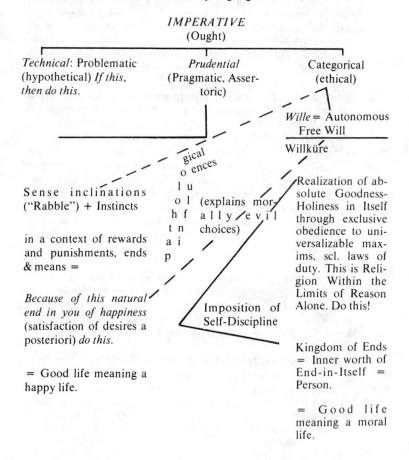

Since all talk of morality finally refers to the good, as we saw earlier, Kant relates all these ideas to that of the moral good, at the same time that he makes sure his point of morality as simply self-enclosed in the will in complete disregard of an act's consequences is not missed.

Universalizability: The Moral Norm

The moral law which the will yields out of its own depths, so to speak, (no other determining objects will do or heteronomy results) takes the *form* of a universal command. That is to say, any genuine moral law or command is a command for all rational beings. Why? It is hard to produce a text which gives a clear, precise and direct answer, but we can perhaps reconstruct the idea in this way. Reason qua reason cannot be different but must be of one and the same nature in every rational being. One may object by pointing out the various contents in men's minds, their obviously varied experiences, or even their divergent customary ways of reasoning. The answer would be that the pure reason which Kant uncovers here as the source of morality has been reached precisely by putting apart all empirical objects of reason, all experiences, everything that belongs to the factual, experiential side. This was the whole import of the insistent distinction between the moral *ought* and the *is*. To recall the point:

> *Even though there might never have been a sincere friend, yet not a whit the less is pure sincerity in friendship required of every man, because, prior to all experience, this duty is involved as duty in the idea of a reason determining the will by a priori principles.*[49]

What then is the basis for saying that anything genuinely moral is also an act that every rational being can do? The basis is simply that pure reason is of the same nature in all men. We do not want to go any further and say pure reason is the same identical reality in all men and indeed in everything, as Hegel did after Kant.

Is reason, one might insist, of the same nature in a native Tibetan and a, say, Sicilian? The answer is yes. Given the sufficient and necessary conditions, the two can understand one another at least to some degree, can they not? Take the Israelis and the Arabs. With all the time and opportunity they already have had in the United Nations and heaven only knows how many other meetings, why do they find it so impossible to understand one another if reason be truly of the same nature in both of them? Here one can answer first, that it should be clear that these two opposing factions are by now pretty clear between themselves on what precise points they disagree. Now *that* could have only come from the intensive use of reason and understanding present in them both. To agree on the precise point at issue is, after all, most of the difficult work in resolving disputes and arguments as any amateur diplomat or debater knows. In other words, to agree on what we precisely disagree shows reason in you and me to be of the same quality, the same nature. Second, the fact that the Israelis and the Arabs keep on arguing and debating their differences show that somehow they see it as within their powers of rational understanding both one day to arrive at a reasonable solution. And if someone counters by pointing to their moments of despair when they have resorted to war, the retort would be to point right back to the self same rational nature on both sides which enabled them to conclude that further reasoning would be unproductive of any practical result in those given circumstances. That same reason, let us add, also led the two sides to see the wisdom of disengaging from war. No matter what objections a persistent sceptic may advance, the retort is always that of pointing to reason as reflective consciousness on both sides and thus as one and the name nature in all men, irrespective of their varying environments, customs, experiences, etc. Even now I read of Alfred Lilienthal, a prominent Jewish man who accepts almost entirely the Arab arguments on the whole dispute. So too, King Hussein of Jordan seems able really to hear what the Israelis are saying. And, finally, there is John .Henry Newman's point on how on the level of informal inferences people could be in agreement even as they disagree while talking. The trouble is one of language.

> *Half the controversies in the world are verbal ones; and could they be brought to a plain~ issue, they would be brought to a prompt termination. Parties engaged in them would then perceive, either that in substance they agreed together, or that their difference was one of first principles.*[50]

Duty

What is the content of this moral law which springs from pure reason? What is this Kantian duty which keeps out all empirical effects and material objects from itself and adheres only to the universal "form" of reason itself? Furthermore, since obviously not all statements are necessarily rational (in the sense of *reasonable*) how does one sort out what is genuinely a moral law or duty from what is not? We will now attend to these two questions, keeping in mind with regard to the second question that what we seek when we claim that a proposition is a reasonable one is not necessarily a *de facto* universal agreement (since as we just said people make conclusions on many other bases than reason) but *de jure* agreement. A reasonable proposition should be one which any rational being ought to see as reasonable. Now the argument could go on indefinitely by asking again who, when, where, etc. decides a proposition *ought* to be universally seen as reasonable. But since we encounter reason only in individual human persons and never in any other form, the answer is that the decision is obviously made by individuals. We, you, I and others, decide whether what is claimed as reasonable is indeed such. We do this by the employment of our reason. There is no other alternative, and that is really the last that can be said on the matter. To sum up then, Kant would maintain that really rational propositions *can be* and *ought* to be seen by all rational beings as such, even though not every one in fact sees those as such for now.

We move on now to the two questions of (1) the formulations of the moral law or the categorical imperative; and (2) the method by which we sort out genuine moral duties. Here we are dealing with the *objective* aspect of duty, the content of the moral act itself as distinguished from the motivation or subjective aspect of duty which we have already pointed out to be always pure *respect* for that law.

(1) *Formulation of the Categorical Imperative.* Kant gives various formulations for the categorical imperative. Commentators disagree on whether there are only three or five or more formulations.[51] There is also disagreement as to whether the various formulations Kant gives in the *Fundamental Principles* are ultimately reducible to only one formula; or whether they are really different among themselves, each one enunciating its own distinctive aspect of moral reality. All this even though Kant himself says there really is *only one* categorical imperative.[52] For us what is essential is the understanding of each of the various formulations (whether they be many or reducibly one) as all involving the essential concept of *universalizability*---with regard to every genuine moral duty or law. Here are various enunciations of the categorical imperative:

> **1.** *Act only on that maxim whereby thou canst at the same time will that it should become a universal law.*[53]
> *Or, as he puts it later:*
> *Act always on such a maxim as thou canst at the same time will to be a universal law.*[54]
> **2.** *Act as if the maxim of thy action were to become by thy will a universal law of nature.*[55]
> *Or, as he puts it later:*
> *Act on maxims which can at the same time have for their object themselves as universal laws of nature.*[56]
> **3.** *So act to treat humanity, whether in thine own person or in that of any other, in every case as an end withal, never as means only.*[57]
> *Or, as he puts it in another place:*
> *So act as if you were by your maxims in every case a legislating member in the universal kingdom of ends.*[58]

All those formulae revolve on the crucial characteristic of law as universal and universalizable, and of mere maxims as by themselves not yet necessarily laws, but merely subjective principles or policies of action which an individual has set up for himself.[59]

First Formulation. Because reason is the same in all men, and moral reason stands apart, as it were, from all individual experiences or anything else other than itself, its determination or law can only be the same in all men. There is nothing else conceivable that can possibly pluralize pure reason within itself. Hence a genuine moral duty or categorical imperative has to be one that holds true, binds and obliges every rational being. A genuine moral obligation for any given individual must also be an obligation for all who are rational beings − the only beings able to function according to the *conception* of laws. All other beings in nature function deterministically according to mechanical laws.[60] Any obligation valid for one is valid for all. This is the point of the first formulation.

Second Formulation. We recall how in Kant the mind contributes the elements of universality and necessity in our rise from individual events and situations to generalized experiences and scientific laws. We recall that "nature" for Kant means "rule-determined behaviour." The rule too is contributed by the mind. It is the generalization, universalization and necessity we find in scientific propositions which gather the sense manifold of individual experiments into the unity of a scientific formula or law. The law therefore is a combination of both a priori elements from the mind or reason, and the individual elements of sensuous intuition. Hence Kant's term for such generalizations or laws, namely, synthetic a priori propositions. This is what is behind the second formulation of the categorical imperative. The moral law is a universal necessity imposed (and thus combined with) upon the sense manifold, namely, our sensual desires, inclinations and all other considerations hinging on the "dear self" as the motivating interest for our action. There is thus an analogy here between the laws of "nature" and the categorical imperative. Both are synthetic a priori propositions.

Third Formulation. This statement of the categorical imperative opens up a whole new dimension. We will therefore follow Kant's own method of presentation and illustrate how the *universalizability* principle works in the four various examples he gives, before returning to the third formulation and reviewing those same four examples in its light.

The test for moral duty is simply the question: Can I universalize the act I am about to do? Note how while every moral act is universalizable, the converse does not necessarily follow. It is not true that all universalizable actions are moral ones. Many trivial activities we perform in the course of a day can obviously be willed universally by every man. It would invite ridicule to term such acts "moral duty." When we talk of moral duty we are obviously talking of deliberate and what William James would call "momentous" options, the final Either/Or choice in Kierkegaard, or what some call acts of vertical freedom. It is horizontal freedom, for instance, to choose among the dishes spread out in a smorgasbord. Vertical freedom is at play, however, on matters of good and evil, v.g., should I beat up this man who provokes me so now that I've finally met him alone in a dark alley. It is this latter kind of choices we are questioning here. We are asking how the universalizability test is applied to them.

Before proceeding to Kant's four examples, it will be helpful to touch on some ideas essential to the context of those examples. First of all, we should note that universalizability and non-contradiction go together as well as non-universalizability and contradiction. If the act I contemplate on doing, when tested by the norm of universalizability ends up contradicting itself, or as Kant says in one place, "annihilating itself"[61], then I can conclude that it is not genuinely a moral law. It will be sufficient here to refer back to our examples in the preceding chapter on shoplifting, extra-marital affairs, etc. Kant was the very first to remark that the mental rehearsal of an act according to the universalizability principle is not the same thing as the actuality of every human being doing the deed. The question is not whether all men will in fact do the same action I am about to do. It is whether they can all be allowed the same thing as though the action were right. If conceived in this way a contemplated deed "annihilates itself," then it is not and cannot be a moral duty.

Now everyone knows very well that if he secretly permits himself to deceive, it does not follow that everyone else will do so, or that if, unnoticed by others, he is lacking in compassion, it does not mean that everyone else will take the same attitude toward him...If the maxim of an action is not so constituted as to stand the test of being made the form of a natural law in general, it is morally impossible, (even though it may still be possible in nature.)[62]

Next, we note that aside from the test of internal contradiction in one's maxim (subjective principle of acting), Kant also talks of contradiction of the "will." An act, he claims, may not suffer internal contradiction when universalized, but it still could suffer contradiction if universally willed. Here he takes the classic position of things in the world, and especially man, as having *natural ends*. Indeed he even talks of special situations and occasions in life as having ends "willed" in them by nature. We cannot at this point take up Kant's theory of ends or teleology. Suffice it to say here that this is the second kind of contradiction the universalizability test must undergo. You cannot, Kant says, will that all men will something that obviously is against the natural intention of things. It is a point which is bound to stir up scepticism and controversy. The best way to answer is simply to go over the examples themselves reflectively. Kant explains that by perfect moral duties he means those which bind all the time without exception or "room for play."

We transgress perfect duties by treating any person as a means. We transgress imperfect duties by failing to treat a person as an end, even though we do not actively treat him as a means.[63]

Examples of perfect or negative duties would be the prohibitions against suicide, lying, stealing, etc. Imperfect or positive duties, on the other hand, would be those with room for play, affirmative duties commanding us to do certain actions *whenever* (as our sense of discretion dictates) the right circumstances are present.

The Four Examples

In the first example a man contemplates suicide due to desperate misfortunes visited upon him. He contemplates suicide on the maxim that one should take one's life when he can foresee only evil for the most part ahead of him. So we put this maxim to the test and ask whether it is universalizable. Can he will that *all* persons adopt this maxim? No, he cannot. Why?

For a law to destroy life by means of the very feeling whose special nature it is to impel to the improvement of life would contradict itself.[64]

And elsewhere he writes:

For if we were never led by a representation to apply our powers before

One must admit that the contradiction pointed to here is not as apparent as Kant thought it was. The idea seems to be that a "system of nature impels towards the improvement of life, specifically by means of crises, even desperate ones." To universalize suicide in such situations would in effect set up a new "system of nature" which would in fact be anti-nature (obviously a use of the term "nature" not in the technical sense of "rule-determined behaviour"). Nature that is really anti-nature---therein is the contradiction involved when we universalize the maxim of suicide. Therefore, suicide is against the supreme principle of duty, the moral law.[66]

His next example, still on self-love, is that of a man who is forced to borrow money under false pretenses of repaying a loan when all the time he knows repayment would be impossible. Can such a maxim be universalized? If you say yes, then no one would ever believe promises made during times of hardship. When promises should mean most, they would thus mean least. When they should mean everything, they would mean nothing. Promises, in short, would not be promises if this action were universalized. We conclude then that this act too is immoral.

With the third example, we come to the impossibility of *willing* some thing that in itself may not be contradictory. The question is whether someone who has the means to do it may simply spend his life in luxurious enjoyment and laziness without exerting any effort to develop the gifts nature has endowed him with, as v.g. the "South Sea Islanders." Can this maxim be universalized? The answer again is no. Though there is no contradiction here ("a system of nature could subsist with such a universal law") in itself, there is a contradiction against the "natural" direction of the human will. As a rational being man's will moves towards the development of his own talents and gifts. To see Kant's point we should perhaps ask ourselves whether we do not experience within ourselves a natural impulsion towards the full exercise and play of our abilities, power, capabilities, etc. That would be a most unusual person whose will goes against the use and development of his own abilities. The natural movement to develop one's self is as natural as it is for any organism to move towards the maximization of its own being. It is this "natural will' which would be contradicted, if the maxim of lazing around during the entirety of one's life were universalized.

For as a rational being, he necessarily wills that his faculties be developed, since they serve him, and have been given him, for all sorts of possible purposes.[67]

Finally, there is the self-made type who wishes to universalize his maxim: never assist those in distress. Can this maxim be universalized? Again, there is no internal contradiction. The proposition does not "annihilate itself." Yet it still would contravene morality in that it would be contradictory to *will* it as a universal law.

74

*inasmuch as many cases might occur in which one would have need of
the love and sympathy of others, and in which by such a law of nature
sprung from his own will, he would deprive himself of all hope of the
aid he desires.*[68]

One commentator, R.P. Wolff, as we saw, does not think these
examples are convincing.[64] But perhaps Kant could defend his point by
answering that such "forswearing" of aid from others when one is in
straitend circumstances is assumed by Wolff in his exceptional individual as taking place without going against a prior natural tendency within
him to long for such aid. That prior natural tendency is there. Surely, it
can be forsworn on the basis of an individual's policy. But the very
observation that such an individual seems exceptional alerts us to the
situation as one which goes against the natural direction of his will.

This idea of a natural direction of the will (or nature; or even
circumstances) seems pivotal whenever Kant puts the universalizability
principle into play. As we said, it would take us outside our scope here to
go into the concept of teleology or finality in natural things in Kant's
theory to see how it fits in consistently with his doctrine on morals. For
our purpose it suffices to see that Kant clearly takes our experience of
"natural movements" and tendencies to be valid enough for use in
reaching moral conclusions.

We come now to the third formulation of the categorical imperative:

*So act as to treat humanity, whether in thine own person or in that of
any other, in every case as an end withal, never as means only.*

Several questions come up about this formulation, among them (1)
How did Kant derive or arrive at this formula? (2) Why is man an
end-in-itself? (3) Why did Kant put in that qualifying phrase "as means
only?"

(1) *The Derivation of the Formula.* We have seen how all heteronomous moral theories are inadmissible. This leaves pure practical reason
alone, i.e., the will, as the sole ground of morality. The free will issues the
moral law, the categorical imperative. It also wills to obey that law solely
out of duty whenever a person acts morally. Pure practical reason,
stripped of all extrinsic determining objects and experiences, cannot in
fact be conceived otherwise than as universally the same nature in all
other rational beings. This unity of pure practical reason in all rational
beings provides the ground for the first and second formulations of the
categorical imperative. The same is true for the third formulation.

The concept of an autonomous will, a will producing its own
determining principle, namely, the moral law, reveals a self-determining
being. The self-determination we are concerned with here is not along
qualified lines of goodness, such as that of being a good engineer,
mathematician, or politician, etc. Rather, it is along the unqualified and
categorical line of human goodness itself. Now a being who determines
himself to his own ultimate goal along the categorical lines of duty,
without in any way descending to the hypothetical areas of technical and
prudential imperatives (areas which, let us recall, are confined to the

means-and-ends context) shows itself to be its own end. It produces its own law for its own determination into an absolute good, a good will. This holds for every human person.

> *Beings whose existence depends not on our will but on nature's have, nevertheless, if they are nonrational beings, only a relative value as means, and are therefore called* things; *rational beings on the contrary, are called* persons, *because their very nature points them out as ends in themselves, that is, as something which must not be used merely as means, and so far therefore restricts freedom of action and is an object of respect. These, therefore, are not merely subjective ends whose existence has a worth for us as an effect of our action, but* objective ends, *that is, things whose existence is an end in itself, an end, moreover, for which no other can be substituted, which they should subserve* merely as means, *for otherwise nothing whatever would possess absolute worth; but if all worth were conditioned and therefore contingent, then there would be no supreme practical principle of reason whatever.*[70]

From the last sentence above we can see how Kant rejects a philosophy in which everything is merely means without there being an end-in-itself. He thus grounds all the means in the end-in-itself, the human person.

Systems of nature then and natural tendencies are used for the universalization test. Now since man is by nature an end-in-himself, to will that he be otherwise is something that one cannot *morally* (physically, of course, he can) will all men to will. Yet, that is precisely what one who uses another as means *only* in effect wills. He disregards and totally cancels, as it were, man's nature as an end-in-itself. He treats a human person as good only for some further end set up whether by himself or some one else. Thus it is impossible to rise to universality. The action in question cannot qualify as moral. By the same token man's nature as morally autonomous is positively affirmed. Man is affirmed as a good-in-himself, an end-in-himself. But again it should be carefully noted that not every act which does not contradict the principle of man as an end-in-himself is thereby moral. There are trivial yet universalizable acts we do all the time which simply are outside the area of morals.

In a sense the various formulations are really identical. They all point up practical reason, purified from anything that might make it individual or provincial, as the essential ground of morality. This pure reason is of the same nature in all men. From it issues imperatives which, if valid for that *one person* from whom it in fact issues is, by that very fact, also valid for *all persons*. And this pure reason, as issuing the same laws for all, organizes human inclinations into rule-determined behaviour or nature (the first formula). This pure reason, as generating its own laws and, decision to be moral or not, is an end-in-itself and not a means only to some further end (second formula). This leads to the concept of a "kingdom of ends" (third formula).

The essential identity of content in all three formulations of the categorical imperative may be viewed in another way. What is the

76

implication behind the test required for assessing moral acts, i.e., the universalizability principle? What does it mean to pause before acting so as to ask yourself whether this act which you are about to do is something that you can will every other person to will also? Is this not in effect to think of everybody else as if you were they and they you who stand absolute at the moment with regard to both the production of and subjection to the moral law? Is this not to consider oneself an end-in-himself, and everybody else as of the same nature? How else explain the complete interchangeability?

> *The will is conceived as a faculty of determining oneself to action* in accordance with the conception of certain laws. *And such a faculty can be found only in rational beings.* Now that which serves the will as the objective ground of its self-determination is the end, and if this is assigned by reason alone, it must hold for all rational beings.[71]

(2) *Why is Man an End-in-Himself?* Again, it is difficult to produce a clear and direct text which answers this question. Instead we have to think our way through such texts as the following.

> *Supposing, however, that there were something whose existence has* in itself *an absolute worth, something which, being an* end-in-itself, *could be a source of definite laws, then in this and this alone would lie the source of a possible categorical imperative, that is, a practical law. Now I say, man and generally any rational being exists as an end in himself,* not merely as a means *to be arbitrarily used by this or that will, but in all his actions, whether they concern himself or other rational beings, must be always regarded at the same time as an end. All objects of the inclinations have only a conditional worth.*[72]

Man and/or any rational being is an end-in-himself not because of his inclinations. These are only of conditional worth. They can only be means to ends. Why then is a rational being not a means only? Why is he an end-in-himself? We can answer negatively by pointing out that if everything else including man were just a means only, without there being any end-in-itself, we would have an absurdity. For we must ask of this strange universe in which everything is a means: a means to what? Now some philosophers (v.g. Dewey) would retort that this kind of question is inherited from the Greek mind which could not rest satisfied until it posited ultimate things. Now, obviously, Kant did not have to reckon with Dewey. But he still was clearly a philosopher of the classical set who positively pushed for an ultimate explanation to the extent allowed by his epistemological doctrine. He is thus one who would not accept a universe in which everything was merely a means.

> *...otherwise nothing whatever would possess absolute worth; but if all worth were conditioned and therefore contingent, then there would be no supreme practical principle of reason.*[73]

Is the point here being merely asserted without further clarification?

77

Perhaps we need to focus for a while on the self-determining nature of reason.

Means are obviously specified by the ends to which they are pointed. In a world where everything is conceived to be mere data or means, specification and determination would come only with human decisions on how to handle them as instruments. This metal in front of me, for instance, is a typewriter when I use it for printing. But it could also be a weapon should I drop it on the fellow standing below my window. *I* determine its end. I determine what my own determination shall be finally, no matter how many preliminary opinions and inlfuences are brought to bear on me. What then shall we say of a being who determines not another being but itself? One who determines itself not toward another being but toward its own self? Furthermore, this being determines itself not only along qualified lines of goodness, but on the unqualified level of moral goodness, the absolute goodness of a "good will." That is the nub of the idea here. For such a being the only adequate concept is that of an end-in-itself. It no longer can be thought of as merely a *means*. In sum, man is an end-in-himself because as a rational being he is a *self-contained will*, able to conceive its own goodness as the one and only absolute good "in the world or even out of it."[74]

To be an end-in-himself it is neither sufficient nor necessary that a person have the physical strength to resist being used by others. It is sufficient and necessary that resistance arise from reason, that is to say, the *humanity* present in him. In brief, if with Kant we hold that morals must ultimately be explained not by sensual inclinations which cannot be universalized, but by that sole power alone in man which makes universalization possible, namely, reason, then we should also see how every man is necessarily an end-in-himself. By his reason which is self-contained and has its own laws, he makes his own decisions. Thus he is autonomous. His object in such decisions, as we saw, cannot be subsumed under some other end without ceasing to be itself. Its end has to be its own goodness, its own "good will." This ultimately is what makes a human person an end-in-itself. At no time in a person's existence may his worth be evaluated, precisely as a person, in terms of "usefulness." This is a position of tremendous implication for anyone who would care to bring it down to the specifics of the moral debate on abortion, euthanasia, human genetics, etc.

We would also agree with those who defend Kant against such ridicule as the following.

> *(Kant) thought it absolutely, unqualifiedly wrong for a starving man afloat on a raft to eat a rotting can of beans to which he had no commercial claim*[75]

To which J.R. Silber comments:

> *It is inconceivable that Kant would regard the claim of the absentee owner of a can of rotten beans as superior to the claim of a rational being to life.*[76]

(3) *The Qualification, "as a means only."* The business of life cannot be carried forward without interpersonal relationships involving exchange

of services, feelings, positions, obligations, resposnibilities, etc., endlessly in an ever spreading network of influences which boggle the mind. Even if we had nothing else but his second, third and fourth illustrations of the universalizability principle, we would still clearly see how Kant placed interpersonal dependency at the very heart of human development and enterprises. Men have to *use* one another. But *how*? How are ends-in-themselves to be used in a way different from mere things which cannot be anything else but means? Interpersonal use is indeed necessary. However, it is only moral when based on interpersonal *respect*. What is "respect?"

Respect

In a very effective section of the second *Critique* called "The Incentive of Pure Practical Reason," Kant describes respect as a "feeling." He is careful to restrict the object of this feeling to the moral law.

> *Respect for the moral law, therefore, is a feeling produced by an intellectual cause, and this feeling is the only one which we can know completely a priori and the necessity of which we can discern.*[77]

There is in every person a propensity to self-esteem, to self-conceit, to arrogance, to being puffed up. The one thing that constrains or checks this tendency is the internal consciousness a man necessarily has of his own moral size or stature. Kant is saying in effect: "The whole world may be applauding its head off in frenzied approval of you (for whatever visible successes you may have achieved), but if *internally*, according to the standard of what is right and wrong, good and evil, you know full well that you are a failure, you cannot but feel humiliated." And frankly, who among us do not in fact come to see ourselves as less than what the moral law demands of us?

> *As striking down, i.e. humiliating self-conceit, it (the moral law) is an object of the greatest respect and thus the ground of a positive feeling which is not of an empirical origin.*[78]

There we have a definitive text in which "feeling" mixes, as it were, with morality. Everywhere else Kant insists on holding morality apart from any inclination or feeling. Indeed, even now he classifies this *feeling* as rooted not in the sensual inclination and appetite but in the *intellectual* acknowledgement of one's diminished stature before the majesty of the moral law within himself. Because of the intellectual parentage of this particular respect, it is something that cannot be found in subhuman objects which are all merely *things, means*. Nor can it be directed towards such *things*. Respect is not for objects, but for human subjects, for ends-in-themselves, in whom dwells the sacred majesty of the moral law. Thus Kant is careful to differentiate even feelings of *sublimity* directed towards subhuman realities of awesome grandeur or natural perfection like lofty mountains, the starry heavens, seas, volcanoes, swift and strong animals, etc.[79] Respect is directed only to the presence of the moral law in a human person.

The matter gets complicated when we talk of the respect we give to our moral superiors, that is, those morally better than we. Elsewhere Kant had talked of the disgust we feel at the sight of an immoral man thriving in worldly prosperity.[80] We could ask: is respect due only to our moral superior? What ultimately is this respect which ought to control our interpersonal exchanges of services?

We need to distinguish a twofold meaning of the term. "Respect" refers to the universal presence of the moral law in every man endowing him with *dignity* (not *price*[76] which refers only to objects). In this sense, every man, as the temple of the moral law, also has dignity. He is worthy of respect, morally autonomous, and a self-legislating agent. In this primary sense every man is *worthy* of respect, respect*able* absolutely and without any qualification.[81]

To use other persons with *respect* is not to coerce them into our services (and heaven knows there are a variety of ways in which a person can coerce another into submitting to his wishes). Coercion uses another person with ourselves as the end. Yet my obligation is to accord him what he is in reality. In reality he is a free being able and morally obliged to choose his own destiny. Again, respect also means that I do not do anything to another person which I cannot also will to be done universally to all men including myself. Obviously, there could be other ways men could devise to show respect for one another, but at least these two constitute the essential minimum for respect to obtain between persons exchanging services, each with his own end in view.

The second derivative meaning of "respect" refers to one's moral betters. This points directly to the moral law itself. If I respect another as my moral superior, either secretly or openly, it is because I see in him a greater fulfillment of the selfsame moral law which is within us both. My respect for this moral law therefore is the reason why I "bow" to him as morally superior to me.

Now a question. After all of Kant's diclaimers about the impossibility of recognizing a moral act from the outside or even inside oneself,[82] how can we talk of recognizing another as morally superior to me? In one long section, for example, Kant carefully develops the idea that youngsters should be reared uprighteously by impressing on them Kant's "duty for duty's sake" morality. However, he goes on to say that, to highlight this principle, examples of great moral deeds must be used. But the problem is that he has told us in no uncertain terms that we have no way of ascertaining the genuinely moral character of any deed. How explain this inconsistency?

The answer we get is not without sarcasm, given as though Kant had forgotten his earlier assertions.

> ...*I must confess that only philosophers can put the decision on this question in doubt. For by common sense it is long since decided, not by abstract general formulas but rather by habitual use, like the difference between the right and the left hand.*[83]

80

We are brought back to the fact that we do actually experience right and wrong deeds, whether in ourselves or from others. We can through clues go step by step:

from mere approval to admiration, and from admiration to marvelling, and finally to the greatest veneration and lively wish that he himself could be such a man (though certainly not in his circumstances)[84]

There is a delicately close affinity between admiration and respect. There is also a distinction. Some unachieved innate talent seems involved in an object of admiration. Whereas *respect* bears first of all on the actuality itself of the moral law in a person and secondly on his free realization of that moral law in his life. Note, for instance, the two meanings of "respect" in the following text:

This respect which we have for a person (really for the law, which his example holds before us) is, therefore, not mere admiration. This is also confirmed by the way the common run of men give up their respect for a man (v.g. Voltaire) when they think they have in some manner found the badness of his character, while the true scholar still feels this respect at least for his talents...[85]

In sum, while there is a close affinity between respect and the feeling of admiration we experience whether for objects, human talents or even the "face and beauty of virtue,"[86] one is still not the other. First, respect refers to our feeling of submission to the moral law which is in every person. Second, it also means our submission ("we bow") or acknowledgement of the moral superiority of another when *somehow* we perceive such superiority. Respect is a feeling different from all other feelings even up to and including admiration. Admiration refers only to objective realities which are not morally brought about. In its secondary sense, respect may mean esteem of character. In this latter sense it could be called *admiration* or aesthetic appreciation of virtue, usually in another.

Respect in its secondary sense then is irrelevant to the idea of treating every person as an end-in-itself and not a means merely in the context of interpersonal exchange of services. What is involved rather is the primary meaning of respect. This means that in the nitty-gritty of life, with all the human drives for survival, happiness, advantages, gain and whatever, men ought to make sure the other is never coerced and that the norm of universalizability prevails at all times.

Respect applies always to persons only, never to things. The latter can awaken inclinations, and even love if they are animals (horses, dogs, etc.) or fear, as does the sea, a volcano, or a beast of prey; but they never arouse respect. Something which approaches this feeling is admiration, and this, as an emotion (astonishment) can refer also to things, e.g. lofty mountains, the magnitude, number and distance of the heavenly bodies, the strength and swiftness of many animals, etc. All this, however, is not respect. A man can also be an object of love, fear or admiration, even to astonishment, and yet not be an object of

81

respect. His jocular humor, his courage and strength, and his power of rank may inspire me with such feelings, though inner respect for him is still lacking.

Fontanelle says, "I bow to a great man, but my mind does not bow." I can add: to a humble plain man, in whom I perceive righteousness in a higher degree than I am conscious of in myself, my mind bows whether I choose or not, however high I carry my head that he may not forget my superior position. Why? His example holds a law before me which strikes down my self-conceit when I compare my own conduct with it.[87]

We can conclude this section by again remarking on the almost infinite number of ways and devices to which men can resort, to make the exercise of free choice in others less than really free. "Really free" is of course a judgement of prudence which a reasonable man would have to figure out from a given situation. How free, for instance, is an illegal alien in Chicago to make a contract with an exploiter of alien labor who ruthlessly reminds his employee that he could pick up the phone any time to turn the victim in to Immigration inspectors for deportation should the employee refuse to work the long hours and little pay offered him? Prudential judgement must assess each situation. But a human person has been treated inhumanly "as a means only" when in one way or another, no matter how ingeniously, he has been coerced into submitting to the manipulation of another for this other's end and own advantages. That the other so exploited is in a way saved from the worst by the other's manipulation cannot cancel the essential immorality of the situation. Seducing another person sexually is another example of using the other person as merely a means. By contrast, some sexual relations between husband and wife are usually not a case of one using the other as a means merely, but rather one of upholding the principle of "respect." Both partners enter with mutual freedom into a context of lifelong sharing. A butcher who deliberately shortweighs his customers is reducing them to a means merely. Whereas a butcher who gives his customers honest weights and answers their questions about his products truthfully is respecting them as ends-in-themselves. Both freely enter into an interpersonal exchange of goods and services as he takes their money and they take his goods.

What of cases where one person offers all the options open to another among which is an immoral universalizable one, which immoral option the other freely chooses? Is it moral for two persons to go off together toward the execution of a deed both of them freely chose, even though they both knew the deed to be immoral? How are these questions answered on the basis of the third formulation? Here the questions probably answer themselves since the issue is about immorality which, by definition, is not morally permissible no matter how freely it is chosen. Kant would be aghast at the idea that one can even conceive of two persons agreeing to commit an immoral deed as possibly a case in which each respected the "majesty" of moral law present in both. The condition of free choice is not the whole of morality. Freedom is inseparable from its own laws, those of morality. Beyond this point the argument can be prolonged only by disagreeing with Kant's ethics altogether.

> *Freedom, the causality of which is determinable merely through the law, consists, however, only in the fact that it limits all inclinations, including self-esteem, to the condition of obedience to its pure law.*[88]

We can now enhance our grasp of this third formulation of the categorical imperative by applying it to the previous four examples.

First, is a person morally allowed to commit suicide when he finds himself in straitened circumstances from which no escape is foreseeable? No. For "if he destroys himself in order to escape from painful circumstances, he uses a person merely as a means to maintain a tolerable condition up to the end of life."[89] We should note however that the question here is not about therapeutical amputation or mutilation, etc. which clearly aims at preserving the person himself, but rather about the destruction of a person's entire being for the sake of a tolerable condition. "Man is not a thing, that is to say, something which can be used merely as a means...I cannot, therefore, dispose in any way of a man in my own person."[90]

Second, can one in dire circumstances make a lying promise in order to get a loan he secretly has no intention of repaying? No. For this is to use the other merely as a means. This other could not possibly assent to my action if I furnished the information to which any lender has a right. Similarly, it is immoral to attack the freedom and property of others.

> *For it is clear that he who transgresses the rights of men intends to use the person of others merely as means, not as ends, that is, as beings who must be capable of containing in themselves the end of the very same action.*[91]

Third, is it moral to be lazy, not to develop my natural gifts all my life long? Now this does not violate the principle of humanity, or end-in-itself in me. But it does violate the natural tendency, present in every human person to, not only maintain oneself, but also to cultivate and advance oneself.

> *There are in humanity capacities of greater perfection which belong to the end that nature has in view in regard to humanity in ourselves as the subject; to neglect these might perhaps be consistent with the* maintenance *of humanity as an end in itself, but not with the* advancement *of this end.*[92]

Then comes the controverted fourth example. Is it moral to refuse all aid to someone who needs it, provided I scrupulously take care not to stand in his way in any way? The answer parallels that of the third example. It is not enough to be "negatively" free from violating the rights of others. Human persons also have a positive duty to advance the "ends" of nature in man, among which ends is happiness. (We will go into the relation of happiness to morality as human ends later). The issue here is not that of violating others, but of positively advancing the ends of humanity in them in the same way that I am obliged to advance them in me. To treat another as an end-in-himself is to treat him as I treat myself. Therefore, I should positively help when I can in the advancement of the happiness of others just as I do so morally in my own case.[93]

At the end of these four examples, Kant appends an interesting footnote pointing out that his principle of universalizability and of rational beings as ends-in-themselves is not the same as the "golden rule." For it is immediately evident that the motivation of the golden rule is self-advantage. The motive for doing or not doing unto others is the fear or desire of the same actions being done to me also. This is worlds apart from the demand that the sole motive for a moral act be duty simply and exclusively. I must because I must. Duty is duty, that is why I must be moral, period. Whereas the golden rule boils down to a motive of personal convenience or inconvenience, advantage or disadvantage for oneself. This actually relegates it to the side of the inclinations. Humorously, Kant observes that if morality came down to the golden rule, the convicted criminal "might argue against the judge who punishes him, and so on."[94]

It is clear now why this theory can claim that morality does not depend on the consequences of an action. Because a man is a creature of the imagination and of the senses, he cannot help but drag consequences into the picture when pondering the universalizability of an action. But this is only a "typic" of the moral assessment.[95] The essence of moral assessment lies elsewhere; namely, in the formal consideration of an action as to its universalizability, whether as to its contradictory "self-annihilating" formulation, or to its contravening will-act which goes against the system of natural tendencies or will implanted in human nature. To repeat, man has an absolute, unqualified worth or value, *apart from all considerations of his usefulness*. All subhuman objects are just that, objects. They are therefore means to further ends. All they have is a *price*. They are correctly assessed according to their usefulness or non-usefulness for any given end. But man in his being is a subject. He is the living temple of the moral law. As such he is an end-in-himself, an absolute worth and value needing no further justification as to usefulness or non-usefulness in order to command the respect of others.[96]

From this absolute worth of man flows his list of inviolable rights, duties and responsibilities. Inviolable because it is absolute and therefore dependent on no other being for its reality. Dependent on no other being because, as we saw, the moral law in us is autonomous and cannot be dependent on any other being than one's own free will itself; and also because the very conception of a rational being as such makes it like everyone else of the same nature a living source of the moral law absolute in its own right. Heteronomy (dependence on something other than the will itself) for the moral law has simply no place in Kant's moral doctrine.

One can ask what this or that object is good *for*. That would be a good question. But it would be absurd to ask what he, regardless of everything else, is good *for*. He does not have to be good for or good at anything at all to be a good-in-himself. He is a value in himself, an absolute and unqualified good simply because he *is* a *man*. Rising above all utilitarian values, we term this unqualified value of humanity "sacred."

> *There is nothing more sacred in the wide world than the rights of others...If everyone did this (i.e., respect the rights of others) there would be no misery in the world except sickness and misfortune and other such suffering as do not spring from the violation of the rights of others. The most frequent and fertile source of human misery is not misfortune, but the injustices of men.*[98]

And, based to a great extent on this Kantian idea, John Rawls wrote his extensive work *A Theory of Justice* as an argument against utilitarianism and a development of the idea packed into the following statements:

> *Each person possesses an inviolability founded on justice that even the welfare of society as a whole cannot override. For this reason justice denies that the loss of freedom for some is made right by a greater good shared by others. It does not allow that the sacrifice imposed on a few are outweighed by others...this rules out justifying institutions on the grounds that hardships of some are offset by a greater good in the aggregate.*[98]

And it certainly would be well for a society where crime runs more and more rampant to ponder a point Kant used to impress upon his students.

> *Let a man be kind and generous all his life and commit but one act of injustice and all his acts of generosity cannot wipe out that one injustice.*[99]

Such then is the core of Kant's moral doctrine. It remains for us now to delve into some of its significant implications, namely, (1) the notion of the kingdom of ends and the postulate of freedom; (2) the notion of virtue and the postulate of immortality; and (3) the notion of happiness as man's end within the "highest good" and the postulate of God's existence.

4

IMPLICATIONS

A Kingdom of Ends

By kingdom here is meant "a union of different rational beings in a system of common laws."[1] It is fascinating to explore Kant's idea that the more individual appetites and inclinational desires are abstracted from, and the nearer we come to the conception of a pure reason all by itself issuing forth moral laws unto itself, the more also we see that all human persons, indeed all rational beings, form a unity on the basis of that pure reason which they have in common.

As we saw earlier, the idea of a solipsistic reason so private and individual as to have nothing in common with reason in other men is indefensible. Like money reason is essentially social. A really valid reason is valid anywhere for anybody rational to see. Reversely, a reason so privately valid that is a "good" reason only to the one individual holding it and to nobody else, or only to an exclusive few, is not really good. Or, we can analogate reason to language. Both are essentially social. A language so private as to be the language only of one individual and incommunicable to anybody else would no longer be language, would it? So too, reason, as essentially social, forms the basis for unification among men. Human beings are all rational. Hence pure practical reason, though existing only individually in each of them, nevertheless issues moral legislations valid for everybody.

It does not matter that the moral law is enuntiated at any given time by one given individual in a concrete set of circumstances. If it is rational, its content will be *universal*. Etymologically, *universal* means precisely that: the many gathered into a unity. In Kant's moral doctrine we see how each man, while standing alone as an end-in-himself, inviolable and sacred above all price and needing no further justification, is yet far from being an island unto himself. The reason in him that is the source of the moral law is the same reason that is present in everybody else- - - a tremendous insight which G. Hegel, another German philopher, was quick to exploit.

Since all rational beings stand under the same system of laws, they belong to one same realm of kingdom of ends-in-themselves. Each is *sovereign* simply as a bearer of humanity. But each is also *subject* to those same laws. To seek exemption from these laws is the very definition of immorality, just as reversely universality defines morality.[2]

> *A rational being belongs as a* member *to the kingdom of ends when, although giving universal laws in it, he is also himself subject to these laws, he is not subject to the will of any other.*[3]

Always that note of reason possibly existing in beings other that men. If there are such, the universality of reason would be just as binding upon them. They too would be members of the kingdom of ends. Actions commanded by the moral imperative of human persons would also be the same actions that would be right for them. Later on, we will note how the law may not exactly apply to them in the same form as it does to human beings who are always found with counteracting inclinations.

Kant talks in various ways about man's freedom vis-a-vis morality. Earlier we saw how he talked of the moral law as the *ratio cognoscendi* (reason/ground for our knowledge) of freedom, and freedom as the *ratio essendi* (reason for being) of the moral law. That is, it is ridiculous to talk of a man being obliged unless he is free either to obey or disobey the law. Moral law as a constraint corresponds to a physical ability to abide by this constraint or not. Thus, though the philosophical arguments for or against the reality-in- itself of man's freedom goes on forever on the theoretical level (according to Kantian theory), on the practical level of morality, we find a basis for believing that man is in fact *free.*

> *A rational being must always regard himself as giving laws either as member or as sovereign in a kingdom of ends which is rendered possible by the freedom of the will.*[5]

The sense in which man is at once member and sovereign in this kingdom of ends ties in with the third formulation of the categorical imperative.

> *For all rational beings come under the* law *that each of them must treat itself and all others* never merely as means *but in every case at the same time* as ends in themselves. *Hence results a systematic union of rational beings by common objective laws, that is, a kingdom which may be called a kingdom of ends, since what these laws have in view is just the relation of these beings to one another as ends and means. It certainly is only an ideal.*[6]

Note how we only *postulate* that we *are* free. Freedom itself is outside the valid limits of knowledge. (recall how we cannot transcend phenomena/appearances.) In the phenomenal world of nature everything moves deterministically. We cannot go beyond these appearances. But the moral law is *not* merely an appearance. It is an objective reality. Every human person finds it within himself. We could not account for this without the postulate and presupposition free to obey or not obey the obliging law.

Now I say that every being that cannot act except under the idea of freedom *is just for that reason in a practical point of view really free, that is to say, all laws which are inseparably connected with freedom have the same force for him as if his will had been shown to be free in itself by a proof theoretically conclusive. Now I affirm that we must attribute to every rational being which has a will that it also has the idea of freedom and acts entierely under this idea.*[7]

Moral practical knowledge then has the same operative force as theoretically proven propositions. Our conviction about the reality of the moral law is so overriding that beside it we deem all else as "nothing." Hence too our conviction about our freedom. Beyond this conviction, however, all else is darkness. We know nothing of the ultimate ground of moral laws.

For if we were asked why the universal validity of our maxim as a law must be the condition restricting our actions, and on what we ground the worth which we assign to this manner of acting --- a worth so great that there cannot be any higher interest --- and if we were further asked how it happens that it is by this alone a man believes he feels his own personal worth, in comparison with which that of an agreeable or disagreeable condition is to be regarded as nothing, to these questions we could give no satisfactory answer.[8]

Virtue and Immortality

Virtue is "moral disposition in conflict."[9] A disposition toward duty, the tendency of the will to obey rather than disobey its own moral laws, the disposition habitually to fulfill moral obligations --- this is virtue.

Strengh of character is strengh of virtue; indeed it is virtue itself.[10]

A perfectly good (holy) will cannot be conceived as subject to moral obligation. For obligation (constraint) can exist only in a being where there are counterforces to an autonomous will. How could a being without inclinations be "tempted" to go against its own moral commands? Indeed why the moral commands at all since there is nothing there to constrain?

But clearly, man is not such a being. In him autonomous will is coupled with inclinations, those "pathological" appetites which remain potential swayers of the will away from moral duty. Pathological desires, as we have seen, always have individualized objects, wheareas moral imperatives move on the universal level. This "mob" of sensual appetites influence the will away from duty by dragging it down to the level of self-centered satisfaction. Admittedly, both autonomous will (i.e. pure practical reason) and inclinations are of man's essence. Hence his ever present possibility of acting immorally, of exempting himself from the universal law to satisfy individual passion. Hence too the impossibility of man ever achieving a holy will. What he can aspire to and perhaps achieve is virtue, a habitually good disposition pointing the will towards duty but never quite getting over the possibility of a moral lapse. The inclinations and the *willküre* could at any time subvert the goodness of a saint. As St. Augustine's famous saying has it, when the best collapse then we have the worst.

> *If a rational creature could ever reach the stage of thoroughly liking to do all moral laws, it would mean that there was no possibility of there being in him a desire which could tempt him to deviate from them, for overcoming such a desire always costs the subject some sacrifice and requires self-compulsion, i.e. an inner constraint to do that which one does not quite like to do. To such a level of moral disposition no creature can ever attain. For since he is a creature, and consequently is always dependent with respect to what he needs for complete satisfaction with his condition, he can never be wholly free from desires and inclinations which, because they rest on physical causes, do not of themselves agree with the moral law which has entirely a different source.[12]*

The diverse sources of inclinations and duty is what produces the conflict between them. Moral law is from pure reason (*wille*)[13]: the nuomenal intelligible world of things-in-themselves. Whereas inclinations are from the sensuous phenomenal world of nature and appearances. Thus there will always be in man the experience of the higher power constraining the lower. This constraint, habitually obeyed and submitted to, is virtue: moral disposition in the face of inclinations.[13]

We now have the link to the second postulate. If indeed moral goodness is what man is commanded by the moral law to attain, and not only moral goodness but *complete* moral goodness (recall how the categorical imperative points to the absolute good as its object); and if, on the other hand, men live and die, every one of them, without ever achieving this complete goodness or holiness, we can conclude to only one of two things. Either the moral endeavor is "fantastic, directed to imaginary ends, and consequently inherently false" since death overcomes every man without his ever achieving the total goodness the moral law unceasingly drives him toward in his lifetime. Or, the moral goal is not merely a utopian dream but makes sense in a realm of being impenetrable to our knowledge (since it lies lodged in the intelligible world). Obviously, Kant who expended long years in the strenuous labor of writing and thinking out his ethical theory with utmost seriousness and dedication, could not accept the idea of moral endeavor as futile and mere pipestuff dream. Repeatedly he talks of the moral will as the highet good, the good-in-itself that is the goal of human life. Repeatedly he talks of man's moral duty to promote and realize it, as we shall see presently. What then does he say on this dilemma?

> *This holiness of will is, however, a practical ideal which must necessarily serve as a model which all finite rational beings must strive towards even though they cannot reach it. The pure moral law, which is itself for this reason called holy, constantly and rightly holds it*

before their eyes. The utmost that finite practical reason can accomplish is to make sure of the unending progress of its maxims toward this model and of the constancy of the finite rational being in making continuous progress. This is virtue, and as a naturally acquired faculty, it can never be perfect...[14]

The moral law commands us to make the highest possible good in a world the object of all our conduct. This I cannot hope to effect except through the agrrement of my will that of a holy and beneficent author of the world.[15]

Kant was always clear on there being no obligation to the impossible. "I ought" means "I can." How then explain this moral drive towards absolute goodness? In one place he even talks of the Gospel of love as the peak of the moral life which no man attains in this life, but only strives "to approach and imitate in an *uninterrupted infinite progress."[16]* Clearly he thinks of moral endeavor as going on even after death. Because of the moral life we have reason to *believe* in a life after death. That life would sustain the moral effort toward a life of complete goodness. The goal of life then is infinite progression in moral goodness both before and after death.[17]

Kant is in between the futility of moral endeavor on the one hand, and its culmination in holiness on the other. He holds for "infinite progression in eternity toward "complete fitness to the moral law," all the time protesting that this is merely a reasonable postulate and thus no intrusion of knowledge into the unknowable. "Endless progress from lower to higher stages of moral perfection is possible to a rational but finite being.[18] We hope in God's justice "in the share He assigns to each in the highest good."[19]

Kant's other remarks on this matter are enigmatic. Perhaps necessarily so since the afterlife is beyond the pale of knowledge.[20]

All that can be granted to a creature with respect to hope for this share is consciousness of his tried character. And on the basis of his previous progress from worse to the morally better, and of the immutability of intention which thus becomes known to him, he may hope for a further uninterrupted continuance of this progress, however long his existence may last, and even beyond this life. But he cannot hope here or at any foreseeable point of his further existence to be fully adequate to God's will, without indulgence or remission which would not harmonize with justice. This he can only do in the infinity of his duration which God alone can survey.[21]

Or, as he puts it in a significant footnote:

But naturally one who is conscious of having persisted from legitimate moral motives, to the end of a long life in a progress to the better, may very well have the comforting hope, though not a certainty, that he will be steadfast in these principles in an existence beyond this life.[22]

Happiness and the Existence of God

Like the ideas of freedom and immortality, Kant held that we can have no resolution of the philosophical controversies on the existence of God. But here too we find a basis for postulating what otherwise would be beyond our ken, namely, that God exists. But first we need to clairfy the role happiness plays in this moral doctrine. For God's existence is postulated on the basis of happiness being due to a moral being who is in an infinite progression toward complete moral goodness. We need to go step by step through three concepts:

(A) Complete Moral Goodness as the end of man (to be shown mostly by Kant's own text); (B) Morals are not about Happiness but about Worthiness to be happy; (C) The concept of man's Highest Good consists in the composition of (A) and (B), namely, complete moral goodness together with the actual happiness proportionate to this worthiness to be happy.

(A). *Man's End: Complete Moral Goodness.* We start with the observation we made at the very beginning: nature clearly marks out a goal for man superior to that of any other object. This is based on the fact that nature has endowed man with reason as his main means for achieving his end.[23] Thus man's end is morality. It is to be attained through practical judgements of good and evil and their will-acts.

> *If human nature is called upon to strive for the highest good, the measure of its cognitive faculties and especially their relation to one another must be subsumed to be suitable to this end.*[25]

> *Philosophy as well as widsom itself would always remain an ideal, which objectively is represented completely only in reason and which subjectively is only the goal for the person's unceasing endeavors.*[26]

Man's end is called his "highest good,[27]" a loaded word in Kant which we will need to unpack later.

> *The achievement of the highest good in the world is the necessary object of a will determinable by the moral law... But complete fitness of the will to the moral law is holiness, which is a perfection of which no rational being in the world of sense is at any time capable. But since it is required as practically necessary, it can be found only in an endless progress to.that complete fitness...*[28]

Not happiness then, but the attainment of complete moral goodness itself is the direct destiny and end of every human person. For this nature had endowed man with reason.

(B). *On Morals and Happiness.* Kant concludes by drawing together the various elements he has been careful up to now to hold apart from each other. Earlier, he had emphasized the completely different natures of morality and happiness. Indeed even in the concluding pages of the second *Critique* the point is still held.

But the moral law does not of itself promise happiness, for the latter is not, according to concepts of any order in nature, necessarily connected with obedience to the law.[29]

The connection between the two is not a necessary one, but there *is* a connection. We saw earlier how the relationship between the two was never said to be one of mutual exclusion or opposition, any more than any such intrinsic opposition could be said to obtain between Reason and inclination. Morality and happiness are ends of a different sort for man. We should now see how not only are the two *not* opposed but in fact they are positively *harmonized*.[30]

Morals as the *worthiness for* happiness can also be called the *condition* for happiness.[31]

Almost from the start we heard Kant say:

Thus a good will appears to constitute the indispensable condition even of being worthy of happiness.[32]

Later, when contrasting the price of things and objects to *dignity* in man as an end-in-himself, Kant had again pointed to the inseparability between the notion of *worth* and that of *dignity*.[33] This dignity and worth has its source in the nuomenal world of freedom, something men could never stop believing in even though they may be unable to explain it.[34]

Recall the distinction between respect which centers on the presence of the moral law in every human person, and respect in the secondary sense which bears on one man's actual moral superiority. An analogous distinction seems to be made here as regards *worth*. There is the primary gratification which each one must feel when he has performed his duty regardless of consequences, and this we should call *self-contentment*.[35] It derives from man's deepest sense of worth, namely, the quality of his morals.

It is true that the upright man cannot be happy if he is not already conscious of his righteousness, since with such a character the moral self-condemnation to which his own way of thinking would force him in case of any transgression would rob him of all enjoyment of the pleasantness which his condition might otherwise entail. But the only question is, "How is such a character and turn of mind in estimating the worth of his existence possible?" For prior to this no feeling for any moral worth can be found in a subject. A man, if he is virtuous, will certainly not enjoy life without being conscious of his righteousness in each action, however favorable fortune may be to him in the physical circumstances of life; but can one make him virtuous before he has so high an estimation of the moral worth of his existence merely by commending to him the contentment of spirit which will arise from the consciousness of righteousness for which he as yet has no sense?[36]

The connection then of happiness to morality lies deeper than just the negative sense of self-contentment felt when one knows he is reproachless because he has done his duty. Even though duty is often denied ensuing *actual* happiness it still deserves such. It was this that led to the postulates of endless moral progress in the state of immortality.[37]

Worthiness thus mediates morality and happiness. These latter two are only indirectly related. But this is enough to make us wonder whether *extrinsically*, through the power of another being, this indirect relationship may not be brought to positive fruition and unity of the two. This is where God and religion insert themselves.

> *...and a moral wish has been awakened to promote the highest good (to bring the kingdom of God to us) ...then only can ethics be called a doctrine of happiness, because the hope for it arises with religion.[38]*

> *From this it can also be seen that, if we inquire into God's final end in creating the world, we must not name happiness of rational beings in the world, but the highest good, which adds a further condition to the wish of rational beings to be happy, viz. the condition of being worthy of happiness, which is the morality of these beings, for this alone contains the standard by which they can hope to participate in happiness at the hand of a wise creator.[39]*

It is time now to bring these two concepts together in the notion of the "highest good."

(C). *The "Highest Good."* Man's highest good, destiny, end, goal, virtue, even complete happiness --- all are synonymously intertwined. We want to go further now and say that duty and happiness are not only indirectly related but *harmonized*. They are the contents of man's "highest good."

> *...happiness and morality are two specifically different elements of the highest good...[40]*

> *In the highest good which is practical for us, i.e., one which is to be made real by our will, virtue and happiness are thought of as necessarily combined, so that one cannot be assumed by a practical reason without the other belonging to it.[41]*

For man to attain his highest good, virtue or moral fulfillment is necessary. This is the good-in-itself to which the categorical imperative drives him unceasingly. However, moral fulfillment as worthiness to be happy also shows that virtue is not sufficient. It would mock man's whole moral enterprise if worthiness to be happy never in fact converted to actual happiness, i.e. the actual happiness proportionate to one's moral achievement. For what could "worthiness" or "deserving" mean if to the condition there is no corresponding object? They would really mean "worthy of" "deserving" nothing, would they not? And since it is fatuous to take man's most serious task in life as tantamount to nothing, we have to say that actual happiness and virtue are combined as man's highest good,[42] that to which man is directed. Yet even at this final moment of unity, the priority and autonomy of duty must be safeguarded. The two concepts must always have to be kept distinct.

93

But it is self-evident not merely that, if the moral law is included as the supreme condition in the concept of the highest good, the highest good is then the object, but also that the concept of it and and the idea of its existence as possible through our practical reason are likewise the determining ground of the pure will. This is because the moral law, included and thought of in this concept, and no other object, determines the will as required by the principle of autonomy. This order of concepts of the determination of the will should not be lost sight of, for otherwise we misunderstand ourselves and believe we are contradicting ourselves when everything stands in the most perfect harmony.[43]

Thus the term "highest good" contains the twofold components of virtue as man's *supreme* good or end and of happiness as its *perfecting* complement. The first without the second is necessary but not sufficient. And vice versa. The two are both sufficient and necessary to constitute the concept of man's end in its entirety. But we must be careful to distinguish even as we unite the two lest we confuse one or the other alone by itself to be highest good.

The concept of the 'highest' contains an ambiguity which, if not attended to, can occasion unnecessary disputes. The 'highest' can mean the 'supreme' (supremum) or the 'perfect' (consummatum). The former is the unconditional condition, i.e. the condition which is subordinate to no other (originarium); the latter is that whole which is no part of a yet larger whole of the same kind (perfectissimum). That virtue (as worthiness to be happy) is the supreme condition of whatever appears to us as desirable and thus of all our pursuit of happiness, and consequently, that it is the supreme good have been proved in the Analytic. But these truths do not imply that virtue is the entire and perfect good as the object of the faculty of desire of rational finite beings. For this happiness is also required... For to be in need of happiness and also worthy of it yet not partake of it could not be in accordance with the complete volition of an omnipotent rational being, if we assume such only for the sake of argument. Inasmuch as virtue and happiness together constitute the possession of the highest good for one person, and happiness in exact proportion to morality (as the worth of a person and his worthiness to be happy) constitutes that of a possible world, the highest good means the whole, the perfect good, wherein virtue is always the supreme good, being the condition having no condition superior to it, while happiness, though something always pleasant to him who possesses it, is not of itself absolutely good in every respect but always presupposes conduct in accordance with the moral law as its condition.[44]

After this clarification on the various elements which constitute the end of man, we can resume the thread of thought which leads to the postulate of God's existence.

Once morality is seen to be identically *worthiness* to be happy, and once the final end of man has been sorted out as unending moral progress

94

toward complete goodness of the will, we have the makings for a dialectical problem as well as for its resolution along the lines of faith (reasonable postulate). We start with the problem.

Happiness belongs to the realm of inclinations and their gratification. There everything moves along individualized lines of desire. Kant observes cynically that if inclinations ever do happen to have a unified object, it is merely the kind of unity which emerges when someone in a theatre starts a contagious yawn. Or the kind of unity "existing between a married couple bent on going to ruin."

> *Oh, marvelous harmony, what he wants is what she wants; or like the pledge which is said to have been given by Francis I to the Emperor Charles V, 'what my brother wants (Milan), that I want too.*[45]

Inclinations, in brief, can never rise from individualized appetites to the universality of pure reason where alone morality resides.

That being so, we can see how it is impossible to derive by mere analysis of the concept of virtue the concept of actual happiness. One is not contained in the other. The question is whether we can combine the two *synthetically,* i.e. from actual experience. We ask the question in the light of the self-contentment which we have shown to follow whenever one does do a moral act.[46] But no sooner do we ask the question than we can recall that this "self-contentment" is not really an inclinational gratification. It is rather the consoling consciousness of having done one's duty. Thus it seems that neither analytically nor synthetically can the two concepts of virtue and happiness be brought together. Let us try a third route.

Our clue this time comes from the fact that virtue, while indeed different from happiness, is nevertheless indirectly linked to it through two concepts. First, morality in a person is a good beyond any price. It cannot be interchanged along lines of various means to ends. It is a -good-in-itself which we term *dignity.* Hence it would be out of place to ask about virtue as worthiness, "worthiness *for what?"* This would reduce it to a *means.* So Kant's question takes a slightly different form, namely, "worthiness *to be* what?" With that morality and happiness are joined.

But why this interest in uniting the two after all the insistence on holding them apart? Well, there was the point all along that nature herself had made happiness an end of man, so much so that it would be absurd to oblige men to seek happiness since they had no choice on the matter. Then too it had been mentioned how a person has the obligation (although only an indirect one) to work for circumstances wherein he will be happy. In the human condition moral duty is more apt to be realized in circumstances of happiness than in those of misery. Hence there were indications all along pointing to the unity between the two.[47]

Nature thus inscribes both morality and happiness in us. Our problem is to understand their relationship. Says Kant:

> *For to be in need of happiness and also worthy of it and yet not partake of it could not be in accordance with the complete volition of on omnipotent rational being, if we assume such only for the sake of argument.*[48]

We probably have a *"deus ex machina"* here. Or do we? Let us follow Kant's solution.

The "highest good" is an ambivalent term whose two meanings include those of morality and happiness. Man's highest good is morality. To attain it nature has given man the suitable and unique equipment of reason. "End" and "good" are thus interchangeable. Any end you propose to yourself you can so propose only because you see it as good, as desirable. So, the highest good or end of man is, in one sense, moral goodness or perfection. We have seen how the human peak on this line is *virtue*, the first component in the highest good. The other component is brought out by equating the term *perfect* with the Latin word *consummatum*. A consummated act is one that is finished, acted through, *per* (through) *facere* (do, make). It is an action brought to ultimate completion and fruition, like the various phases of a weddling ceremony from the public formalities to the consummation of the act between the spouses.

In the first sense of "supreme good," man's ordination toward the highest good of virtue is a fact, "an objective reality" for Kant. But this is the same as saying man is destined to be *worthy of* something, namely, the *consummation* or ultimate fruition of virtue. That is, actual happiness proportionate to the degree of virtue achieved. We heard Kant say it would make no sense for man to be ordered to the highest good (which includes actual happiness) especially by one infinitely wise by supposition, if in fact actual happiness never came about. The two components of the highest good are thus seen to complement one another harmoniously.[49]

If virtue is worthiness to be happy, and this is man's final end not only in this life, but in the infinite progress toward *complete* moral goodness after death, does it make sense to say that simply is the last word on the matter? Do our minds really accept the idea of men completely worthy of happiness to which they have been driven all along and to which they shaped and hewed their existence both in time and beyond time, without at any point attaining (perfecting) the happiness corresponding to it? With those questions virtue and happiness are "harmonized."

> *This order or concepts... should not be lost sight of, for otherwise we misunderstand ourselves and believe we are contradicting ourselves when everything really stands in the most perfect harmony.*[50]

Why cannot the two, though intrinsically other to each other not be harmonized *efficiently*, i.e. through an extrinsic cause? Why cannot some being actualize the potentiality that lies lodged in the very meaning of *worthiness* to be happy? The only objection would be that in our experience there is no such being who can award *complete* happiness. As we saw earlier, complete happiness would demand more than finite widsom to comprehend it. Kant would agree that no such being is found in our experience. But he would ask in turn whether nature or the phenomenal world of experience is, after all, the whole of reality. Is there not in addition the nuomenal intelligible world out of which nature appears? If morality has shown us anything, it certainly has shown us that nature is *not* everything, nor even the most important. There is the world of freedom, of moral duty, an entire realm of things-in-themselves which, though we cannot penetrate speculatively, neverthless shows itself to be actual and, through our moral experience, to produce effects in the sensuous world of nature. There is thus an other world of morality.

Why not say then that in that world there exists a being able and willing to do what nature cannot do, namely, award corresponding actual happiness to beings worthy of it? Why not fall back on the familiar phrase, Author of Nature, and say that such a being effects the required harmonization at the final stage? That would make more sense than to leave all these concepts in loose shambles at the end when they show every sign of coherence. On this basis we postulate the existence of a power beyond nature who is able to award deserved happiness to moral beings.[51]

In brief, although speculatively pure reason cannot prove God's existence and thus finds itself dialectically neutralized by these seemingly disparate ideas, the concept of the highest good as the final end of man, with its twin components of virtue as worthiness to be happy and correspondingly actual happiness, provide a reasonable basis for the self-same reason on *practical* grounds to put them all together in a harmonious whole through the concept of an Author of Nature. God, in his infinite wisdom and ability to survey a timeless existence and endless progression of virtue toward complete goodness, awards actually proportionate happiness to morally deserving agents. All this is merely saying that though speculatively I cannot prove God's existence, practically, on the basis of morality now seen to be worthiness to be happy progressively even in timeless duration, I have a sound basis for believing or postulating the existence of God, the Author of Nature, who can and does what nature cannot do.[53] But down to the end, Kant insists on both the primacy and autonomy of morality even when it is brought into combination with actual happiness through God's power.

> *The moral law commands us to make the highest possible good in a world the object of all our conduct. This I cannot hope to effect except through the agreement of my will with that of a holy and beneficent Author of the world. And although my own happiness is included in the concept of the highest good as a whole wherein the greatest happiness is thought of as connected in exact proportion to the greatest degree of moral perfection (which, in fact, sternly places restricting conditions upon my boundless longing for happiness) which is proved to be the ground determining the will to further the highest good.[54]*

Kant stoutly rejects objections that he has forced all these seemingly disparate ideas into a unity.

> *Granted that the pure moral law inexorably binds every man as a command (not as a rule of prudence), the righteous man may say: I will that there be a God, that my existence in this world be also an*

existence in a pure world of the understanding outside the system of natural connections, and finally that my duration be endless. I stand by this and will not give up this belief, for this is the only case where my interest inevitably determines my judgement because I will not yield anything of this interest. I do so without any attention to sophistries, however little I may be able to answer or oppose them with others more plausible.[55]

So strong is his belief in the objective reality of moral obligation in man and of all his other beliefs built on it, that twice in the second *Critique* we find him breaking forth into passionate and poetic paeans to duty. In the middle of this work we hear him exclaim:

Duty! Thou sublime and mighty name... what origin is worthy of thee, and where is to be found the root of thy noble descent which proudly rejects all kinship with the inclinations and from which to be descended is the indispensable condition of the only worth which men can give themselves? It cannot be less than something which elevates man above himself as a part of the world of sense... It is nothing else than personality, i.e. freedom and independence from the mechanism of nature regarded as a capacity of a being which is subject to special laws (pure practical laws given by its own reason)[56]

And on the final pages of that work again be exclaims:

Two things fill the mind with ever new and increasing admiration and awe: the starry heavens above me and the moral law within me. I do not conjecture them and seek them as though obscured in darkness... I see them before me, and I associate them directly with the consciousness of my own existence.[57]

After we reach the existence of God as the benevolent Author of Nature on practical grounds, we cannot but wonder whether we have allowed "religion" to intrude into ethics. The pursuit of this topic will take us beyond the scope of this book. We will simply have to refer the reader to Kant's work on the subject: *Religion Within the Limits of Reason Alone*. Kant never takes back his contention that morality is autonomous and as such prior to the concept of God and religion.

Religion is the recognition of all divine commands, not as sanction, i.e. as arbitrary and contingent ordinances of a foreign will, but as essential laws of any free will as such. Even as such, they must be regarded as commands of the Supreme Being because we can hope for the highest good (to strive for which is our duty under the moral law) only from a morally perfect (holy and beneficient) and omnipotent will; and therefore, we can hope to attain it only through harmony with his will. But here again, everything remains disinterested and based only on duty, without being based on fear or hope as incentives, which, if they become principles, would destroy the entire moral worth of the actions.[58]

Conclusion

There are indeed many points of tension and perhaps even incoherences (a philosophical failing he despised) in Kant's position on the nature of morality. All of them revolve on the theory of knowledge he had so painstakingly laid out previously, in which he separated the world of appearances and the senses from those of Reason and reality-in-itself. Still Kant was by nature a unifier. Some of the great philosophers before him like Descartes, Spinoza and Hume had either separated the worlds of Intellect and Sense, or had reduced one to the order. Kant tried to bring the two worlds together through his critical method. He showed the function, contribution and legitimate limit of each faculty in the process of human knowing. "Consistency," he notes, "is the highest obligation of a philosopher and yet the most rarely found."[59] It was only natural then that in his moral doctrine he should attempt to bring all the various loose and separated strands of his system into harmony. Whether he succeeded or not will always be a question each of his readers must answer for himself. What he said of his theory of knowledge, we can also say of his moral doctrine. You may disagree with him. But the serious-minded will find it impossible to ignore him on the questions each person must come to terms with at some time or other in his life: What can I know? What ought I to do? What may I hope.

To end on a note of balance, we may cite Sir W.D. Ross' objection to the doctrine. Among all others it seems to strike at the heart of the theory, namely, the universalizability principle. Ross contends that every human act is so concrete and particularized that to think about it, as Kant requires, means to render it more and more abstract to the point where universalizability comes in only under conditions where it has lost touch with the very individualized character of the act from which it all started in the first place.[60]

Let us exemplify this by going back to the case of shoplifting. Ross is saying that Kant all too quickly goes to the abstract and most general characterization of the act as "shoplifting." In fact, this is practically an arbitrary categorization. The act is a very concrete act. It happens in a given case, perhaps performed by a mother forced to this act because she is out of work yet has to feed her starving family, whose father has just walked out of the picture, etc. etc. ad infinitum. Why then go with Kant and simply call her act "shoplifting?" Do not these lower specifications also cry out to heaven for consideration as decisive factors? Yet once we take them as decisive, then the theory would end up in a paralysis. We couldn's act, according to the principle in the abstract, and yet we could legitimately act according to the same universalizability principle in the concrete, since there would be consistency and encouragement that men do the deed when so specified in its physical concreteness, taking "all" the circumstances into consideration.

This is a good objection to reflect upon at the end of our study of Kant. It makes for a good transition to Dewey's theory which, like contemporary theories of situation ethics, holds that absolutistic ethics such as that of Kant should be rejected. An ethics must be worked out which deals with the given actual case as it emerges in its concreteness with all sorts of considerable relationships extending in every direction.

Why? In a way the whole of the next section is an attempt to answer that question. Here it will suffice to sketch out two reasons.

First, an individual is constituted by his relationships to others. True, an individual is ultimately ineffable. At the kernel of his being there lies lodged that ultimate solitude which defines him as only himself and no other one else. Still, in the human condition, he would not last very long if he decides to get away from it all and live by himself among barren rocks, would he? If he does, and then decides to descend to the sea to fish; or if he goes off to the forest to hunt; or to the plains to plant, then he would need *tools*, would he not? These he could not realistically manufacture all by himself. Moreover, he would need words, language inorder to think, and that is social. Thus we need others *essentially*, not merely in a superficial incidental way. Indeed, even Kierkegaard's individual stands alone before the Alone, a relationship which again defines him. If, therefore, it is impossible to begin and to continue to exist without a relationship of dependence upon others, then why should not these relationships be considered essential in resolving a moral problem, as Ross insists? It is not enough to admit that an individual is indeed consituted by these referential strands and then go on as though these can be handled in an abstract universalized way. True, to think is inescapably to universalize. But at least we should make the effort to get back to the actual *concrete* situation by making our specifications really more and more particular, as Ross asks. To do otherwise would be to deny what we already admitted, namely, that those particularizations are essential, not merely incidental to a person's existence.

Second, not merely is an individual defined by relationships to others but every moral problem he has arises out of a network of social influences whose strands sometimes criss-cross and counter one another. We shall hear from Dewey how genuine thought can only arise out of genuine questions. Moral perplexity comes out of moral conflict, that is, two or more claims each of them apparently right. Apparently, but not really. For two contradictory obligations both *really* right would make no sense at all. They would be mutually annihilative, by now a familiar idea after our study of the universalizability norm in Kant. To resolve opposing claims from others all converging on me simultaneously, I will invariably need to sort out the priorities of my relationships to those others. From beginning to end in the process of moral decision thus, both my physical and moral selves are enmeshed in essential relationships with others. These cannot be treated abstractily through set categories. They must be handled, taken in hand, as the individual moves along in the series of experiences we call *his* life. The question is: can this be really done philosophically? Can all these various strands of our "selves" be brought together coherently into an organic unity? Indeed, can the moral *ought* be fused with the *is* without producing a bastard with limbs of various derivations? We turn now to Dewey.

Part II: DEWEY

1

A DRAMATIZATION

It was John Dewey's insistent point that the advent and rise of the scientific experimental method revolutionized the human mind. The old-world view had things immoveably fixed through their "forms." Beings were constituted each with its own independent existence under inflexible categories. With science, all these *collapsed.* Reality thenceforth had nothing more than the hypothetical status of things under experimentation to find out what *uses* they will serve, what they will *do* under such and such conditions. In this new view knowledge starts not with repetition of accepted doctrine, but with a *shock,* a disturbance actual or imaginary of one's ordinary field of action. It may be worth our while to exploit this metaphor by going into some length at an imaginary scenario which will expose the highlights of Dewey's philosophy. Needless to say our scenario is no exception to the adage that all analogies limp.

When we look at ourselves in this classroom, what do we notice? Well, before anything else we notice that we are about to notice things we never noted before! Yet they have all been here, huge as life, all the times we have sat here. Why then are we somewhat uncertainly noticing them now? To go to the point quickly, is it not because we have a problem, namely, that of grasping Dewey's thought --- a problem we did not have before?

Look at those blackboards. So perfectly framed, finished predictable. When I need to write I don't even think of its wide-spreading presence. It's second nature to pick up a piece of chalk and simply write on it. Blackboards are blackboards to be written on; chalk is chalk to write with. The light switch there by the door is exactly that, nothing more. You flip it up for light when you need to, and flip it down when your need ceases. There's the lectern, here's the professor's table, the chair behind it, and over there are your desks in straight rows, each a sturdy piece of furniture made of metal and plastic. On the north side are those huge glass windows which look out to a spectacular view of Lake Michigan. Some days you draw those curtains shut, often you leave them open. But they are always there regardless, predictable and ready for use. Windows are windows, drapes are drapes, and we hardly ever even notice they're there *except* when one day we need to draw the drapes and they are stuck. They don't draw no matter how hard we tug at them. Then we scrutinize the situation to see what is the matter. So too with all the other things in this room. We don't give them a second thought. We are all each in our usual place. I am the professor, you are the students, the maintenance people are outside. The same can be said of the dozens of other classrooms in this building. Everything is set and definite, perfect, completed. We all move within a network of relationships we call our "campus." For many of us campus life has become so predictable that we do what we have to almost somnoambulantly. In four years we have been pushed into habitual grooves by, to use Dewey's phrase, "the heavy arm of custom."

For our purpose let us turn our imagination loose for a while. Let us "bracket" (suspend, pretend) the fact that there is the whole of Chicago, Illinois, U.S.A., etc. of which we are only a part. Let us imagine ourselves in this campus as an island, self-sufficient and very well organized with everything in its place, as we have said. Suddenly, a titanic earthquake occurs. Within seconds every building, wall and floor in this entire campus collapses. By a great stroke of luck, however, no one is killed. We, the survivors, find ourselves deep in dust and debris each piece of which once stood correctly and precisely in its appointed place. There it had performed its function with predictable regularity, as we saw. Now everything is in shambles. Windows are no longer windows, switches no longer switches. We see plumbing pipes and electric wires and cables bent and twisted all over the place --- everything just an amorphous mass, sheer matter devoid of shape, pattern or form.

Since, in our supposition, no outside help is forthcoming our first thoughts amidst our isolated ruins would turn to *reconstruction,* would they not? We'd first have to reconstruct shelter for ourselves. Then we would need to think about our means of sustenance: fundamental human necessities. Our thinking process in such a situation would not be one in which thought followed clearly and neatly on a previous thought. Rather, our heads would be simply swarming with all sorts of ideas, all of them directed towards the construction or production of goods to satisfy our needs. We swarm with such ideas because of our swarming needs. Needs, thoughts, actions, movements, direction, interest, etc., all arise simultaneously from the same matrix of a difficult problematic situation.

Guidance and direction are obviously required as we all start pulling together toward the task of rebuilding. Now, *whom will the group turn to for leadership?* Will they look to me, a philosophy professor, who in happier unchallenged times was accepted as having had the training necessary to analyze such problems as "Being and Northingness?" Will they not turn instead almost instinctively towards the *scientists* to reconstruct our world, to do everything correctly, "scientifically?" Given the materials at hand, we need use them in such a way that they give both the most and the best quality of shelter, food, clothes, etc. Thus we will need the know-how main and expertise of our maintenance crew. All of us former students and professors now find ourselves lining up under their leadership --- on the supposition, of course, that their training on these matters have been "scientific." Thus they are superior to any guess-job-amateurs at construction like us. This would hold true of every phase of the reconstruction work. When it comes to animal husbandry, or gardening, for example, we would look around again for those in the biological, zoological, agricultural, etc. sciences for expert guidance. Always we find ourselves turning to the scientists.

But wait. Is it true that we would *always* turn for everything to the scientists in the job of reconstruction? For *everything?* If so, then it would behoove us to remember those words of George Santayana now emblazoned in many languages at the arched gates of Dachau: "Those who cannot remember their past are condemned to repeat it." Have we forgotten all too soon our resentment against scientific products in our recent hue and cry about environmental pollution? Have we forgotten all our slogans about going back to the simple life, to the farming communes which sprang up in all parts of the country practically overnight in disgust at the situations a technological society has produced? Why now all over again entrust *everything* to the scientists? That seems absurd. Well, what then, specifically, should we entrust and what not to them? There we have it: the nub of problem.

Let us now take off the brackets from our scenario. Our community is back as a part of the "great city of Chicago." As such we are part of Illinois, the U.S.A. etc. And, of course, we are a Jesuit University. Through the Jesuits we have affiliations to the Catholic Church which is spread all over the world. If, therefore, in our disaster we appealed for help to the great world community which surrounds us, the work of restoration would happen quickly. But, we would also from beginning to end find the same values, the same goals, ends --- the same everything which contextured our lives before the fall, so to speak, would automatically be reinserted, restored into our lives. If *restoration* were what we wanted, why, we would know exactly how to restore our buildings: what things to install in our classrooms, labs, gym, library, etc. For we have fixed and set ideas about what things are necessary for "education." We even seem to know clearly what education is *for*. For the most part, education for us is for money, for making a living, for qualifying at good-paying jobs. In a restored campus, this same fixed end of the society in which it existed would be built right back, *restored* into it.

But what would "better-paying jobs" be for? Why, they would be for a home in Suburbia, U.S.A., where the father of the house can pridefully pull at the ripcord of his power-mower of an early morning on July 4, and work his motorized way merrily along the patches of green he has so meticulously manicured at the front and back of his house. If a few stubborn ones risk displeasure by asking just what living this way in Suburbia is for, then the plot thickens. Our answers begin to wobble. However, in every group there is always bound to be those to whom the question is not difficult at all. For instance, we could be told, that successful living (and unsuccessful) is destined like human life for where it originated, namely, the hands of God. God is the beginning and the end, the Alpha and the Omega of man. In this view the world is for helping man in his pilgrimage of life to the one great End which itself will be without end, and without change. The really *ultimate* value thus does not lie in this world and this life, but rather in the next life and the next world.

And since all things in this world came out of God including and especially human life, they are products of God's perfect ideas. To know them then is to know the divine ideas they reflect, both as to their richness, since things in the world are of infinitely individualized variations; and as to their eternity, since each species of things come and go while the species endure. We need go no further. If a *restoration* took place, the same old ends which had governed society all along would also be restored. Society and its various means and supports are not separate entities. Rather, they are all entwined into a living unity.

To go back now to our question: what shall we entrust to the scientists and what not in our imaginary world of dust and debris? If it is true that war is altogether too important to leave entirely to the generals, is it not also true that life is altogether too serious a matter to leave entirely to the scientists? Yet, to ask this question is to presuppose that there are areas of life demarcated from science, does it not? Should we then relegate science to the area of mere *physical* reconstruction, mere manual labor? Should we then turn to others for enlightenment on the more serious matters, the more profound questions in life? Which others? Those whose profession it had been to spend their time thinking on the nature of *ends,* the ends of things in the world, the *ends* of human life? Is it not the precise business of philosophy, and beyond philosophy, theology, to cast light on these ultimate and all important matters?

We see how in our scenario we cannot simply move forward without thought on all these matters which surge up simultaneously. It seems we would need to discuss and agree first on what ends we want in our reconstructed world. Do we want a world new only in its physical being but a carbon copy of the old world as regards its ends and beliefs? In that case we want *restoration,* a relatively easier task. But if we want a really new world, new both in its physical being and its ends, then the task will not be as easy.

The old world, after all, traced its being back to prescientific days. Though science had made massive inroads into it to the point where our buildings, for instance, had everything scientifically set about it, still all these scientific techniques and gadgets were all subsumed to the service of those old ends. Old modes of thought still prevailed, old certainties were still clung to by a great many. Very few had the raw courage and nerve to put all those ends themselves into question. Very few dared submit everything to question, to the status of mere *hypothesis,* i.e. possible material for yet-to-be-discovered ends. Very few dared treat the world, including human beings, not as finished natures with their own intrinsic intelligibilities already embedded in them waiting only to be penetrated, grasped and understood by the intellect --- but rather as mere data. That is, as matter for scientific hypothesis and experimentation to find out what can be done with them, what would result if we mixed them this way and that, etc. Because of this failure of nerve science always came to be relegated and restricted to its own "limit." It was treated as a lower type of action, namely, that of discovering procedures for solving men's practical difficulties. It was held suspect anytime it "intruded" into those serious and lofty realms of art, the profound matters of morals, religion, etc., in short, into the domain of ends. There was thus this ingrained bias in the minds of old-world people to keep science and the humanities apart. Each must have its own separate chief who recognized, so to speak, the sovereignty of each one *in his own field.* It was simply taken for granted that it is not the role of the sciences to spell out the lofty ends of the university, of society, human life, morals, or the nature of the noble, the good and the beautiful. But *should* this be so?

Let us imagine our scenario one last time. Here we are, isolated from the rest of the world, aswarm with immediate needs, thoughts, and also expertise of many sorts. Can we realistically believe that in such a situation men will split into groups, one group each with its own assigned expertise apart from others? Now, where would the philosophers fit? Should they sit away by themselves to contemplate the situation all the better, and to come up with a list of the ends the new society should have? Since the shapes and sizes of everything must conform to those ends, should evrybody stop and wait for the philosophers to produce such a list before engaging in *reconstruction?* If the philosophers were silly enough to do that, the scorn and disrepute they would bring down on themselves and their discipline would be richly deserved. For the result would be predictable. After days of discussion among themselves, they will predictably end up with nothing to report or list except their own disagreements among themselves as regards the ultimate nature of reality. They report that they first had to face that question before they could specify the ends of the lesser reality, viz., society. The reaction of the group too is predictable. In disgust and disappointment they will ask the philosopher to take their places, just like the rest, in the work forces. Without further ado the whole group starts the work of reconstruction, this time with everybody agreeing to work under the direction of scientists. What has happened is that under the term "scientists" we now include both the theoreticians and their allied artisans, i.e. both the science professors and the maintenance crew.

Note how in this scenario no one thinks it necessary to define good and evil and the "ends" of life *first,* before engaging in the work of reconstruction. Indeed action, work had actually been going on every moment from the instant the first man started pulling himself up from the wreckage. Action of one sort or other had never really stopped. But now as everybody pools his effort with the rest even the philosophers gain admiration as they roll up their sleeves and plunge directly into the work of bettering the conditions they are in. Lo and behold, we find out there really is no need to define the natures of things around us before we can use them. We simply assault them, manipulate them, *bring them under our own hand* (literally), regardless of whether they had a divine origin or not. Clearly, things have come unstuck and must be dealt with not as neatly categorized, but as just plain material to be shaped by human ingenuity; not as things already shaped and formed for us to accomodate ourselves to. There is no time for idle contemplation and nothing really to contemplate. The need is not for intellectual spectators but for realistic participators in the task of *reconstruction.*

We have seen the futility of debating the natures of "good" and "evil" before setting our hand to the task at hand. What is other than the present situation is seen practically intuitively as "better." And since no one has really ever stopped from action what we call *reconstruction* is in effect a rechannelling, a redirecting of all those activities towards the new project. This re-direction, as we noted, cannot be effected by pure thought or reason alone. Rather, reason operates amidst the swarming needs of all and each person as the momentum of work builds towards the better state, the state envisioned as providing satisfaction for all concerned.

Note how in this situation it would be silly for anyone to accuse any other one else of "selfishness" simply because this other one deisres "satisfaction." Everyone's immediate needs are similar. When anyone desires the satisfying objects of those needs, it is exactly that and nothing more: *desiring those satisfying objects.* This is not the same as snatching those objects only for oneself and explicity wishing to keep them away from others. This latter would indeed be "selfishness," and the selfish individual would undoubtedly be the target of very swift and effective social disapproval. Yet, everyone will understand that in a way their immediate satisfaction entails further consequences which may no longer be approvable to the group as a whole. For the kind of consequences each one will want depends on the quality of character or conduct he possesses.

We can say, for instance, that in our scenario all need food, drink, clothes and shelter. The scientists can, with their expertise, produce these quickly and effectively, in our supposition. But in the process they may have had to rape the environment. This would be execrated by some who remain steadfast purists even in such a crisis. These, in turn, will be mocked by those aggressive types who have no time for such niceties, and merely tolerated by yet others who have learned the art of straddling controversial issues. The group will see that if life is not going to be nasty, short, and red in tooth and claw, then it is best for them to organize their desires. They should have to harmonize them in such a way as to honor and include as many of the desires as is possible in the line of action they decide to pursue. They leave out only those which are incompatible with this largest, most enduring and inclusive framework of satisfaction for everybody. This framework of shareable and enduring goods would then be clearly perceived by everybody as the legitimate objects or ends of desire. Anyone subsequently seen pursuing an object of individual desire incompatible with that larger framework of shareable goods would be deemed "selfish," this time with swift social sanction.

But what if there are stubborn individuals who simply refuse to accept this democratic decision with regard to the framework of shareable goods? What if these few insist that their minority view is what ultimately will reap better harvests for all? Well, we should recall, first of all, that the term "better" is not something abstract and academic to this group who are engaged in the work of survival. They can practically *feel* what is "better" as they work from one step to another step, and to another, as they work out of their predicament. Confusion attends the term "better" only when it is analyzed prospectively toward an imaginary ultimate ideal by which all goods are measured by varying degrees of distance or proximity to it. Thus it may not be clear whether it is better simply to move ahead unmindful of the rape of the environment so long as steady provisions come in; or whether the voices of conservation should be heeded under pain of having less provisions. The situation is one of two goods towards which, seemingly, there are legitimate desires which apparently are in conflict. What decision should be made? It will not do, as we saw, to turn to philosophers as a separate group for an answer. On the other hand, it would be clearly wrong to listen one-sidedly whether to the unscrupulous environmental rapists, or to the hardheaded conservationists, both of whom are undisguisedly "hot" about their convictions. How then resolve the conflict?

Well, we should note once again that things around us which we never noticed before now loom large in our perception. For we have a problem. We also note that the material for the resolution of the problem is woven into the problematic situation itself. Our need thus is not so much for a final solution as for a rearrangement of priorities and desires. We want to do away, or at least reduce the conflict to the minimum. Thus the group themselves will see that to listen to hotheads on either side onesidedly will not do. Partisanship, by definition, tears away from the legitimate framework of a commonly shared goal. The need is rather for everyone to cool off, to stand apart at least mentally, from hot convictions and grasp what the other side is saying. There is need for cool and impartial thinking on the issue.

We should note that what is demanded is not for "pure reason" to bring forth an answer from whatever rarified atmosphere it inhabits. We need instead reflective consciousness assessing oneself in the situation itself from the viewpoint of truly shared goods, not of merely individualized satisfaction. We note four points as we reflect on the group's ongoing activities.

First, reflective thought dismisses physical might and superiority exercised against one another ("survival of the fittest") as the desirable procedure. The consensus is rather on reflective and democratic thinking combined, indeed united, with scientific procedures as the best line of action. Without separating the two (reflection, scientific experimentation) the group has already engaged in the task of scientific reconstruction. All the while they question themselves as they better themselves, step by step, on the largest framework of shared goods possible. Means and ends are not separated. They are merged in one reality: reconstructive work, which is a living blend of reflection and experimentation.

Second, it becomes clear to everybody that with the dismissal of physical might as the norm of arbitration, predictable behaviour becomes a necessity. No forward movement can be effected if each one had no idea whatsoever from moment to moment what kind of action is forthcoming from the fellow nearby. Thus claims on one another necessarily arise. Each one can see how he stands to the persons around him. And that concrete relationship itself, not some abstract idea or power of reason, reveals the claims and expectations which may be legitimately demanded of the persons concerned. Is one, for instance, leading or led? Claims will arise accordingly as to the expected behaviour from each consistent with his concrete social responsibility. And so on along the line of the various groups at work.

Third, we should notice how, as the work moves forward, we draw from memories, traditions, habits of the old world even as we set about fashioning our novel world. Funded experience and know-how come into play countless times. The engineers, scientists, maintenance crew --- everybody in the group has to rely on his past experiences as he does his job. Those who are so hidebound to the past so as to be able only to repeat it --- those who see the fallen pipes, switches, blackboards, glass windows, etc. as still nothing else but those selfsame things, will soon find themselves at a deadend, since in our supposition they have collapsed. How much more effective it would be to employ an imaginative cannibalization of parts, some creative artistry! Experimentation, improvisation, not slavish repetition of the past is the need of the hour.

Finally, we have to note how the greatest future for the greatest number in the group lies in everyone pitching in toward the commonly shared good. There is an almost airtight unity in the whole picture. None of any individual's powers are compartmentalized from one another. In every man reason, imagination, emotions, needs, desires, objects of satisfaction, etc., all are fused into the struggle for better living. Reason, as the reflective guide out of the 'buzzin' bloomin' confusion" is not isolated in some contemplative corner. It is right there at the heart and center of actual desires, needs, inclinations. All in fact function together spontaneously as one power seeking a better life for the organism.

There are no separate ends to be acquired by separate means. Means and ends are all intertwined in a complex unity as rich as life itself. There is no demanding call for answers to contemplatively ultimate questions about the nature of reality, man, the world and the world beyond. *This world*, the very human interest of seeking a better life is what matters. No one disputes the most effective method available. It is science. And if someone suggested that it might be a good thing to stop and think up ways of being charitable to one another, that person would be laughed to scorn. Of course anyone in dire need and emergency would be a center of concern. But on the whole, everyone sees that charity is a side-issue. The best way of furthering any one's well-being is precisely to go ahead and do the task that is his assignment in this whole work of social reconstruction, of rebuilding the common good and shared interests of all. Each one can then draw, for whatever particular interest he might want to pursue, from the situation of common welfare all worked for and achieved.

As the work of reconstruction goes on from day to day, those who work devoutly and dedicatedly at bettering the conditions for everybody get spontaneous admiration from all around. They are persons clearly driven by the vision of a better life for everyone. Their unusual fervor at trying to bring those aspirations into reality reminds everyone of what "religious" people were meant to be in the old world. And yet those of the oldworld religion in the new situation who still persist in the belief that everything in this world is *merely* fleeting and transient, that not even the task of reconstruction is worth all that total devotion given it by others would soon arouse the group's antagonism. Who then should succumb to whom? Or is the solution to revert right back to the divisions of knowledges each in its own sphere valid but nowhere else? With that we draw the curtains on our scenario to see the analogies in Dewey's own presentations.

2

PHILOSOPHICAL
RECONSTRUCTION

Even the most conservative philosophers and theologians today lament the fact that our moral and humanistic studies have not kept up with our technical achievements. There is agreement on all sides that our age needs to engage anew in the quest for certainty about things in nature and our experiences of them. We need to reconstruct our views such that they will take full advantage and march hand in hand with scientific method as its equal partenr. Obviously, this cannot be done by perpetuating the ageold divisions between the sciences on one side, and the arts, morals and religion on the other. Nor can it be achieved by philosophy repudiating science and vice versa. Why then not come out boldly and ask for the integration of all modes of human thought and operation with the scientific method?[1]

Here and in the chapters of this part we will first recall and explain the old classic view of reality with its penchant for the *separation* of realities from one another. Next, we will point to the advent and rise of the new science. Then we will present Dewey's instrumental characterization of knowledge. Finally we will bring all these into a focus on Dewey's melioristic ethics.

Dewey calls the old-world view of knowledge and reality the "classic" conception.[2] We can explain this view *genetically* as the end result of human knowledge as it refined itself through a series of separations from the only matrix and starting point of all authentically human knowledge, namely, *experience*. Roughly, these separations were those of (1) romanticized knowledge from actual experiential knowledge; (2) "higher" from "lower" knowledges and social classes; (3) the real world of fleeting and changeable beings and the philosophical world of fixed and immutable beings.

Romance, Poetry and Symbols.

We start by noting how no being, no organism at any rate, is ever inert. Appearances to the contrary notwithstanding, every organism is at every moment a plenum of action. Most fundamental among these actions are those which reach out towards objects which sustain the organism's life. In the case of men we know that these activities in the most primitive stages took the usual form of the chase and the hunt.

Essential to the nature of the hunt are danger and risk, peril and uncertainty. Hunting is also hard labor. In primitive conditions lack of sophisticated weaponry reduced the odds of victory for the hunter. He faced nature, as it were, alone and naked. It was largely a question of pitting the physical strength of the hunter against his prey. The fact that men have come to call both the experience itself and the quarry as a "game" indicates that with hardship also came sport, adventure. The whole enterprise was fraught with uncertainty, suspense, and a literally breathtaking drama in which the outcome was totally in the balance. Anything was possible: success as well as tragedy.

It is reasonable to imagine that at the dawn of human knowledge, whenever the chase was over, the hunters would sit around a fire as the slain animals were prepared for a festive homecoming. Invariably the "irrepressible human tendency toward storytelling" took over.[3] For celebration is an intensely social phenomenon. The meal and effusive conversations are its staples. All the high moments of the hunt's perils and triumphs are relived. Not in action and hardship, of course, but in word, song, and oftentimes dance. All these had their roots in *memory*. It is not unrealistic then to suppose that in the group the women, children, elders, everyone soon joins in the common merrymaking. All are regaled by the memories which they re-enact in song, talk and narrative rhythmic mimes.

This transformation of the real hunt into a merely verbalized and remembered one has its obvious advantages. For one thing it is free of all actual dangers. It is purified from all the ineluctable labor of the actual hunt. In triumphal celebration and song, reality is transformed into memory and symbols. From symbolic memory the way is open for fantasy and dreams which, as Freud has shown, is man's special device for escaping from the pains of the harsh workaday world.[4] Thus we can surmise how in time memories of the hunts, especially the more spectacular ones, are preserved in a special way among the tribe. The finer the hunt and the finer the retelling, the deeper etched also it becomes in the group's memory. Slowly the stories accumulate about the tribesmen's finest hours on the field. And formalization of tradition has begun.

Now, fine stories come into being only because of fine story-tellers. It is natural to assume then that in those times even as today, those gifted with the art of storytelling, and those who are expert at the art of symbolizing, soon acquire a privileged status among the group. Experience and actuality are harsh, slow, often unmanageable and lengthy. Whereas words and symbols enable men to deal with experience quickly. The gifted storytellers then are set apart as the special living deposits and experts of the group's tradition. More and more they are relied upon in moments of uncertainty and perplexity to draw, from out of their store of knowledge, the best ways of dealing with a present crisis. In the light of what the group has done most effectively in similar situations in the past, they are expected to have special access to the hidden truths that will resolve perplexing situations at hand. In primitive times the overriding problem was that of sustaining life. Yet, even then the eternal human longing for certitude, for *sure* knowledge appeared in the special status the tribe accorded its expert storytellers and keepers of tradition. They exempted these gifted few from manual labor and toil. It was for them merely to read omens and prognosticate, to appease mysterious powers which control what is humanly uncontrollable, and most of all to be the deposits of sure knowledge. They were usually gifted with a vivid imagination, retentive memory and powers of symbolization and expression.[5] To them the members of the group came for afvice, for information on how to act in perplexing circumstances, for future plans. In them was the repository of the group's best experiences.

Men usually base their plans on realistic expectations. Since those privileged few were deemed as enjoying a special grasp of reality, they were consulted. People like to be *sure*, since experience shows how "the best laid plans of mice and men gang aft agley." Not that men dislike uncertainty in itself, but rather "uncertainty involves us in peril of evils."[6] In return then for their privileged functions, the tribe did not begrudge the keepers of their tradition exemptions from lowlier tasks. After all, did they not need the time to improve their skills too? With this we have the fatal admission that a general knowledge of the chase was superior to engaging in the actual chase itself.

From this we see how the social phenomenon of an aristocratic few, possessing authority and prestige and separated from the majority, was spontaneously effected. With this social stratification came corresponding divisions of labor, as well as divisions of knowledge "with the holy and the fortunate and their opposite, the profane and the unlucky."[7] Now there were the *selecti quidem*, the elite who had a "higher" calling than the completely physical and completely laborious one of the actual hunt.[8] Human knowledge went from raw experience to poetry, then to romanticized accounts. In a word, the first separation of thought from its experiential matrix was effected. From this logically followed the social class divisions of "higher" and "lower" folk, depending on whether the task performed was "intellectual" (white collar) or not.

"Higher" and "Lower" Knowledges and Classes.

The myths and legends of a group of people invariably cohere into a body of spoken or written literature after centuries of story-telling, poetizing and symbolizing among the most gifted of the tribe who dedicate themselves to nothing else but this specialized task. From poetry to consolidated tradition, to customary ways of doing things are easy steps.[9] Now to be responsible for the consolidation of customs and traditions is a fulltime job. Those who engage in it cannot also be expected to take part in the hunt. Rather they must busy themselves with the purely mental task of portraying the group's experiences in symbols such as its totem, its rituals, supernatural beliefs, religion and taboos. The community itself approves of this separation of knowing from doing, of seers from doers. Seers and knowers are naturally deemed the "higher"

111

class with a "higher" task which they discharge in an atmosphere of leisure and safety from all peril.

By contrast, the world of the hunter and the doer remains one of harsh unpredictability where nothing is guaratneed. Death stalks every moment of existence. Danger lurks everywhere. This great difference in styles of living is, of course, not lost on the leisure class themselves, the special people with "brains." They naturally enjoy and appreciate their special status with all its perquisites of power. Hence they will strive to perpetuate their standing. And the surest way to achieve this is to maintain the separation of tasks,knowledges and classes in society.

We can confirm all this by looking at the ancient classical world of Greece, for instance. There the social classes of free men and slaves corresponded exactly to the tasks and knowledges assigned them. There the great division between *knowing* and *doing* was a *fait accompli* economically, socially and, in an inchoate way, philosophically.[10]

We thus have traditions, myths, legends and both homespun and tribal wisdom all congealing into symbolic deposits of social heritage and possession. This tradition becomes the norm to which everyone must now conform. Naturally it is the learned "higher" class who will be the principal guardians of this tradition. They will have the powerful say over those who conform and those who refuse to conform. All too soon we observe the phenomenon of power seeking to extend itself to its furthest limit.

Ancient Judaea, Greece and Rome are good examples. Through their prestige and authority and political power, they extended their traditions to the western world and assimilated new elements that could harmonize with their own traditions. From this arose larger cosmogonies and cosmologies as well as ethical expansions.

> *Whether this is literally so or not, it is not necessary to inquire, much less to demonstrate. It is enough for our purposes that under social influences there took place a fixing and organizing of doctrines and cults which gave general traits to the imagination and general rules to conduct, and that such a consolidation was a necessary antecedent to the formation of any philosophy as we understand the term.[11]*

Such then is Dewey's surmise of how, in the main, the view became deepseated in the western mind that knowing is different from doing; that knowing was the "higher" calling, "doing" the lower. Expressed or not, the workman's world of daily manual toil was looked upon as "lowly," full of unpredictable dangers and uncertainties, and on that account the least desirable. The secure existence of the privileged class, on the other hand, was certainly the desideratum. It was immunized further and further away from the actual peril of the chase and hunt for the necessities of life. It kept meticulous watch to make sure that everything and everybody stayed fixed to his post as tradition demanded---tradition which was to their advantage and which they, the intellectuals, had shaped for the group in the first place!

112

Separation of Metaphysics from
Unquestioned Belief.

Dewey writes:

Man can never be wholly the creature of suggestion and fancy. The requirements of continued existence make indispensable some attention to the actual facts of the world.[12]

The human mind has countless concepts. It can conceive, as Aristotle had noted, "all things." Correlatively, it also has the propensity to wonder whether what it has conceived *is really so*. With that philosophy is born.

Change is a fact. It is inescapable, and it poses a constant threat to tradition. The mills of the mind, impeded and frustrated by normative customs, may grind ever so slowly, but the ineluctable day comes when discrepancies are pointed out between ageold and fixed traditions and the facts of daily life. By definition, tradition tends towards fixed and immutable views of the world, towards *withstanding change*. On the other hand, the common laborer and working housewife see that *everything* around them comes to be and passes away into something else.[13] Trees become deadwood. Wood burns to ash. Animals are hunted and become food which in turn becomes living human flesh. All organisms eventually cease to exist. Nothing in experience thus remains fixed and permanent. Rather *change* rules all of human existence and experiences.

This seemingly innocuous and commonplace observation nevertheless posed a direct threat to a society built on the basis of immutability. For if change did indeed rule the world, then solidified social values are immediately up for questioning. What passed as "higher" knowledges are likely to be exposed as either false or irrelevant. Indeed it might come out that only the "lowly" arts which dealt directly and actually with changing things were the ones on the track of truth. What is called for in a changing and changeable world then was to find out what really was going on, what things *do*. To ask what they are as though they were fixed and immutable will be seen as a mere exercise in irrelevance. This danger did not escape the keen eyes of the social aristocrats.

In the ancient sophists we have a historical record of how the traditionalists reacted to the threat we have just described. The Sophists were the first ones to question the set and fixed social beliefs of Greek society. There was the trial and execution of Socrates. This was evidence, once and for all, of the retaliation a society unleashes on those who dare question its traditions.[14] The only trouble was that while Socrates was physically disposed of, his message (which was by no means mere sophistry) got across, namely, "the unexamined life is not worth living;" "to be awake is better than to be asleep;" (i.e. to be in the comatose grip of unquestioned tradition). These Socratic dicta made it impossible to escape a thorough evaluation of the foundations on which the class-structure of Grecian society was built. Questions now came thick and fast.

What was the basis for holding the view that reality was fixed and

immutable? Why not go to experience which belied such a characterization of reality? Is it possible that the only real way to find out what
anything is is simply to test what it will in fact *do* in various and sundry
situations? Clearly, the potentially revolutionary situation which the
Socratic event ushered in was from the beginning a radical challenge to
the unquestioned view of the Greek world which then prevailed and
which formed practically every phase of society. Was the basis for that
structure sound? Was reality in truth static? Or, were the "lowly" arts right
after all in insisting that experience showed nothing fixed at all in
anything? Some crucial rethinking was now necessary. Then Plato and
Aristotle came on the scene.

As everyone knows, those two great philosophers set the course for
the western mind. Unfortunately, from Dewey's viewpoint, these two
thinkers were themselves too much the products of their own civilization.
Their philosophical geniuses took the predictable turn of searching for the
stable and secure ground of reality. They had an eye always for upholding
the Greek social institutions in which they lived, moved and had their
being. It became their aim to purify these institutions from all the
imaginative accretions, whether from custom or superstition, which could
not withstand the rigor of intellectual and logical scrutiny.[15] Henceforth,
they held, only reason should prevail.

The only trouble was that instead of focusing on the objects of the
workaday world where alone the interaction of experience took place,
Plato and Aristotle focused the eyes of philosophy on the permanent
forms of thing, forms visible only to the eyes of the intellect. These were
forms the lowly artisan could neither see with their eyes nor comprehend
with their "untrained" minds. For the *forms* pruned away all their
connections with anything contingent and unpredictable---the precise
characters of the artisan's world. Plato placed the foundations of stable
being in a world beyond this world seen only by the eyes of the
philosopher. There dwelt the eternal forms, imperishable, perfect, themselves the very essence of reality. The fleeting transient things of earth
were deemed insubstantial, mere shadows unfit to be taken seriously. As
for Aristotle, we know that he made some drastic revisions in this Platonic
metaphysics by bringing the forms "back to earth." Nevertheless, with an
ingenuity truly worthy of the Greek intellect, he still retained the doctrine
of immutable forms, of eternally perduring being which continued to exist
in the *species*, even as individuals came and went, existed and perished.
Both philosohers considered matter "non-being," the principle of corruption and change. And since in the material principle as potency there was
nothing directly intelligible, the objects of genuine knowledge became
fixed not on the immediate objects of experience (which obviously were
material and fleeting) but on these immutable forms.

We see then how philosophy rose up to Socrates' challenge to live the
examined life. It examined the foundations of Greek social life and
experience. It submitted reality to thorough questioning. But alas, it ended
up ironically with a metaphysics of immutable being which merely
supported the prevailing traditions of the time.[16] Furthermore, all this
served to effect a further severance of thought and its objects from the
matrix of experience. In this sense, both Plato's and Aristotle's philoso-

114

phies were truly *metaphysical*. They assigned reality not to the changeable and unfinished materials men held in their hands, but rather to their metaphysical forms which escaped observation and yet remained their selfsame specific selves forever and ever, in another world. Clearly philosophical knowledge had been severed from common experience.

There were now the eternal world of pure and unchanging being revealed only to a chosen few (whether in this world or beyond it did not matter, since in either case the forms were not physically visible), and the world of the workaday level where nothing was permanent, and everything submitted to the manual toil and dexterity of workers who worked for the satisfaction of men's needs. It is understandable how such a separation of knowledges encouraged the formalization of primitive beliefs in animism and divinities as sources of mysterious events beyond man's control. Sophisticated Greek thought assigned the element of chance, peril and evil to "matter" in this world---matter, the formless unintelligible principle. Nevertheless, the original idea of assigning *separate* worlds for the uncontrollable elements in experience persisted. The controllable was relegated completely to the realm of thought and its objects of fixed forms.[17] We can perhaps best summarize the results by going through a series of adjectives which describe this "classic" worldview.

A. *Teleological.* In the classical view, every single thing has its own fixed end, its telos towards which all its natural activities converge as to a goal. Prescinding from the technical differences between the Platonic other-worldly forms and the Aristotelian thisworldly ones, we can say that in this view each thing is what it is by virtue of its *form*. This form which composed with matter to constitute the complete being is the principle of stability. It makes each thing capable of being known, i.e. intelligible. Even as a being changes, it remains the same *kind* of being it is. Matter or potency, on the other hand, is the principle of change or non-being, and thus of unintelligibility. For what is there to know in something that is *not-yet*?[18] When the complete being corrupts altogether and passes away, we can see that while the individual passes away, its species or kind perdures. It is upheld through other individuals who continue to bear that same specific form.

Since the form is held to perdure through all the stages of change each thing undergoes, it is in fact intensified rather than altered in a changing being. The upshot is that change is seen merely as a realization of an end *already* imprinted and prefixed in the texture of each thing. Experience itself seemed to bear out this metaphysical assertion. After all, great oaks (not rabbits or anything else) from little acorns grow. Great Danes (not cherries or anything else) from little Dane-puppies come. Each being in the universe follows its own specific line of being with its activities pre-set and predetermined for it from the start by the kind of being it is, i.e. by its *form*. A man was a man from beginning to end. His form perdured until the final breakdown of the individual.

B. *Spectator.* In the classical view, philosophy's task was not to make or remake being ("to change the world" as Karl Marx's grave at Highgate in London proclaims) but simply to discover it. Thought probed being, broke it open, so to speak, so as to penetrate to its inmost structure. Once understood, that structure functioned as an ethical norm. The question, "of what use would such a knowledge be?" would have been irrelevant.[19] For, as we saw, it was the task of the privileged few, the philosophers, to engage in knowing for knowing's sake, to contemplate being, not tamper with it. To know what things are and how they stand in relationship to each other's forms; to see how they flow from one original source of pure being---that was the exalted calling of the philosopher. Hence Plato had dreamed of making kingship an exclusive privilege of philosophers. Aristotle had written beautifully also on how no human experience can quite equal in quality the few ecstatic moments philosophers experience when they succeed in contemplating the orderly centralization of all things in that most perfect of all forms, God.

Aristotle deemed God the supreme model of contemplative thought since God was Thought Itself at its purest as he thought of his own thinking---his own thinking which was also his own being. In Aristotle's beautiful words:

> *And God is in a better state. And life also belongs to God: for the actuality of thought is life, and God is that actuality; and God's self-dependent actuality is life most good and eternal. We say therefore that God is a living being, eternal, most good, so that life and duration continuous and eternal belong to God. For this is God.*[20]

Finally, not only is each thing defined and driven by its own *telos*, but all beings collectively move in one grand cosmic teleological harmony, each in its fixed specific line by virtue of a "desire" in each to approximate the perfection of that divine Being set above and beyond them.[24]

C. *Archetypal*. The archetype of all things was the eternally pre-existing object of desire, God, the form of forms, who ultimately causes (through final causality of desire) change and motion in all things. Individually, the archetype for each thing is its own specific form already existing within itself. That form determined all its activities in one fixed line throughout the span of that being's existence. What a being is at its point of fulfillment or maturity is what it was programmed by nature to be from the start. That program in turn was imprinted beforehand in the texture of that being.

D. *Finalistic*. Since everything in the classical view is preset and preformed both individually and collectively in a given species, any change in a thing during its span of existence is deemed to be merely accidental. This is because things are taken as finished (*perfecta*). Over and above all things there is *the* End, the Absolute Most Perfect Being who is the ground of all beings. No infinite regress of ends deriving their finalities from one another is possible here, whether in unending linear succession, or in circular fashion.[22]

E. *Idealistic*. Classical thought is biased towards thought. It prefers the idea which fixes on its immutable objects over against the immediacy of sensible experience where everyday living takes place. Since the *idea* of the whole is primal, the particularity, indeed the *partial* character of evils in experience becomes secondary to the whole as viewed by the intellect. Man, it seems, is ever in quest not merely of certitude but of *perfect*

116

certitude. And obviously this latter cannot be had on the level of experience where everything is contingent. The classical mind, therefore, turns towards a realm beyond experience. It revels in metaphysical immutable objects of thought.[23]

> *Perfect certainty is what man wants. It cannot be found by practical doing or making; these take effect in an uncertain future and involve peril, the risk of frustration and failure. Knowledge, on the other hand, is thought to be concerned with a region of being which is fixed in itself.[23]*

F. *Retrospective.* Being is always traced back and better understood in terms of its causes, its origins, its ground and preexisting explanatory principle. To understand the world in which we live we would always have to fall back on antecedently existing causes. And finally everything is explained by reference to the Supreme Cause of all, God.

G. *Classificatory.* Since each being is fixed to its own line of natural action through its specific form, it follows that what things *are* can be known with enough assurance so as to justify classifying them in fixed categories.[24] It is a metaphysical contradiction for one form to be ever any other but itself. To know the forms of things (remember, *form* is the principle of intelligibility, matter of unintelligibility) is to know once and for all that they are *that* and never anything else. It is this fixity of forms which makes things eminently suitable for permanent classification.

We have said enough of the classical philosophical view such as Dewey describes it. It only remains to add that for him this ancient conception of knowledge and reality continued on throughout the Middle Ages in ever magnifying, ever deepening proportions of formalization and institutionalization. All the metaphysics fashioned in that long stretch of centuries called the Middle Ages were totally Greek in cast and substance. Mediaeval philosophical thought in short was, according to Dewey, merely a prolongation of Greek speculative thought and bias. Of course this was in a different setting and in deep unity with the prevailing social structures of the time.

> *Metaphysics is a substitute for custom as the source and guarantor of higher moral and social values--- that is the leading theme of the classic philosophy of Europe, as evolved by Plato and Aristotle--- a philosophy, let us always recall, renewed and restated by a Christian philosophy of Mediaeval Europe.[25]*

This apologetic spirit in philosophy is even more apparent when mediaeval Christianity, around the twelfth century, sought for a systematic and rational presentation of itself. It utilized the classical view, especially Aristotle's philosophy, to justify itself to reason. Philosophy then became "insincere."[26]

> *But for over two thousand years the weight of the most influential and authoritatively orthodox tradition of thought has been thrown into the opposite scale. It has been devoted to the problem of a purely cognitive*

117

certification (perhaps by revelation, perhaps by intuition, perhaps by reason) of the antecedent immutable reality of truth, beauty and goodness. [27]

Theologians of the Christian Church adopted this (Greek) view in its form adapted to their religious purposes. The perfect and ultimate reality was God; to know Him was eternal bliss. The world in which man lived and acted was a world of trials and troubles to test and prepare him for a higher destiny. Through thousands of ways, including histories and rites, with symbols that engaged the emotions and imagination, the essentials of the doctrine of classic philosophy filtered its way into the popular mind. [28]

Before closing this section, we should in fairness say a few words to explain how epistemologically (i.e. as a theory of knowledge instead of the "genetic account" we just saw) the classical mind equated genuine ("higher") knowledge with the characteristics of permanence, immutability, fixity, etc., not only in the subject knower who possessed it, but even more importantly in the objects known, the world of the "really real" as it has come to be called ever since ancient times when Plato talked of the "world of forms." Since we have heard Dewey's side of this theory, and since aspects of this theory still command a considerable number of followers even today, it miglt be in order here to look ad the other side briefly.

The ancients believed that genuine knowledge referred to unchanging objects; or, in the case of changing objects, to them insofar as they are unchanging. Now, what is change? Motion. Change is the transition from not-yet being something (potentiality) to *being* actually that thing. Thus it is a process, a motion from a point of rest (*this* being) to another point of rest (*that* being). Now, that in-between process or motion *by itself* would be completely unintelligible, since it would simply be pure *becoming*. Unless we answer the question *becoming what?* there is nothing much we could say about the process by itself. This really was what was at the heart of the classic position. Once we discover where a process originated we can start to say intelligible things about it, v.g. what things probably caused it to start becoming another thing. Moreover, if we could anticipate and project the future product of the process (its end or goal to which the motion is tending), then again we would have something intelligible to say about it. But to prescind from either the point of rest in the beginning or the end of the process; simply to try and understand that process by itself is impossible.

Try to understand *pure potentiality*. You cannot do it. It would be like trying to understand me if I met you and said, "You are potential," then abruptly walked away. You would be befuddled, would you not? Now if you ran up after me and asked what I meant, and I replied, "You are a potential Ph.D. in philosophy," then suddenly there is something to be understood, is there not? The same you whom I have come to know and categorize as a fine student will *move* towards the goal or end of a Ph.D. That in turn is categorized as an achieved state of rest in relation to the motion which preceded it and led up to it, namely, your studies to fulfill

118

the doctoral requirements. This is simply the way our minds work, the way we understand things around us.

Take another example. Shots ring out suddenly infront of me. I notice a bullseye stand sustaining hit marks from its peripheral circles closer and closer to the center spot. I look around and see no one. I am mystified. I look some more. Now I see a man aiming his rifle at the bullseye. The whole situation instantly clears up. The process is made intelligible in the light of the man's goal or end: to try and hit the center dot.

Can you not retort and say that you can certainly say something intelligible about the process itself, namely, "holes are happening on this surface"? If so, then that would seem to concentrate purely on the process of *becoming* and still have some definite intelligibility about it. But wait. Note how you are merely saying that the painted surface is in a condition where "holes are happening to it." We have in effect even here *rested* our minds on the holes themselves and their appearances as the end of whatever process it is that is taking place. We can go on with other examples and the same point will obtain. It is only *rest*, stability, permanence of a sort which enables us to utter intelligible statements about objects. The mind in its natural dynamism to understand things understands them through points of rest, or what comes down to the same thing, categories, classification, etc., those various characteristics we saw Dewey mention earlier. It was this fundamental point which the classical thinkers evolved into a fullblown mindset which even to this day still characterizes much of the western mind.

Once we understand this, we can then begin to appreciate the enormity of the philosophical task one undertakes in moving the fulcrum of knowledge out of and away from a world of immutable objects back to the actually experienced world where every instant change, not rest, is king. How do you go about showing philosophically that genuine knowledge ought to center itself on *change?* Of course, one easy way would be to admit right off that *intellectual* knowledge is not to be trusted precisely because it is naturally programmed to undertsand only the unchanging. Thus, it may be contended, as some in fact have contended, that the way to genuine knowledge is feeling, intuition, the heart, etc., which enables us to "flow along" with an onflowing universe without freezing its *élan* into categories. We all know how common the feeling and saying is that we are dynamic personalities, ever growing, ever changing, etc., and therefore are perceived distortedly when stuck into some generalized description. We opt to be known, "related to" through "vibes" not ideas. For an idea, as Plato noted, is indivisibile and thus unchanging. Whether this object infront of me is an animal or a plant I perhaps am not sure. But the ideas themselves of "plant" and "animal" are obviously indivisibly distinct from one another. To be mistaken about those ideas themselves (not their application) is simply not to have grasped either one at all in the first place. This then is one easy way out: admit that the intellectual ideas are by nature classificatory, and thus untruthful in a world of change. This Dewey did not do. He chose instead to attack the fundamental "bias" the Greeks injected into their theory of knowledge.

Dewey insisted that with the advent of science, man at last has in his possession the instrument and tool he needs to focus his knowledge on precisely the world as unfixed and *changing*. The classical world of fixed objects and things determined distinctly from one another in their various natures ---all these came unstuck with the coming of science. The scientist now approached things with a genuinely "open mind" without bias as to what they have been by their very natures antecedently programmed to do. "Handsome is as handsome does" says Dewey. Far from the world being a "cosmos" of things, each changing according to the eternally unvarying cycles of their fixed natures, the world now is to be viewed as initially nothing but a "buzzin' bloomin' confusion." On this, at any rate, Dewey does not seem to escape the logic of the classic position: dismiss rest, and with it you dismiss intelligibility. It will be interesting to watch how Dewey uses science to elaborate a theory of knowledge based on a world of change and unfixed objects, and from there go on to propose his moral theory. But first, let us follow his account, this time a historical one, of how both the mind and nature were "opened up" as it were, and liberated from the classical bias, how man was enabled to look on things around him adventurously, with fresh eyes and fresh enthusiasm about novel possibilities in the world.

The Advent of Science.

Dewey points to Francis Bacon (1561-1626) of the Elizabethan Age as the forerunner of the kind of scientism he advocates.[29] Before Bacon there had been the great "Copernican Revolution." Bacon himself had for contemporaries Galileo (1564-1642) and Kepler (1571-1630) who corresponded with each other and whose works and writings went a long way towards abolishing the Ptolemaic theory. Too, Bacon was contemporary with Descartes (1596-1650) who earned a permanent place in philosophy by fathering a new method based on mathematics. Through Descartes' "universal doubt" came the unprecedented opportunity to wipe clean off the mind all past thoughts and beliefs and get a fresh start. Cartesian philosophy proclaimed its aim as that of building the edifice of human knowledge on an absolutely new foundation, namely, that of pure certitude. This was not all. This edifice of knowledge was itself subordinated to a further end. Whereas before Descartes the classic ideal of knowledge for its own sake was in general still the unchallenged doctrine, with Descartes philosophy was henceforth launched on the novel course of "mastering nature;" of man wresting nature's secrets from her bosom by *force majeure*, if necessary, for his uses and convenience. Cartesian *method* aspired to make its users "lords and masters of nature" who would assault nature and tame her into being a servant. This is the general picture we have to keep in mind to grasp Dewey's assessment of Bacon:

> *What makes Bacon memorable is that breezes blowing from a new world caught and filled his sails and stirred him to adventure in new seas.*[30]

With his famous statement that "human knowledge and human power meet in one"[31] Bacon steered the primary focus of thought back to actual experience. He advocated the inductive method to find out in a strictly scientific way what forces things have locked secretly within themselves. Not for him the quasi-magical "sciences" of his day which took the easy way out. His was a serious effort to unlock nature, to lay her bare to human understanding---the only way man could ever hope to control natural processes. Discovery of new facts, new truths was what knowledge was all about, not repetitious demonstrations of old truths which was hardly productive of novel ideas.[32] To penetrate into the secrets of nature so as to wrest them away from her for use towards man's needs, active experimentation, under a carefully thought out technique, is necessary. A complete overhaul and thoroughgoing reclassification of things was the order of the day. Henceforth knowledge was not to be construed in the manner of a spider spinning its web out of its own substance (like rationalists are wont to do with "pure thought"); nor should it be conceived like a pile of materials which individual ants industriously gather (as empiricists are wont to do with sense impressions). Rather, the true and new method must be "comparable to the operations of the bee who, like the ant, collects material from the external world, but unlike that creature attacks and modifies the collected stuff in order to make it yield its hidden treasure."[33]

Even logic, which supposedly dealt only with mental operations, should be subsumed under the new aim of all human knowledge, namely, ever-renewed progress.

> *Where, Bacon constantly demands, where are the works, the fruits, of the older logic? What has it done to ameliorate the evils of life, to rectify defects, to improve conditions? Where are the inventions that justify its claim to be in possession of truth?[34]*

In Bacon we find a method which calls for careful technique and attention to facts so as to be able to use them more powerfully: "to obey nature intellectually in order to command it practically."[35] This new enterprise was to be carried forward to success not on an individual but rather on a collective basis.[36]

Dewey takes Bacon's spirit in the pursuit of knowledge as a prophetic anticipation of William James' theory of pragmatism in which truth was conceived to lie solely in its melioristic results.

These were all revolutionary conceptions of the nature of human knowledge. We can see, if only cursorily, the mutual interdependence between the psychological, scientific, social and industrial revolutions. After all, what is modern science but so much applied science?[37]

> *The mind became used to exploration and discovery...This psychological change was essential to the birth of the new point of view in science and philosophy.[38]*

The industrial revolution with its steam and electricity became the reply to Bacon's prophecy.

The growth of this new technique which made control of natural energies its preoccupation was everywhere followed by the "fall of feudal institutions,"[39] i.e. the divisions of social classes according to their possession of "higher" and "lower" knowledges. For it is in the nature of applied science and its results to be open for anyone to verify and enjoy. It was knowledge to be shared, in clear contrast to the old views of restricting knowledge only to the elite.[40] Knowledge ceases to be *aristocratic*. Instead it becomes democratic. Instead of people continuing to think of themselves as assigned to a social class for life, or to the religion in which they happened to be born, political and religious individualism arose as witness the social contract theory and the Protestant break from Roman ideas. In this new spirit, men questioned old beliefs everywhere. They began to think, observe and experiment for themselves.[41] This was the buildup for what later on in the eighteenth century French thinkers would call the "indefinite perfectibility of mankind on earth." Everywhere, on every level of reality, *progress* was the aspiration of all those who embaced the new method.

A question seems to arise naturally at this point. If, as Dewey says, feudal institutions did indeed "fall everywhere"[42] with the emergence of the new knowledge, why has not scientism triumphed completely? Indeed why has Dewey's whole philosophical mission been to point to the lamentable mentality which has continued powerfully even to our own day to hem science in to a restricted territory, to its own "legitimate" domain? Why have the artistic, moral, religious and humanistic disciplines continued to stand apart from the scientific method? What happened to the seemingly all-engulfing fascination for the new method? Why, after these hundreds of years since Francis Bacon, has not science taken over *completely*?

Whenever this question is asked nowadays, it is fashionable even in Roman Catholic communities to conjure up the memory of Galileo, and the spirit which produced that sorry event as *the* explanation for the setback of science. And Dewey would probably agree that the explanation does indeed lie in that direction. But in truth the matter is not that simple. For we should not overlook the fact that Copernicus was an ordained Catholic clergyman. His great book *De Revolutionibus* (which Galileo stoutly defended) was published by his permission in Leiden by a Protestant and brought to him when he was practically on his deathbed. Galileo and all those other luminaries of that age had not yet been born when Copernicus was already working out his theories. Why then was Copernicus' theory not deemed a threat by the Church while Galileo's was?

From what we said earlier of Socrates' case, we know that institutions do not necessarily act decisively until they have to. And they have to only when a new idea and movement threatens their existence. This was the case with Galileo, while it apparently was otherwise with Copernicus who preceded Galileo by some twenty years.[43] The threat in Copernicus' ideas seemed to be, in his time, only implicit, and subtly implicit ideas can always be hidden from the masses. But when these germinal ideas developed and came into explicit and convincing expression in Galileo, action had to be taken. Galileo confidently announced that all reality was composed of geometrical figures, and that while the same God wrote both the books of Revelation and of Nature, whenever there was a conflict between the two, *nature*, understood and interpreted mathematically and geometrically, was to have the last word, not *revelation*. God was then proclaimed to be the Geometer Creator of everything, and there was no hope of ever fathoming any natural thing unless one fathomed it through mathematics and geometry. In cases of conflicting interpretation Galileo insisted that the right answer is in the book of nature, not in Sacred Scriptures.[44] It was then that the religious institution saw the grave threat these positions posed, and it acted in the interests of its tradtiions.

The upshot of the confrontation was not a total victory for one side over the other. A sort of truce or compromise was worked out which merely perpetuated the classic separation of knowledges. While the onslaught of the new scientific movement could not be squelched, neither could the weight of traditions be forced out on matters of morals and religious faith, man's "spiritual" life. The notion thus became prevalent that while the new scientific method was indeed powerful and incontestable in the realm of physical natural things,[45] it had no competence as regards man's "spiritual" life. Here other ways of knowledge, not experience, won the day. And so, the old separation of the social classes and their corresponding specialties was kept intact. The realm of sacred being still belonged to an elite versed in its own systematized body of knowledge, while the realm of the mundane and the profane belonged to the scientists. In the latter, experience was indeed king. But each realm was clearly and strictly demarcated from each.[46]

We see then how a traditional view of nature undergoes questioning and challenge from science, yet manages to survive, prevail and hem science in to its *own limits*. This was merely a courteous way of saying the new knowledge ought never leave the level of the experimental, the manual. It ought never intrude into "spiritual" affairs. Here truth was to be reached by other ways such as revelation, "pure reason," demonstration, logic, etc.

Finally, we should note how the new science offered no substantial view of what things are *in themselves*. In the new context such a view was irrelevant. The new knowledge had its eyes turned in another direction, namely, to *method*, rather than to the *content* of things. If it dealt with the substantial content of things at all, it was merely in a negative fashion, to challenge the traditional claims that things were already known and classified and catalogued through an immutable knowledge of their antecedent forms. Science now declared that what things are remains to be found out through carefully measured and exactly repeatable observations. No significant definition of these beings is possible before experimentation. In short, the new science did not offer any metaphysical or epistemological version of what things are. It ushered in only a method of dealing with things under the controlled circumstances of an experiement. In doing so it moved away from deductive demonstrations which all too often were nothing more than repetitions of traditional belief. Several distinct steps made up this new method as it energetically sought out the power of things: what they can really do when released by effective technique.

1. Analytic reduction of the gross total situation to determine data, i.e. qualities that locate the nature of the problem.

2. Formation of ideas or hypotheses to direct further operations that reveal new material.

3. Deductions and calculations organizing old and new subject matter together.

4. Operations that finally determine the existence of a new integrated situation with added meaning, and in so doing test or prove the ideas that have been employed.[47]

Clearly, the old-world view of looking at things as though they were once and for all fixed and permanent through forms which merely awaited discovery and contemplation had been surpassed. Experimental method emphasized instead the *search* for new knowledge about things.[48] The interest was now in *power* in nature, what things can *do* at the behest of and for man. All things were seen not as defined and delimited beings, but as endlessly promising instruments to serve man's needs.

> ...*henceforth the quest for certainty becomes the search for methods of control; that is, regulation of conditions of change with respect to their consequences.*[49]
> *Science is not constituted by any particular body of subject-matter. It is constituted by a method, a method of changing beliefs by means of tested inquiry as well as of arriving at them.*[50]

Now that the aim of knowledge has shifted to control and exploitation of nature for man's needs, the idea of both thought and its objects as instruments calling for ever more refinement, efficiency and economy is evident. *Discovery is* now, paradoxically, *inquiry.* Technique (formerly a *means* only) producing calculated results publicly repeatable, now becomes the substance (end) of things present and to come.[51] Technique, as it were, aims at itself.

> There is thus no a priori test or rule for the determination of the operations which define ideas. They are themselves experimentally developed in the course of actual inquiries. They originated in what men naturally do and are tested and improved in the course of doing.[52]

If someone objects that this sort of knowledge is so transient since experiments continue on progressively in an endless series and that thus no knowledge (rest) is possible, there is a ready answer. The results of each experiment at each stage becomes the solution to the problem which prompted that particular experiment in the first place. One ought to be satisfied with this relatively stable and consummatory piece of knowledge, namely, the problem-solution contextual series. To look for more stability than this is to reveal one's incapacity to transcend the classic view of fixed forms in reality.

> We know whenever we do know; that is, whenever our inquiry leads to

conclusions which settle the problem out of which it grew. This truism is the end of the whole matter---upon the condition that we frame our theory of knowledge in accord with the pattern set by experimental methods.[53]

Certified as it is by public verification, the new knowledge is also purified of myths and superstitions. It becomes the "final arbiter of all questions of fact, existence and intellectual assent."[54] Without publicly verifiable evidence, nothing is to be assented to, everything is to be first submitted to doubt.

The scientific attitude may almost be defined as that which is capable of enjoying the doubtful; scientific method is, in one aspect, a technique for making productive use of doubt by converting it into operations of definite inquiry.[55]
Moreover, in experiment everything takes place above board, in the open. Every step is overt and capable of being observed. There is a specified antecedent state of things; a specified operation using means, both physical and symbolic, which are externally exhibited and reported. The entire process by which the conclusion is reached that such and such a judgement of an object is valid, is overt. It can be repeated step by step by anyone.[56]

In sum we can say that with the advent of science man found a new way of conceiving thought and nature together as conjoined in the manner of an experimental instrument. In subsequent centuries this had an enormous social impact upon the conditions which govern men's associations with one another.

The social changes that have come about through application of the new knowledge affect everyone, whether he is aware or not of the forces that play upon him. The effect is the deeper, indeed, because largely unconscious. For, to repeat, the conditions under which people meet and act together have been modified.[57]

It may be good to end this chapter by interrupting this quasi-historical treatment of science briefly to look at ourselves in the United Stated today to see how technology has indeed modified the conditions in which we meet and act together. From the time we wake up to our automatic radios to the moment we take our sleeping pills, at almost every step in-between we depend on the push of this or that button to keep us going. It is all "largely unconscious." It is all just us, alive and in motion. Hence it is not easy, while doing the same things day after day in an almost mechanical way, to realize how far technology has taken us, or even how different we have become from almost all the rest of the world.

But break the routine. Go the living museums of early Puritan life at Plymouth or Sturbridge Village in Massachusetts. Those costumed Pilgrims may look cute and their chores fascinating, but to live that sort of life? Or visit an Amish settlement in Iowa or Pennsylvania. There in seemingly purer form than even Christian Scientism we observe the full force of Dewey's critique (as we shall see) when dogmatic religion rejects science outright. We admire what we see, but who would really want to stay? Or set foot in other countries. The way people drive in continental Europe remains a challenge and a vital threat to an American. After conducting our lives by the clock, we get confused when we find out that other people take the appointments they make with charming insouciance. We are distraught when our schedules are thrown awry because we must now do manually what we did at home with the flick of a switch before stepping out on our way to work. For their part, other people too are puzzled by us. Why all the hurry? To hurry sometimes, yes. But always? What philosophy is that which makes punctuality a cardinal virtue? Why can't Americans really *relax* even as that word also happens to be their favourite expression? They take a table on the sidewalk cafes of Via Veneto, lean back, stretch their legs to cool off those hush puppies, join the fingers of both hands tip to tip and sigh, *"la dolce vita"* --- all the time taking apprehensive glances at their watches before the waiter has had a reasonable chance to hurry back with their gin and tonic with "lots of ice." It's even more startling when we see the rapid Americanization of almost everything everywhere as we travel, all the protests to the contrary notwithstanding.

How great the need is for philosophical vigilance can be surmised from *homo Americanus* himself. Has not the scientific obsession for quantitative measure and calculation worked itself so deep into his soul that he tends to equate bigness and "more" with "better?" Has he not by now unconsciously equated reality with time, and time with money, money with success? And has not this tended to make our friendships superficial, calculating and utilitarian because genuine friendships take time with usually no money in them? But let us stop before we get too far ahead of our presentation. We go back now and resume our philosophical chronicling of what happened when science was born and advanced in the West so we can follow what Dewey makes of it all.

Key to abbreviations*

TML   = *Theory of the Moral Life*, New York, 1960.
RP   = *Reconstruction in Philosophy*, Boston, 1962.
QC   = *The Quest for Certainty*, New York, 1960.
EN   = *Experience and Nature*, New York, 1958.
TV   = *Theory of Valuation*, Chicago, 1966.
CF   = *Common Faith*, New Haven, 1972.

All the above are in paperbacks.

For secondary works on the various aspects of Dewey's thought as culled from his wide range of publications, see the twin paperback volumes, *The Philosophy of John Dewey: The Structure of Experience*, by J. J. McDermott, New York, 1973.

For Dewey's ethics, see the hardback, *The Moral Writings of John Dewey*, by J. Gouinlock, New York, 1976.

The critical editions of all of Dewey's writings are being published serially by Southern Illinois University Press, Carbondale, Illinois. To date nine volumes are out reaching to the Middle Years.

3

INSTRUMENTALISM

Galileo's public declarations that Copernicus was right and Ptolemy wrong were full of portents much later for Dewey's philosophy. The heavens, specifically the moon, were not made out of a fifth essence (quintessence) but of merely the same corruptible matter and elements as the earth. With this equalization between the heavens and the earth, the separating categories of "higher" and "lower," which had heretofore held apart practically every level of classic thought from one another, became suspect. Quickly the heavens themselves were included among the objects to be probed, assaulted and brought under control to serve man's needs.

> ...the work of Galileo was not a development, but a revolution. It marked a change from the qualitative to the quantitative or metric; from the heterogeneous to the homogeneous; from intrinsic forms to relations; from esthetic harmonies to mathematical formulae; from contemplative enjoyment to active manipulation and control; from rest to change; from eternal objects to temporal sequence.[1]

And what of this new man, now standing in this immense field of the universe armed with his new "metric" method and intent, as we saw, on the indefinite perfectibility of himself, on conquering all of nature? Was he really so different from nature the way the old classic view since the Middle Ages had made him out to be? Was he really a creature unique among all others around him in that he had a divine origin and destiny? We know how in time the new method yielded Darwin's *Origin of Species* --- a deadly blow to this classic view of man. Man was not a separate being set over against nature. He was shown to have arisen merely from nature's lowliest of conditions: primal slime. He had evolved slowly, phase by natural phase. Finally, lest man still insist on separating himself from nature by vaunting his intellectual consciousness and freedom, there was Freud. Here was one who insisted on the identity of psychic desire with the cosmos at its original point of emergence. Through his theory of the universal compulsion-to-repeat, and the twinning of desire and death in all living things, Freud was to show how man is not even master of his own house and self. Man must turn his new method in on himself also. just as he does with all other things around him. Does he not wrest secrets out of nature's hidden recesses? Then he also must plumb his mind's own dark depths through the new techniques of psychoanalysis. He must throw light on his behaviour, explain it in as purely naturalistic and scientific terms as possible. Freud pronounced all resort to supernatural theories illusory and without a future. In a word, the inexorable advance of science had shaken habitual beliefs about reality as forever fixed and immutable. Nothing now could be considered fixed and immutable, not even man. All the world is merely a "buzzin' bloomin' confusion" which needs to be submitted to the hypothesizing and tentative approach of science for decision on what it *can* do[2]. Everything is to be further and further known through new experimental combinations and interactions with other beings.

John Dewey comes on the scene with a call for a "Ministry of Disturbance, a regulated source of Annoyance; a destroyer of routine; an underminer of complacency" to prevent any slackening of the scientific spirit.[3]

> *For discovery and inquiry are synonymous as an occupation. Science is a puirsuit, not a coming to possession of the immutable; new theories as points of view are more prized than discoveries that quantitatively increase the store on hand... the great innovators in science are the first to fear and doubt their discoveries.[4]*

To put it another way, reality has now come unstuck. Everything is now material and datum with no form except the tentative one scientific experiment may give it openendedly from stage to stage. Everything in thought and nature is now to be regarded as an *instrument,* a tool for the betterment of the human condition. Thus we come to two essential concepts in Dewey's philosophy: *instrumentalism* and *meliorism.* The first comprises his philosophical theory on experience and nature, the second his ethical view. We will treat each of these two ideas separately. However, it should be pointed out that Dewey, the philosopher, has an aversion for "separation" of practically any sort. Perhaps the only separation we find him allowing is the one necessary for scientific analysis of data. This, in fact, is not so much a separation as merely a phase in the ongoing process of inquiry. Always Dewey's outlook is marked not only by the unity but the *continuity* of all things, especially that of experience and nature.

Instrumentalism

Dewey always acknowledged his indebtedness to William James for many leading ideas in "pragmatism."[5] Where James broke ground for that philosophical theory. Dewey cleared up the rest of the site and engineered the construction of a philosophical edifice befitting the greatness of the whole pragmatic movement. James was the brilliant lecturer and polemical essayist, Dewey the steady thinker and systematic writer on the pragmatic approach.

Dewey cleared up the site with *"malice prepense,"*[6] he frankly admits, for the purpose of a good show on his all-out attack on the old classical view of reality as fixed and immutable. Such a spectator type of philosophy seemed utterly irrelevant and useless. It made high claims to truths which made no difference whatsoever as regards the real world in which man breathes, moves and makes his home. Understandably so. For if things were indeed immutably fixed in their being, the only logical thing to do was look at them, contemplate them. Efforts to change them and make them work for man's betterment would be futile. How could anyone change the unchangeable? No wonder classic philosophy yielded nothing towards the realization of man's immemorial desire to lessen his pains, increase his pleasures and provide for the necessities of life. By contrast, the products of applied science for the betterment of the human condition, since the scientific revolution, are so overwhelming we cannot even begin to catalogue them today. On this indisputable power of scientific knowledge to be of service to man Dewey erects his new philosophy.

> *It is not too much to say, therefore, that for the first time there is made possible an empirical theory of ideas free from the burdens imposed alike by sensationalism and a priori rationalism. This accomplishment is, I make bold to say, one of three of four outstanding feats of intellectual history.*[7]

Today there are those who are greatly disturbed by the destructive effects of scientific products, especially on nature around us. Dewey anticipated this objection. These destructive effects ought to be blamed he insisted, not on science, but rather on the social institution and traditional mindsets which have refused to heed his call to give up their old beliefs. Dewey has been asking all along that thay join in the task of reshaping everything in the light of the scientific method. What destructive effects we are complaining about now can be laid squarely at the doors of those who have stubbornly clung to the "separation" of knowledges.[8] The reply to those who flaunt environmental "pollution" against scientism today would be the same as the one Dewey gave those who objected to his scientism because of the holocaust visited upon mankind by the atomic bombs.

> *The destructive use made of fission of the nucleus of an atom has become the stock-in-trade of the assault upon science. What is so ignored as to be denied is that this destructive consequence occurred not only in a war but because of the existence of war, and that war as an institution antedates by unknown millenia the appearance on the human scene of anything remotely resembling scientific inquiry. That* in this case *destructive consequences are directly due to pre-existent institutional conditions is too obvious to call for argument.*[9]

What then does it mean to look on everything --- ourselves, our experiences and all the universe arounds us --- in the scientistic instrumental way that Dewey advocates? It is, as we said, to look on (1) the world as *data* (not as fixed entities) for scientific experiment and inquiry; (2) man as an organic unity of needs and desires; (3) the world as the only setting there is for man's satisfaction of his desires and needs; (4) man and nature, human experience, thought and its objects not as separate beings, but as one ongoing, instrumental and scientific process.

1. *The World as Data.* There was a time when man saw himself as standing over against nature. He was the intellectual, that being *other than* mindless nature around him. Hence he tried to think out what things *are basically,* regardless of the countless ways there may be of viewing those same things on a superficial level. From the ancient Greek philosophers to Edmund Husserl, the father of presentday Phenomenology, man has never given up on this effort to lay bare the fundamental structure of "the things themselves." All of which seems illusory to Dewey.[10] For any question man asks of nature he asks out of some interest or need on his part. Thought comes out of questions. Questions in turn are nothing more than the problematic situation of the questioner. If I ask "what is that?" of a long yellow object in front of me which looks like a banana, I ask it probably out of hunger. That object looks potentially satisfying to my physical condition of tension and disequilibrium. This flows right into a mental disequilibrium, the *question.* The whole set is one problematic condition. If, after eating the banana and recovering my equilibrium I still ask, v.g. what constitutes a banana chemically, then I am asking from an interest obviously other than that of hunger, namely, curiosity. And curiosity surely is a problematic situation looking towards an answer. Again, I can look on this same piece of fruit as a weapon. I can lay it on the sidewalk with precise carelessness so that my enemy will slip on it. This would yet be some other problematic standpoint. And so on. Indeed, even the supposedly *basic* viewpoint which seeks to know the banana in itself *fundamentally* cannot but also arise from an interest. In short, no question we raise is ever free of interest. Without interests men do not ask questions. Before interests and problems arise, it seems idle to ask what things are in themselves. They can be most anything. They are there, in other words, merely as data (the buzzin' bloomin' confusion we mentioned earlier) awaiting careful and effective use.[11]

It follows that nature, when considered apart from men's interests (an impossibility, as we just showed) would be meaningless, "ineffable."

> *Immediacy of existence is ineffable. But there is nothing mystical about such ineffability; it expresses the fact that of direct existence it is futile to say anything... because knowledge has no concern about them. Immediate things may be pointed to by word, but not described or defined.[12]*

In their immediacy then things *are* simply, and that's that.[13] To talk of basic structures within things out there as though they existed with their own fixed forms apart from human consciousness only reveals the interest the talker has of knowing those things in his supposedly uninterested way. Indeed, historically, this was the professed interest of the classical mind before the scientific age. It wanted merely to know, knowledge for knowledge's sake. This extends to the mediaeval saying, *"Credo ut intelligam"* (I believe so I may understand). But it would be self-deception to take such knowledge as interest-free. Of course the interests here were other than the interests *after* the rise of science and man proclaimed his intention to assault nature and tame her for the satisfaction of human needs. Nevertheless, in both situations knowledge stood as what satisfied human interests. Prior to interest and question it is otiose to talk of "nature."

Meaning therefore appears only as answers to questions.[14] Questions arise only when human situations become problematic, when "shock" breaks routine. A need whose satisfaction is in doubt startles us. Such shocks

> *are stimuli to reflection and inference. As interuptions, they raise the questions: what does this shock mean? What is happening? What is the matter? How is my relation to the environment disturbed? How shall I alter my course of action to meet the change that has taken place in the surroundings? How shall I readjust my behaviour in response... shock of change is the necessary stimulus to the investigating and comparing which eventually produce knowledge.*[15]

Thus questions and satisfaction of needs are correlatives. The former control the latter. We pass over a bridge hundreds of times without even noticing it is there. But we miss it very badly, and we think about it intently, if day after day we are forced into a very long traffic-jammed detour because the bridge has collapsed. Then we are late for work. The boss is upset. Our job is threatened. The family could starve---all because of a bridge we took for granted and never noticed!

Now, however, the bridge-problem must be engaged in thought. What to do about it? In a more primitive setting, we would probably notice the trees along the gully banks, trees we never noticed before. Will they *do* as materials for a bridge? Will they *do* for the new kinds of bridge beams we have in mind? And so forth. Our need triggers off hosts of questions *in* the problematic context. Solutions to the problem are sought and referred right back to the heart of the situation in which the question arose.[16]

Needs, interests, questions, problems, solutions, satisfactions--all converge to make things previously meaningless now meaningful.[17] This in precise proportion to their capacity to solve or *re*-solve the tension in the situation.[18] With the solution, however, things settle back again into the old routine. We are back where we started: we take things for granted, we do not notice them. They recede, are just there without meaning. Clearly then what a thing is is defined by its capacity to satisfy a need. What can it *do* to resolve a problematic situation? Things are their powers of doing.[19]

Note how Dewey does not say the world exists only when man thinks about it or perceives it. He does say the world has meaning only in relation to man's need. Before that need the world is just there and there is nothing to say about it. It is a mistake to talk of things in themselves in isolation from human interest. To say for instance that one has understood things *basically* is merely to reveal one's interest as stemming from a *basic* standpoint, namely, that of a spectator and a contemplative. But cannot one object that *prior* to our interests and needs things are obviously there providing the setting for our interests and questions? Is not this sort of meaning prior to the emergence of needs? Does not even Dewey himself talk of them in this prior stage as *data*, material for solutions? Is this not a priori intelligibility? The reply would be a retort. Obviously, the objector has an interest when he refers to things in their preproblematic state as data. It serves his interest at the moment to view them as data!

The "world" thus has neither meaning nor antecedent forms prior to its insertion into a problematic context.[20] It is only data awaiting contact with instrumental thought. Hence the question is: what sort of thought has been decisively shown to be the most effective, economical and efficient at working out solutions? The answer is obvious: scientific thought, method, technique and manipulation.[21] In this connection, no one sets up an experiment with a mind already biased as to the outcome. An experiment is by definition a tentative, hypothetical and open approach to a situation. Its focus is not so much on the matter being brought under control as on the *method of control* itself being employed. This must be publicly repeatable. The products must be producible on demand. If something accidental results, it is not really considered a result since the method of producing it escaped the observer. Thus results and methods of production are interchangeable. The experimental method is equivalently its product, and inquiry is correlated to discovery. We see thus how thought and its object are intertwined. Between man and nature there is no break.

> *Instead of a knowing subject over against an alien world as object, we have intercourse between a living organism and its physical and social environment, interactions so integral to the events related that distinction between them becomes largely functional rather than one involving a confrontation between hard and fast, sharply defined, relatively unmodifiable individuals that change in little but position. And, of course, not merely two, but commonly many events may interact at a time so that we have a web or complex of relations, connections, referential strands and vector qualities.[22]*

> *Matter, life and mind accordingly are not separate and distinct kinds of being, but rather are different modes of interconnection and operation, properties characterizing diverse particular fields of interacting events.[23]*

So much for the continuity between thought and the situation in which it arises. We turn next to the continuity of thought in man with everything else that is in man.

2. *The Organic Unity of Man.* The separations of reason and thought from sensation, and of "higher" from "lower" powers and appetites in man are

belied by the unity of experience. Thought, to repeat, emerges only from problems. In that "shock" feeling and thought in man, impulse, emotion and rational consciousness are all merged components of one reaction the organism undergoes in the tension-producing situation. Let us illustrate this point by dramatizing one of Dewey's own examples, namely, that of reacting to a noise I hear.[24]

During the Christmas holidays of 1977, I spent a couple of days on Mt. Athos, the "holy mountain" in Greece. This is an independent state of sorts, consisting of twenty-one ancient and colorful monasteries and many dozens of hermitages (sketees), all dotting an enormous mountatin peninsula. A visitor there walks miles of absolutely lonely mountain trails from one monastery to another. Athos is one of those rare places where indeed one goes back a thousand years in time and even further. Nothing seems to have changed here since then. The monks go on and on forever in their routines of prayer and work, sometimes alone, many times together. Early one morning as I walked meditatively by myself in those high mountains, far away from "civilization" in the Grecian mainland (or from any monastery for that matter) I was startled by a dog which leaped at me ferociously from out of some bushes. It was obviously from one of the sketees, but its hermitowner was obviously not going to be around to control the wild animal as it charged barking and with fangs bared at me. I remember having flashing visions of myself torn to bits and bleeding away up there in the mountainous middle of nowhere where, literally, only God knows when next there would be another human being passing by. But that was only for an instant, Suddenly I felt my whole body tense up and my hair stand on end as I lifted my stout walking stick with both hands to deliver a blow. My panic was such, however, that before I could swing at the animal (which had momentarily hesitated), I cried out, more in terror than anything else, "Get out of here!" I can still see that dog now. Instantly, it turned back cowering, its tail between its legs as it fled in fright to the valley below never again to cross my path. With knees wobbly with relief and cold sweat pouring down my spine, I continued my walk. Slowly I began to reflect on the strange incident. How explain that dog's odd behaviour? And then it dawned on me! It must have been my voice, my scream of terror. In that holy place where human beings are as silent almost as the skies, the dog had never heard a human shout before, not to mention one emitted in full terror. The explanation satisfied me. Farther down the road I sat down to rest and make a note on this most unusual incident.

Notice how in this experience at no time at all was I engaged in "pure thought" alone without feelings. (Remember the philosophers in our earlier scenario who tried in vain to think by themselves?) Both thought and feelings were riveted on the dog. Nor, on the other hand, were there feelings without thought. Even if there were, there would be nothing significant to say about such feelings. For this would be the parallel of "nature" before the emergence of thought. Feelings, thought, impulses and reflexes all occurred at once, as one action, namely, the organic reaction to an unusual stimulus. No moment can be pinpointed in this ongoing process in which one phase ended and the next one started. Just so, there is no way of pinpointing limits or moments in our experiences when reason and feelings are divided each from each. Both flow simultaneously to constitute one behavioural action.[25]

Admittedly, we have depicted an extreme situation. But essentially the same description would apply to every shock situation, any startling departure from routine. The intensity of the reaction would of course vary with the situation. But the unified activity of thought and feelings, of interests and needs, impulses, reflexes all suddenly thrown into tension, and all impelled together in organic unity toward readjustment and relief from tension---these would be the same. Naturally, to understand the situation better we resort to analytic separation of "reason" from feelings. In actuality, the two are by no means separate. Like any other organism, man does not react piecemeal and separately power by power to his environment. Rather, he reacts as a whole unity, "homogeneously," as we shall see shortly, with his environment.

3. *The World as the Setting for Human Satisfaction*. Man is a being of needs. Many of these needs he satisfies through impulsive or habitual interaction with his environment without any explicit attention. We breathe, walk, enjoy a day in spring or a temperate day in summer. We use the darkness of night for rest, the light of day for work. We usually do not even advert to these actions unless something unusual turns up. And why should the unusual, the problem arise at all? Since, as we saw, meaning and thought come only as answers to questions it is clear that we have had quite a lot of them if we have lived any reasobable length of time. Quickly, however, thoughts recede to the back of consciousness once the needs which triggered them off are over. Like the rest of the world before thought arises, they then become mere *data* for future possibilities.

Interestingly enough this receded world of data is not altogether inactive. It comes through to satisfy our needs almost effortlessly through our habits. We habitually rely on things in the world and to a great extent they do not fail us. They satisfy some of our recurrent needs steadily. This is so evident that we tend to overlook it, unless and until someone directs our attention to the fact. Then we remind ourselves that "despite everything" we should be grateful for life's simple and elemental satisfactions.

What does "despite everything" mean? It really means despite *troubles*, does it not? Troubles attend our existence. We are in pain of one sort or another. We seek and cannot for the moment find the right solution. To console ourselves in this state of frustration we fall back on the realization that there are "despite everything" the same old *stable* satisfactions to fall on.[26] They do not cost anything, these elemental joys from nature itself: the reliable return of springtime, the warm rains and breezes of summer, the shade of trees, the colors of fall, etc. Why do we savour them so much "despite everything?" We can perhaps answer in the words Sakini (Marlon Brando) speaks at the end of the film *Teahouse in an August Moon*.

> *Pain makes men think.*
> *Thought makes men wise.*
> *Wisdom makes life*
> *A little more bearable.*

Recall how every problem contains the norms and reference points for its own solution discoverable through technique. In the lived world problems are rarely abstract. Indeed "abstract" problems do not really become problems until they bite, until they touch ground. Then they make a difference in our existence. They threaten the familiar. What we never dreamed could alter comes unstuck, and we unstuck with it. We are at a loss. We flounder around for a solution. We become desperate, grasp at straws. When all else seems to fail, we fall back on the rockbottom consolation that "despite everything" there are still life's simple joys. In short, a steady and stable world provides us our routine satisfactions. At the same time this same world has an unpredictable way of coming unstuck, or becoming unreliable. How then should we characterize such a world? How picture its structure? Is it all stability? Then what of our troubles? Is it nothing but troubles? Then what of its continuing comforts "despite everything?" What of the great solutions we often find *because of* troubles so that we look back and call those troubles really "blessings in disguise?"

The world is constituted neither of security solely, nor of peril solely, but rather of both elements. It is the field of the stable and unstable at once. It is a place where man builds optimistically, and yet also his place of never-ending hazards.

> *Consequently, it will surrender the separation in nature from each other of contingency and regularity, the hazardous and the assured; it will avoid that relegation of them to distinct orders of Being which is characteristic of the classic tradition. It will note that they intersect everywhere; that it is uncertainty and indeterminateness that create the need for and the sense of order and security; that whatever is most complete and liberal in being and possession is for that very reason most exposed to vicissitude and most needful of watchful safeguarding art.*[27]

This is the experience of anyone who has lived a fair number of years. "You can't be sure of anything in this life." But we quickly correct ourselves, "except death and taxes," we say. Seemingly light banter and mere words. But they reveal a conviction in the human mind, built on the collective experience of the race, that the world is a mixed scene.

The world is full of peril and danger. At the same time it offers good things, a setting stable enough to encourage efforts at improving satisfactions, at making them securer and more enduring. Reflection thus leads from "trouble" to the insight that this world is a mixture of the secure and the hazardous, the stable and the perilous, the predictable and the unpredictable. There would be no setting to interrupt, no field for troubles to arise in, were there not the steady routine of habitual existence built on the familiar world.

Indeed "troubles" themselves can have no reality apart from the world as familiar. In this sense we said the norms and references for a solution already lie in the problems themselves, even though for the moment they may be still unrecognized. To be exact, this mixture is not that of the *secure* as finished beings in themselves, and the *insecure* as likewise finished in an opposite way and both shaken together, as it were, and scattered over the field we call the "world." Rather, reality itself is mixed both of the secure and insecure *at once* in a unity as of one root. This mixture is a *living* unity, since, as we saw, it is otiose to talk of reality in separation from man's life and thought.[28] The world is at once the scene of risk and security, of hazard and success, of potential innovation in the midst of goods already conserved and secured.[29]

> *We live in a world which is an impressive and irresistible mixture of order and uncertain possibilities, processes going onto consequences as yet indeterminate. They are mixed not mechanically, but vitally like the wheat and tares of the parable. We may recognize them separately, but we cannot divide them, for unlike wheat and tares they grow from the same root.*[30]

Dewey notes how impressed even the most primitive men were by by this characteristic of the world as at once predictable and unpredictable as shown by their proverbs.

> *Germanic tribes had over a thousand distinct sayings, proverbs, and apothegms concerning luck. The world is a scene of risk. It is darkest before dawn; pride goes before a fall; the moment of greatest prosperity is the moment most charged with ill-omen, most opportune for the evil eye. Plague, famine, failure of crops, disease, death, defeat in battle, are always just around the corner, and so are abundance, strength, victory, festival and song.*[31]

Let me recount an incident related to these beautiful lines in Dewey. One spring afternoon in 1964 I was reading that very passage to a class at Holy Cross College in New England. Its full force was borne in upon me when upon driving up to my garage, my wife met me with the terrible news of John F. Kennedy's assassination. At the very height of his victory parade in Dallas, the *numero uno* in the world was brought low by Lee Harvey Oswald's evil eye.

To say this mixture of good and evil is "living" means that life's chain of events keeps on moving. There are those who, for instance, claim that the immortality the young President gained through his premature and tragic death may in fact be greater than any he might have gained had he lived. We will never know. Either way the point is made that the world is not composed ultimately of elements separately classed apart from each other as the stable and the unstable. Only a classic spectator mentality which is always bent on tracing things down to a fixed and immutable base would say that. Dewey takes men as they live, toiling, enjoying, succeeding, losing etc. in a world *at once* friendly and hostile. Hence the ambiguity in the question: "Is the universe friendly to man?" Anyone expecting an absolute and unqualified answer to the question is bound to be disappointed. For the universe is *both* simultaneously. It is the scene of human growth taking place amidst conserved goods, suddenly unsettled by problems and hopefully moving, through scientific effort, towards a better state.

The question is an ambiguous one. Friendly to man in what respect? With respect to ease and comfort, to material success, to egoistic ambitions? Or to his aspiration to inquire and discover, to invent and create, to build a more secure order for human existence? In whatever form the question be put, the answer cannot in all honesty be an unqualified one. Those who will have all or nothing cannot be satisfied with this answer. Emergence and growth are not enough for them. They want something more than growth accompanied by toil and pain. They want final achievement.[32]

Dewey's melioristic position, as we shall see, looks not to final achievement (this is repugnant to his whole inspiration) but to a realistic attitude of working for the best out of every situation. Wisdom then is not a gift nor an achieved finished state in which one knows what to do already even before a problem, any problem, has actually come up. Rather we have here an attitude of reflective and pragmatic balance, a readiness to use the funded experiences of past generations as guidelines for working out new goals out of trying times. The main means to these goals is, as always, the scientific method. In almost poetic lines we read about this Deweyite sort of wisdom in a world at once dangerous and reliable, the only setting available to man for growth.

This fact is nothing at which to repine and nothing to gloat over. It is something to be noted and used. If it is discomfiting when applied to good things, to our friends, possessions, and precious selves, it is consoling to know that no evil endures forever; that the longest lane turns sometime, and that the memory of nearest and dearest grows dim in time. The important thing is measure, relation, ratio, knowledge of the comparative tempos of change.[33]

4. *The Instrumental Unity of Man and Nature.* Experimental methods illustrate the homogeneity and continuity of thought and its object. Thought functions as part and parcel of any experimental operation in its entirety.[34] At no point is an experiment independent of thought. It is merely thought in action; thought is its essence. Not "pure thought," however. Far from it. Experiments are controlled and closely-monitored operations. Hence their public verifiability and repeatability. A laboratory of some sort, a material setting forms the matrix of experimental thought.

We cannot stress often enough that the arm-chair type of thought which views reality *classically* does not interest Dewey. He dismisses it as outdated since the advent of the scientific method. Consequently, if some persist in philosophizing that way even today, or in depicting man as other than and set over against nature, their ideas would simply not interest Dewey. To him nothing but reflective scientific thought is ultimately authentic.

What then do we see when we enter a laboratory? All sorts of instruments, dial clocks, measuring devices, vials, gadgets of every description, all of them with finely calipered measurements. The question naturally arises in the mind of one who picks up any of these instruments, "what is this *for*?" What is it meant to *do*, *produce*? There we have it. An instrument is embodied thought. Like thought it comes out of the past. Skill is needed to make it. The more sophisticated and refined the instrument, the greater the skill and experience needed to produce it. The same holds for thought. To be really sophisticated and refined, thought must grow out of a rooted appreciation of what other great men have already thought out. Instrument and thought thus carry this essentially *retrospective* dimension.

An instrument is also *prospective*.[35] It points towards action, towards use, production. *Meaning* (merely another word for *thinking*) thus makes itself real, embodies itself in a tool, an instrument. Indeed even if thought did not thus embody itself in an instrument it still would be instrumental of its very nature since, as we saw, its whole genesis marks it as *the* means for reaching a solution. The point is not difficult to see provided the contemplative spectator approach to things is abandoned, and intellectual resources are concentrated towards the arduous task of finding out what things actually can *do* through technical control.[36]

> The invention and use of tools have played a large part in consolidating meanings, because a tool is a thing used as a means to consequences, instead of being taken directly and physically. It is intrinsically relational, anticipatory, predictive. Without reference to the absent, or "transcendence" nothing is a tool...to be a tool, or be used as means for consequences, is to have and to endow with meaning; language, being the tool of tools, is the cherishing mother of all significance.[37]

Thus thought is not set over against its object any more than man is against nature. Both are "homogeneous." To object at this point that this cannot be since one is "spiritual" while the other is "material" is again to lapse into the rejected spectator classical view. Such philosophizing does nothing to ameliorate the human condition. Thus it decisively reveals itself as outdated, irrelevant. The amelioration of man should be the touchstone of any genuine philosophizing today, and only the scientific method is equal to that task. Only applied science with all its refinements and sophistication will *do*.

But what is applied science? Is it not simply the scientist at work with his instruments? Detached and separated from his hands an instrument ceases to be such. It points to nothing at all. Nor would it be an instrument when handled without a trace of consciousness, like worry beads or iron balls in the neurotic hands of a Captain Queeg. No, things are instruments only when and if they are put into actual operation towards controlled production. Before that, what would they be? Well, they may perhaps be called "tools" or "instruments." But this pre-production status, this non-use state may be paralleled to that of things or nature in the pre-problematic stage. They are just there. Nothing significant can be said of them.

Just as man is *in* nature, and the elements of a solution somehow are already indicated in the problem itself, so too thought is in one continuous unity with the physical tools being actually used. There is a unity of action in the *desired* end. Everything lines up according to the end to be achieved. There is also the unity of the world as the field of inquiry, as available data for man's organizing consciousness. Each is implicated in each, one entails the other. Neither one in isolation could give rise to either thought or the products of thought.

Clearly then, genuine philosophical thinking is always *anticipatory*. It looks forward towards ever better consequences. It is also *participatory*. It places thought and nature both in the same ongoing process of measured observation. It is *hypothetical* and *tentative* even when it does reach conclusions. For conclusions are intrinsically conditioned by the problems to which they are conclusions. They may be themselves the setting of new thoughts, new meanings, new questions. Thus reality is never taken as finished at any stage. Instead it is seen as vitalistic, pragmatic, regulatory. It may help at this point to list side by side the various characteristics of Dewey's philosophy in contrast to the classic type.[38]

Reality as Known Antecedently (Greek, Mediaeval, Classic)	**Reality as Known Consequently** (Scientific Activity)
1. Spectator	1. Participator
2. Archetypal	2. Interactive
3. Contemplative	3. Anticipative
4. Categorical	4. Hypothetical, Tentative
5. Finalistic, End-in-itself	5. Consummatory, End-in-view
6. Compensatory	6. Vitalistic
7. Idealistic	7. Realistic
8. Speculative	8. Pragmatic
9. Fixed, Immutable	9. Problematic, Mutable
10. Retrospective	10. Prospective
11. Classificatory	11. Regulatory

All the adjectives on the right side describe a philosophy which takes *growth* as the human desideratum. Both the quality of the enjoyer and the things enjoyed are in proportionately progressive motion. There is never any time when one can demarcate certain objects as unchangeably *the* properly human and virtuous goods, with their opposites as also unchangeably undesirable. This realistic outlook admits to a more hypothetical view of things.

Growth is change. We cannot predict absolutely the lines growth may take. Correspondingly, the objects to be enjoyed and found enjoyable in various stages of growth may also change, even though, as we shall see, Dewey also talks of enduring comprehensive human goods. The term "compensatory" refers to the classic view whereby the ills of this world are promised solutions not from within the setting of the problem itself, but in another world. Needless to say, this is in diametrical opposition to Dewey where the insistence is on achieving the solution right at the heart of the "bads" and "pains" of the problem. Dewey repudiates the attitude which makes "resignation" to life's ills a virtue, since the presumption here is that by doing nothing more than simply waiting patiently and resignedly to one's fate, a happier state awaits the suffering subject at the end of life. If mankind has not moved itself forward and out of its many ills and evils, the blame can be laid to a great extent on this sort of compensatory acceptance of what otherwise would be worked at and improved on the spot.

Now it may be true that there are even today cultures in which "religion is the opium of the people." There may still be masses of the poor who believe that the pie now missing on their tables will, "if they are good," eventually be theirs in the Great Beyond, "the sky." But by and large, no sophisticated religion worth its name inculcates such silly passivity among its adherents. Rather, they all try, not infrequently with heroism, to solve the bads and pains where these exist. Indeed they are only too happy to utilize the latest scientific know-how in their humanitarian zeal. For what then can Dewey fault them?

For one thing it may be fairly asked on behalf of Dewey whether it is not true no matter how sophisticated a believer has become technologically, that he still has that last area in his soul and spirit whereby he considers "resignation to God's will" a virtue. Yes or no? When everything within a man's power, be it financial, scientific, physical, etc. has been done, and still the problem remains, does not the believer then consider it plain wisdom to be resigned and accept the situation? Even the ancient Stoics taught this. And as long as we are going to be resigned, we might as well be resigned to God's will. Thus at least we have maximum solace. And there you have it. Those last two sentences constitute the parting of the ways with Dewey. He would consider them not only meaningless but the sort of attitude which ultimately impede the amelioration of mankind.

The point is this: can you reserve, so to speak, such a space in your spirit for "resignation" as a virtue, while at the same time *totally* dedicating yourself to the kind of technological meliorism Dewey demands? To ask the question is already to see the incompatibility between "reserving" and "totally dedicating." In truth, back of it all is a fundamental difference in persuasion. One holds that it is within the power of science eventually to solve all human problems as they come. The other insists on the intrinsic limitation of scientific solutions when it comes to certain areas of huma existence. It is only natural then to assume that such a difference in persuasion will also heave their respective impacts on actual behavior. But this is an assumption. Is there *in fact* a difference in the way believers and scientific meliorist behave as regard using all their energies for the improvement of man's lot through technology? We will hear Dewey say that after all we all want the same things: the banishment of the ills we feel and the multiplication of the goods we enjoy. We need only mention the word "abortion," however, and immediately we know that the differences between the two mentalities on the matter of the bads and goods in life remain vast and deep.

4

MELIORISM

A Philosophical Landmark

In one place Dewey writes sarcastically about Kant's claim to a "Copernican revolution" in philosophy. Kant believed that his theory of knowledge (which had the human mind contributing the organizing categories that make scientific generalizations possible) had turned the old way of understanding knowledge completely around.[1] But as far as Dewey is concerned, Kant achieved no revolution at all. He had merely thought up a new theory which ultimately supported the tired, old classic view of the world. In Kant both knowledge and its objects still remain fixed and unchangeably categorized. Nothing of the classic view was thus transcended. Certainly nothing at all is changed by this theory in the world in which we live. Instead there is merely the strengthening of the already stubborn view that every being was fixed in its place with an unchanging nature and essence.

If any theory qualifies as a "Copernican revolution," Dewey claims, it ought to be his own instrumentalist, melioristic philosophy.[2] It is here that reality comes unstuck from an eternal other world to which everything was rigidly referred as to an undeviating norm---whether it be a Platonic world of forms, a mediaeval conception of a beatific heaven, or a Kantian insistence on a nuomental world with its own higher laws of freedom and morality. All such "other" worlds are now brushed aside. Real being is brought down instead to *this* world, restricted to it as its one and only center. No being is granted a fixed form. Everything awaits the outcome of scientific experimentation, remains tentative, ever cumulative, never final. Everything is submitted to the never-ending process of wresting a securer life from an insecure environment. This is *the* real Copernican revolution in philosophy. For together with the coming unstuck of reality in the eternal world of fixed forms also comes the unsettling of prefixed moral values. All antecedent ethical norms, everything that was based on the classic notion that both reality and value lie lodged in a world other than the only one where in fact we make our home, an other world taken as completely finished and as a model of value and reality to which everything must conform---all these must now dissolve and submit to the searching eyes of science with an eye to human use and service.

Henceforth things must be characterized only from the context of an experimental process.

We have already touched on the reasons why, inspite of its convincing credentials for alleviating the ills of mankind, and as human knowledge par excellence, the new scientific method somehow still failed to gain complete supremacy over all the domains of human knowledge. The difficulty lay in the truce and compromise that was effected when the new science found itself not strong enough to overcome the traditional beliefs in religion and morals, the humanistic arts and studies in general. As a result, religion, morals and art hygienically cordoned off their regions of knowledge from the intrusive claims of the new method. The new knowledge was relegated to its "legitimate" sphere of dealing only with what things *do*. The old classic separations persisted. Something other than science was held to be competent when it came to morals, art, religion, etc. where the subject matter was other in kind than what is scientifically observable, verifiable and measurable. Indeed the *is/ought* dichotomy, originally expressed by Hume and driven home by Kant, is by now so deeply settled in the mind that it seems well-nigh impossible for Dewey to succeed in showing that moral value could only lie in the sensible verifiable world of human experience itself. That was the precise place where Kant said it could never be found.

> *The notion that valuations do not exist in empirical facts and that therefore value conceptions have to be imported from a source outside experience is one of the most curious beliefs the mind of man has ever entertained. Human beings are continuously engaged in valuations. The latter supply the primary material for operations of further evaluations and for the general theory of valuation.[3]*

How can morality be excised from experience when human beings are *always* making value judgements from and within experience itself? Can people escape the funded experience of the society in which they move and grow? Value judgements refer to experienced satisfaction or dissatisfaction of some sort. And while every experience and value judgement is made and undergone only by individuals, it would be an abstraction of the absurdest sort to think of an individual making them in isolation from the society in which he supports his life. An individual cut off and isolated from the network of social relationships around him would be nothing more than a dead stick. Realistically then, we should see that people are saturated with the institutional beliefs in which they have been nourished.

As we saw, they are mistaken who blame science for the atomic holocaust rather than society's institutionalized belief in war. In the same way men cannot escape from the traditional beliefs as to which satisfactions are worthy and which ones not. The ethical task lies not in separating satisfactions from experience, but rather in assessing the value judgements men do make.[4] *Ought we to continue making them, or are they due for a change?* What Dewey finds puzzling is the continuing prevalence of the classic view, reaffirmed in Kant, that antecedent reality outside experience, all finished and perfect, should act as the standard for moral value. This seriously hinders the long overdue takeover of science in ethics. Today the peculiarly human task is to submit the values in which people have been brought up to reflective and scientific inquiry. No more time should be lost in joining the endless quest for better and better human satisfactions which become more enduring and more comprehensive as they grow out of the matrix of experience.

We must forget once and for all the separation of reason from experience, the ideal from the real world. We should start from thought as it is born out of experience itself, that is, *integrated* with all of man's powers and faculties, indeed with the environment itself in which the meliorating consequences are sought. It is the philosopher's task to integrate the mental and the real, not in an abstract way, but in action, production and experience. It is the philosopher's task to point out that all thought starts in experience, from a human need and problem. No matter how abstract thought may become as it tackles this or that problematic situation, "clear and distinct" ideas should never be taken as replacing the reality of original experience. This even though the latter may be cloudy and obscure by comparison with its mentalized termination. It is also the philosopher's task to point out that gross experience ought to turn to science for the best solutions of the problems it encounters.

Recourse to Science

Science uses "selective emphasis;" some aspects of experience are singled out as pertinent to experimental consideration, some others left out as irrelevant. But the scientific enterprise is all continuous with the original experience. It should be brought back to that experience.

The failing common to rationalists, like Descartes and Spinoza, of taking clear and evident thoughts about a situation as revealing a reality superior to the situation itself, may also attend the scientistic person who forgets that the scientific method is, after all, only an instrument (albeit the best) for the satisfaction of man's needs. The important point then is to keep the unity of experience itself, as it presents itself originally and all throughout the process of reflection; to stay with experience concretely, not as it is refined and abstracted by thought. That is, we should affirm things as changeable and changing, instead of succumbing to the intellectual temptation of transferring the characteristics of permanence and immutability (which are proper only to clear and disrinct ideas) to reality itself. This latter breaks, separates thought from experience. This is a rather sticky point. Perhaps it will help to look at Dewey's own explanations.

> We begin by noting that "experience" is what James called a double-barrelled word. Like its congeners, life and history, it includes what men do and suffer, what they strive for, love, believe and endure, and also how men act and are acted upon, the ways in which they do and suffer, desire and enjoy, see, believe, imagine---in short, processes of experiencing. "Experience" denotes the planted field, the sowed seeds, the reaped harvests, the changes of day and night, spring and autumn, wet and dry, heat and cold, that are observed, feared, longed

for; it also denotes the one who plants and reaps, who works and rejoices, hopes, fears, plans, invokes magic or chemistry to aid him, who is downcast or triumphant. It is "doublebarreled" in that it recognizes in its primary integrity no division between act and material, subject and object, but contains them both in an unanalyzed totality.

Now empirical method is the only method which can do justice to this inclusive integrity of "experience." It alone takes this integrated unity as the starting point of philosophic thought. Other methods begin with results of a reflection that has already torn in two the subject-matter experienced and the operations and states of experiencing. The problem then is to get together again what has been sundered.[6]

Dewey illustrates his point on how ideas quickly replace original experience.

An author writes: When I look at a chair, I experience it. But what I actually experience is only a very few of the elements that go to make up a chair, namely, the color that belongs to the chair under these particular conditions of light, the shape which the chair displays when viewed from this angle, etc. "Two points are involved in such a statement. One is that 'experience' is reduced to the traits connected with the act of experiencing, in this case the act of seeing. Certain patches of color, for example, assume a certain shape or form in connection with qualities connected with the muscular strains and adjustments of seeing. These qualities which define the act of seeing when it is made an object of reflective inquiry over against what is seen, thus becomes the chair itself for immediate or direct experience. Logically, the chair disappears and is replaced by certain qualities of sense attending the act of vision. There is no longer any object much less the chair which was bought, that is placed in a room and that is used to sit in, etc. If we ever get back to this total chair, it will not be the chair of direct experience, of use and enjoyment, a thing with its own independent origin, history and career; it will be only a complex of directly "given" sense qualities as a core, plus a surrounding cluster of other qualities revived imaginatively as 'ideas.'[7]

How then avoid this sort of separation between experience and ideas?

The only way to avoid a sharp separation between the mind which is the center of the processes of experiencing, and the natural world which is experienced is to acknowledge that all modes of experiencing are ways in which some genuine traits of nature come to manifest realization.[8]

How things in nature come to "manifest realization;" how we come to observe traits, aspects, etc. of things which never struck our attention before, we know by now from our previous explanation of problems as the starting point of meaning and thought.

144

We take up next the step of "selective emphasis" as necessary to any thinking process.

> *Selective emphasis, with accompanying omission and rejection, is the heartbeat of mental life. To object to the operation is to discard all thinking. But in ordinary matters and in scientific inquiries, we always retain the sense that the material chosen is selected for a purpose; there is no idea of denying what is left out, for what is omitted is merely that which is not relevant to the particular problem and purpose in hand.*[9]

On selective emphasis Dewey warns about the "hypnotic influence exercised by the conception of the eternal."[10] We need say nothing further on this point.[10] This kind of mistake cannot take place in the empirical method of the sciences, even as they too emphasize aspects of experiences selectively according to the utilitarian purpose of their experiments.

> *...empirical method points out when and where and how things of a designated description have been arrived at. It places before others a map of the road that has been travelled; they may accordingly, if they will, re-travel the road to inspect the landscape themselves.*[11]
> *The scientific investigator convinces others not by the plausibility of his definitions and the cogency of his dialectic, but by placing before them the specified course of searchings, doings and arrivals, in consequence of which certain things have been found.*[12]

As so we come to the final step, which is that of bringing back scientific thought with all its refined and sophisticated conceptions of an experience, back to that experience itself in all its rawness.

> *What empirical method exacts of philosophy is two things: First, that refined methods and products be traced back to their origin in primary experience, in all its heterogeneity and fullness; so that the needs and problems out of which they arise and which they have to satisfy be acknowledged. Secondly, that the secondary methods and conclusions be brought back to the things of ordinary experience, in all their coarseness and crudity, for verification. In this way, the methods of analytic reflection yield material which form the ingredients of a method of designation, denotation, in philosophy. A scientific work in physics or astronomy gives a record of calculations and deductions that were derived from past observations and experiments. But it is more than a record; it is also an indication, an assignment, of further observations and experiments...The recorded scientific result is in effect a designation of a method to be followed and a prediction of what will be found when specified observations are set on foot. This is all a philosophy can do.*[13]

Ethics and Satisfaction

We come back now to the ethical question: how to improve the human condition; how to improve satisfactions and lessen dissatisfactions and, if possible, eliminate them.[14] Here we should distinguish between two kinds of satisfaction: *immediate* and *reflective*. About immediate or casual satisfaction or values, nothing more can be said beyond the immediacy of *having* them. You either are satisfied or not. You either want for nothing at the moment, or you do. Such satisfaction is casual, unreflective. Unless one brings up the topic the satisfied condition is not even noticed. Ethical axiology (value theory) does not deal with this state. For satisfaction is rooted in need. Casual satisfaction of a need tells us nothing at all about whether the satisfying object, though desired, was desi*rable* or not. Because of our constantly shifting experiences, we do not and cannot know beforehand how satisfactions, rendered causal either through habit or impulse, may be enriched and better secured through reflective calculation. The one thing we know, though, is that all these values and satisfactions, casual though they be, are fit subject for ethical assessment.

As in all cognitive experiences, our meliorating method on the matter of values should be that of the empirical sciences, especially those which obviously and directly deal with man, such as biology, sociology, anthropology, experimental psychology, etc. Reflective values thus, in contrast to merely casual and habitual ones, are synonymous with the concept of bettering any given concrete situation through the instrumentality of the sciences, hand in hand and in continuity with a philosophical assessment of the truly desi*rable* and worthwhile ends. As we have said often, the one and only human task which we can safely state with absolute certainty is the relative one of rendering the human condition more and more satisfying in an endless process. There is no way of achieving this except through the partnership and continuity of philosophical reflection with the empirical scientific method. Reflective thought cannot be viewed as though it were one operation which sets up ideal ends for the betterment of a situation, and then turns to science as though this latter were something separate for the execution of those ends. The ends to be set up have to be realistic, really achievable. That is, the ends themselves are to be discovered within the experimental process, not a priori and in separation. Even though for purposes of clarity and analysis we may have given the impression earlier of turning to science as though it were a subsequent and separate step for the realization of an end already thought out, the actuality of the thought process involved no separation at all. There is only one fluid continuity of one experience in which both reflective and scientific thought merge in a "living mixture" to alleviate the problematic situation.[15] But why this obsessive and exclusive stress on science?

If we train our eyes on consequences, there can be no doubt as to what sort of knowledge has really lifted man up from his primitive ways of accommodating his needs to the present level when so much power and natural force have been harnessed to work and produce for him. But has not Dewey in effect absolutized science? Is this not a contradiction since science is incapable of transcending its own hypothetical status? How then can it be *the* best instrument for man? The reply would point out that the objection is plainly academic. On the pragmatic level where men undergo their burdens of life, there simply has not been any better method of thought which has produced goods and diminished the bads of human existence than the method ushered in by the scientific revolution. Academic objections are a waste of time. What behooves us all is the fullscale and massive employment of science in every area of human endeavor.

For a better grasp of Dewey's scientific *meliorism* (from the Latin *melior*, better) it will help to understand his ideas on (1) ends-in-view; (2) means-and-ends; (3) religion.

Ends-in-view.

For Dewey "end-in-itself" is one of those leftovers from the classic account of reality which so many find impossible to shake off. In many ways it has been perpetuated by those who somehow have successfully maintained the separation of knowledges. The concept of an "end-in-itself" presupposes reality to be antecedently fixed and finished, a view Dewey repudiates. The classic idea that unless a last absolute end exists everything becomes a *means* in an infinite regress and therefore is impossible should be rejected likewise. For this is merely an abstraction without basis in experience. True, abstractly, if everything is a *means* one can ask "a means to *what*?" and the question would be unanswerable if everything is by admission a *means*. However, to say that everything is a means without an absolute end-in-itself does not in actuality involve an infinite regress. For a means does not always stay only a means. What is a means now may be an end next time, and so on. Here is where there may be an infinitely regressive succession. And experience *is* lived succession. No one ever employs or encompasses all means *at once*. Hence to insist on the existence of an absolute end-in-itself is to abandon the empirical realm of experience. It is to separate thought from actuality, and then to take that hypostatized thought as mistakenly reality itself.

Abandon such abstractions. Look only to experience. Note how an end arises out of a condition of need, deficit, conflict, tension. In this condition it may happen that we grab directly at the object of satisfaction without the intervention of reflective thought. This is what we termed earlier "casual" satisfaction. On the other hand, it is also possible that thought intervenes. Then it will function instrumentally towards not only the object desired immediately, but towards the truly desirable object, an end-in-view.[17] Thus reflective thought invariably looks at the larger picture. It aims at the more comprehensive and enduring satisfaction that may be brought about from the problematic situation. Either way, it would be false to say a last end-in-itself is necessary to complete the picture. The satisfaction of an existing need seals off a situation.

consummates it. This is so even when reflective thought is involved. For though it operates towards the more comprehensive and enduring satisfaction, reflection does aim at actually stopping need. It does not abandon need to search contemplatively for what is ultimately and absolutely an end-in-itself. After all, what is in question are organic needs. These are rooted in vital impulses which of themselves are not yet ends-in-view nor desires/acts of valuation. These latter come only with the start of reflective thought.[18]

A doctor, for example, cures a patient's "trouble" by restoring him to health. Certainly there is the notion of health-in-general. But this is merely the outcome of a great number of definite empirical inquiries, not an a priori preconditioning "standard for carrying out inquiries."[19] Thus need, impulses towards immediate satisfaction, reflective thought towards more enduring and comprehensive solutions---all these, whenever they are all in fact present, intertwine in the human organism's forward movement out of an experienced tension. But they need not be *all* present in every situation.[20] Dewey explains the connection of desires and needs to ends-in-view.

> *...desires arise only when 'there is something the matter' when there is some 'trouble' in an existing situation... when things are going smoothly, desires do not arise and there is no occasion to project ends-in-view, for 'going smoothly' signifies that there is no need for effort and struggle. Now vital impulses and acquired habits often operate without the intervention of an end-in-view or a purpose...Behaviour is so often direct that no desires and ends intervene and no valuations take place...Organic tensions suffice to keep the animal going until it has found the material that relieves the tension. But if and when* desire *and an end-in-view intervene between the occurrence of a vital impulse or a habitual tendency and the execution of an activity, then the impulse or tendency is to some degree modified and transformed: a statement which is purely tautological, since the occurrence of a desire related to an end-in-view* is *a tranformation of a prior impulse or routine habit.[21]*

Action or vital impulse arises out of need. It moves, we can say, mechanically towards a satisfying object. This is purely organic reaction or reflex activity.[22] It may happen that one does think casually of the satisfying object in the process. There would still be very little difference between the two situations. In the former case satisfaction merely happens, in the latter it is merely *had*. Dewey seems to reserve the term "end-in-view" only to situations where the ideational is definitely present: an action, that is, which *adequately* appraises an object in terms of its comprehensiveness, relative stability and quality. This end-in-view, functioning in our experience as terminating objects of desire, takes the place of the older concept of an ultimate and absolute end-in-itself. It is accurately phrased since our desires do not wander off into abstract chains of goods ultimately anchored at some fixed and absolute good from which all others derive their goodness. This is precisely the usual rationalist-idealist contention. In fact our desires and interests actually cleave to

148

satisfying objects, whether immediately or mediately, through reflection. They are seen to be terminal, consummatory for *that* particular concrete situation of need. Needless to say, different situations and different experiences call for discretely diverse ends-in-view. It is part of being virtuous to integrate as many of one's ends-in-view as possible into the truly desir*able* character that is the goal of all ethical efforts.

There is an advantage to this concept of an end-in-view. It shifts man's attention away from an other world of finished ends (which merely awaits man's coming to attain it) back to the conditions in which desire emerged in the first place. It stakes out in realistic fashion the reasonable limits of human effort. It stays within the perimeters of experience. Man is not required to foresee anything beyond his actual powers of seeing. That much, however, he ought to foresee, namely, calculate as best he can the ends of a projected action. He should weigh the factors which enter into a foreseen goal as to their genuine desireability. There is nothing abstract nor abstruse in all these. The experiences of the race themselves, accumulated in wise sayings, show that men have recognized this procedure to be the desireable one.

> *There is an indefinite number of proverbial sayings which in effect set forth the necessity of not treating desires and interests as final in their first appearance but of treating them as means---that is, of appraising them and forming objects or ends-in-view on the ground of what consequences they will tend to produce in practice. 'Look before you leap;' 'act in haste, repent at leisure;' 'a stitch in time saves nine;' when angry count ten;' 'do not put your hand to the plow until the cost has been counted.'...They are summed up in the old saying,* Respice finem.[23]

But even the foreseen ends indicated in these proverbs need to be assessed further by a reflective imperative. That an end simply because it is an end is prized goes without saying. The question is whether it *ought* to be prized, valued. What really is it worth?[24] Again, we must be careful not to let our reflection mislead us into contemplative norms which have been disengaged altogether from the context of the situation itself.[25]

Freud had talked of maturity as ability to postpone gratification. This contrasts with the childish disposition to demand instant gratification. Dewey gives a more positive view by talking not of "postponement" but of reflective discrimination among the satisfying objects offered.

> *All growth in maturity consists in not immediately giving way to such tendencies but in remaking them in their first manifestation through consideration of the consequences they will occasion if they are acted upon---an operation which is equivalent to judging or evaluating them as means operating in connection with extrapersonal conditions as also means.[26]*

Thus ends-in-view may be divided into adequately or inadequately reflective ones. In either case desire exists with thought of the end. Only in the former is there, strictly speaking, mature thought, the union of the desired with the desirable, of the end-in-view with value. In an adequate end-in-view the generally accepted separation of the "is" and the "ought" vanishes. An adequate end-in-view is homogeneous with the situation in which it arises through the continuum between means and ends. In this sense it "is." At the same time, because it approves itself to reflection as desirable *on the whole*, it is what "ought" to be.[27]

> *There is no value except where there is satisfaction, but there have to be certain conditions fulfilled to transform satisfaction into a value.*[28]

Dewey notes that what is in question, when reflective choice operates on the level of morals, is not an object as "good" or "evil" but conflicting objects.

> *Most conflicts of importance are conflicts between things which are or have been satisfying, not between good and evil. And so to suppose that we can make a hierarchical table of values at large once and for all, a kind of catalogue in which they are arranged in an order of ascending or descending worth, is to indulge in a gloss on our inability to frame intelligent judgements in the concrete. Or else it is to dignify customary choice and prejudice by a title of honor.*[29]

It may help to illustrate this distinction between mere satisfaction and reflective evaluation which leads to an adequate end-in-view.

> *Take, for example, the gratification of learning that one has been left a fortune by an unknown relative. There is enjoyment. But...there is no valuation...the latter coming into being only when there arises some desire as to what shall be done with the money and some question as to the formation of an end-in-view...Value begins when the finder begins to consider how he shall prize and care for the money.*[30]

Or again,

> *...take the case of a child who has found a bright smooth stone. His sense of touch and of sight is gratified. But there is no valuation because no desire and no end-in-view, until the question arises of what shall be done with it; until the child treasures what he has accidentally hit upon. The moment he begins to prize and care for it he puts it to some use and thereby employs it as a means to some end, and, depending upon his maturity, he estimates or values it in that relation, or as means to end.*[31]

We know how Dewey takes an individual as shot through and through with social relationships and influences. We can even say that these relationships define him. The same sociality should not now be overlooked in the concept of an end-in-view. The individual cannot help but extend his own social makeup into whatever end-in-view he may be framing for himself at the moment. Indeed this is to a large extent what it means to search, through reflective inquiry, into "more comprehensive" ends: "the valuation capacity of any one is a function of the set to which he belongs."[32] Needless to say such influences are not to be accepted uncritically. Not infrequently they deserve resistance if not outright rejection.

Means-End Continuum.

Dewey asks some interesting questions on Charles Lamb's famous essay on how roast pork was discovered through the accidental burning of a Chinaman's pighouse. If an end were really separate from the means to it, what is absurd about burning pighouses down inorder to get roast pork? Real separation means real disconnection, does it not? And to be without connection is to be unrelated? Well, why say burning pighouses down for roast pork is absurd if in truth we conceive roast pork in itself as something without connection to the preceding conflagration? Yet we do call the act absurd. This shows not only that the two acts are related, but that they are inextricably intertwined with each other such that the means or process enters into the very makeup of the result itself.[33] The concept of an *end* includes within it that of the means which makes it possible. And of course it is impossible to conceive a *means* without including the *end* to which it is precisely the *means*. The whole thing seems clear. Why then the continuing belief in some circles that *ends* and *means* are separate both in fact and in concept?

Again, the classic view must bear the blame. If the end of man is taken as already existing in a Perfect Being, then it is this end and this being alone which will necessarily be *prized*. This makes all other beings fall into line as merely relative to that Absolute End. This means they are to be appraised merely as means towards the Perfect Being,[34] a position which may be verified in almost any ascetical literature of any Church which teaches God to be the true and final end of man. The situation is really no different in a Kantian perspective of man as an absolute end-in-himself. Man is taken there to be a fixed and immutable nature. All else then become separated from man and are regarded as means for him, while he never is a means merely. The difference and separation between the two are complete. It is this preferential view for antecedent and unchanging being that taints absolutist and rationalist philosophies at the core. Immutable Being is regarded as "first class" reality, while beings as they actually enter into living commerce with the human organism, and often the human being himself is taken as "second class" by comparison.

Let us relate this to Dewey's idea of thought as instrumental. Thought is a tool, indeed the tool of tools for reaching solutions. Intrinsic to thought is some end-in-view, namely, the solution or restoration of equilibrium which an organism has lost momentarily. However, even as thought is locked in to an end-in-view, equally locked in with its contents are the *means* for the realization of that end-in-view. In the example, presupposing that the subjects knew no better, roast pork to a hungry man would in its very conception include the idea of a burnt house, and obviously he conceives a burnt house in this situation *only in relation* to roast pork and to his hunger for it.[35] No separations here. Indeed if we remember that thought itself even in its ideality is "homogeneous" with its problematic setting (there is only one movement in the dissatisfied thinking organism, namely, towards satisfaction which is one and the same reality as the solution) we should be able to see that there is no separation at all or break in the single process. It goes on from the time dissatisfaction arises and moves through and in thought to satisfaction. A series of texts should bring this point out.

> When he perceives clearly and adequately that he is within nature, a part of its interactions, he sees that the line to be drawn is not between action and thought, or action and appreciation, but between blind, slavish, meaningless action and action that is free, significant, directed and responsible. Knowledge, like the growth of a plant and the movement of the earth is a mode of interaction; but it is a mode which renders other modes luminous, important, valuable, capable of direction, causes being to be translated into means and effects into consequences.[36]

If we insist on any separation at all, it should be not within the single ongoing process of conscious search for satisfaction, but rather in the kind or quality of satisfaction elected. Is it significant or not? Either way, the process is an unbroken unity between the mental (psychical) and the physical.

> The distinction between physical, psycho-physical, and mental is thus one of levels of increasing complexity and intimacy of interaction among natural events. The idea that matter, life and mind represent separate kinds of Being os a doctrine that springs, as so many philosophic errors have sprung, from a substantiation of eventual functions. The fallacy converts consequences of inter-action of events into causes of the occurrence of these consequences---a reduplication which is significant as to the importance of the functions, but which hopelessly confuses understanding of them. "Matter," or the physical, is a character of events when they occur at a certain level of interaction.[37]

The mistake liable to be made is that of picking out certain elements of a situation as it is actually being thought out, then treating these as though they had their own discrete meanings. This way lies confusion. But,

> ...change the metaphysical premise; restore, that is to say, immediate qualities to their rightful position as qualities of inclusive situations, and the problems in question cease to be epistemological problems. They become specifiable scientific problems: questions, that is to say, of how such and such an event having such and such qualities actually occurs.[38]

152

...body-mind simply designates what actually takes place when a living body is implicated in situations of discourse, communication, and participation.[39]

A need then, when raised to the level of reflective consciousness, does not divide itself into two levels of need, much less into two needs: one for the body and one for the mind. There is only one organic need of a self-reflective organism. It is a disastrous philosophical error to lose sight of this unity at any point in our analysis of a situation.

...to see the organism in nature, the nervous system in the organism, the brain in the nervous system, the cortex in the brain is the answer to the problems that haunt philosophy...they will be seen not as marbles in a box, but as events in history, in a moving, growing, never finished process.[40]

This sort of unity should not stop short of but indeed encompass that of aims and ideals.

The aims and ideals that move us are generated through imagination. But they are not made out of imaginary stuff. They are made out of the hard stuff of the world and of physical and social experience. The locomotive did not exist before Mr. Stevenson, nor the telegraph before the time of Morse. But the conditions for their existence were there in physical material and energies in human capacity. Imagination seized hold upon the idea of rearrangement of existing things that would evolve new objects.[41]

To put it concisely:

Consciousness is *the meaning of events in the course of remaking.*[42]

Thus the processes of ethical evaluation, the reflective appraisal of goods toward the amelioration of a condition of want, and of scientific experimentation are by no means exempted from this analysis of the mutual containment of means and ends in one another.[43] The same holds for ordinary "vulgar" experiences. Here means are like elevators used to haul material for the erection of a building but which themselves become incorporated into the finished building. Only in unintelligent actions are means and end separated as in the weaving of utopian fantasies, or in physical works of drudgery.[44]

Even prizing and appraising, as processes, intertwine in reflection.[45]

For what is deliberation except weighing of various alternative desires (and hence end-values) in terms of the conditions that are the means of their execution, and which, as means, determine the consequences actually arrived at?[46]

Clearly, the practice of attributing the word "intrinsic" to something which supposedly exists as an end or good-in-itself, and the word

153

"relational" as defining the nature of *means*, i.e. goods only for the achieving of some good-in-itself, is fallacious. If we look to experience, we find this supposedly derivative and relational character of means as something equally applicable to the end. The "intrinsic" goodness of an end may be applied to a means which can at any moment be itself the prized object, the end.[47]

There could be some confusion here. If, in the continuum of means and ends, the means are in the ends, does it not also follow that the end-in-view is in the means? Yes. We can even say the means itself can be viewed as an end-in-view. It happens that at certain stages it becomes a terminating object of desire or interest. Only a fatal loss of contact with experience will deny that our processes of driving for satisfaction can flicker on and off between the larger picture of means-to-end, and that of getting hold of the means, of bending one's total energy toward bringing it into being. When this latter happens, the means for the moment becomes the terminating focus of desire. It is the end-in-view.[48]

In a scientific experiment the mutual containment of means and end can be seen in that the consequence or end result is merely the terminating point set by the experimenter for the preceding conditions which all flowed into it.

> *An end as an* actual *consequence, as an existing outcome, is, like any other occurrence which is scientifically analyzed, nothing but the interaction of the conditions that bring it to pass.*[49]

We should now ask how this way of viewing means and ends as united in one continuous process relates to meliorism.

To consider all things in the universe as on an equal footing without designating some as ends and others merely means beforehand enables one to view everything without exception as merely material for the improvement of the human condition. "How" is, of course, what man must try to find out in experience through the twin tools of science and reflection. Since man is not outside and over against nature but rather "homogeneous" with it, instrumental thought cannot be such except as it is in continuity with its environment. Conversely, nature or environment takes on the aspect of instrumentality only through conjunction with thought. Both as instruments point to the realization of the good and the elimination of the bad in any given situation.

> *Ends-in-view as distinct from ends as accomplished results, themselves function as directive means; or, in ordinary language, as* plans. *Desires, interests, and environing conditions as means are modes of action, and hence are to be conceived in terms of energies which are capable of reduction to homogeneous and comparable terms.*[50]

> *The only excuse for reciting such commonplaces is that traditional theories have separated life from nature, mind from organic life, and thereby created mysteries.*[51]

The constant emphasis thus is on the organic unity of the life processes themselves within the organism and with its environment.[52] These unities in turn are subsumed into the process of meliorism. No privileged being, not even man, stands as a static and separate already-finished something to be simply prized and enjoyed. Everything is submitted to the continuous ever-changing stream of means and ends in the context of social betterment through intelligence.

The much abused and disputed adage, "the end justifies the means" resulted from the classic view of ends as already preset unilaterally. Objects "below" were then classed as merely means for "higher" ends. The task allegedly was to sort out among all these objects below those which fit the preset ends above. Reject this and it follows that man must himself work out his ends-in-view contextually with means and ends intertwined. If further we take this over into the scientific procedure, we see how discovery and inquiry are identical, as also experiment and result, method and product. This identity between product and method enables the result to be repeatable and publicly verifiable. It is not hard to see then how powerful this approach is towards changing the world for the better. For we are now to look on all ourselves and on nature as unfinished, material waiting for the realization of ever progressing ends which only concrete situations can reveal. This does away once and for all with the antequated notion of an end-in-itself.

If the notion of some objects as ends-in-themselves were abandoned, not merely in words but in all practical implications, human beings would for the first time in history be in a position to frame ends-in-view and form desires on the basis of empirically grounded propositions of the temporal relations of events to one another.[53]

In this unending process of improvement, the end (consummation) of one set of circumstances (one situation) becomes the point of departure for the next stage of development. Hence "end-in-itself" is devoid of meaning here. Instead we have every end-in-view becoming a means to further ends, just as every tried and tested scientific method calls for further refinement and improvement on itself. In the physical sciences, for instance, it is now taken for granted that all "effects" are also "causes;" that nothing happens which is final. Everything is part of an ongoing stream of events.[54]

The sole alternative to the view that the end is an arbitrarily selected part of actual consequences which as "the end" then justifies the use of means irrespective of the other consequences they produce, is that desires, ends-in-view, and consequences achieved be valued in turn as means of further consequences.[55]

Religion.

Man has an unquenchable longing for an ideal world. "We long, amid a troubled world, for perfect being."[56] Classic thought fastened on this longing, and sought to satisfy it by positing an antecedently existing, all perfect and absolute Being, God, with whom man was destined to be united. All otherwordly outlooks share this same approach vis-a-vis this human longing, namely, to focus its gaze on untroubled rest upon arrival at an already existing and waiting perfect world.

The trouble is that such an outlook promotes a passive attitude among men as regards their experimental powers "to advance the good life."[57] Furthermore, this perfect being is perceived in diverse ways by men, as history up to our own time amply attests. These diverse perceptions of the perfect being breed diverse cults of exalting, adoring, worshipping and obeying the deity, cults which in time become socially ingrained. An individual born into one of these religions then becomes a devotee of *a* religion. Yet interestingly enough all these particular religions appeal, each in its own way, to that other perfect world for a favorable intervention in their mundane affairs. Such appeals deflect the energy which could have been concentrated on the basic ideal of moving the human condition forward through the life of intelligence.[58]

Even today not only *the* divinity, but any divinity will do for those who have been taught to await betterment and salvation from another world instead of utilizing the tools at hand to do the job. Recourse to the supernatural becomes the order of the day.

> *Demons were once appealed to in order to explain bodily disease and no such thing as strictly natural death was supposed to happen. The importation of general moral causes to explain present social pheno-mena is on the same intellectual level. Reinforced by the prestige of traditional religions, and backed by the emotional force of beliefs in the supernatural, it stifles the growth of that social intelligence by means of which direction of social change could be taken out of the region of accident...Accident in this broad sense and the idea of the supernatural are twins.[59]*

Instead of the exact, painstaking research of science for the solution of human ills, rare and unpredictable interventions from mysterious sources (which by definition can never be brought within man's direct control) come to be relied upon. We need only express this attitude explicitly to see its error.

Yet the longing for the ideal world persists. It forms the basis for the so-called religious attitude in man. What we need to do is not to deny its presence but to intensify it---but of course, only after uncovering the authentic value in it through reflection.[60] The classic approach is incapable of discovering that authentic value in human religiousness. It always ends up in divisions among men on the basis of their diverse religious perceptions of the perfect being. Men divide themselves invariably according to diverse religious affiliations. And everyone knows how much evil has been committed in the name of a religion's claim to exclusive truth and connection to the Absolute.

In opposition to the classic view, Dewey would cultivate the perfectly natural human longing for an ideal world by using science to find out how best to realize those ideals; how to produce them; how to translate them into really enduring goods for the whole of mankind. If every "religious" man were to give up his particular *religion*; and if everyone in the world joined together in the enterprise of realizing a better world for one and all through the instrumentality of science, then a new *religious* dedication to ideals would be born. Something really and truly powerful would be around to deliver men out of their conditions of want. And this power would be at the disposal of man not only rarely and accidentally but *always*. Thus we invest the term "God" with a new meaning.

> *We are in the presence neither of ideals completely embodied in existence nor yet of ideals that are mere rootless ideals, fantasies, utopias. For there are forces in nature and society that generate and support the ideals. They are further unified by the action that gives them coherence and solidity. It is this* active *relation between the ideal and actual to which I would give the name 'God.' I would not insist the name* must *be given.*[61]

This "God" who functions as the point of juncture between aspiration and action obviously needs explaining.

> *...On one score, the word can mean only a particular Being. On the other score, it denotes the unity of all ideal ends arousing us to desire and actions. Suppose for the moment that the word 'God' means the ideal ends that at a given moment and place one acknowledges as having authority over his volition and emotion, the values to which one is supremely devoted, as far as these ends, through imagination, take on unity. If we make this supposition, the issue will stand out clearly in contrast with the doctrine of religions that 'God' designates some kind of Being having prior and therefore non-ideal existence.*[62]

Lest this new conception of "God" appear fictitious since it is rooted merely in the imagination, Dewey is quick to explain.

> *An ideal is not an illusion because imagination is the organ through which it is apprehended. For* all *possibilities reach us through the imagination... The unification effected through imagination is not fanciful, for it is the reflex of the unification of practical and emotional attitudes. The unity signifies not a single Being, but the unity of loyalty and effort evoked by the fact that many ends are one in the power of their ideal, or imaginative quality to stir and hold us.*[63]

Dewey hesitates to apply the term "God" to this new concept because that word has too long and too deep a tradition opposed to Dewey's new meaning. God in the tradition produces no ameliorating consequences which can verifiably and publicly be traced back to his own peculiar causality. Only private testimony and belief, rare inexplicable "interventions" do duty here. Of course there is is also the classic problem of as many, if not more, accidental evils happening. Believers themselves are the first to attribute these to the deity with the mystified comment that it all escapes understanding.

If by contrast we set about doing things Dewey's way, the attribution of ideals realized to a being other than the components of the situation itself would be seen to be superfluous. Not only superfluous, but the circularity in the traditional reasoning would be evident. For then it will be seen how the question is begged whenever "mystical" experiences are taken as proof of God's existence. Clearly "God" is already inserted in the word "mystical."[64] Why not dispose of all these tautologies and and employ instead a method that can produce, not accidentally and infrequently, but at man's bidding?

Interestingly enough, all religions and churches, despite their supernatural focus and mutual differences, agree with practically everything naturalists uphold when it comes to the nitty-gritty problems of helping the wretched of the earth improve their condition. There is no debate about wishing to bring these improvements about in the most effective and quickest way possible. Religious and irreligious people are one in a common aspiration to improve the human condition through science, the only tool at hand equal to the demands of that aspiration. How then explain the lag in employing scientific technique fullscale melioristically?

Here we should note how even liberal theologians among the various religions stand in the way of scientific takeover. They look on science as just one more means toward the realization of fixed, separate traditional ends. There is an inability to disengage from the classic view of ends antecedently existing in a perfect world. Therefore everything else (including science) becomes a means merely among countless others, all already prefinished and merely awaiting use. Clearly this view offers no realistic answer as to how one is supposed to discover the "right" ones among all these various means.

Furthermore, religious pluralities effect divisions among men and their endeavors, divisions which clearly retard sorely needed improvements. It is understandable then how an energetic naturalist, surveying this sorry scene, desires the abolition of all beliefs in the supernatural. At the same time he wishes to retain the fervor on the part of all for the ideals they all share in common: bettering the human condition. The melioristic consequences would be incalculable should people really turn a single eye toward science, man and the earth. With the dismissal of the supernatural would also come a truly "common faith" for the first time in human history.

> *I cannot understand how any realization of the democratic ideal as a vital, moral and spiritual ideal in human affairs is possible without surrender of the conception of the basic division to which supernatural Christianity is committed. Whether or no we are, save in some metaphorical sense, all brothers, we are at least in the same boat traversing the same turbulent ocean. The potential religious significance of this fact is infinite.*[65]

We should now ask what "good" and "evil" could possibly mean in this context? If fixed and settled beings, whether in this world or in another, are banished permanently from man's consciousness, and no preset model of goodness is allowed in the picture, how does meliorism get started? *Meliorism* means improving, bettering. Now "better" derives, as a comparative, from "good." If "goods" are not antecedently existing, how do you jump to the "better?"

The answer revolves on that phrase "not antecedently existing." Obviously to *better* something is to suppose *that* something as originally *good* and expand it whether intensively or extensively. There is no difficulty here. Men *do* experience immediate goods and bads, regardless of whether these can be defined with philosophical nicety or not by those undergoing them. But it is only a misguided academicism which would insist on a clear definition of "good" and "evil" beforehand to know that what one experiences as bad is indeed bad and vice versa. In experience goods and bads are directly had and udergone. In reflective experience they are moved into the larger context, *meliorated*. The "bad" (i.e. the problem) is bettered (i.e. solved). They are not antecedent therefore in the way of being already defined as good or bad before experience, at least not in the way some rationalists and idealists sometimes love to catalogue the do's and dont's, the goods and bads of life.

> ...*what I have tried to show is that the ideal itself has its roots in natural conditions; it emerges when imagination idealizes existence by laying hold of possibilities offered to thought and action. There are values, goods actually realized upon a natural basis---the goods of human association, of art and knowledge. The idealizing imagination seizes upon the most precious things found in the climacteric moments of experience and projects them. We need no external criterion and guarantee for their goodness. They are had, they exist as good, and out of them we frame our ideal ends.*[66]

As for "evil," it is a negative concept. It is simply what in experience we find ourselves wishing were otherwise.

> *The significance of ideal ends, meanings is, indeed, closely connected with the fact that there are in life all sorts of things that are evil to us because we would have them otherwise. Were existing conditions wholly good, the notion of possibilities to be realized would never emerge.*[67]

Genuine religiousness is thus dedication to melioristic ideals, no more, no less. Why indeed linger on pre-scientific attitudes with its bias for separate knowledges of separate realities? Already we have come to the point where liberal clergymen today themselves look to what Dewey calls the life of "intelligence" to improve the lot of mankind.[68]

> *But if it be once admitted that human relations are charged with values that are religious in function, why not rest the case upon what is verifiable and concentrate thought and energy upon its full realization?*[69]

> *The values of natural human intercourse and mutual dependence are open and public, capable of verification by the methods through which all natural facts are established. By means of the same experimental*

159

method, they are capable of expansion. Why not concentrate upon nurturing and extending them? Unless we take this step, the idea of two realms of spiritual values is only a softened version of the old dualism between the secular and the spiritual, the profane and the religious.[70]

Gone then ought to be the classic belief in a Supernatural Being who exists as all perfect beforehand and whose power will save mankind. Such a negative attitude tends to foster a "pessimistic" belief in the corruption and impotency of natural means themselves to do the job of saving mankind.[71] It encourages the far too optimistic idea in "conversion and in the objective efficacy of prayer, too easy a way out of difficulties."[72] Dewey would replace this with his brand of scientistic optimism.[73] Then we would have a melioristic interaction between our ever improving ideals and the conditions from which they spring, and also between the generations of men as they succeed one another.[74] The good impulses which already exist in human beings are grounds for continually growing optimism.[75] "Ideals change as they are applied to existent conditions. The process endures and advances the life of humanity."[76] In this view we have an integration of all man's powers, funded experiences and religious attitudes under the unifying instrumentality of science.[77]

Dewey notes how his characterization of the reflective life as inclusive of the scientific method, philosophical criticism and even *feeling* as "intelligence"---all in unfied interaction with the concrete environment and without connection to anything "supernatural"---is quite different from what the classical writers termed "reason." "Intelligence" can even include *passion* for social improvement in its meaning.

There is such a thing as passionate intelligence, as ardor in behalf of light shining into the murky places of social existence, and as zeal for its refreshing and purifying effect.[78]

We have by now grasped enough of Dewey's philosophy to see how his rejection of any separations whether in the world, or in man, or in man-within-nature; and his constant emphasis on unity in all those areas conclude to the unity also between ethics and all of man's activities, between the empirical *is* and the moral *ought*. His Meliorism makes all philosophy a part of morals as contrasted to the separation advocated by older views.

In the next and final chapter we shall survey the high points of Dewey's own lectures in ethics which he taught in his younger years. As we shall see his main ideas stayed with him to the end of his life. But it will help to hear him, as it were, *teach* ethics systematically. As we do so, however, it will help immensely to keep in mind the rich concept of GROWTH which we can extract from the preceding pages as the encapsulation of Dewey's philosophy and/or ethics. In the next and last chapter of this part, the same thrust of thought will again be evident. Always, in pleading for the adoption of science and reflection, Dewey advocates an advance out of small, restricted separately compartmentalized knowledges, social classes, religious bodies, philosophies of man and nature, etc., toward the broad, harmonious larger picture. This is what science and reflection do: move toward the larger picture. Science does this by removing the notion of authentic knowledge away from an elitist class toward *public verification*. His method calls on nothing less than the whole human race itself to cooperate by active participation in experiments or at any rate in constructive hypothesizing. If scientific procedures are conducted secretly, as they often are these days, this is extrinsic to the nature of scientific procedure as such and can be attributed only to national motives. Science is of its nature *open* knowledge. The scientific mind is ever alert to the possibility that there may be other and better ways of viewing reality than the ones presently obtaining, ways that anyone could, at least in theory, discover and which everyone, upon its discovery, can verify. Both quantitatively and qualitatively, therefore, in terms of increasing information, the Deweyite concept of GROWTH springs directly out of the scientific method.

Through reflection, too, the larger picture is attained. For to reflect is to pause, to take a step back, as it were, from the immediately confining pressures of a situation so as to see it in "context," in the larger picture, indeed the "scheme of things entire," as the ancient Stoics loved to say---as far as it may reasonably be demanded of mere human minds to grasp the whole. The difference can be briefly illustrated in the case of being angry. If I step back and reflect on my anger, immediately I cool off as I view myself in context, in the larger picture. In Dewey such habits of reflection go hand-in-hand with GROWTH, a person's contant reassessment of what he is and whether he should continue to be that or change directions.

Finally, both the scientific method and reflection may be seen as leading up the idea of *democratization*. Knowledge is democratized when, in addition to science, those who existentially feel a problem in their flesh and bones are called upon to solve it, to develop the political art of consensus, the virtuous habit of balancing out the conflicting desires of selfish individualism toward the larger demands of society's well-being from which the individual, as a member, also profits. Needless to say, there is always the other dimension of constantly appraising whether the group consensus is in fact for the betterment of all. Here Dewey's optimism in his procedure is based on the fact that experience is a good teacher. Satisfactions as well as the "cries of the wounded," to use W. James' phrase, are there to pass judgement on ongoing programs of action.

Perhaps the only area where one may forcefully object to Dewey's preoccupation with the larger picture is that of religion. Why, if indeed he is for the larger picture, did he rule out the transcendent dimension of the Supernatural in man? Why did he restrict himself only to nature? Is this not in fact to look at the smaller non-transcendent picture? A good objection, but Dewey's answer can perhaps be gathered from what we have seen in the previous chapters. He would retort that the Supernatural is too confining. It breaks people and their loyalties up into separate competing religions with all the terrible results we see in history. Dewey wrote before the contemporary spirit of ecumenism. So, the reader will have to judge for himself whether ecumenism today supersedes the contention that religions always divide. What is not in dispute is that we, as fellow-humans are in the same perilous sea of life together. We have common needs and troubles which we can the more easily solve and conquer if we have loyalty to one another. This is the common faith Dewey sets up as the ideal. It is an ideal with its roots spread out in living growth deep in the soil of experience, science and communal reflection. It is also the merging point of the *ought* and the *is* too long held apart by philosophers before Dewey.

In the final section of this book we will take this matter up again at greater length. There we will point out that religious persons like Mother Teresa today, for instance, may perhaps be living critiques of those philosophers who believe that time spent by "contemplatives" in the direction of the Supernatural is time lost for the betterment of the world here and now. If a person works day and night to help alleviate the sufferings of others, the poor in this world; and if that same person tells us that she and her fellow-sisters get their energy from a few hours of "prayer" each day, then has not the Supernatural broadened such persons instead of confining them? Has not religion then brought people together in the warmth of their common humanity instead of dividing them?

In reply Dewey could say that this is all true but that it evades the point he is making. What he is questioning is, first of all, their *method* in arriving at their "knowledge" of the Supernatural. Once that method is accepted as valid, then the separation of the various knowledges necessarily follow. Once that is established, there is invariably a tendency to classify these knowledges into "higher" and "lower" according to the "perfection" of their objects. What follows from that is the corresponding human attitudes to both the practitioners and the objects of such stratified knowledges. And so on. These are separations Dewey cannot accept. Nor will it do to say such knowledges are not stratified statically but rather they enjoy a dynamic interdependence. Some order of priority and subalternation will eventually have to be set. And who, in his right mind, will subordinate the already Perfect to the one striving toward that perfection?

Second, Dewey has insurmountable difficulty with regard to that idea of an already finished, perfect and immutable Being. Invariably those who believe in such a Being also identify man's final end or destiny with that Being. How can this be compatible with our experience of ourselves as having to change our ends or goals in life whenever circumstances and reflection demand it? How can we avoid looking on everything else "below" that Perfect Being as merely a means for reaching that already perfect world? True, a stout believer, more often than not, also has ready answers against Dewey here. But if the truth be told, are not theologians today, even the most liberal of them, still laboring on this Immutability-mutability complex of questions? Dewey would probably pre-judge it all as a case of wanting to eat one's cake and have it too.

5

THEORY OF THE
MORAL LIFE

Against Kant

Dewey devotes a section of this book to an explicit criticism of Kant's ethics. He notes how in Kant the meaning of the moral *good* is subordinated to that of what is *right*. This means "the concept of good and evil must not be determined before the moral law, but only after it and by means of it."[1] Now it seems true that the mutual interchangeability of morality, freedom and its laws, reason and pure practical will, in Kant, makes the categorical imperative *the* defining principle of the moral good. Too, Dewey notes how in Kant "the moral good is not only different from the natural goods which man experiences in the regular course of living but is *opposed* to them."[2] Here Dewey's accuracy can be questioned, since we saw how Kant himself talked of inclinations as sometimes generating actions in conformity with duty and mixing themselves into the motivation of what otherwise would be a moral act. However, this does not necessarily render the act "immoral," though that motivational mixture does take the act out of the area of morality. We recall how the relation between Kant's moral will and the inclinations was not one of *intrinsic opposition*. What we can say is that moral obligation or constraint in Kant, *whenever it is in fact experienced*, opposes any private exclusively self-centered individualistic interest of the subject, which for the most part arises from inclinations. Dewey interprets this point in Kant to mean that "morality is a struggle just because men in their native make-up and capacity naturally seek to satisfy their desires, while their higher nature imposes a complete check on this tendency."[3]

Thus for Kant no two-sided resolution of the struggle between reason and inclination, whenever the struggle does occur, is possible. Morality, to be itself, must completely cut off any interest the pathological mob of inclinations may clamor for. This, Dewey objects, is impossible. Why? Because any realistic resolution would necessarily have to be mixed, an integration of both reason and desire (interest). For:

> *No idea or object could operate as an end and become a purpose unless it were connected with some need; otherwise it would be a mere idea without any moving and impelling power.*[4]

We need only recall Dewey's inflexible rejection of all sorts of separation perpetrated by pure thought or reason to understand his reaction here. Dewey considers fictitious Kant's pure reason which produces moral acts purely for the sake of the law in hygienic isolation from any of the lower influences of the sense appetites. Having been somewhat of a Hegelian in his youth, Dewey knew well how to combine opposites and subject both to the higher synthesis of reflective thought with a view to action. He uses this method consistently in all his writings. He thus could not accept the Kantian separation of moral reason from inclinations. Instead he combines both the longer-ranged and the shorter-ranged interests of both reason and inclinations, respectively, as equal components of moral action. Anything less than this unity would be a departure from the reality of human action as it actually happens in experience.

The same difficulty obtains against Kant from the standpoint of *consequences*. Dewey thinks that there is an opposition in Kant between will (motive) and consequences. Hence Kant could locate the morality of an act totally in the motive.[5]

> On the one side stand those who, like Kant, say that results actually attained are of no importance morally speaking...only the will can be good or bad in the moral sense. On the other side are those who, like Bentham, say that morality consists in producing consequences which contribute to the general welfare, and that motives do not count at all save as they happen to influence consequences one way or the other.[6]

Dewey will have none of this either/or. As is his wont he synthesises both: consequences and motives.

> Our analysis shows that both views are one-sided. At whichever end we begin we find ourselves intellectually compelled to consider the other end. We are dealing not with two different things, but with two poles of the same thing.[7]

We can recall how Kant always *imaginatively rehearsed* the consequences of a universalized act and in fact held this "typic" to be unavoidable in our human makeup. Yet, finally, it was not those consequences which were decisive for either the morality or immorality of an act. The dutiful act must be done regardless of consequences. The question is, can the inseparable, namely, motive and consequences, be separated as Kant would have them? Unless we put consequences into the very essence of a moral act, it is impossible to explain how the particular event we call the moral act issues out of pure reason by itself.

> Ignoring technicalities in the Kantian theory, the difficulty is this: when all regard for consequences and for all ends which desire sets before us is excluded, what concrete material is left to be included within the idea of duty? Putting the question in its precise form, how shall a man go from the mere idea of duty in general to that of some particular act or mode of conduct as dutiful?[8]

Kant answered that pure reason by itself, with its universalizability idea, is able to effect particular actions which appear in the sensible world of nature. But Dewey insists that the universalizability idea, realistically speaking, contains consequences after all, though under the guise of generality.

> But this method, instead of excluding all reference to consequences is but a way of securing impartial and general consideration of consequences. It does not say: Ignore consequences...It says: Consider as widely as possible the consequences of acting in this way; imagine the results if you and others always acted upon such a purpose as you are tempted to make your end, and see whether you would then be willing to stand by it.[9]
>
> When it is recognized that 'motive' is but an abbreviated name for the attitude and predisposition toward ends which is embodied in action, all ground for making a sharp separation between motive and intention---foresight of consequence, falls away.[10]

Dewey then goes on to say how foresight of consequences is inevitably controlled by the kind of character a person has. What aspects of consequences will be highlighted in one's moral calculation, and what deemphasized will obviously depend on the kind of person making those considerations.

> Othello and Iago foresee different consequences because they have different kinds of characters.[11]

Finally, Dewey's objections find support in a consideration of the second and third formulations of Kant's categorical imperative. There we are commanded to treat every human person never as a means only but always as an end in itself, within a kingdom of ends. This in effect says that the idea of what is good for me cannot be simply equated with what is morally Right except by referring that idea as good also for every rational being. Now this may not appear at first sight to be the same as the idea of consequences, but really it is. In stopping to reflect whether the deed I am about to do is good not only for me individually but also socially for everybody else, I have already shifted my consideration away from myself alone to the "impartial and general consideration of consequences." I have already widened "the area of consequences to be taken into account in forming ends and deciding what is Good."[12]

Counter Consideration

From these objections to Kant, we can make three points. One, in all moral consideration there is a shift of outlook away from the individual self toward the impartial and general consideration of consequences. It is in this shift of focus that Dewey locates the essence of moral thinking. The phrase "wider consideration of consequences" refers to society, to other persons surrounding the moral agent. These persons necessarily enter into the agent's consideration in two ways and from two directions: one, prospectively, as those who will in some way be affected by the results of his action: two, retrospectively, as those who in countless ways through the prevalent mores of a society, through the socialization process, language, etc. etc. have in some way shaped our "stable and formed character," our *conduct*. It is as impossible to put our conduct aside, when making moral considerations and assessments, as it is to prescind from ourselves as the source of thought itself. Our conduct is in a real sense *ourselves*. In stands decisively at the center of our moral condierations, indeed of our whole lives: "...*potentially*, conduct is one hundred percent of our conscious life."[13] What consequences we deem desirable or not then will depend in a significant measure on the quality of our conduct. All this is merely another way of stating that one cannot really leave out consequences from moral consideration.

Secondly, Dewey insists that the pure universality of reason by itself has to mix in with appetitive needs and actual impulses in a person in order to issue forth as a particular event in the real world. The pure reason, which can be traced back to Descartes' "I think" (cut off, supposedly, from all the senses during the exercise of the "universal doubt"), is a fiction. Very few today hold such a "ghost in a machine" theory of man. The truth is that we, as organisms, do not ever find ourselves in an actionless state even when we do pause to consider what action to undertake. Rather, we are always acting in one way or another every moment of our existence. Reason then does not create action. It merely redirects them according to its more comprehensive vision. Of course, reflective thought needs to sort its way *through* principles, not only those which happen in fact to govern our values for the moment but also those which *ought* to govern our action. How does this moral reflection come about? How does it ever get started seeing men are already in action from the first moment they are born?

Just as all thinking starts with a question or problem, as we saw, so too moral thinking arises from the concrete experience of moral conflict. It may help to recall here a point we heard Kant make, namely, "I ought" means "I can." No one is obliged to what is impossible. Yet when we have two conflicting moral obligations imposed upon us, we seem to be precisely in the predicament of having two contradictory actions, an impossibility. Clearly, in such a situation only one obligation is real, the other must be merely apparent. But which is which? In this puzzlement, reflective moral thought is born. To settle the issue we begin to search for the foundational principles which not merely govern the actual obligations that are supposedly exerting claims, but for the principles which *should, ought to* give birth to genuine obligation. This is necessary because of the socialization processes we have all undergone. Dewey quotes Greek thought about our parents and teachers constantly admonishing us, "pointing out that one act is just - another unjust; one honorable and another dishonorable; one holy - another unholy. When a youth emerges from parental tutelage, the State takes up the task for the community compels them to learn laws and to live after the pattern of the laws and not according to their own fancies."[14]

This socialization process begets "customary morality." To maintain and preserve such a morality an elite is formed, in the exact same way we saw earlier an elite being formed for the preservation of tradition. No one in the beginning escapes customary morality. Later, one could escape it but only through the instrumentality of reflective moral thinking. Reflection puts customary morality in question. It searches for the principles behind and beneath customs so as to hold them up for reevaluation.

Moral theory cannot emerge when there is positive belief as to what is right and what is wrong, for then there is no occasion for reflection. It emerges when men are confronted with situations in which different desires promise opposed goods and in which incompatible courses of actions seem to be morally justified...For what is called moral theory is but a more conscious and systematic raising of the question which occupies the mind of any one who in the face of moral conflict and doubt seeks a way out through reflection. In short, moral theory is but an extension of what is involved in all reflective morality.[15]

Now we should distinguish the experience of moral conflict which starts the process of reflective morality from mere rationalization. A banker, for example, who wants to embezzle funds and "reflects" on the situation only to argue himself into doing what he already wants and has decided to do "is not really thinking but merely permitting his desire to govern his beliefs."[16] It is otherwise with a conscientious objector who in time of war is drafted and obliged by his country to enter combat.

He is torn between two duties; he experiences a conflict between the incompatible values presented to him by his habits of citizenship and by his rebellious beliefs respectively. Up to this time he has never experienced a struggle between the two; they have coincided and reinforced one another. Now he has to make a choice between competing moral loyalties and convictions...He is forced to reflect in order to come to a decision. Moral theory is a generalized extension of the kind of thinking in which he now engages.[17]

All through the process of puzzling one's way through a moral confict, it is clear that thought or reason functions *in connection with*, not separation from, the situation of need. This is so because thought here is constituted precisely by the interest or need of the moment, not by a comparison of mere ideas.

Thirdly, Dewey's reflective moralist, once shocked into thought by the experience of conflicting duties, necessarily takes consequences into consideration, i.e., "wider consequences." This distinguishes the selfish narrow view of one who merely follows his impulses from that of a reflective person. Whereas Kant was constantly searching for the uncondi-tin behind the conditioned, the ground that makes our experiences possible, Dewey is well content to talk simply of reason seeking the larger more comprehensive view, the possibility of replacing customary morality with perhaps someting better. Reflective morality never arrives at any set of moral obligations which holds true for all men for all times---a view possible only on the classic bias that the natures or essences of man and things in nature are fixed and unchanging. Rather, a reflective man not only focuses on the principles which govern the currently prevailing moral beliefs. He also is ready to question whether those same principles should continue to prevail or be replaced by new ones.

> *(This kind of appoach) does not offer a table of commandments in a catechism in which answers are as definite as are the questions which are asked. It can render personal choice more intelligent, but it cannot take the place of personal decision, which must be made in every case of moral perplexity...the attempt to set up ready-made conclusions contradicts the very nature of reflective morality.[18]*

The work then of ethical theory is never finished. Its conclusions are never permanent answers binding on all ages for all time which men must either conform to or use as absolutes for deducing specific answers to puzzling situations. It is not as if thought is disconnected from the situation and connected instead to an abstract absolute from which a solution is to be deduced. The call for constant reflection comes from its concrete genesis in experience.

> *Realization that the need for reflective morality and for moral theory grows out of conflict between ends, responsibilities, rights and duties defines the service which moral theory may render.[19]*

We can see then how any set of prevailing morals arises from either (1) conceptions of the ends of man; or, (2) man's duties, rights and responsibilities; or, (3) obedience to actually prevailing mores as what is good (virtue), and disobedience to them as evil (vice).

> *Roughly speaking, theories will be found to vary primarily because some of them attach chief importance to purposes and ends, leading to the concept of the Good as ultimate; while some others are impressed by the importance of law and regulation, leading up to the supremacy of the concepts of* Duty *and the* Right; *while a third set regards approbation and disapprobation, praise and blame as the primary moral fact, thus terminating with making the concepts of Virtue and Vice central.[20]*

We will now follow Dewey's critique of each of these moral schools in succession. At the same time we will keep an eye on his own doctrine which he interweaves with his critique, and which of course issues out of his whole philosophical outlook, familiar to us by now.

Moral Theory as Centered on Ends

Each organism is in unceasing activity every moment of its existence. Human beings are no exceptions. It is a mistake to think that men first think, *and then* set about to satisfy their desires. Prior to reflection and to any sort of thought, men are already acting out the satisfactions of their various desires for "food, a companion, money, fame and repute, health, distinction among their fellows, power, the love of friends, the admiration of rivals, etc."[21] Now, whatever objects a man tends to, he tends to only because "value is attributed to them; because they are thought to be good."[22] But initially these goods are not objects of thought and reflection (recall our earlier mention of "casual" vs. "reflective" values). It happens that men are often brought up short on objects they automatically appropriated but which now have turned out to be ashes in their mouths, so to speak.[23] It is then that reflective consciousness emerges to ask: what objects are *really worth* striving for?

To ask that question is already to have the insight or wisdom to see that not all goods anticipated by our desires are in fact desi*rable*. We thus have two meanings of "desirable." One, any objects of our actual desires are by that very fact desirable. In this sense the word contains no moral elements in it, despite John Stuart Mill's insistence on the opposite in his famous text where he in effect gave the charter to the utilitarian theory in ethics.

> *The only proof capable of being given that an object is visible is that people actually see it. The only proof that a sound is audible is that people hear it; and so of the other sources of our experience. In like manner, I apprehend, the sole evidence it is possible to produce that anything is desirable is that people do actually desire it. If the end which the utilitarian doctrine proposes to itself were not, in theory and practice, acknowledged to be an end, nothing could ever convince any person that it was so. No reason can be given why the general happiness is desirable, except that each person, as far as he believes it to be attainable, desires his own happiness. This, however, being a fact, we have not only all the proof which the case admits of, but all which it is possible to require, that happiness is a good, that each person's happiness is a good to that person, and the general happiness, therefore, a good to the aggregate of all persons.*[24]

The other sense of "desirable" comes when the experience of conflicting goods is undergone so that one has to ask which good is really and truly desirable, i.e., which objects *ought* men to desire? Dewey replies: "That which in the eye of impartial thought *should* be desired."[25] And what is that?

With that question reflection is underway in its search for principles that will answer to the situation. It is this second sense of "desirable" which is properly the ethical one. Correspondingly we have two sorts of values or objects of desire: those accepted prereflectively, and those accepted only *after* deliberate consideration of the differences between short and long range consequences as well as the differences in the quality of various satisfactions. This is saying that in human experience there are "specious" and "real" goods: goods men move to in animal-like fashion without conscious choice, and goods men move to precisely as men, that is, with due deliberation and choice, with recognition of them as truly desirable. It is this distinction between the actually desired and the ideally desirable which defines the difference between customary morality when no longer subjected to reflection, and the reflective morality which Dewey espouses.

Recall how every organism is in constant action, satisfying its many needs one way or another, though without thought. However, this is not altogether an accurate way of putting it. Human needs and desires have a certain regularity and pattern to them. They are not a hopeless tangle of unrelated acts, each a totally unique event. If this latter were so, no one could survive under the chaos of claims we would make upon one another, claims for the most part unsatisfiable because of their utter unpredictability. No, we do recognize patterns in our desires, and slowly, through time and experience, we evolve ways of coping with them in the most efficient and effective way possible. These ways of coping will naturally vary from one setting to another depending on the resources available, both human and natural. For instance, the ways people evolve for coping with hunger in a highly industrialized level are quite different from the ways hungry people provide for themselves in underdeveloped countries. People in a technological level eat from refrigerators, while those in the underdeveloped countries of the tropics, for instance, eat salted and sun-dried fish and meat. Human ingenuity finds ways of regularizing ways of coping with its recurrent needs. Repetition, through long stretches of time and through generations, solidifies into that what the poor man Tevya, in *Fiddler on the Roof*, approvingly calls "tradition."

> *A fiddler on the roof...sounds crazy, eh? But here in our little village of Anatemka, you might say that every one is a fiddler on the roof trying to scratch out a simple pleasant tune without breaking his neck. It isn't easy. You might say, why do you stay if it is so dangerous? Well, we stay because it is our home. And how do we keep our balance? That I can tell you in one word: Tradition!*

It is into this hardbound state of doing things that each one of us comes at birth, and which each of us inescapably internalizes in the process of growing up. Without tradition for protection, a human infant is sure to "break his neck" and die. If we are around today, it is certainly because from our infancy onward we have submitted (first passively, then cooperatively) to the ways of coping with natural forces which our elders before us had themselves internalized. Our beings thus are woven in with those of others around us. We become part and parcel of the whole social fabric.

> *The human being is an individual because of and in relation with others. Otherwise, he is an individual only as a stick of wood is, namely, as spatially and numerically separate.[26]*

> *The idea that individuals are born separate and isolated and are brought into society only thru some artificial devise is a pure myth. Social ties and connections are as natural and inevitable as are*

physical. Even when a person is alone he thinks with language that is derived from association with others.[27]

Clearly then, thought is at the origin of traditions. Its intent is positive: to enable us to deal with the dangers to life posed by the hostile forces of nature to our particular "village" where we stay because it is our "home." Hence we can appreciate why anyone in a community who defies and despises its traditions, especially if young, is execrated as an ingrate or worse.

If time stood still and things simply never changed from the day of our birth to the day we die, it would probably be true that our lives would be passed in their entire length in a kind of zombie-like state of routine without the intervention of any social questioning, defiance or novelty. That is the danger in traditions. Through routine it can make deadwood out of human imagination. It can reduce what originally was a thoughtful movement toward objects of desire, to animallike unthinking actions. Reflective thought soon disappears where no conflict of duties, nor perhaps even of the goods of desire, occurs.

Fortunately, time does *not* stand still. Things change. People change. There is a constant cycle. People change their environments. In turn, changed environments change people in little ways often hardly noticeable; i.e., "additively." Changes, no matter how infinitesimal, become cumulative through generations. New ideas appear. New inventions produce new tools which again produce other inventions. And so on. Even the Stone-Age people in Mindanao, Philippines, are discovered one day and brought into interaction with the world of canvass tents, clothes, blankets, canned goods, firearms, cameras, etc. While outwardly they may seem to go on unchanged in their ways in the midst of strangers using all these strange instruments, the dawn of new ideas in their minds is inescapable. By that very fact they have already been altered, no matter how imperceptibly for the moment. Gone forever are their days of original innocence.

So too, invariably, there comes a day in every Anatemka of the world when some brainy fellow questions heretofore blindly accepted traditions. Needless to say, the community's perception of his loyalty to them, and the depth and extent of his criticism, will arouse proportionate reaction in the community. But the questions will be posed. Once posed and reacted upon, it is an illusion to think the community remains unchanged no matter how this may seem so outwardly. Changes have been effected, we can bet on it, in the consciousness of traditional innocence. Now the question arises whether it is *really good* to keep on surviving merely according to the ways of the past in the light of alternatives. Can things be improved? Can they be *bettered*? What's the sense of making tradition an end in itself when its very nature is instrumental? Traditions are for life; the "good life." If new ways and new tools can achieve a better life, why not use them?

To these questions, communities usually react on the side of tradition. Institutional ways become so deeply internalized that it becomes impossible to abandon them merely on the say-so of some social innovator. Indeed for quite a few tradition becomes an ultimate. To put it in question is, to their minds, equivalent to betrayal or treason. On the other hand, there will always be some open-minded members in the same community whose desire will be that the path of inquiry and dialogue be not blocked; that cool reflection be exercised on the new proposals. Probably too there will be a spectrum of emotional reactions in between these two extremes of being completely closed or open. At any rate, it is out of such a conflict situation that the search for the moral standards or principles which lie underneath traditions begins. It is now necessary to bring them out into the daylight of public dialogue so that their usefulness can be assessed. Of course, reflective study and discussion can be painful and cumbersome. At times more heat than light is generated.

> *Deliberation and inquiry take time; they demand delay, the deferring of immediate action. Craving does not look beyond the moment, but it is of the very nature of thought to look forward to a remote end.*[28]

What should not be lost sight of is that the quest is for goods[29] as against merely apparent goods. By real goods here is not meant unchanging good. We know Dewey's thought too well by now to make that mistake. Rather, we mean goods which are always in growth just as people grow and change. In such changes, goods really good for one time and situation may turn out to be merely apparent ones for other generations, and so on. This is the nature of the moral search when it is conducted in a context of reality as changeable, *not yet in any way* finished, not perfect and therefore unchangeable. What directions growth will take, when it will take place, and what principles to enunciate vis-a-vis various changes and movements, the balance between tradition and innovation---all these cannot be answered beforehand and graven into tables of stone. They can only be arrived at by reflective conscious-ness operating within experience which looks to principles that could enhance growth and make life better.

> *The business of reflection in determining the true good cannot be done once for all, as for instance making out a table of values in a hierarchical order of higher and lower. It needs to be done, and done over and over and over again, in terms of the conditions of concrete situations as they arise. In short, the need for reflection and insight is perpetually recurring.*[30]

However, all this is not to say we are incapable of identifying, at least in general, certain types of goods which enter into the makeup of any genuine human progress.

> *In a general way, of course, we can safely point out that certain goods are ideal in character: those of art, science, culture, interchange of knowledge and ideas, etc. But that is because past experience has shown that they are the* kind *of values which are likely to be approved upon searching reflection. Hence a* presumption *exists in their favor, but in concrete cases only a* presumption.[31]

172

Specifically, what goods are people after? The immediate reply is "pleasure" or "happiness." This now we need to discuss.

It seems true that the end of any human action is pleasure (or to put it negatively, "avoidance of pain.") This certainly seems true of our impulses. Even in the wider context, it seems evident that if a man willingly submits to a momentary deprivation, he does so only in the hope of greater satisfaction or pleasure to come. Why then not simply agree with J.S. Mill that the moral end is the general happiness of all: the greatest amount of pleasure for the greatest number, or negatively the minimum amount of pain for the least number possible?

The matter is more complex than at first appears. We need to distinguish between pleasure and happiness, not simply use them interchangeably. Pleasure looks only to immediate satisfaction, whereas happiness is the result of choosing an end on the larger basis of its *reasonableness*, the attainment of an end which "in the eye of impartial thought *should* be desired;"[32] an end approved "by an impartial and undisturbed spectator" in "a moment of calm reflection."[33] Secondly, Dewey notes the correction J. S. Mill makes on why pleasure, in disregard of reflection, fails as *the* end that men should desire. Pleasure, says Dewey, is so ridden with accidental features beyond anybody's control that it really cannot be brought under the "cool and far-seeing" judgement that is required of any genuinely human goal.

Pleasures are so externally and accidentally connected with the performance of a deed that attempt to foresee them is probably the stupidest course which could be taken in order to secure guidance for action.[34]

There is a remark to startle any hedonist. What does it mean? Cannot one foresee displeasure by accepting an invitation to a party where all one's enemies will be in attendance? Cannot one foresee pleasure by going instead to the other party where all are friends? What basis is there for not trusting the same foresight to deliver pleasure in other settings?

The answer lies in that phrase "accidental connection." There is no intrinsic or essential connection between pleasure and that party of friends, nor between pain with that party of enemies. "There's many a slip between cup and lip." How many parties among friends end up in a sour evening or worse? And, have there not been pleasant surprises in parties among enemies? Of course there are physical settings that are sure to inflict pain. You just do not intrude into a buzz saw. The point we are discussing, however, is the laying out of scenarios where one will be happy. This, startlingly, Dewey calls "perhaps the stupidest course of action." No better reason can be given than the one we already saw in Kant, namely, that we are so changeable ourselves that we really cannot foresee what in a future setting would make us happy. To repeat, look at the copious tears shed in the end over a piece of good luck, "answered prayers," etc. Who knows whether the pleasures of touring that you so excitedly anticipate now as you pack up for the trip are really going to materialize? They could. But then again you could end up "running" (having the "turistas" as they say in Mexico about "Montezuma's revenge") all throughout the trip and wishing to God you had stayed home in the blissful comfort which you found so "boring."

The same could be said of riches, social prestige, etc., things which are usually connoted with pleasures beyond the reach of the poor. Who knows whether they are really right for you? Of course, it's natural to want to try. ("I've been rich, I'm poor. Rich is better.") Well, all other things being equal, "rich" is indeed better. The only trouble is when are "all other things" ever equal? Hardly ever. Things change; you change; other people change. And this brings us back to Dewey's point. There is no way of insuring that you will achieve the pleasures you foresee through all your careful planning. The connection between them is too "accidental" to be completely amenable to such plans. So many things could intervene and do intervene before the hour appointed for the consummation of pleasure. As a policy of life, the pursuit of pleasure is unrealistic.

Moreover, pleasures are relative to the *conduct* of the experiencing subject. No moralist, not even the most hardbitten hedonist, will claim that all pleasures are moral. As the existentialist Albert Camus observed:

> *If we believe in nothing, if nothing has any meaning, and if we can affirm no values whatsoever, then everything is possible and nothing has any importance. There is no pro· or con: the murderer is neither right nor wrong. We are free to stoke the crematory fires or devote ourselves to the care of the lepers. Evil and virtue are mere change or caprice.[35]*

What follows from the fact that Hitler's Nazis found pleasure in throwing innocent human beings into crematory ovens and stoking their fires, while dedicated saints like Mother Teresa today expend their lives in the care of diseased human beings whom everybody else shuns? Dewey notes:

> *There are certain kinds of happiness which the good man enjoys which the evil-minded man does not---but the reverse is true. And this fact is fatal to the theory that pleasures constitute the good because of which a given object is entitled to be the end of action.[36]*

There are, in other words, noble and ignoble conduct with their respectively different kinds of enjoyment. Whatever noble conduct may be, it certainly includes reflective thought within itself. The ensuing state of satisfaction when such a conduct brings forth deeds according to its nature is what Dewey considers "happiness."

Not any old pleasure then, but only those which result from noble conduct and action ought to be termed "happiness." The action and conduct themselves would have other objects as their ends, but the resulting condition of the agent would be a happy one.

> *Happiness is a matter of the qualities of mind and heart with which we greet and interpret situations. Even so it is not directly an end of desire and effort in the sense of an end-in-view purposely sought for, but is the character which is interested in objects that are enduring and intrinsically related to an outgoing and expansive nature.[37]*

174

Descending to details, Dewey quotes from a novel:

> *It is only a poor sort of happiness that could ever come by caring very much about our own narrow pleasures. We can only have the highest happiness, such as goes along with being a great man, by having wide thought and much feeling for the rest of the world as well as for ourselves; and this sort of happiness often brings so much pain with it, that we can only tell it from pain by its being what we would choose before everything else, because our souls see it as good.*[38]

"Alright," a stubborn hedonist might reply, "I'll prescind from all your talk of conduct, happiness, etc., and simply be an Epicurean of the sort who goes for the pleasures of the simple life. I mean pleasures enjoyed by me *now*, simple pleasures available to everyone *now*, without having to wait, save and plan. Therefore, *carpe diem*. Sufficient for the day are the evils thereof; enjoy yourself. Whatever food and drinks are at hand, enjoy them. Stop all those plans." An Epicurean of this type knows that:

> *Pleasures of the appetites, like sex, may be more intense, but they are not so enduring nor so likely to give rise to future occasions of enjoyment as those which come from books, friendships, the fostering of esthetic delight...Enjoyment of sunlight, moving waters, fresh air, is tranquil and easily obtainable. The simple life is the good life because it is the one most assured of present enjoyment.*[39]

The difficulty with this position is that it is a retreat from the world of action in which a man's character is to be forged. It opts for passivity and seclusion. The separation it advocates of the present from the future, and of itself from the rest of the world (all the while living off that world) is impossible.[40] Think of it: only people with means can ultimately afford to talk with such "disinterestedness" at the world around them.

> *It is a doctrine which can appeal only to those who are already advantageously situated. It presupposes that there are others who are doing the hard, rough work of the world, so that the few can live a life of tranquil refinement.*[41]

Hard words those. At the same time, Dewey admits that there is some wisdom in Epicureanism. For it rejects the always "busy" attitude which so engulfs many people that they forget the simple life of contemplation altogether.

We come next to the great American drive for "success." What can we say about it as the end of human life? Well, if by "success' we mean "achievement," then of course it comes within the scope of morality. Any prudent person is concerned about success in his line of work. But we can hardly fail to notice the superficiality of this idea which all too often finds its way into advertisements and slogans.

> *It hardly rises above the mere external aspect of life; it encourages the idea of 'rising,' of 'getting on,' of 'making a go' while it accepts*

without question current estimates of what these things consist in. It does not criticize the scheme of values which happens to be current, say, in an age when men are devoted to pecuniary gain. It encourages conceiving of gain and loss in tangible material terms...It pins its faith to certain values at the expense of others more human and more significant. [42]

Dewey, an all-American philosopher certainly, criticizes this tendency among his fellow Americans toward materialism which grabs "any seeming near-by good."

This state of affairs is characteristic of many phases of American life today. Love of power over others, of display and luxury, of pecuniary wealth, is fostered by our economic regime. Goods that are more ideal, esthetic, intellectual values, those of friendship which is more than a superficial comradeship, are forced into subordination. The need of fostering the reflective and contemplative attitudes of character is therefore the greater. Above all, there is the need to remake social conditions so that they will almost automatically support fuller and more enduring values. [43]

Values therefore more enduring and significant than "external power, repute, making money, and attainment of social status"[44] are to be sought. What are such values? They are what reflective reason must uncover as it goes from situation to situation. They cannot, as we have repeatedly seen, be specified any more than in the general way Dewey does here. Certainly they cannot be written down once for all in "tablets of stone."

If neither pleasure nor success can qualify as *the* objective of life, why not reverse direction and go to the "ascetic" theory? This holds that it is fallacious to submit everything to the inhibiting effect of thought. Rather, one must go directly to action, specifically, to the discipline of all our desires. In support of this point, Dewey quotes John Locke and William James on the importance of developing the habit of disciplining desires in the young.[45] Again there is some wisdom in this position. However, to propose "discipline" as *the* end of life is to fail to see that its negative wisdom has to be for something positive, namely, the enabling of reason and desire both to rise to more enduring, comprehensive and inclusive goods, goods above those of narrow self-centeredness.

And what is the new good? Here Dewey follows John Stuart Mill in holding that:

...a cultivated mind finds sources of inexhaustible interest in all that surrounds it, in the objects of nature, the achievements of art, the imaginations of poetry, the incidents of history, the ways of mankind, past, present and their prospects in the future... [46]
The proper course of action is, then, to multiply occasions for the enjoyment of these ends, to prolong and deepen the experiences connected with them... [47]

However, there has to be a parting of the ways with Mill when he insists on the distinction between "higher" and "lower" pleasures:

*It is better to be a human being dissatisfied than a pig satisfied; better
to be Socrates dissatisfied than a fool satisfied. And if the fool, or the
pig, are of a different opinion, it is because they only know their own
side of the question. The other party to the comparison knows both
sides.*[48]

Dewey corrects Mill.

*There are times when the satisfaction of hunger takes precedence of
other satisfactions; it is at that time ...for the time being...'higher.'
We conclude that the truth contained in Mill's statement is not that
one faculty' is inherently higher than another, but that a satisfaction
which is seen, by reflection based on a large experience, to unify in a
harmonious way his whole system of desires is higher in quality than a
good which is such only in relation to a particular want in
isolation...Mill's argument points not so much to a different quality in
different pleasures, as it does to a difference in quality between an
enduring satisfaction of the whole self and a transient satisfaction of
some isolated element in the self.*[49]

We should note than when Dewey requires reflection as the way to
the moral good, it is always reflection in unity with natural, even material
goods. We know enough of his thought by now to think he would agree to
the separation of the ideal from the natural, of the "cultivated mind" from
merely organic needs. Hence he reinterprets Mill's famous passages so as
to assimilate their meaning into the framework of the reflective morality
he himself (Dewey) espouses. Each of the positions discussed here does
have its truths and its errors. In general their truths will be found
whenever they do unite the ideal and the natural, their errors whenever
they separate the two.

Thus in hedonism, what must be remembered is that present
enjoyment already occurs at the mere thought of a future object.

*A man in order to cultivate good health does not think of the pleasures
it will bring to him; in thinking of the various objects and acts which
will follow from good health he experiences a present enjoyment, and
this enjoyment strengthens his effort to attain it...*[50]

The same is true of "success" as the moral end.

*Error lies in restriction of the domains of value in which achievement
is desirable. It is folly rather than wisdom to include in the concept of
success only tangible material goods and to exclude those of culture,
art, science, sympathetic relations with others. Once a man has
experienced certain kinds of goods in a concrete and intimate way, he
would rather fail in external achievement than forego striving for
them. The zest of endeavor is itself an enjoyment to be fostered, and
life is poor without it.*[51]

177

Finally, in Epicureanism the ideal and the real unite by "nurturing the present enjoyment of things worthwhile, instead of sacrificing present value to an unknown and uncertain future."[52] It goes without saying that the goods under discussion are the "kind of goods reflection approves."[53]

Dewey sums up his thought:

> *Wisdom, or as it is called on the ordinary plane, prudence, sound judgement is the ability to foresee consequences in such a way that we form ends which grow into one another and reinforce one another. Moral folly is the surrender of the greater good for the lesser; it is snatching at one satisfaction in a way which prevents us from having others and which gets us subsequently into trouble and dissatisfaction.*[54]

Or, put more simply:

> *In conclusion, we point out that the discussion enables us to give an empirically verifiable meaning to the conception of* ideal *values in contrast to* material *values. The distinction is one between the good which, when they present themselves to the imagination, are approved by reflection after wide examination of their relations, and the goods which are such only because their wider connections are not looked into.*[55]

The natural impulsion of men toward ends that satisfy their needs and desires gives rise to a morality centered on the concept of the Good. What is *really* good, i.e., which good will really bear reflecting upon? The reference here is to the standpoint of a cool and impartial spectator. The moral "ought" cannot be identified with the quick grab for goods we make on impulse to satisfy our need. We should make room for the refining fires of rational assessment. We see how from this, the idea arose that moral duty has nothing to do with man's object of desires or ends (the Good) in a *teleological* ethics. Rather, moral duty in its essence talks only of what is Right (deontological ethics) of obligation regardless of the various objects of desires, indeed, often in the face of those desires. The attitude typifying this theory is that of a person who believes in doing right simply because it is right, period, all his desires to the contrary notwithstanding. Such an attitude virtually separates the concept of *good* or end-object of desires from that of *right*. Kant immediately comes to mind, and we have already seen Dewey's criticism of him.

We know enough of Dewey by now to see that he would object to any separation of reason from desires in man. His focus is rather on the *whole* self. This necessarily includes the social relationships which are always an essential constituent of any individual, even as an individual.[56] How then can the concept of what is right be separated from that of what is socially good? Even Kant, we now see, was really forced to bring the two together under the rubric of his third formula of the categorical imperative. To do what is right conduces to the good, does it not? However, deontologists perceive correctly that; there is something in the concept of "right" which is not quite encompassed in that of the "good." This we should now try to bring out.

As an idea, "right" introduces an element which is not in that of the good, namely, *exaction, demand*. To say something is good does not necessarily mean it must be striven for. It is only a *possible* object of desire; whereas to say something is right means it is what one *must* do and strive for. This element of exaction or demand calls for some clarification. For why should an act, simply because it is right, impose exaction, a demand on me? Or, as Dewey puts the question in a startling way, "Why not be foolish if I want to be?" To answer means already to repudiate the idea that one is indeed a fool. But more to the point here, to answer one has to explain the nature of moral exaction, demand, claim or obligation---all of them terms for one and the same reality. One also needs to show the connection between the authoritative claim of what is reasonable to what is good.

> *Our discussion will accordingly be directed to showing that it is possible to maintain the distinctness of the concept of right without separating it from the ends and the values which spring from those desires and affections that belong inherently to human nature.*[57]

Moral Claims

Let us say at the outset that a moral claim cannot be based on sheer might. Might is not necessarily right. It is the other way around: "mere compulsion has no moral standing."[58] The exercise of might has to be first of all right, if it is to be moral, i.e., exert a moral claim, in this case its justified application. On the plane of morals (*de jure*) right is prior to might, even though physically and historically (*de facto*) it may happen to be the other way about. Here we have a problem. If moral claim or right is not based on might, on what is it based? Reason? This is much too simplistic an answer. It tends to "split man into two disconnected parts:" reason and whatever else is not reason in man; v.g., inclinations. What then is a moral claim based on?

Whatever that basis may be, it has to be located in actual experience. It must affirm and not negate the unity of man within himself and with his environment.

> *The way out is found by recognizing that the exercise of claims is as natural as anything else in a world in which persons are not isolated from one another but live in constant association and interaction.*[59]

Dewey, in other words, refuses to find the basis for moral claims in anything other than the human person's concrete social relationships. These relationships themselves as they reveal themselves to our understanding provide the basis for claims. They generate the demands we make on one another. They spell out our mutual rights and responsibilities. They generate moral obligations.

Take a college classroom. It is actually a little community. It is unified by one purpose, namely the understanding of a certain subject matter. This is a social enterprise in which there is a teacher and his students. In this relationship, the teacher has to be heard. This in turn calls for some silence on the part of the students. The teacher, thus exercising his function, lays a claim on the class. This is a claim based not on reason alone, nor even less on physical superiority, nor from some teacherly psychological compulsion to be heard. Quite simply the claim arises out of the classroom situation itself. Reversely, this very same social relationship between teacher and student both bent on learning, also demands that the teacher listen whenever students are explaining their own intellectual apprehensions. For that too is part of the relationship. The same analysis will yield similar conclusions as regards the demands friends make on one another, parents make on their children and vice versa, citizens on the state and vice versa, etc. etc.

> The Romans spoke of duties as offices. It is as a parent, not just as an isolated idnividual, that a man or woman imposes obligation on children; these grow out of the office or function the parent sustains, not out of mere personal will.[60]

We have here a realistic account of how obligations in fact arise from actual situations to their generalized expressions in books and codes of law, rights, obligations and responsibilities.

> If we generalize such instances, we reach the conclusion that Right, law, duty arise from the relations which human beings intimately sustain to one another, and that their authoritative force springs from the very nature of the relation that binds people together.[61]

A moral claim then is not based, as other theories would have it, on the will of God, nor on the will of the State, nor on the fixed and unchanging nature of things including man, etc.; nor can it be based on reward and punishment which would only be another way of saying that might makes right. And certainly it cannot be based on individual hedonism.

The fact that social relationships themselves form the basis of moral claims means that the natural evolution of human affairs moves toward institutionalizing whatever moral claims are in fact already prevalent in societies. Hence our books of laws. We cannot simply leave the hundreds of different sort of claims in all our various levels of relationships dangling, so to speak, in an informal state. The recurring needs of daily life compel men to spell out their claims on one another explicitly for the effective functioning of society.

Thus *law* is necessary to every social structure. But any given particular *law* is not necessary, at least not in the same way as Law in general. That is, society cannot be lawless. But the particular laws which are in fact promulgated can be so promulgated only on the basis of actually existing social conditions, needs and relationships. Hence these *particular* laws always call for periodic scrutiny and reassessment to make sure they do indeed continue to conduce to what Law is supposed to effect, namely, the carrying forward of the common goal agreed to by the members of that community. That again is merely another way of affirming the relationships among the members already in existence.

> *Law is necessary because men are born and live in social relationships; a law is always questionable, for it is but a social means of realizing the function of law in general, namely, the institution of those relations among men which conduce to the welfare and freedom of all.*[62]

The same can be said of Right, which is only another word for claims and demands.

> *...while Right in general has an independent status because of social claims which attend human relations, any particular claim is open to examination and criticism.*[63]

Constant reflective vigil over particular laws must be kept because the institutionalizing of laws tend to make certain individuals more powerful than the great majority of society. Once in power, they tend to equate their views with what is *right*. Why? Dewey's reply is as enlightening as it is perceptive.

> *It is difficult for a person in a place of authoritative power to avoid supposing that what he wants is right as long as he has the power to enforce his demand. And even with the best will in the world, he is likely to be isolated from the real needs of others, and the perils of ignorance are added to those of selfishness. History reveals the tendency to confusion of private privilege with official status.*[64]

Another way of looking at rights or moral claims is to see them simply as the *shared good* of everybody involved in a given relationship, both those on whom a claim is being exercised and those exercising the claim. Hence the invocation of any particular moral claim should be subjected to this reflective criterion of *shared good* to test its validity.

> *Does the conduct alleged to be obligatory, alleged to have the authority of moral law behind it, actually contribute to a good in which the one from whom an act is demanded will share?*[65]

An act which goes against a shared good at the very same time that the doer profits from that shared good cannot have moral justification on its side. It would be wrong, publicly wrong, and not wrong merely because of "private conscience."

> *A man would not steal if there were no value placed on property; even a thief resents having what he has stolen taken from him. If there were no such thing as good faith, there could be no fraud; otherwise there*

would be nothing beneficial to him in violating these ties. Wrong consists in faithlessness to that upon which the wrongdoer counts when judging and seeking what is good to him.[66]

The criterion of *shared good* then shows how laws protecting property and forbidding perjury are true laws. Their violators seek to profit from these laws even as they violate them. In every case of wrongdoing what is supposed to be a bilateral good is subverted toward private gain at the same time that the private gain itself invokes protection for itself on the basis of the bilateral good it unbalanced in the first place. Needless to say it is not always easy to unravel the skeins of relationship which support a moral claim in any given particular situation, any more than it was easy to apply Kant's test of universalizability.

The points of this chapter can now be summarized in three topic sentences.

(1) There is a school of thought in moral studies which identifies morality not with the concept of the Good directly (teleological), but rather with the concept of what is Right (which inhibits desire). This concept of the Right as having priority to all else has given rise to a deontological ethics of Law, Duty, Loyalty to Principles, which relates to the good only indirectly.

(2) The basis for Right (which is the same thing as a moral claim or justification for a demand) is not an abstract principle but rather the concrete social relationships themselves which go into the very being and definition of any human individual. These are relationships which in various ways and from countless aspects frame themselves within the context of a *shared good* among those encompassed by the claim.

(3) It is the task of reflective morality therefore to, a) temper the tendency to isolate Duty from its concrete matrix and set it up in abstract isolation, as is done by those with attitudes like "Duty for duty's sake; and b) to guard the concept or Right from those who because they possess the resources to carry out their views automatically identify "right" with their own views. *Law* is a social necessity, but particular laws need to be constantly checked out as to their validity, usefulness or non-usefulness, as times change and people with them.

Approbation, The Standard And Virtue

We shift now from the concept of morality as centered on satisfaction of desires (the Good or teleological ethics), or their inhibition in the name of what is Right (deontological ethics) to the concept of morality as what men intuitively approve, and of immorality as what they "naturally" disapprove.

Every child willy-nilly internalizes the attitudes prevalent in his infancy. With those internalizations also come the equation of what is good with what pleases the elders, and of bad as what displeases them. Any observant parent can verify this point many times in the course of a day. Should a precocious child for instance ask at this stage why such and such acts are encouraged and others discouraged, this act allowed and that forbidden, the reply probably more often than not is, "that's the way it is;" "that's how the ball bounces' and the cookie crumbles;" or worse, that one-word non-sensible reply, "Because!," an answer meant to block any further inquiry. For the unreflective individual virtue thus is equated with what is socially accepted, vice with the socially unaccepted; good with what is praised, evil with what is blamed.

> In customary morality, acts and traits of character are not esteemed because they are virtuous; rather they are virtuous because they are supported by social approval and admiration.[67]

One then does not praise an act because it is virtuous, but the other way about. It is conceived as virtuous because it is praised. It is conceived as vicious because it is blamed. We have here a morality of "conventionality," of "respectability." It is so interwoven with our own consciousnesses as we grow up that we hardly ever detect its presence in us. Those who protest most vigorously to be free of any taint of such conventionalism are not infrequently those deeply affected by them. Conventional morality is everywhere. For no one escapes the protective embrace of tradition. Indeed,

> Customary morals naturally 'make it hot' for those who transgress its code, and make it comfortable for those who conform.[68]

But men are reflective beings. They can transcend their present limits of thought. No society thus can be immune to the appearance of the moral rebel who questions its conventional judgements of right and wrong. Why is this act good simply because others say so? Why is this act evil simply on the say-so of my elders? Why do the elders say what they say anyway? What is their basis? Ought we not lay bare such bases for traditions so reflective examination can see whether indeed they characterize acts correctly as either praise*worthy* or blame*worthy*? These are the sorts of questions a reflective individual is bound to ask. Implicit in them are two meanings of the word "to judge."

To "judge" can refer either to the factual judgements a society makes unreflectively when it simply repeats the readymade convictions of its traditions. Or, to "judge" can mean a philosophically reflective assessment of the principles underlying tradition as to their moral validity.

> In respect to knowledge, the word (judge) has an intellectual sense. To judge is to weigh the pros and cons in thought and decide according to the balance of the evidence. But in human relations, it has a definitely practical meaning. To "judge" is to condemn, approve, praise, or blame. Such judgements are practical reactions, not coldly intellectual propositions...Reflective morality notes the inconsistency and arbitrary variations in popular expressions of esteem and disapproval, and seeks to discover a rational principle by which they will be justified and rendered coherent.[69]

Dewey is wont to characterize reason as "cool, impartial, disinterested, comprehensive" etc., in contrast to the impulsive desires which are characterized by opposing adjectives, such as "narrow, selfish" etc. Cool reason is said to be the primary tool of reflective morality.

The very idea of a standard is intellectual; it implies something universally applicable.[70]

But reason is not in pure seclusion as in Kant. Rather, reason is taken in its overall inclusion and unity with everything in man that is not reason, and with all the concrete relationships which converge toward the making of a individual. What then does reflective morality do with conventional morality? Two things. (1) It seeks out and clarifies the moral standard that *ought* to generate social approval or disapproval. (2) It seeks to clarify the true nature of virtue.

1. *Moral Standards.* By "standard" is here meant "the principle upon which the assignment of praise and blame rationally rests." It is what makes practical judgement possible. Standards can be of two sorts: a) those which *actually* (*de facto*) control moral conventions already formed here now; b) those which should, *ought to* (*de jure*) govern those conventions. Obviously it is impossible to study each and every social morality existing in the world. Hence Dewey concentrates only on the characteristically "English" moral theory and takes it as a prototype of conventional morality.

In English moral theorizing, the manifestation of commendation and condemnation, and their influence upon the formation of character, are for the first time made central (just as End in Greek, and Duty in Roman philosophy). [71] Dewey points to Shaftesbury's moral sense intuition, strictly comparable to "good taste" in esthetic matters; to Hume's "what pleases on the general view;" and to Adam Smith's "what satisfies the 'impartial spectator' as variants of the same conventional morality typical of English thought. The difficulties with these theories are that they are (1) too narrow, rarely extending beyond those near us; (2) superficial, taking note only of short-ranged and spectacularly striking consequences; (3) they ecnourage habitual acceptance of established laws and institutions unmindful of their beneficial and/or hurtful consequences.

To remedy these three defects, utilitarianism comes in with its emphasis on the welfare of everyone as the desirable consequence. It demands an expansive view in which every human person is to be taken seriously as counting for one.

But the utilitarian theory, in addition to its insistence upon taking into consideration the widest, most general range of consequences, insists that in estimating consequences in the way of help, harm, pleasure and suffering, each one shall count as one irrespective of distinctions of birth, sex, race, social status, economic and political position.[72]

To this early Benthamite version of utilitarianism, J.S. Mill had added the corrective of qualitative to a purely quantitative measure of happiness, "a wider, if vaguer, idea of well being, welfare, as the proper standard of approval." Earlier Dewey had objected to Mill's idea of "higher" and "lower" satisfactions in man, as though man were compartmentalized into different faculties, when in fact "higher" and "lower" needs were really interchangeable according to the prevailing needs of the organism. Dewey now admits, however, that Mill was certainly correct in drawing attention away from consequences by themselves to the *sources* themselves of pleasure and pain. For the condition, quality and development of these sources (the human doers) certainly are essentially determinative of those almost unmanageable terms, "pleasure" and "pain."

> *Mill accordingly brought utilitarianism in closer accord with the unbiased moral sense of mankind when he said that 'to do as you would be done by and to love your neighbor as yourself, constitute the ideal perfection of utilitarian morality.' For such a statement puts disposition, character, first and calculation of specific results second... Emphasis upon personal disposition also appears in Mill's desire to see certain attitudes cultivated in and for themselves...Intrinsically, and by our very makeup, apart from any calculation, we prize friendly relations with others...In other words, Mill saw that a weakness of Bentham's theory lay in his supposing that the factors which make up disposition are of value only as moving us to special acts which produce pleasure; to Mill they have a worth of their own as* direct *sources and ingredients of happiness.*[73]

To Dewey it seems apparent that Mill had correctly surrendered (though never quite explicitly) the "untenable" hedonistic element in utilitatianism. Untenable because "pleasure" and "pain" as resultant states are not really aimed at directly---not to mention how the ongoing processes of reality keep transforming pleasure and pain into each other in a seemingly unending chain. In its place Mill had installed the notion of welfare "widespread and impartially measured."

> *This revised version recognizes the great part played by factors internal to the self in creating a worthy happiness, while it also provides a standard for the moral appraisal of laws and institutions.*[74]

All this shows that to reflective morality not merely what is appro*ved*, (*de facto*) but what is approva*ble* (*de jure*) should really constitute the moral standard. In the concrete, that standard is the widest possible welfare or happiness for the greatest number in the context of a "shared good" such as we have explained it. This is the essential objective of LAW, the provision of conditions conducive to everyone's working out his happiness. For happiness is a very individual matter, as we nave learned well from Kant.[75] And welfare can be assessed in its generality, away from the necessarily constricted view of individual interest, only if the standpoint is disengaged from the interested individual and then idealized impartially.

> *An ideal spectator is projected and the doer of the act looks at his proposed act through the eyes of this impartial and far-seeing objective judge.*[76]

We should bear in mind, however, that this seeking of the standard which ought to prevail (as preferable to mere conformity to conventional morality) is not meant to effect a separate respect for a standard by itself in isolation from the ends of action. This would bring us back to a "duty for duty's sake" morality. Rather, the ideal standard here which constantly brings all factual standard to the test is intimately intertwined with ends and/or desires. They are two poles of one reality. Desire assesses itself through reflection.

> *Desire points to a definite and concrete object at which to aim. After this end has occurred to the mind, it is examined and tested from another point of view: Would the action which achieves it further the well-being of all concerned?*[77]

The words "for all concerned" are significant. The standard approved by reflective morality does not say the happiness of most should be had at the painful expense of the ones producing it. That would be a wrong way of phrasing it, just as it would be wrong to defend conduct which makes others suffer simply because it "yields happiness to the one who injures others."[78] What is required is that both standard and individual ends merge in the one reality of a chosen action...when an individual does deliberately choose and approve objects which harmoniously produce goods for others also, not only for himself. Even if such a sort of happiness may be less than it could have been otherwise in a narrower and selfish context, it has this invaluable characteristic, namely, that it is the *only* moral sort of happiness that could approve itself and pass the searching test of the moral standard.

> *By personal choice among the ends suggested by desires of objects which are in agreement with the needs of social relations, an individual achieves a* kind *of happiness which is harmonious with the happiness of others. This is the only sense in which there is an equation between personal and general happiness. But it is also the only sense which is morally required.*[79]

To understand this intertwining of the ends of desire and the standards of moral approbation is also to undersand that justice, if it is to function effectively in morals, cannot have a meaning separated from the concrete consequences which make for the harmonized welfare of all.

> *The meaning of justice in concrete cases is something to be determined by seeing what consequences will bring about human welfare in a fair and even way...To put ourselves in place of another, to see things from the standpoint of his aims and values, to humble our estimate of our own pretensions to the level they assume in the eyes of an impartial observer, is the surest way to appreciate what justice demands in concrete cases.*[80]

2. *Virtues.* People are interested in human virtues "since no community could endure in which there were not, say, fair-dealing, public spirit,

regard for life, faithfulness to others" etc. Customary morality has no difficulty drawing up its lists of virtues as though they were truly many, and as though it were possible to cultivate them single and separately. But can a person be, for instance, really publicspirited if he is devoid of the spirit of fairdealing? Can we trust one who is faithless to others to have due regard for life? Are the virtues really many in atomic isolation from one another? Or are they more like fruits in one tree nourished by one common root?

Unity of Virtues

Reflective morality holds that virtues at their root can never be more than one. Virtue is the *wholehearted, singleminded, persistent, impartial and enduring interest a person has of acting according to the moral standard which intelligence approves as the Right End to strive for.* In that definition desires, standard and reflection are combined, all three of them. And since we are familiar by now with Dewey's aversion for separation and his preference for unification, it will suffice to quote two of his texts on why virtue has to be persistent and impartial here.

> *Hence the interest which constitutes a disposition virtuous must be continuous and* persistent. *One swallow does not make a summer nor a passing right interest, no matter how strong, constitute a virtue. Fair weather 'virtue' has a bad name because it indicates lack of stability. It demands character to stick it out when conditions are adverse, as they are when there is danger of incurring the ill-will of others, or when it requires more than ordinary energy to overcome obstacles. The* vitality *of interest in what is reflectively approved is attested by persistence under unfavorable conditions.*[81]

Without reflection interest tends to restrict itself only to the well-being of one's self, family and friends. Only a character made strong by reflective convictions can rise above these partisan and divisive limits to the desirable level of impartial universality where the moral norm of the *shared good* is extended to all men simply because they are that, human persons. On the other hand, we must be realistic.

> *Complete universality of interest is, of course, impossible in the sense of equality of strength or force of quantity; that is, it would be mere pretense to suppose that one can be as* much *interested in those at a distance with whom one has little contact as in those with whom one is in constant communication. But equity or impartiality or interest is a matter of quality not of quantity as inequity is not a matter of more or less, but of using uneven measures of judgement. Equity demands that* when *one has to act in relation to others, no matter whether friends or strangers, fellow citizens or foreigners, one should have an equal and even measure of value as far as the interests of the others come into the*

reckoning. In an immediate or emotional sense it is not possible to love our enemies as we love our friends. But the maxim to love our enemies as we love ourselves signifies that in our conduct we should take into account their interests at the same rate of estimate as we rate our own.[82]

Moreover discussions on virtue usually go into the nature of love or friendship. Various traditions must be intuiting something sound here. In one way or another they express the proverbial insight that "love is the fulfillment of the law." They point to love or charity as either the living root whence come all virtues, or else the crowning point of them all in which they meet in architectonic unity.

> *For in its ethical sense, love signifies completeness of devotion to the objects esteemed good. Such an interest, or love, is marked by temperance because a comprehensive interest demands a harmony which can be attained only by subordination of particular impulses and passions. It involves courage because an active and genuine interest nerves us to meet and overcome the obstacles which stand in the way of its realization. It includes wisdom or thoughtfulness because sympathy, concern for the welfare of all consideration, for examination of a proposed line of conduct in all its bearings. And such a complete interest is the only way in which justice can be assured. For it includes as part of itself impartial concern for all conditions which affect the common welfare, be they specific acts, laws, economic arrangements, political institutions, or whatever.[83]*

The upshot of all this then is that:

> *...virtuous traits interpenetrate one another; this unity is involved in the very idea of integrity of character. At one time persistence and endurance in the face of obstacles is the most prominent feature; then the attitude is the excellence called courage. At another time, the trait of impartiality and equity is uppermost, and we call it justice. At other times, the necessity for subordinating immediate satisfaction of a strong appetite or desire to a comprehensive good is the conspicuous feature. Then the disposition is denominated temperance, self-control. When the prominent phase is the need for thoughtfulness, for consecutive and persistent attention, in order that these other qualities may function, the interest receives the name of moral wisdom, insight, conscientiousness. In each case the difference is one of emphasis only.[84]*

In a word, the virtuous life is the life of moral excellence. It is the life in which reflective thought embodies itself, with its moral norm of the *shared good*, within the concrete human desires and interests. In a tradition which goes back to St. Thomas Aquinas,[85] and before him to Aristotle and Plato, the virtues (habitually good human dispositions) have been reduced to four. They come under the heading of *cardinal* virtues, from the Latin *cardo*, a hinge or pivot, since various other virtues pivot or revolve on them. They are usually listed as *prudence*, which seeks out the *mean* between what is excessive and deficient in a line of human action, and then points out the right means towards right ends; *temperance*, which moderates or controls our appetites for food, drink and sex; *courage* or fortitude, which pushes on, without giving up in a chosen line of virtuous conduct despite great dangers and toil (sometimes in what Aristotle would call a maganimous manner when one would rather die than betray others or lose honor); *justice*, which is the social virtue of giving to each human person his due.[86]

Here we can recall Aristotle's celebrated text on "unselfish" love as the high point of human nobility.

> *It is true of the good man too that he does many acts for the sake of his friends and country, and if necessary dies for them; for he will throw away both wealth and honours and in general the goods that are the objects of competition, gaining for himself nobility, since he would prefer a short period of intense pleasure to a long one of mild enjoyment, a twelve month of noble life to many years of humdrum existence, and one great and noble action to many trivial ones. Now those who die for others doubtless attain this result; it is therefore a great prize that they choose for themselves. They will throw away wealth too on condition that their friends will gain more; for while a man's friend gains wealth, he himself achieves nobility. He is therefore assigning the greater good to himself. The same is true of honor and office. All these things he will sacrifice for his friend.*[87]

Given Dewey's polemic against any existence of a Perfect Being, or any other world than that of experience, we can see why there is no treatment of the theological virtues of faith, hope and charity. He has, however, reinterpreted the unity of virtues according to his theme here of reflective morality. The virtues are many, let us repeat, only in emphasis. At base, they all come down to the same reality: persistent excellence in the moral life.

Moral Judgements

We come now to conscience: the ultimate source of a person's moral judgement. Conscience clearly involves thought on moral matters. The question is "how is it related to experience?" Is conscience an intuitive faculty independent of experience? Or, "is it a product and expression of experience?"[88]

If conscience were independent of experience, it would indeed be ultimate and there could no appeal from a community's moral judgements as stored in its traditions. For any appeal would itself be a moral matter. As such it would be forced back on the intuition of conscience for judgement, the selfsame intuition which produced it in the first place. If intuition were independent of experience, then judgements it once made it will make again. No appeal to changing times and experiences could effect any difference. On the other hand, if we go along with the theme of Dewey's reflective morality, we should see that conscience is located at the very heart of experience as its searcher of motives and assessor of far-ranging and inclusive ends. No domain of human activity, no matter how banal or prosaic, is alien to it. All the stuff which goes into our everyday lives is grist for the mill of conscience. For experience grows nowhere else except in the concrete and actual web of relationships in the family, neighborhood, community, etc...all sorts of communities which go to make the fabric of any human individual.

Judgements of conscience are *value* judgements, not judgements of fact. Now we make value judgements in all aspect of our lives, from art objects to weather, to credit rating, to our states of health, to the statements of others (scientific or otherwise) when we characterize them "true" or "false," etc.,[89] whereas on judgements of fact, we are usually careful to defer to experts in their given fields of specialization. It is a point Descartes had indicated when he made his famous remark at the start of his *Discourse on Method* that "good sense is of all things in the world the most equally distributed," and which Kant had reaffirmed when he observed, as we saw earlier, how in social gatherings and parties, moral debate is the stample of conversation, the one way people love to entertain themselves.

> *Those who otherwise find everything which is subtle and minute in theoretical questions dry and vexing soon take part when it is a question of the moral import of a good or bad act that is recounted; and they are exacting, meticulous, and subtle in excogitating everything which lessens or even casts suspicion on the purity of purpose and thus on the degree of virtue to an extent we do not expect of them on any other subject of speculation.*[90]

A distinction is necessary as regards value-judgements. It is one thing to judge *factually*, and quite another to judge *valuationally*. In the former we deal with an emotional and practical act; in the latter with an act that is continuous with reflective thought. We should make the same distinction between "esteem" and "estimation," between "prizing" and "appraising." The distinction really comes down to that of reflex spontaneity and reflective intellectuality. Dewey of course opts for the latter, but always inclusively of the former. Things after all can be distinct from one another without being separate. Thus all the paired expressions above are intertwined as judged and judging in the process of moral growth.

> *We esteem before we estimate, and estimation comes in to consider whether and to what extent something is worthy of esteem. Is the object one which we should admire? Should we really prize it? Does it have the qualities which justify our holding it dear? All growth in maturity is attended with this change from a spontaneous to a reflective and critical attitude.*[91]

The difference between spontaneous or reflex action (v.g. toward an object or end of desire) and reflective thought consists in the latter moving beyond mere spontaneity to a consideration of *relations*, of the chain of consequences and their desirability under the norm of maximum inclusiveness and enduring satisfaction (the Good). An illustration would be a person who, after careful consideration, submits to the extreme pains of a radical surgery (which he would spontaneously reject) to save his life. Here we see how a constructive view of ends is essential to a reflective conscience.

Secondly, while we distinguish conscience from merely spontaneous intuition, we should also bear in mind that accumulated experiences in moral matters become a fund, as it were, from which one can draw for his purposes, often with the ease and rapidity of intuition, Funded experience, especially among the old as Aristotle had noted long ago, can take on the characteristics of intuition even while in fact it issues out of reflective judgement. But we must be careful here. Everyone, as we said, is born into this world in helpless submission to the all-engulfing tutelage of elders in whom reflective judgement (presupposing it was indeed exercised) has often regressed to customary morality. Invariably, these elders impress their ideas of good and evil upon the child with dogmatic certainty. "Extreme intuitionism and extreme conservatism often go together,"[92] an attitude chronically averse to change. For change entails the pain of "ungrooving" from deepset habits.

We have already stressed how traditions, including customary morality, are not lightly to be dismissed. People do not evolve ways of coping with the business of life senselessly. Hence Dewey is careful to *presume*, at the start of moral reflection, correctness in favor of tradition.[93] They can serve well as "guides and clews" for reflective judgement. But reflection has to be on the alert vis-a-vis tradition in a world of change. For tradition all too easily hardens into narrowness and bias, to inordinate attachment to its own objects. This in turn gives rise to *ipse dixitism* (literally, he himself says so). Needless to say, the reflective person can see that it is not right to say an act is moral simply because "that's the way we do it around here."

If reflective morality concedes a presumption in favor of tradition at the start, how does it get started? Recall how thought does not start off except with problems. Moral thought arises only within a situation of moral conflict. How then does thought penetrate tradition so as to reconstruct and guide it toward new ends required by changed times? What ignites moral conflict? *Sensitive feelings*, says Dewey. Sensitive feelings for

> ...*an idea of the object which is admired or despised; there must be some perceived cause or person that is cared for, and that solicits concern.* Emotional *reactions form the chief materials of our knowledge of ourselves and of others. Just as ideas of physical objects are constituted out of sensory material, so those of persons are framed out of emotional and affectionate materials.*[94]

Indeed this is how revolutions themselves get started. Such movements are not set off by mere abstractions. Rather, they are always charged with emotional valuations springing from sensitiveness, not toward a selfish object, but toward what is perceived as a worthy cause, so worthy that it is perceived as one with their agents and their deeds. This emotional, sensitive and unselfish beginning of reflective thought, as it arises amidst the conflicting demands of tradition and innovation, is akin to the sentiment of *sympathy* and generosity, or to aesthetic feeling, as we heard Kant say. Like Kant, Dewey is eloquent on this point.

> *It is sympathy which saves consideration of consequences from degenerating into mere calculation, by rendering vivid the interests of others and urging us to give them the same weight as those which touch our honor, purse and power. To put ourselves in the place of others, to see things from the standpoint of their purposes and values, to humble, contrariwise, our own pretensions and claims till they reach the level they would assume in the eye of an impartial sympathetic observer, is the surest way to attain objectivity of moral knowledge.[95]*

In this kind of sympathy we can see the fusion of intelligence with emotions and impulses, not their separation.

> *In this fusion there is a broad and objective survey of all desires and projects because there is an expanded personality. Through sympathy the cold calculation of utilitarianism and the formal law of Kant are transported into vital and moving realities.[96]*

In this perspective, "self-control" (Latin, *temperantia*; Greek, *sophrosune*) is the *effect* of a comprehensive and reflective estimation rather than its *cause* though the two are intertwined. We can understand this better by thinking of the Greek ideal of the beautiful and the good (*Kalokagathia*)...obviously an aesthetic ideal. Artists are controlled by their vision of the beautiful and the good. So too in morals. Our vision of what is truly desirable influences our behaviour. It takes an artist to see beauty in subtle art, just as it takes a moral man in the first place to be "a judge of what is truly good" as Aristotle had noted. However, in such an admittedly good man reflective reason must prevail. For like the rest of mortals, he too does not escape the hazards of rigidifying customary morality into absolute stansards.

Genuine moral deliberation or "conscientiousness" then is not a scrupulous comparison of an act to a permanent set of laws so as to judge whether conformity has been achieved or not. Rather:

> *The truly conscientious person not only uses a standard in judging, but is on the outlook for something better...is concerned to revise and improve his standard...He is on the lookout for good not already achieved.[97]*

With this statement we finally join this treatise explicitly to our earlier section on "meliorism." It is a doctrine which always calls for looking beyond goods already achieved to other new goods more comprehensive than the present which are within the instrumental capabilities of human beings in a changing world to achieve. Meliorism is a sort of *idealism*, i.e., one which ever reaches beyond goods already achieved to goods desirably achievable after critical reflection. However, as we saw in Dewey's criticism of the American obsession for "success," the question here is less about acquiring or possessing goods and accumulating material possessions, and more about character and conduct formation, about *being* rather than *having*.

I once heard a student equate Dewey's thought with the well-known DuPont slogan: "Better things for better living through chemistry." The reader of the following passage should see how that is not quite fair to Dewey.

> *(Moral) deliberation involves doubt, hesitation, the need of making up one's mind, of arriving at a decisive choice. The choice at stake in a moral deliberation or valuation is the worth of this and that kind of character and disposition. Deliberation is not then to be identified with calculation, or a quasi-mathematical reckoning of profit and loss. Such calculation assumes that the nature of the self does not enter into the question, but only how much the self is going to* get *of this and that. Moral deliberation does not deal with quantity of value, but with quality.*[98]

Moral deliberation consists of an *imaginative* (as opposed to actual) experimentation or "rehearsal" of the various courses of conduct open to the agent who asks: "which one will produce better results according to the standards of reflective morality."[99] Again the distinction here is between reflective and customary morality. We distinguish between a moral principle which is intellectually evolved out of experience and is thus open to the demands of changing experiences and changing times versus "rules" which are ready made, prefixed and permanent. Obviously Dewey opts for the principle rather than the rule. We should note how abstract notions, v.g. of justice, give us no specifics on how to act *here and now* in these very precise and particular circumstances of an actual situation...the only ones, after all, we are called to act in. Even the moral theoretician who has to decide what moral theory to espouse is making a very specific and particularized existential and situational decision. All moral decisions are like that. Hence, if we are to reach specifics, we must opt for principles rather than rules.

The choice is between rigid, absolute, conformistic and customary morality and a morality based on intelligent reflection upon experiences in a changing world of intensifying socialization processes, in an age of technology and mass media. The former magnifies the letter of the law at the expense of the spirit. It tends to reduce morality, which by nature must be constructive and creative in a moving world, to mere legalism. Thus it deprives the moral life of freedom. It conceives morality not as loyalty to ideals, but as conformity to commands which as intuitive need no defense or justification. Principles relate constructively to specifics, while rules yield the kind of specifics which may be characterized as wooden conformity, much like a scrupulous cook going meticulously by "cooking recipes."

> *The fundamental error of the intuitionalist is that he is on the outlook for rules which will of themselves tell against just what course of action to pursue;* whereas the object of moral principles is to supply standpoints and methods which will enable the individual to make for himself an analysis of the elements of good and evil in the particular situation in which he finds himself. *No genuine moral principle prescribes a specific course of action.*[100]

Or put another way:

> *Rules are practical; they are habitual ways of doing things. But principles are intellectual; they are the final methods used in judging suggested courses of action...A moral principle, then, is not a command to act or forbear acting in a given way;* it is a tool *for analyzing a special situation, the right or wrong being determined by the situation in its entirety, and not by the rule as such.*[101]

Moral conformism is on the side of rule morality, while constructive reflective morality is on the side of principles. This says that there really are no realms of human endeavor which can be set aside as exclusively the moral realm over against other areas of human life. Rather, everything in life can be brought within the realm of morals "whenever they are discovered to have a bearing on the common good." Such a scientistic universalism separates itself once and for all from Kantian ethics and all ethicians who in one way or another insist on the separation of science from ethics, of the *is* from the *ought.*

> *Probably the great need of the present time is that the traditional barriers between scientific and moral knowledge be broken down, so that there will be organized and consecutive endeavor to use all available scientific knowledge for humane and social ends.*[102]

While this text is a loose enough way of speaking so as to allow even Dewey's philosophical opponents to subscribe to it without giving up their own contrary positions, we know that Dewey does not mean merely the use of science for ends already spelled out beforehand, but rather the assimilation and refashioning of those ends themselves within science. Conformistic customary morality disagrees. It prefers to separate science from sets of permanent moral values. It holds that some areas of human life, like scientific experimentation, are simply other than the moral sphere where absolutes, whether based on tradition, moral intuitionism, the will of God or whatever, prevail. Such separation must be rejected. Everything in human experience, both tradition and innovation, should be submitted to the constructive judgement of reflective morality as it periodically identifies, isolates, clarifies and even promotes the ideal common good.

> *Where will regulation come from if we surrender familiar and traditionally prized values as our directive standards? Very largely from the findings of the natural sciences.*

194

For moralists usually draw a sharp line between the field of the natural sciences and the conduct that is regarded as moral. But a moral that frames its judgemetns of value on the basis of consequences must depend in a most intimate manner upon the conclusions of science.[103]

Does all this come down to moral relativism? Yes. Does it follow that moral obligations are not real since it is based on a universe constantly at flux? No. For the moral obligation toward the common good reflective morality concludes to in any given situation is *really binding only for that situation and for that society.* Not necessarily binding *forever,* but still truly binding at that precise moment and situation. To go beyond this to absolutes is to fall victim to the classic contemplative view. To settle for less reveals a lack of intelligence.

It is stupid to suppose that this signifies that all moral principles are so relative to a particular state of society that they have no binding force in any social condition. The obligation is to discover what principles are relevant to our own social state. Since this social condition is a fact, the principles which are related to it are real and significant, even though they be not adapted to some other set and style of social institutions, culture and scientific knowledge.[104]

We can now see Dewey's and Kant's ethics standing in stark contrast to one another. We might well ask then what implications and practical corrolaries may be drawn from this sort of relativistic ethics.

The Moral Self

At stake in the moral life is the quality of *self* which a person achieves. Ethics does not compile an informative and factual catalogue of men's actions whether in the past or in the future. It deals not with what men do in fact desire, but with what actions they *ought* to desire, what they ought to hold up to themselves as their *ideals.* Here the danger is that of making the actions and ideals which men do choose appear as though they were *separate* from their selves.

Of course there is a sense in which ideals and actions, which have not yet taken place and are merely contemplated or "imaginatively rehearsed," are not yet a part of the self. One *is* actual, the other one *is not* yet. But to disconnect ideals and action from the existing self altogether so as to really think of the self as merely *having* ideals is wrong. It would lead logically to the position that when we act according to those ideals, the resulting actions which we deliberately choose for ourselves become merely our possessions, some things we *have.* And surely our moral choices are not possessions that we *have.* They are rather expressions of our very being, our genuine selves such as we have chosen, formed, and shaped them. For the human self is not something finished, delivered automatically by nature. That is evident. Unlike subhumans, a person

195

does not achieve a self simply by maturing physically,. This sort of mere physical maturation, if ever it happened in a normal human being, would still carry an authentically human imprint, namely, the *decision*, expressed or not, of the person not to take pains to shape himself by any further choices. Choices thus constitute the core of the human self. And the ideals as well as the actions a given self chooses clearly correlates in the most intimate fashion to this self. The relation is one of continuity. Action and ideals are nothing more than outpourings, expressions of the self that actually exist and constitute the base for action.

For just think: would dedicated Marxists internalize the ideal of a theistic world such as Pope Paul VI or any other dedicated Pope would identify as his reason for existence? When a Marxist and a theistic missionary like Mother Teresa do the same deed objectively such as caring for the poor of the world, the acts though seemingly identical from an objective standpoint (whatever objectivity may be) are quite different. In one it is a theistic expression and witness. In the other, it is the opposite. The selves in operation are opposite because all along the line they have formed their selves precisely into the kinds they are through choices. These choices in turn were greatly influenced (not mechanically determined) by their already existing selves which were intensified through being affirmed in deeds.

> But every choice is at the forking of the roads, and the path chosen shuts off certain opportunities and opens others. Consequently, it is proper to say that in choosing this object rather than that, one is in reality choosing what kind of person or self one is going to be. Superficially, the deliberation which terminates in choice is concerned with weighing values of particular ends. Below the surface, it is a process of discovering what sort of being a person most wants to become.[105]

This is a key point in morals missed by many ethicians. The self in whatever quality of being it has moved itself to is integral with both the deeds which issue from it and with the pleasures, if any, which accompany the deeds. Recall a point made earlier, namely, that any organism is always in action. "Choices" are not creations issuing out of nothing, but rather redirections, rechannellings of activities and energies already in operation.

> It is not too much to say that the key to a correct theory of morality is recognition of the essential unity of the self and its acts, if the latter have any moral significance; while errors in theory arise as soon as the self and acts (and their consequences) are separated from each other, and moral worth is attributed to one more than to the other.[106]

We can look at this point by approaching it from another angle. It certainly seems more correct to say that we see the world according to the kind of *beings* we are, rather than according to what objects we may or may not *have*, Marx and his followers to the contrary notwithstanding. *being* cannot altogether be identical with *having*. Now man's being is

196

continuous with his free acts. If a man with possessions values them beyond anything else in this world, then that is the kind of being he is. If a poor man knows in his wisdom that external possessions are certainly not what constitutes a man's true worth, and that thus it is folly for him to work day and night in order to amass earthly goods, this decision is an expression of his deepest self. His free choices reveal the ideals which are in him. We are dealing then with a person's *being*, his *self*, his free choices, his ideals all as one unit *without any separations*, whenever we talk of a man's moral self, his true self. To grasp the point even better, we might look at how this unity might be disrupted.

Recall how Kant severed the realm of freedom, where the moral self resides, from the consequences of an act---certainly in the sense of those consequences being the determining factors for the morality or immorality of an act. There the realm of the true self, the free self, is in that of pure practical reason, a reality other than that of the man's action in the empirical world. We thus have a will or a self closed in on itself and perfecting itself essentially through its own pure acts of willing, actions and events in the empirical world be what they may. This Dewey rejects. "For goodness and badness could, on this theory, be attributed to the self apart from the results of its dispositions when the latter are put into operation."[107]

In the utilitarian theory also we have a reverse kind of separation, that of the consequences from the self. True, J. S. Mill had insisted that the quality of the self correspondingly qualifies the kind of pleasures a person enjoys, but the emphasis here was still essentially on the *consequences themselves* as still the determining and decisive factors of morality. The quality of the self functions only as a *means* toward those consequences which were the real *ends* of action. There was a manifest demarcation between the two. It is this sort of disruption and separation which Dewey decries in the idea of a moral self.

> The opposed point of view (to Kant and those who make virtue their end) is found in the hedonism of the earlier utilitarians when they assert that a certain kind of consequences, pleasure, is the only good end and that the self and its qualities are mere means for producing these consequences.[108]

How then are the self, end, ideals, free choice and a person's resulting action united?

> There is a circular arrangement. The self is not a mere means to producing consequences because the consequences, when of a moral kind, enter into the formation of the self and the self enters into them. To use a somewhat mechanical analogy, bricks are means to building a house, but they are not mere means because they compose a part of the house itself; if being a part of the house then reacted to modify the nature of the bricks themselves the analogy would be quite adequate.[109]

197

Clearly then a man's self does extend or express itself in his choices and ideals. Those ideals and choices themselves as they are successively realized within the self in turn modify that self. And so in "a circular arrangement" toward future choices. We can now turn to some implications of this position on the actual unity of a person's self and his actions.

We should first get rid of the notion that motives to action are external to the agent as if this latter were completely passive and then aroused by those outside motives. This makes motives like alien forces to any organism. To repeat, a human person is the matrix of unceasing and multiple activities at every moment of its existence. "The organism moves, reaches, handles, pulls, pounds, tears, molds, crumples, looks, listerns" etc.[110] Motives therefore do not move man from not-acting to acting. Rather they redirect, channel toward new directions, actions already in operation. This point is significant especially when we come to the perennial debate in ethics on selfishness and altruism, a debate that has been called "the crux of moral speculation," as Herbert Spencer put it.[111] Somehow all moral doctrines, no matter how disparate among themselves, seem to agree on the point that the unselfish act is the moral act, and the narrow and exclusively selfish act the immoral. Dewey's reflective morality which always looks melioristically at every situation would certainly subscribe to this notion of "altruism." Now what is "selfishness?" Since we cannot really call a man "selfish" when his motive is clearly unselfish, it is clear that our clarification must revolve on the meaning of "motive."

Is motive some force external to the self which then ignites action in an otherwise actionless self? This we have seen is erroneous. Motive is really the movement of a person's whole being, such as he has already shaped it and endowed it with the quality it is, toward a class of objects called for accordingly by his needs because of the kind of being he is. The need may be purely an organic one. On this level, it is manifestly absurd to attribute "selfishness" to some actions which do not even enter the realm of motivation of free choice. Thus for a hungry man to reach out for food, or for a tired young lad to dive for a vacated seat on the bus ahead of a weaker, elderly lady, is perhaps simply a direct movement of the organism toward satisfaction, without any choice coming into play. If we call this selfish at all, it would have to be only in a roundabout way, namely, by pointing out that free choice *should*, *ought* to have come into play. This shows that the central meaning of "selfishness" involves free choice *positively*. In our example, we would say that habitual inconsiderateness for elderly people in a young person could not have become habitual without a choice coming in somewhere along the line of either sticking to such inconsiderateness or not even bothering to think about correcting it. Either way the choice is positive. Only with such antecedents may we call those sorts of apparently spontaneous acts "selfish." When, however, such positive free choice *does* come into play, we should keep the unity of the self with its actions. Thus we should not conceive a politician who accepts a bribe to vote for an unjust bill as though he were being moved by an alien force from the outside. If he accepts the bribe and acts on it, it is because that acceptance and that unjust action is integral with the self he already is, to wit, one who puts more value on bribes, on narrow self interest than on justice and a shared common good.

> *The case is no different when we say that a man is moved by kindness, or mercy, or cruelty, or malice. These things are not independent powers which stir to action. They are designations of the kind of active union or integration which exists between the self and a class of objects. It is the man himself in his very self who is malicious or kindly and these adjectives signify that the self is so constituted as to act in certain ways towards certain objects. Benevolence or cruelty is not something a man has, as he may have dollars in his pocket-book; it is something which he is; and since his being is active, these qualities are modes of activity, not forces which produce action.[112]*

It is wrong thus to characterize an act which an organism does merely mechanically as "selfish." For that a free choice which produces a self that is insensitive to others' claims and obsessed only with one's own self-satisfaction as one's ideal in life is necessary. Instead of unselfishness and altruism then, it is better to chatacterize a moral act as "disinterested." For "an act is not wrong because it advances the well-being of the self, but because it is unfair, inconsiderate, in respect to the rights, just claims of others."[113]

> *In short the essence of the whole distinction between selfishness and unselfishness lies in what sort of object the self is interested. 'Disinterested' action doeas not signify uninterested...the only intelligible meaning that can be given to disinterested is that interest is intellectually fair, impartial, counting the same thing as of the same value whether it affects my welfare or that of someone else...About the only general proposition which can be laid down is that the principle of equity and fairness should rule.[114]*

Nor is it necessary that this "disinterestedness" be always explicit in a moral man's consciousness as he acts, though of course at some time or other it needs explicitation and deliberate appropriation.

> *It is not easy to convert an immediate emotion into an interest, for the operation requires that we seek out indirect and subtle relations and consequences. But unless an emotion, whether labeled selfish or altruistic, is thus broadened, there is no reflective morality. To give way to kindly feeling without thought is easy; to suppress it is easy for many persons; the difficult but needed thing is to retain it in all its pristine intensity while directing it, as a precondition of action, into channels of thought.[115]*

The resulting action "channelled by thought" is not satisfactorily described by the terms "egoism" or "altruism," terms which arose, thinks Dewey, in an era when the economic principle of rugged individualism prevailed. Rather we should now see that

Selfhood is not something which exists apart from association and intercourse; (hence)...regard for self and regard for others are both of them secondary phases of a more normal and complete interest: regard for the welfare and integrity of the social groups of which we form a part.[116]

We can get a further clarification of this point from another work of Dewey.

...now it is true that social arrangements, laws, institutions are made for man, rather than that man is made for them: that they are means and agencies of human welfare and progress. But they are not means for obtaining something for individuals, not even happiness. They are means of creating individuals. Only in the physical sense of physical bodies that to the senses are separate is individuality an original datum. Individuality in a social and moral sense is something to be wrought out. It means initiative, inventiveness, varied resourcefulness, assumption of responsibility in choice of belief and conduct. These are not gifts but achievements. As achievements they are not absolute but relative to the use that is made of them. And this use varies with the environment.[117]

The individual person is such only by fitting into a whole social network. It is the interest of this social whole which should be the primary focus of a person's intelligent assessment of the worth of human action. Thus neither exclusive self-advantage, nor exclusive benevolence will do as authentic moral interests. Both need to be sublated to a primary focus on the community's shared and enduring good.

Regard for self and regard for others should not, in other words, be direct motives to overt action. They should be forces which lead us to think of objects and consequences that would otherwise escape notice. These objects and consequences then constitute the interest which is the proper motive of action. Their stuff and material are composed of the relations which men actually sustain to one another in concrete affairs...Interest in the social whole of which one is a member necessarily carries with it interest in one's own self. Every member of the group has his own place and work.[118]

It should be the individual's primary concern that the work he has within the context of the whole should be as well-discharged by him as possible. This means it is the person's responsibility not to confuse his efforts at keeping himself fit for the discharge of his obligations for "selfishness." Nor should he be distracted from this work and responsibility by a false benevolence or altruistic sympathy. In promoting the good of the social whole, both the interests of self and others are taken care of in a moral fashion.

When selfhood is taken for what it is, something existing in relationships to others and not in unreal isolation, independence of judgement, personal insight, integrity and initiative become indispensable excellencies from the social point of view.[119]

There is a warning here on the danger of the so-called "charity" of the rich and mighty in society toward the poor and the weak. Such "charity" is fine provided it does not become merely a cover for brutal economic exploitation and an investment really for the perpetuation of an unjust system favorable only to those few rich ones.[120]

How then should we regard acts of "charity," "altruism" and "benevolence?"

> *...overt acts of charity and benevolence are incidental phases of morals, demanded under certain emergencies, rather than its essential principle.* This is found in a constantly expanding and changing sense of what the concrete realities of human regulations call for.[121]

In the light of all this, slogans about "self-fulfillment" can be terribly erroneous if they are taken to mean that the self is to be the target of efforts at fulfillment. If we have said anything at all here, it is that the fulfillment of self is something that results from a moral life, a life reflectively focused always on the larger and enduring interests and satisfactions of the social whole *into* which an individual is related. The self is certainly not some separate entity that awaits fulfillment through a series of actions stimulated into being by outside motives. The same holds for the "pursuit of happiness." Paradoxically, happiness eludes those who aim for it explicitly as their exact end-in-view. For happiness is nothing more or less than what accompanies and rewards acts well done.

> *The final word about the place of the self in the moral life is, then, that the very problem of morals is to form an original body of impulsive tendencies into a voluntary self in which desires and affections center in the values which are common; in which interest focuses on objects that contribute to the enrichment of the lives of all. If we identify the interests of such a self with the virtues, then we shall say, with Spinoza, that happiness is not the reward of virtue, but is virtue itself.[122]*

How is this focus on the common social good of the whole as the moral good to be fostered in members of a society? Here the idea of *responsibility* enters in.

The true role of social approbation and disapprobation (censure, blame) should be to foster this attitude of always looking to the larger commonly shared good as the moral good among its citizenry. Thus responsibility is *prospective*. It looks to inculcating right concerns, to cultivating and making these grow among members of a community. Unfortunately, it is easy to look at responsibility only retrospectively, i.e. as holding citizens to the just consequences of their deeds. The fact is overlooked that the very nature of retrospective retribution would mean nothing, *unless learning for the future of the real goals of action* is possible in the one being disciplined. That this is so can be seen in the fact that we do not charge falling rocks, wild animals or even mentally incapable human beings with retributive responsibility when they cause injuries. They are incapable of learning and growth. What can be clearer than that the role of reflective morality is to assess constantly the methods of inculcating responsibility current in its society as to their desirability, relevance, effectiveness, humaness, etc.

> *One is held responsible in order that he may become responsible, that is responsive to the needs and claims of others, to the obligations implicit in his position. Those who hold others accountable are themselves accountable for doing it in such a manner that this responsiveness develops...Being held accountable by others, is in every instance, an important safeguard and directive force in growth.[123]*

Retrospective responsibility thus looks towards the rehabilitation of a self so as to make it responsive to the guidance of reflective morality. In this context:

> *...mistakes are no longer either mere unavoidable accidents to be mourned or moral sins to be expiated and forgiven. They are lessons in wrong methods of using intelligence and instructions as to a better course in the future.[124]*

Needless to say, none of this can take place unless freedom, choice and voluntary action come into play, both in those holding others as well as those held responsible.

> *Except as the outcome of arrested development there is no such thing as a fixed, ready-made, finished self. Every living self causes acts and is itself caused in return by what it does. All voluntary action is a remaking of self, since it creates new desires, instigates to new modes of endeavor, brings to light new conditions which institute new ends. Our personal identity is found in the thread of continuous development which binds together these changes. In the strictest sense, it is impossible for the self to stand still; it is* becoming, and becoming for the better or for the worse. It is in the quality of becoming that virtue resides. We set up this and that end to be reached, but *the end is growth itself.[125]*

There is a danger in the fact that the end of moral striving is growth itself. Through the erroneous notion of morality as mere conformity to obligations and laws laid out once and for all time, or through discouragement and weariness in the never-ending task of moral reassessment and renewal, good persons begin to fall short of their actual responsibilities. Worse, some even positively shy off from them. Thus while these "saints"

> *...are engaged in introspection, burly sinners run the world. But when self-hood is perceived to be an active process it is also seen that social*

modifications are the only means of the creation of changed personalities.[126]

There can thus be no final end for a truly moral person. For "to make an end a final goal is but to arrest growth."[127] Since tradition, habit and deepset customs ease the weighty burden of reflective assessment of goals, of reconstructing and renewing the ends of a changing society to better fit its enduring needs, it is understandable how many yield to the temptation of arresting their moral growth and "resting on their oars," of moving simply on the basis of the self they have already achieved. But there should be no room for this sort of self. There should be no rest from reflective concern. The genuine moral self must constantly be in dynamic growth toward the ever new goals it fashions reflectively for itself. It is never satisfied with the self it has accomplished. It transcends that self unceasingly, even as it transcends old customary morality to the formation of which it itself perhaps once made invaluable contributions but which it now finds inapplicable.

> *...no matter how 'good' he has been, he becomes 'bad' (even though acting upon a relatively high place of attainment) as soon as he fails to respond to the demand for growth. Any other basis for judging the moral status of the self is conventional...The only distinction, however, that can be drawn without reducing morals to conventionality, selfrighteous complacency, or a hopeless and harsh struggle for the unattainable, is that between the attained static, and the moving, dynamic self...If we state the moral law as* the injunction on each self on every possible occasion to identify the self with a new growth that is possible, *then obedience to law is one with moral freedonm.*[128]

Who then is the good man, and who the bad? Dewey answers:

> *The bad man is the man who no matter how good he has been is beginning to deteriorate, to grow less good. The good man is the man who no matter how morally unworthy he has been is moving to become better.*[129]

In the end, a truly moral man fuses every other end he has on the many other levels he operates in, such as that of the economic level, with the hard work of making a living.

> *...making a living economically speaking, will be at one with making a life that is worth living.*[130]

The moral imperative ("categorical imperative" just would not sound right in Dewey's context) then in a Deweyite ethics can be formulated in this way:

> So act as to attain new growth for yourself based on reflective consideration of the most enduring and shared good possible on every occasion.

The growth Dewey talks about here is of course a "change of self." But he points out the difference between the change of self he advocates and that, for example, of the Aristotelian or classical kind, which as we saw a few pages back in that famous text from Aristotle, talks of a change of self only in relation to the contemplation of a fixed final end.

> But there is a radical difference between a change in the self that is cultivated and valued as an end, and one that is a means to alteration, through action, of objective conditions. The Aristotelian-mediaeval conviction that highest bliss is found in contemplative possession of ultimate Being presents an ideal attractive to some types of mind; it sets forth a refined sort of enjoyment. It is a doctrine congenial to minds that despair of the effort involved in creation of a better world of daily experience. It is, apart from theological attachments, a doctrine sure to recur when social conditions are so troubled as to make actual endeavor seem hopeless.[131]

Summary

The main lines of thought and principles in Dewey's moral theory may be summarized as follows:

In opposition to Kant, Dewey insists that "moral conceptions and processes *grow naturally* out of the very conditions of human life." The conditions out of which moral doctrine evolves are:

(1) human desires and needs tending towards satisfaction in their respective ends, coupled with reflective thought which guides them toward larger, more inclusive ends. It is for moral theory to identify the characteristics of the really moral ends. Such identification is the role of wisdom and prudence.

(2) Human existence is always concretely social. "Even the hermit communes with gods or spirits; even misery loves company." Hence companioship as well as competition, cooperation as well as subordination are natural to man. These relationships express demands, claims, and expectations of people from one another. Hence arise *rights* (justified claims on others) and obligations, the owing to others of their due, their justified claims. Reflective morality should be ever vigilant about the tendency to make these Rights, Duties, and Law into Absolutes severed from their existential matrix of concrete relationships. For these relationships are ever changing in a mobile world. They demand the constant reassessment of existing laws as to their continuing relevance in changing contexts.

(3) No man or woman born can escape customary morality, the approval and disapproval of certain lines of conduct based on tradition. Here reflective morality must seek the genuine basis of moral approval, i.e. the approv*able*. Tradition should be accorded its due value as funded experience of the group, at the same time that it must be transcended when times and moral growth require it.

These three conditions can be viewed as aspects of a naturally growing organism with intellectual powers to direct its own growth and to shape its own conduct as the source of its peculiarly human needs and ends. In thus satisfying its needs, it defines its quality of existence, a definition never final but which, hopefully, conduces toward new growth. Only death or mental impairment could stop this process.

This theory is thus not an ethical heracliteanism in which change and growth are king and nothing whatsoever remains stable and permanent. Always the character of both natural and moral reality is a mixture of both. Hence neither is it a Parmenidean world of immobility in which contemplative thought freezes moral absolutes into tables of laws to which human beings must conform at all times and all ages. In all human living just as in nature, there are both stable and unstable elements. And this should not be surprising. For man, let us repeat one last time, is not set over against nature. Rather he is within and interwoven with natural processes themselves, even as through reflective thought he fashions his growth with the instrument par excellence he has at his hands, namely, science. We do not have therefore either the extreme of moral absolutism, or that of sheer relativism as though nothing stable and enduring is recognizable in human nature, so that everyone may do whatever he thinks is right only for himself. Even Pepsi-Cola after all, which uses this slogan, appeals to a recurrent need in human nature.

> *The facts of desiring, purpose, social demand and law, sympathetic approval and hostile disapproval are constant. We cannot imagine them disappearing as long as human nature remains human nature, and lives in association with others. The fundamental conceptions of morals are, therefore, neither arbitrary nor artificial. They are not imposed upon human nature from without but* develop out of its own operations and needs. *Particular aspects of morals are transient; they are often, in their actual manifestation, defective and perverted. But the framework of moral conception is as permanent as human life itself.*[132]

Here then is the ethics Dewey would have for a technological society. While a lot of this material, notably this chapter, was written in his earlier years, the inspiration and shape of his key ideas remained essentially the same. Far from backing away from them, as we saw, he reiterated their relevance when the horrors of the nuclear age were used as objections against them. And since, as we said earlier, the whole world is rapidly turning to technology fullscale for answers to its problems, it would not be amiss to declare that the moral norm of the *shared* good all around which Dewey proposed, if universally adopted in the various descending levels of communities within communities, would go a long way toward making all men treat one another as brothers in more than just a metaphorical sense. For in truth, not only the problems of America but those of the whole world itself occupied Dewey's mind and pen. It was not mere happenstance that when he went to the Far East he spent most of the time in the industrial giant of that part of the globe. We turn now to a comparative study of Kant and Dewey as well as to some ideas that may help toward forming our own guiding moral principles.

CONCLUDING REMARKS

Dewey's philosophy may be seen as a repudiation of any movement away from experience such as Kant's "regressive method" to the supreme principle of morality typifies. We have already seen some of Dewey's refutations of Kant whose doctrine Dewey certainly knew well since he wrote his doctoral dissertation on "The Psychology of Kant" in 1884.[1] Interestingly enough, in another early essay, "Kant and Philosophic Method,"[2] he characterizes Kant as the turning point, "the transition of the old abstract thought, the old meaningless conception of experience, into the new concrete thought, the ever growing, ever rich experience."[3] This should alert us against any simplistic conclusion that the two are worlds apart with nothing in common between them. True, Kant's ultimate and uncomprimising location of the supreme moral principle in a realm other than the empirical world of experience was obviously an irreconcilable point between him and Dewey. But the mere fact that Dewey himself, after a close study of Kant, concluded that Kant had moved away, though not far enough, from the classic spectator type of philosophy gives us a clue that while there is indeed a philosophical chasm between the two as to their methods and content in philosophizing, the chasm may not be as wide as it may at first seem. It may help then to line up their respective points of differences to see how near, for all that, they are to each other.

1. *Use and Dismissal of Teleology.* Despite his *as if* doctrine on natural teleology, we have seen how Kant in actuality used fixed teleologies, *ends* in man and nature to make absolute moral conclusions. If we look, for example, at his stricture against suicide, laziness and insensitivity in the first, third and fourth illustrations respectively,[4] we see how his absolute conclusions are based on the idea that there are fixed and firm finalities in nature, man, and even the circumstances which befall men regularly. In contrast, we have seen how Dewey considers this the result of an idealizing, abstractionist tendency away from experience. For Dewey who situates everything into the context of scientific experimentation, nothing in this world is ever with a fixed end. There are neither formal nor final

206

causalities in nature. There is only the one causality found in experimentation, namely, productive or efficient causality.[5] Everything is open-ended, an opening which a continuous process of experimentation keeps punctuating periodically. The constant discovery of new subatomic particles; the scientific miracles in agriculture which have never ceased from Luther Burbank to miracle rice today; the experiments on "cloning," artificial insemination, and other new experiments in which new combinations of genes are grafted on to bacteria, a technique "that is going to generate the most exciting thing in biology in the next ten years, if not longer" --- all these Dewey would cite as decisive arguments against fixed ends in nature.

Yet, a close look at Dewey's meliorism shows how close the two thinkers are to each other. For we find a definite strain of meliorism in Kant's use of teleology. For instance, the reason Kant gives for man's avoidance of suicide, laziness and lack of compassion for others is man's natural orientation *towards improvement* of his situation. Though Dewey dismisses intrinsic teleology in everything else, it would be difficult even in his own terms to dismiss the basic teleology in man toward meliorism. For such a dismissal would undermine the entire foundation of his philosophy. Thus, since this thrust towards progressive improvement is the supreme principle which inspires Dewey's whole scientistic account of reality, it would follow that all reality too must tie in with this human finality since, as we saw, life-mind-nature is an organic and continuous whole in his view.[6] The proximity of this position to the Kantian doctrine of teleology as our own mental contribution to our experience of empirical things is obvious.

The divergence too is obvious. Dewey is for reducing everything to empirical pragmatism. Kant, on the other hand, steadfastly maintains the absolute otherness of the nuomenal and phenomenal realms to each other.

2. *Pure Reason Versus Intelligence.* The moral life in Kant moves in the world of freedom which definitely is *other* than the deterministic one of nature and scientific phenomena. In contrast, Dewey rejects this sort of separation which has its persistent root, so he claims, in the classic view of reality. Instead of pure reason, Dewey advocates the life of creative and reflective *intelligence*, that is to say, the merging of philosophical reflection with melioristic scientism. To say the ethical life is one of "intelligence" means that all of man's faculties are integrated in an organic continuity with his environment. Reason is one with inclinational desires and interests, whereas we saw how steadfastly Kant held these two apart. Moral theory in Dewey is immersed in experience, while in Kant the moral *ought* remains untainted with any element from the empirical *is*. For him moral principles and experience are heterogeneous to one another. For Dewey they are homogeneous. There is thus an unbridgeable chasm between them. As Dewey observes:

Reason as a faculty separate from experience, introducing us to a superior region of universal truths, begins now to strike us as remote, uninteresting and unimportant. Reason, as a Kantian faculty that introduces generality and regularity into experience, strikes us more and more as superfluous --- the unnecessary creation of men addicted to traditional formalism and to elaborate terminology. Concrete suggestions arising from past experiences, developed and matured in the light of the needs and deficiences of the present, employed as aims and methods of specific reconstruction, and tested by success or failure in accomplishing this task of readjustment, suffice. To such empirical suggestions used in constructive fashion for new ends the name intelligence is given.[7]

...experience for philosophy is method, not distinctive subject matter. This fact convicts upon sight every philosophy that professes to be empirical and yet assures us that some special subject matter is experience and some other not...[8]

Yet, as we read Dewey, we cannot help but notice how he characterizes moral reflection in terms of "coolness," impartiality," indeed of "spectator." He takes fine moral judgements to be those which are made not in the heat of the moment, but in the high and lofty comprehnsion of one who looks beyond the immediacy of things actually being experienced. True, he does not separate "intelligence" from emotion. In one place he even talks of "passionate intelligence,"[9] but even here the task of intelligence is shown to be that of "purifying" experience. There is thus an almost tantalizing attempt to move reflective thought towards the lofty regions of Kantian pure reason away from experience. At the same time, the organic oneness of intelligence with emotion makes such a movement finally only an elastic distension which never quite snaps free of the experiential matrix and is, in fact, snapped right back to the empirical core in subsequent sentences.

3. *Concepts as A Priori in Kant and A Posteriori in Dewey.* The categories of the mind in Kant are all a priori. Prior to experience itself, they are themselves the formative factors of experience. But they are finished and self-sufficient in themselves to the point, at any rate, where Reason can brood on them in separation from experience and rear up an entire, though insubstantial metaphysics. This is simply unacceptable to Dewey. For him all concepts arise only from actually problematic situations, from "shocks" to the organism which precipitates the tension-relieving activity of thinking, of finding a solution. Ideas thus can come only from experience. Hence Dewey criticizes Kant for holding that that "the concepts of reason are so far above experience that they need and can secure no confirmation in experience."[10] And to show how erroneous such a doctrine is, he points to the practical effects this sort of absolutizing reason had on the German mind which, as everybody knows, has otherwise proved its excellence in science.

That the Germans with all their scientific competency and technological proficiency should have fallen into their tragically rigid and 'superior' style of thought and action (tragic because involving them in inability to understand the world in which they lived) is a sufficient

> *lesson of what may be involved in a systematical denial of the*
> *experimental character of intelligence and its conceptions.* [11]

Thus while the two positions are obviously irreconcilable, it is interesting to recall how Kant himself is well-known for characterizing those a priori concepts of the mind in isolation from sensuous intuitions as "empty," while intuitions by themselves in isolation from the organizing categories are "blind." If that famous Kantian dictum means anything, it means that concepts are for *use* in organizing experience. Indeed concepts have no other realistic function in Kant other than to be *used*, to enter into union with sensation so as to constitute experience. The other established distinction in Kant between the regulative and constitutive use of concepts makes the same point, namely, concepts are for *use*. The critical philosopher is he who knows the valid limits of such uses. And this comes very close to Dewey's idea that abstractions and generalizations are natural to the human mind, but that they must be regarded much in the way that we regard roadmaps. These are concepts not for contemplation but for use in the intelligent organization and direction of experience. In the text above, Dewey does not fault the Germans for not using their concepts in a very pragmatic way. Heaven knows they did! Or, better, anyone who has been to Dachau, Belsen, Mauthausen, etc, knows they did. The tragedy rather was that they used the *wrong* concepts. And they had the concepts wrong because, says Dewey, they picked them out of the rarifield atmosphere of isolated thought instead of from concrete experience itself, from the real world.

4. *The Immutable or Mutable Basis of Moral Claims.* All moral duty for Kant is based on the reality of man as an end-in-himself. The universalizability principle in all its variations is reducible finally to the absolute fact of man as an end-in-himself. Needless to say, for Dewey there is no such thing as an absolute end-in-itself. Man does not stand over against and apart from nature. Rather he is in organic and homogeneous continuity with nature in a context of ceaseless and ongoing process. These processes generate ever shifting relationships among men in social intercourse. But though ever shifting, these social relationships nevertheless recur with enough frequency for men to be able to understand what sort of moral claims they generate in the light of the most inclusive and enduring satisfaction reflective intelligence reveals. Thus the parents-child relationship is not forever, and even while it lasts it is ever shifting. Yet there is enough stability in it while it does last. It recurs in the human condition frequently enough for men to realize what claims must be made of each party if what all want, namely, inclusive and enduring satisfaction, is to be gained from the situation. It is in these ever shifting relationships, not in the persons themselves as unchanging ends-in-themselves that Dewey roots moral claims.

We should note how if one stopped with the statement that man is an end-in-himself, period, then no specific moral conclusion has been reached. To generate specific moral injunctions, the negative correlate of that principle must be spelled out, namely, "therefore, do not ever treat any man as a means only." Only then does the principle come alive, so to speak, and go into action. Only then do we derive from it perfect duties (in which there is no playroom) and imperfect duties (in which there is playroom).[12] Indeed among these duties is eventually that of seeking the conditions conducive to a moral life, namely, that of satisfaction and even happiness which Kant was careful to hold apart most of the time from morality itself.

How closely this correlative meaning of end-in-itself and of "means only" comes to Dewey's idea of moral claims as rooted in existential relationships between essentially social individuals may be seen in the way Paton, one of Kant's commentators, summarizes Kant on this point.

> *We transgress perfect duties by treating any person merely as a means. We transgress imperfect duties by failing to treat a person as an end, even though we do not actively treat him merely as a means.*
>
> *The difference between duties to self and duties to others is commonly recognized, though in some respects it is not easy to account for such a difference. Kant pushes this difference very far in regard to imperfect duties by insisting that our duty to ourselves is to seek as an end our own natural and moral perfection but not our happiness; and that our duty to others is to seek their happiness as an end, but not their perfection. It may, however, be our duty to seek the moral welfare of others in a negative sense. We ought not to tempt them to courses of action which might likely cause them pangs of remorse.*[13]

In others, for both thinkers, morality can never lie in the selfish ends of an individual. It always looks to the act that preserves and promotes the worth and capabilities of individuals based on their *being,* rather than on what they *have.* While concrete social stations obviously vary, the obligation of all and each to do nothing against the general welfare, and indeed to do what one can for its increase is always there.

5. *Kingdom and Communities.* In Kant there is one kingdom in which all men are equal members under the same unchanging set of moral laws. A law valid for one is valid for all. The variety of customs and actually prevailing circumstances cannot alter a law which comes out of a realm impervious to experience. In Dewey, morality is, in the beginning, the habits and customs of any particular group or society which sooner or later undergo "shock," the apparent conflict of moral demands. This moves on to reflective morality which assesses actually prevailing standards and ends as to their desirability. Clearly, not all men are under the same moral laws. As circumstances are different so too are their corresponding moral obligations which, as we saw, arise from the social relationships which actually exist between individuals. The sameness and equality of men in one kingdom are thus a *fait accompli* for Kant even before experiences start. Whereas for Dewey, the community and equality of men is an ideal not yet realized towards which men have been moving historically and epistemologically, through the abolition of the separation of knowledges into "higher" and "lower," together with their corresponding social system of elitism. The ideal community is modeled on the equality that comes from a publicly shared knowledge publicly repeatable through scientific procedures, knowledge that, in principle, is accessible to *all* men, instead of being the secret possession of only a privileged few.

Again, the difference here is in the conception of community as an a priori reality from the beginning in Kant, and only an a posteriori ideal yet to be brought into being through the universal adoption of the scientific method in all matters in Dewey.

The point of near-convergence between the two is the way both men agree that God is not necessary to the conception of all men as equal members of one community. In Kant, the universal nature of pure reason is sufficient to ground both the sovereignty and promulgation of the same moral laws to every human being as a member of the same kingdom. There is no call to ground this sovereignty in any other being beyond the selfcontained autonomy of reason. And of course in Dewey, as we saw, all further grounding of present experiences in a metaphysical or supernatural reality is treated as an unacceptable philosophical bias. Men must work out their unity and community by the sole use of their own powers of intelligence. The condition they all share as inhabitants of a world in which they all seek greater security and more enduring satisfactions democratizes them all to the level of fellow workers and wayfarers.

> *I cannot understand how any realization of the democratic ideal as a vital moral and spiritual ideal in human affairs is possible without surrender of the conception of the basic division to which supernatural Christianity is committed. Whether or no we are, save in some metaphorical sense, all brothers, we are at least all in the same boat traversing the same turbulent ocean.*[14]

6. *Religion and Religiousness.* In Kant's kingdom of ends a reasonable man must of necessity postulate an Author of Nature who finalizes the process of the moral life by granting proportionate happiness to moral achievement. There is also a "religion within the limits of reason alone "purified of all irrational superstitions and meaningless rituals". Nevertheless, it is true religion, the only true one in fact. If it is true that it actually commands no more actions of man than the categorical imperative itself, it is also true that these moral acts, looked on as acts of religion are viewed, no longer as self-contained within reason alone without any further reference. The religious man now sees them as the best acts of worship and adoration he can make to the supreme being. While the force of the Categorical Imperative remains from the beginning rooted in its own entire authority, looked at retrospectively by the moral man who also comes to believe in God, its commands are seen to be the same ones God wills men to do. Indeed, Kant goes so far as to say the Christian religion (presumably the Pietistic brand of Protestantism he inherited from his mother) stands out above all the others as *the* religion most approvable to the reasonble man.[15] In Dewey, on the other hand, all we have is the life of intelligence choosing to redirect actual experiences themselves in the most scientific manner possible towards an end deemed best under the circumstances by a "cool and impartial spectator." Not only does Dewey never extend ends even when actualized to any otherworldly reality. He vigorously condemns any giving in to such classic tendencies of the mind as a failure of nerve to rise up to the challenges and promises of science, an option not open to men before the advent of knowledge par excellence,

211

the scientific method. It is not enough that churchmen take the liberal stance of welcoming science and contending that they are thoroughgoing empiricists "as good as the scientists themselves."[16] As long as they commit themselves to *a* religion they are moribund. They will end up in only one way, namely, considering science as the best tool man has fashioned, but something to be used only to uphold the same old classic traditions and beliefs of institutionalized religions. They would merely be putting new wine into old bottles. Or, to use Santayana's idea,[17] because of this failure to make the ultimate surrender of traditional beliefs in a Divine and Supernatural reality, their supposed welcome of science would in reality be only a harmless poetic attitude which merely "supervenes" in life without really changing anything. To welcome science in such a way as to make it actually *intervene* in life situations, one must decisively give up all and further reference of experiences to anything otherworldly, to any particular religion or religious institution. One must cultivate nothing more than dedication and loyalty to ideals set forth by reflective and creative intelligence, as it seeks to reconstruct the human lot amid the mixture of good and evil in which it finds itself.[18] We can point up this contrast between Dewey and Kant on religious attitude as growing out of pure reason alone in separation from the empirical, and that same religious spirit limiting itself exclusively to the empirical, by quoting what in substance is Dewey's religious creed.

> *For were we do admit that there is but one method for ascertaining fact and truth --- that conveyed by the word 'scientific' in its most general and generous sense --- no discovery in any branch of knowledge and inquiry could then disturb the faith that is religious. I should describe this faith as the unification of the self through allegiance to inclusive ideal ends, which imagination presents to us and to which the human will responds as worthy of controlling our desires and choices.[19]*

From two sides then, Kant's and Dewey's views on religiousness collide. In the beginning, Kant isolates the source of his religious acts from the empirical and bases them on pure reason alone, acts identically those of morality itself. At the end, God is added on to the autonomous moral act as an Omnipotent harmonizer of morals and happiness. Dewey would have no part of such a view.

On the other hand, we can observe how close the two are to each other on loyalty and singleminded dedication to the dictates of morality. For Kant that is all of religion. For Dewey too religion is only that and nothing else. Of course we are concerned here only with human actions, moral deeds. Kant calls these "acts of religion." Dewey calls them "religious acts." But both confine themselves to the one same reality of moral deeds and consider these self-contained realities in themselves, regardless of further consideration. And Kant's emotional hymn to duty, and many other poetic obtbursts in praise of morals certainly come near to Dewey's notion of "passionate intellegence"[20] in the religious man. In addition, Dewey's decisive and matter-of-fact conviction on the futility of importing the Supernatural into the realm of morals, interestingly enough reminds one of Kant's stern calls for "duty" alone, though it dry up cherished beliefs in the wellsprings of the heart.

7. *Professor and Philosopher.* Dewey was an academician all his philosophical life, while Kant left the classrooms quite a while before his death. Yet, interestingly enough, it is in Kant we find the all-too-common professioral pretension that philosophy is some special and privileged knowledge beyond mere empirical experiences. As Nietzsche observes about Kant's "joke:"

> *Kant wanted to prove in a way that would dumbfound the common man, that the common man was right: that was the secret joke of his soul. He wrote against the scholars in support of popular prejudice, but for scholars and not for the people.*[21]

Experiences do contain sound truths. But philosophy has the special task of developing those truths into a coherent and harmonious system of thought which will provide the basis for defending the sheer innocence of experience from seduction. Without the support of philosophical knowledge which in Kant is full of esoteric and highly technical expression --- all Greek to the man on the street --- the common man with his sound inklings of truth would soon be the victim of falsehoods. This same distrust of the common man, if left alone to his experiences, as thoroughly vulnerable to falsehood, is not found in Dewey. Truth, after all, is for Dewey the empirical matter of the consequences of a man's actions, and who else could be a better judge of such existential consequences than the man on the street himself? Because Dewey shuns the sort of abstract thinking which cuts itself off from the empirical matrix of a deed's actual consequences, any sort of "coherent" system of thought which starts out supposedly to prevent the common man from philosophical seduction ends up doing exactly that: it ends up denying the reality to experienced evils in the world in favor of an abstract system which "explains" those evils away on the basis of the *whole* view of reality as viewed through the special light of pure reason. Dewey's books may all be read by the common man. At least he thought so. He never quite understood the distinction between philosophical essays written for professional philosophers and those written for non-philosophers.[22] The difference between such an attitude and that of a Descartes or a Kant who both had to write shorter versions of their *magnum opus* for public consumption as contrasted to the academic philosophical elite who are on to their jargon is obvious. Unlike Kant, Dewey did not have to put out a simplified version of any of his works. He somehow never developed the sort of esoteric jargon which tends to give the impression that philosophers have a special access to being, knowledge and insights beyond the reach of the common man. Indeed he execrates this precise practice as the very reasons for the deserved ill repute of philosophy and the bad times in which, by her own lament, she has fallen. One only has to hear Heideggerians nowadays using kilometric words perhaps in all honesty impenetrable even to themselves to see what Dewey means here. The constrast is between the aristocratic and a democratic view of philosophy. The assimilation of philosophy into the scientific milieu democratizes it. It is henceforth knowledge about empirical consequences which any man, with or without formal schooling, can verify for himself.

But for all these differences, there is in Dewey the idea of philosophy as "criticism." The very word should alert us to a possible similarity of outlook in Kant. For in the last analysis, philosophy in Dewey is not the same thing as actual physics, or biology, or medicine, etc. Philosophy is reflective thought on all these sciences, and on all human experiences. It searches not only what men do, and what they prize, but what they *ought to do,* and what after appraisal they ought to esteem and appreciate. True, it does all these things without ever leaving the empirical realm of actual and experienced consequences. Still, it does go beyond experience as it sets up new ends-in-view, and as it goes about the task of reconstructing experience towards newer and more enduring satisfactions. It seeks to understand not only the actually existing experiences but other better and more desirable consequences. Clearly, philosophy cannot perform this critical function without, like Kant, trying to uncover the principles which ought to underlie experiences. On the other hand, despite his insistence on isolating pure reason from experience, Kant points out that in arriving at his principles, he nevertheless has not "quite the moral knowledge of common human reason."[23] Indeed he used the very same expression as Dewey, namely, that of a "cool observer"[24] as the description of the moral philosopher. Any reader of Kant soon understands why his commentators dispute among themselves whether Kant's ethics is after all a consequential and empirical one, all his protestations to the contrary notwithstanding. Here again we see how close the two are to each other despite their unbridgeable differences.

8. *Conformity and Creativity.* In Kant moral performance is conformity to pre-established, prefixed and immutable moral laws. Since empirical circumstances have been ruled out as determining factors of morals, and since these empirical circumstances are the only causes of change, it is clear that moral laws, once established and enunciated, are established immutably. Whereas in Dewey, every moral imperative is open to change, either by cancellation as something no longer relevant to the situation, or by supersession, namely, as funded experience entering into new moulds and patterns reflective consciousness sets up as new ends-in-view. What novelty there is in Kantian morality is the novelty of a rational deposit either overlooked or as yet undiscovered and lying there hidden in the depths of pure reason itself waiting to be discovered and enunciated. For morality's supreme principle is freedom with its own nuomenal laws which are other than the deterministic and mechanical laws of experimental phenomena. While freedom may and does produce effects in the phenomenal world, the phenomenal world of inclinations in turn may not positively enter in any way into the positive constitution of a moral act. At the most, pathological influences can exercise only a negative influence up to the limits of that unclear and controverted aspect of the will called *willkür.* But the will itself, as pure practical reason itself, is in a realm all sufficient by itself and apart from the sensuous world. We will perhaps be not far from Kant's intention if we compare the relation between the two realms as similar to that of sense experience in Plato serving as an occasion for bringing innate ideas into play. The relationship, in any case,

214

is not an intrinsic one. Whereas in Dewey, there are no two ways about the fact that morality begins, feeds itself from and grows within experience itself. Here all substance and moral content lie in publicly observable and sensibly verifiable consequences of a problematic situation when resolved. No innate ideals exist awaiting merely to be discovered. Thought has no content prior to experience. Indeed thought itself is merely a constituent of one instrumental process that is fashioning an improved situation out of the old.[25] Thus Kant's a priori divergence from Dewey's a posteriori view of morality is clear.

Here perhaps our search for similarities between the two breaks down and it is hard to see any saving aspect between the two views which might possibly draw them towards each other. On the other hand, we should not forget a point we have already noted in Dewey which perhaps comes closest to anything innate or prefixed in man, namely, man's melioristic orientation. Since this is itself the prior condition necessary for the emergence of any problem and its correlative meaning, whether only ideally or in actually achieved satisfaction, it would seem that this is a supreme principle in Dewey which makes all the other factors of experience possible. But to call it *a priori* would be erroneous.

9. *Happiness and Satisfaction.* In Kant happiness belongs to a realm other than that of morality. Any concidence of the moral life with happiness or sensual satisfaction is just that, a coincidence. Even at the end point of man's otherworldly moral progress when the Author of nature is postulated as granting proportionate happiness to the deserving, it is looked upon as something coming to morality from the outside. The unity between morals and happiness never becomes essential. Whereas in Dewey, morality has one and the same root as every meaningful human activity, namely, the problematic situation which arises out of a need for satisfaction. Morality thus and satisfaction are in essential correlation. The performance of a moral deed is identically action or movement towards satisfaction. Morality, far from being separated from satisfaction or happiness, is movement towards maximal intensification and stabilization of reflectively approved satisfaction. Plainly put, morality is organic satisfaction. Of course, not any which sort of satisfaction --- but it *is* satisfaction, reflectively approved satisfaction on the experimental level. There is no other meaningful level for Dewey.

Here I must admit that I have never quite figured out what "happiness" could mean for a moral being in Kant in the state of an immortality which presumably is a disembodied state. And, of course, since this would be a trascendent reality sealed off from human knowledge, Kant himself would be the very first to admit that neither can he. The fascinating question then is why he ever makes this improbable twinning of happiness with a disembodied being, considering his endlessly repeated identification of happiness as essentially sensual and inclinational. The answer probably lies in his conception of morality as identically *worthiness* to be happy. It may be well to linger a bit on this point.

In Kant to be moral is to be worthy of sensual happiness (to put the matter tautologically). What then is the difference between happiness in Kant and satisfaction in Dewey? Certainly the two ideas seem identical, especially if we remember how finally Kant "harmonized" the concepts of happiness and morality in that of the *summum bonum*. In effect Kant admitted that it was meaningless to be ever oriented towards satisfaction without ever achieving it. Now, what is this but simply the admission that meaninfulness after all comes down to satisfaction? And this was Dewey's point all along. Of course the metaphysical framework of Kant's thought on this matter, and the downright refusal of Dewey to accept any such framework of Kant's thought on the matter should alert us against any temptation to fuse the two doctrines on satisfaction into one. They seem to come near each other. But in reality they are unbridgeably apart, with one being located in a metaphysical world which the other dismisses as merely a hangup of the classical mentality.

I would like now at this point to go over some aspects of Dewey's philosophy with which I disagree, namely, his positions on (1) man's *homogeneity* with nature; (2) the non-existence of metaphysical reality and intrinsic finality in pre-problematic being; (3) scientistic reductionism; (4) the tendency to focus ethical considerations disproportionately on empirical consequences; (5) the basis of meliorism in "good" or "bad" ("evil") as *immediately* evident to experience, although admittedly, the melioristic ideal is only established later by reflective inquiry.

1. *Man Over Against Nature.* That there is some deep continuity between man and nature may be seen in the etymological link between "world" and the Old English and High German *woruld* and *wer*, meaning human existence and man. The same insight is found in Freud's concept of psychic desire and cosmic desire being one originally, a state which continues in the stage of infancy and terminates only with the intrusion on the child of its society's prohibitions, totems and taboos. This intrusion is effected largely through the parents who inevitably "socialize" the child consciously and unconsciously in an infinite number of ways. Mother Nature as Death and the Third Woman, in Freud, ever accompanies the eros of life. Man is certainly of earth and must draw sustenance from her constantly. His whole being, through his feet, must maintain this life-giving contact with the earth. We may note, for example, how in times of great danger such as bombings and shellings in modern warfare, human beings literally and physically burrow their beings as deeply as they can into the earth for cover, protection and life. It is as though by some primal instinct they know that the earth which mothered them can also be relied on more than anything else to keep them from harm. There is thus no doubt about a certain continuity between man and his natural environment.

It is another thing, however, to assert that man is *homogeneous* with nature. If Teilhard's evolution theory shows anything, it shows that man is indeed *of* of the dear and precious earth. Neverthless, with the upsurge of consciousness and the appearance of *reflective consciousness* or the "phenomenon of man," something for the first time stood *over against* nature. Of course even that was still *natural* consciousness. But with man's reflective awareness we have nature for the first time being aware of herself, and it is difficult to conceive how else this could happen except in an over-againstness posture.

For reflection means to look at oneself. How else can this be accomplished except by, in some way, standing over against oneself? Not, of course, in successively discrete moments external to one another like an infinite series of watcher and watched. Rather, man stands over against himself *simultaneously* in an identical act of awareness of objects and the act of awareness itself. In the selfsame act that you read these pages you are at the *same time* aware not only of these pages but of your *awareness of* these pages. It is this power of simultaneous reflection that is distinctive of man and that singles him out as unique in nature. In the older idea of the schoolmen, brute consciousness, though it stands also as above the mere passivity of matter, is still reducible to matter since it is incapable of rising above its individual and concrete fixation on surrounding objects. Whereas self-reflection not only knows objects but rises above them in the act of simultaneously knowing it knows those objects. It is watcher and watched in one identical act. It is this for instance which enables man to perform the incredible feat of standing outside himself, as it were, and at the *same* time point to his whole self and say, "I am myself." Nothing like this happens on the subhuman level. The point is simply that though man is continuous with nature both as to his beginning and end and indeed in-between, yet he constitutes the threshhold where nature is able to stand outside herself and engage in self-observation. This is a decisive and essential differentiation of nature from herself. For now with self-reflection comes all sorts of questions and wonderment about everything: the self, the world, and even beyond the world. The reflective spirit enters into the limitless world of human inquiry and adventure.

2. *The Non-Existence of Metaphysical Reality and Intrinsic Finality.* We saw how for Dewey, prior to the appearance of a problematic situation, the world or nature (or whatever you may want to call the field of man's actions) is just a buzzin' bloomin' confusion. Everything is in action, but as yet uncontrolled and unintelligent action. The instrumental nature of thought is such that meaning only appears with the answer or solution to a problem. If one therefore presses his philosophic inquiry into the field of pre-problematic reality, the search for Dewey is at once futile and useless. In addition it carries the inherent vice of classic spectator philosophy, namely, the desire to penetrate being in an ultimate way that rests satisfied only with the attainment of knowledge in unchanging principles or forms in things. This invariably leads to the conception of a static world, usually deemed superior. This superior world underlies or super-venes upon the ever changing and changeable world which is in fact the only one we experience. This sort of procedure Dewey rejects.

The question now is whether Dewey is not being overly dogmatic in being so totally unyielding in his rejection of metaphysical reality. To say one is interested in science and the new knowledge, and nothing else is one thing. But Dewey is saying much more that that, namely, that being is *only changeable being.* And this necessarily entails the position that statements about immutable being and principles are false.

Yet why should we not inquire into *every* area of reality? Is not boundlessness, as we just saw, precisely the characteristic of a reflective mind? To use a thought from Lonergan, even that which we do not know is at least known to us by that much, namely, as unknown. Paradoxically, therefore, the unknown presents an intelligible opening. Hence to say outright that nothing significant can be said or known of being in its preproblematic state is an overstatement, or at least too dogmatic. Worse yet, it is dogmatism at the *start* of inquiry. If philosophical dogmatism must be resorted to at all, it should be only at the *end*, when conclusions have been carefully reached and reviewed for possible mistakes. Now Dewey of course goes over the classic positions of philosophy. But his reader cannot escape the impression that he does so already with his own position and its eventual justification in mind, so that the reviews turn out to be ultimately ways of reinforcing his own preset positions.

After all, pre-problematic and post-problematic beings are beings. Uncontrolled action and scientifically controlled action *are* actions. Whether we want it or not, there is a note they commonly share. It is part of the philosophic enterprise to pry into that being which is common to both. True, such prying eventually led the classical mind to metaphysical realities and to the notion that even those uncontrolled actions flow from set natures as fundamentally diverse as those actions are among themselves. But Dewey should argue against such conclusions by showing where in fact their reasoning in faulty. Instead one gets the impression that he simply insists on the uselessness and insignificance of all that sort of spectator view of reality on the level of meliorism. To say such views are ineffective melioristically is still to leave untouched the question whether on a level *other than meliorism* they may indeed be valid and true. Or are we to assert that Deweyite meliorism is the only permissible avenue to reality? Is it possible that "consequences" may be a multivalent word whose meaning cannot and ought not to be confined solely to that of practical meliorism. In a word, there may be consequential value even in simply knowing for knowing's sake, in what Spinoza so aptly calls the "healing" of an originally ignorant and unknowing intellect.

It is also possible to learn from William James that the conception of a metaphysical reality need not necessarily result in spectator impracticality. We would naturally have to go past the idea of merely an immutable and unchanging God. But the point is that it is possible at once to blend the acceptance of realities beyond experience with practical action, indeed of melioristic action. A living proof of this would, for instance, be Mother Teresa in India. If we may believe the testimony of people like her, they draw their strength to carry on their humanitarian work from their religious conviction. For them to give up these convictions on the existence of the "supernatural", as Dewey recommends, would be to fall not necessarily into the "common faith" Dewey espouses. Certainly, there is no way of showing that they would accomplish more by such apostasy. All their testimony goes the other way.

Since there is a similarity between Dewey's dismissal of metaphysical reality, v.g. God, and the same dismissal by logical positivists such as Ayer, it may be good to refer here to the debate on the subject between the metaphysician Fredrick Copleston and A.J. Ayer.[27] The crux of the matter lies in Ayer's contention that metaphysical realities are meaningless concepts since we cannot in fact point to anything that would be verifiably different whether they exist or not. For Ayer only sensibly verifiable reality which makes sensibly verifiable differences must be accepted as the restricted area of meaningfulness. Copleston, on the other hand, points out the apparent inconsistency in Ayer's pronouncement that knowledge is valid *only* within the confines of the sensibly verifiable at the same time that Ayer violates his own rule by making statements about metaphysical reality which supposedly lies outside the sphere of meaningful discourse. It is one thing, in other words, to say metaphysical reality lies outside the sphere of scientifically and sensibly verifiable things which are the only ones one would accept as the sphere of meaning. It is something else to claim, as Ayer and Dewey do, that any other sphere is false or meaningless.

As Copleston remarks about a metaphysical proposition:

> *It isn't meaningful if the only meaningful questions are those which can be answered by the methods of empirical science, as you presuppose. In my opinion, you are unduly limiting "meaningfulness" to a certain restricted kind of meaningfulness.*[28]

And again:

> *If you say that any factual statement, in order to be meaningful, must be verifiable, and if you mean by 'verifiable' verifiable by sense experience, then surely you are presupposing that all reality is given in sense-experience. If you are presupposing this, you are presupposing that there can be no such thing as metaphysical reality. And if you presuppose this, you are presupposing a philosophical position which cannot be demonstrated by the principle of verification. It seems to me that logical positivism claims to be what I might call a 'neutral' technique, whereas in reality it presupposes the truth of positivism.*[29]

Copleston then goes on the elaborate his point:

> *By cognitive statements I presume that you mean statements which satisfy the criterion of meaning, that is to say, the principle of verifiability: and by non-cognitive statements I presume you mean statements which do not satisfy that criterion. If this is so, it seems to me that when you say that metaphysical statements are non-cognitive, you are not saying much more that that statements which do not satisfy the principle of verifiability do not satisfy the principle of verifiability.*[30]

Finally there is this summary of Copleston's position which I reproduce here because I think it makes the same point that could be made against Dewey.

> *Well, then, in your treatment of metaphysical propositions you are either applying the criterion of verifiability or you are not. If you are, then the significance of metaphysical propositions is ruled out of court* a priori, *since the truth of the principle of verifiability as it seems to be understood by you, inevitably involves the non-significance of such*

The other point which needs comment is Dewey's notion of action as a datum in the world. Indeed the idea is that movement itself, process, action *is* the world. Of course, there is also a relative stability in things, as we have seen. Indeed there is a "living mixture" of motion and rest, stability and instability, etc. "like the wheat and the tares." Nevertheless, meaning for Dewey emerges, strictly speaking, only when these motions are domesticated through scientific solutions to problematic dissatisfactions. Prior to this problematic moment, the actions going in the background of "buzzin' bloomin' confusion" are just not fit matter for philosophical reflection. Now it is very hard to cope with this position if one happens to disagree with it because in effect Dewey refuses to talk about that whole area of as yet scientifically uncharted area of beings in motion. Anyone disputing this attitude would soon find himself out of dialogue with Dewey and talking to himself. Hence we need to fall back on Dewey's basic doctrine on the inescapably social nature of man and language. Hopefully, then, we will not be in a monologue as we try to spell out some metaphysical observations on that preproblematic being which obviously covers a greater area than that of "scientized" being.

We cannot dispute Dewey's position that everything in this world is an individual existent;that abstractions are exactly that, namely, generalizations existing only in the mind. It follows that each action going on in the world of buzzin' bloomin' confusion is also individual action. Action in general, without any specific characteristic, can no more happen than can a horse or any other animal run off in all directions at once. Every action or motion that exists is of a definite, specific line or characteristic. What further results we can get by "mixing" these various sorts of actions in various measurable proportions is precisely what science is all about, and it is understandable that its interests are not about the nature of action itself but about the *results* of variously mixed actions. On the other hand, it seems to be part of the philosopher's essential task to call attention to the fact that in order to have experimental *mixtures,* one presupposes that there are beings of various types with their correspondingly varied actions to mix. If that is so, then it is an admission that even prepoblematic being has more intelligibility than it is credited with, namely, that each one is *itself,* with its own respective actions diverse from those of any other one. After all, we do not construct bridges and overpasses with water. Action is merely the extension, the completion of a being's existence. Hence if the beings are diverse and specified each one as other than the other, so too are their corresponding actions. Action and being are correlatives.

The upshot of this is that the community of being and action in problematic reality and postproblematic reality would be something that a metaphysician would like to speculate about. Both prescientific and postscientific beings certainly exist. They exist as changeable, and as of certain basic types. They have, in other words, a composition of *essence* and *existence* so that we can at least know of each of them *that it is* and that it is *different* from the others. The way is then open for understanding *all* changeable reality as contingent and as demanding the causal influx of a Being who is not contingent, one that transcends change. The path is open from here to what Dewey would call, with obvious disapproval, "spectator" philosophy. But I agree with Copleston when he calls the positivistic approach of Ayer et al. too confined. Philosophy should not block the way of inquiry whether by ukase or bias, but must deal rather with intelligibilities wherever they present themselves. Thus a philosopher cannot help being "eclectic" in this good sense, namely, with a basic principle or principles in mind which serve to organize one's framework of knowledge. In my case this would be the idea of *wholing*[32] based on the position that all changeably existing beings exist ultimately through a Being Who is other-than-the-world and the precise cause of any changeable being's existence. Because of the infinite causality radically at work in each and all of the beings in the world (what Teilhard de Chardin calls "creative transformism"), it follows that there is no end to the intelligibility of things, both individually each in its own existence, and interactively such as the results they give, or *do* when mixed with one another in various measures. And here it is interesting to note that the schoolmen themselves were the first to agree that the essences of things are opened to us only indirectly through their activities. These are metaphysical statements which obviously need quite a bit of explaining, and the interested reader will have to pursue the matter on his own.

3. *Scientific Reductionism.* Our point here is merely a corollary to the preceding section. If beings have an intelligibility other than their strictly measurable interactions with one another in a scientific context (and they do), then one may dispute the claim that the scientific method is the paradigm of all other knowledges. There is a certain infinity of intelligibility in things which makes any one method claiming a corner on knowledge suspect. The fact is that reflective philosophical thought even in Dewey himself cannot ultimately be merged with scientific thought, and scientific thought left to itself cannot even begin to understand itself. Science, in other words, understands its objects, but science itself is not its own object. There is, after all, no "science" just in general. There are only specific lines of scientific thinking going on in the minds of individual scientists, and these specific lines of scientific thought have definite objects to which they are directed, and these objects are never on the scientist's own thinking in those objects. Even the object of introspective psychology would not be, at any given moment, the act of thinking itself the psychologist is focusing on an internal object. Philosophy, in other words, is philosophy and not science. The difference here is closely related to, if not identical with that of confining meaning only to what is positively verifiable or extending it even to trascendent reality.

4. *Consequences as an Ethical Factor.* This is a point which will be included in the lenghty treatment of the two other factors of will and act itself in the section which follows. The reader may judge for himself whether the reasons given there for the validity of considering the motive of an act, as well as the act itself, as two other factors which ought to enter into an ethical consideration are valid. For now it will suffice to recall Kant's whole ethical doctrine which is against this reduction of morals not only to consequences, but to sensibly verifiable consequences. Dewey, of course, distinguishes between conduct/character and the observable deeds of a man which are the expressions or externalizations of character. Should someone say to Dewey that the effects of bad deeds are not confined only to observable consequences but also to that invisible thing called character, he would agree. But, Dewey would insist that we have no conception whether a character is good or bad except through the kinds of actions, i.e. consequences it produces. It would not be easy to object against that point, but we can perhaps insist on Kant's repeated observation that an act cannot be deemed moral simply because it happens to *conform* to a moral demand uncovered by intelligence. There must in addition be the factor that it is done precisely out of respect for the demand. In other words, applying that to our question here, we cannot deem an act moral simply because it happens to conform to the scientifically verified proposition that such actions will precisely produce desirable consequences. There should also be the conviction and will in the agent that he do the action *because* it is the right act to do. Otherwise there can be no real imputability of the action to the moral agent as such. We can recall the example of two politicians bent on constructing the same public library or bridge for their constituents. One is motivated by a genuine sense of social conscience. The other is unmoved by such motivations and habitually works only under the spur of greed for votes, self-aggrandizement and power. The need to consider the motive *in addition* to consequences is evident. Indeed any humane judge does not fail to take sincerely good motivation in a felon as a mitigating factor.

The third factor in an act that is usually considered pertinent to moral assessment is that of the *act itself.* Since this view prescinds from the act's connection to motive or consequences, Dewey understandably would find it an absurdity. However, those who hold that there is a moral assessment possible on the act itself do so because of an immutable moral standard such as the will of God, or human nature, right reason, etc., with which any act freely chosen by an individual can be compared for moral judgement. To go back to Kant we have the immutable standard, for instance, of *universalizability.* Any action that is truly universalizable is an action that anyone anywhere anytime from now till doomsday can and may will morally. Reversely, any action not so universalizable is one which no one anywhere anytime may will under penalty of being immoral. The question thus comes down to this: is it true that provided you *will* to do good, and the consequences of your willed action are good, i.e. produces the greatest happiness for the greatest number, it follows directly that the act is moral? Is there really no need to consider further the morality of the act itself? If so, that would mean that any act is good provided it is willed with a good will and the consequences are good. Here we can rightly ask" what *consequences* do you mean? For, as John Stuart Mill points out,[33] the consequences of an act can be seen within an infinite series of good and evil coming out of one another in an unending chain. Take the case of a father sincerely wanting to shock his erring youngster back to the right path before a clearly impending disaster awaiting him if he continues on the path he is presently taking. The father beats the youngster black and blue, batters him into a curbed and submissive stage so that the impeding disaster is avoided. His will is good and the good consequence is produced. If someone objects that the youngster's battered condition cannot possibly be judged good even as it is admitted that his reformed life is indeed good, at least to the extent it prevented the disaster, then all one is saying is that the produced consequence is a *mixed* good. And the interesting thing is that in Dewey it is a basic principle that everything is a *mixed* good. It shares the basic pattern of all reality as the combination of the secure and the haphazard. The question thus boils down to a consideration of the action itself, since neither the will nor the motive alone nor the consequence by itself, nor the two together can decide the case. Yet everyone knows something is wrong. Something bad or evil has been certainly done. Clearly the only other factor to be considered is the act itself. Somehow, perhaps through an intuitive immersion into the situation or experience itself we know that the act itself needs to be judged as either good or evil. As Alexander Solzhenitsyn expressed it in his now well-publicized BBC interview:

> *I would put it like this: Those people who have lived in the most terrible conditions, on the frontier between life and death, be it people from the West or from the East, all understand that between good and evil there is an irreconcilable contradiction, and that one cannot build one's life without regard to this distinction.*[34]

And again in answer to to a reminder that the great British philosopher, Bertrand Russell, gave his support to the view "better red than dead," the Russian author points out:

> *Why did he not say it would be better to be brown that dead? There's no difference. All my life and the life of my generation, the life of those who share my views, we all have one standpoint: better to be dead than a scoundrel. In this horrible expression of Bertrand Russell there is an absence of all moral criteria.*[35]

This does not of course mean that the act by itself, in isolation from either the will or the consequences, is all that must considered. We still need to clarify a great deal of opaqueness in the meaning of those words "good" and "evil."

5. *Bettering the Bad.* It is fair to say that in Dewey what is *bad* can be pointed to (not defined, nor perhaps even described) in any situation where one has run into a problem. What is good will be the solving of that problem, which means the *bettering* of the situation as it passes from being problematic to being satisfactory, through reflection and the scientific method.

Here we can recall Kant's remark to the effect that crises in life are to be looked on as challenges for improvement. Indeed this too was Dewey's recurring theme. Where then do the two disagree? In this, namely, that Kant has an *ultimate* definition of good and evil, whereas Dewey has none and thinks such a "spectator" type of philosophical definition neutralizes the philosophical enterprise altogether. One maintains that there do exist ends-in-themselves, while the other, faithful to the model of knowledge as exemplified best in the experimental sciences, maintains that there are only ends-in-view. One takes a stand on the absolute definition of certain things, whereas the other leaves no room for such absolutes in a view of reality as a throughly ongoing process. We saw how for Kant the good is the universalizable act, and evil the exception to that universalizable act; that universalizability is ultimately rooted in reason and its own unchanging laws which is the same for all men for all time. Dewey, on the other hand, would have none of that and would simply contend that we know directly in the immediacy of our experiences what the bad situation is which needs to be remedied. We need no notions of *good* and *bad in themselves* elaborated a priori. *Good* and *bad* are adjectives and attach to situations which are always *concrete*. Indeed, since all reality for Dewey is in constant activity, good and bad are, strictly speaking, adverbs. It makes more sense to say that things are going badly or well, than that they are good or bad. Things are going badly when no solutions to their difficulty are forthcoming inspite of scientific efforts to do so. Things are going well when the difficulty is being taken care of in the most efficient and effective and comprehensive way possible. Dewey would concur with the observation William James makes somewhere that the German mind tends to think of Good and Bad as upper case terms (think, for instance of Martin Luther) whereas the British (and Latin) temperament seems more inclined to the concepts of *goods* and *bads* in actual situations, in more prosaic lower case forms. At any rate, such a contrast seems certainly a propos here between Dewey and Kant.

For Kant the issue here would boil down to this: Is it moral to batter an innocent human being? Since every person is an end-in-himself, the answer is "No." Consequences for Kant cannot make any essential difference. The will ought not to will such an act. Whereas for Dewey, the issue would come down to that of the right end-in-view. He would insist on finding a solution that would prevent the impending disaster without going to the extreme of battering the youngster. And, of course, Kant and all the rest of us would go along with that. The difficulty comes with the not unrealistic factor that with some youngster (the type we presumably are discussing) only the battering would prevent the disaster and produce a reformation no matter how unpredictably brief or permanent. It is easy enough for scientific meliorism to spell out the nice results scientific method could produce out of the situation. But the fact is that in many instances the answers science gives are most abstract and thus at a few removes from the demands of the situation at the moment.

The upshot is that I personally resort, at this point, to my "wholing" idea. I suggest that that all three factors, motive, act and consequences be always considered in making a moral decision. We should reject the position that only one of the two, or only two of the three factors will suffice for resolving a moral perplexity. As the schoolmen used to say *"bonum ex integra causa, malum ex quocumque defectu."* An act is good if all the three factors (motive, act, consequences) are each of them good; an act is bad if any one of the three is bad. I would certainly go along with the positive formulation of the principle. But as is evident in the case we are just discussing, it happens sometimes that a decision should be made when one of the factors is inescapably bad, or at any rate *mixed.*

It will not do, for example, to think away the bad by saying the beating and battering cannot really be considered "bad" in the light of the reformed life that resulted from it. This is precisely what Dewey said rationalists usually do. They find themselves able to blink away the reality of experience infront of them in favor of some abstract schema in the mind according to which the very real *bad* in front of them is in actuality *good*, even though to experience it may appear *bad.*

The wholing outlook I am suggesting would instead admit that battering is indeed bad where it is done to an innocent person. Too, the will to save the child, and the subsequent result of the child's reformation are both good. Yet, in that actual situation, there is really nothing that can be said or done except to go by one's best judgement as to how far to punish the child to achieve the desired result. To those who would say that I have here simply evaded the issue, I would ask: what else can one do when one *has to* do something? It seems unrealistic to say we should wait until a scientific method has been figured out, when, as we said, the situation will not allow for that sort of luxury. It also seems absurd to say that battering another human beings is always and everywhere wrong. It is well-known how Kant himself sternly advocates that a community in an isolated island about to disband and go back to join the mainland society, should first make sure they *execute* the lone criminal in their prison whom they have condemned to such punishment.[36] If execution is not battering, then what is? Obviously, despite all his protestations, and as some of his commentators frankly admit, circumstances and consequences figure even in Kant, whenever moral assessment takes place.

What I am maintaining here is that on the "wholing" view, when all the three factors are good, then of course the act is good. And an act may still be good *on the whole* even though one of the factors may be bad. I know this is departure from the natural law tradition, but I think the idea of approaching a moral problem *on the whole* and resolving it on a *wholing* basis, simply makes more sense. This seems so since nothing, after all, is purely good, except perhaps Kant's good will which, he is the first to say, is unattainable in the human condition. Indeed what mere mortal can foresee all the unending chain of goods and bads that keep emerging out of one's action? But it is a part of realistic wholism to agree that the impossible cannot be made morally obligatory on any one. If it is impossible for any man to foresee the final result of an unending chain of goods and bads, and it is --- then all one can be required to do reasonably is to foresee *as much as is in his power.* Naturally, this presupposes the advise and help of as many "wise" men as is realistically allowed by the situation, as to the most comprehensive end-in-view possible. This certainly means looking toward the greatest shared and secured good possible. And having made these wholing efforts, one must then act according to one's best lights. What else could morals be all about?

That no one is obliged to foresee the results of an intended action beyond what is humanly possible is evident in that all morality is a matter of responsability and imputability. Anything that happens accidentally or outside the intention of the agent cannot realistically be imputed to him. He cannot be held accountable for it, unless of course, as we have said, it was humanly foreseeable --- in which case imputability would be still linked beyond possible knowledge to his provable *willing* of those consequences. Could we, for instance, impute the present prosperity of West Germany to Hitler, since in the unending chain of good and bad results the present situation may in a sense be traced back to the big bad result of Hitler's Germany? To repeat, moral obligation can only obtain within the human limits of knowledge. And we have to admit that the limits are those which a prudent man sets, nothing more. But also nothing less. For the same prudence would deem it reasonable to impute to an agent consequences which he *could have* and *ought to have*, therefore, foreseen.

Let us go back to Dewey's point that the *bad* needs no prior definition since it lies revealed in a problematic situation which demands melioration. The most comprehensive melioration here means the most enduring and inclusive goods. The problem, however, is one of distinguishing the morally *bad* from the merely physically bad. Likewise with the *good*. We know that Dewey is against such separation in experience. The only distinction he would make would be between reflective and unreflective goods in experience. We recall how the point of reference for a solution is already contained in the very articulation of the problem itself. But can we really go along with the position that any state of dissatisfaction immediately points to its relief as *good?* Now of course Dewey did not hold this simplicist position. We recall his illustration to the effect that the way a burglar solves or meliorates his problematic situation of want and the way an honest man does the same through honest labor are obviously of different moral quality. The question thus is: how do we come by this judgement?

Dewey's answer would fall back on the nature of a moral claims as already contained in the social relationship in which an individual necessarily finds himself. But if we press the point further and ask what really is the commonly shared good that Dewey is talking about as the basis for moral claims, the answer can only be that it cannot be defined beforehand but must be revealed in experience, though he does say that very general human wants do recur regularly so that thay can be mentioned in the abstract without really meaning too much in the concrete. Thus we come back to the concrete *good* or *bad* as immediately revealed in the experience of a problematic situation. In a word, our difficulty is that physical goods (pleasures) and bads (pains) can in fact be moral evils and goods. The point reverts back to the fact that a physical evil may produce a moral good and a physical good may produce a moral evil and vice versa. We need only recall, without further elaboration, the case of the burglar and the honest worker.

It seems clear to me that we need to go beyond Dewey to the position that both motive and the action itself are relevant considerations in a moral situation, in addition to consequences. Too we should go beyond Kant to the position that consequences also are essential consideration in addition to motive and act. All three (motive, act and consequences) in the concrete situation in which an individual is making the moral assessment must enter into reflective consideration. Whether there is a final end-in-itself transcending this world which must also be considered would naturally depend on whether the agent is a philosophical theist or not. This means it is futile to generalize and contend that every person must take God into the picture when making a moral judgement. To repeat, no one is obliged to the impossible. It would be obliging one who does not · believe in God to the impossible by obliging him to weigh what clearly can have no weight in his own consciousness.

Hence we come back to the point that a moral judgement must take a wholing view of the problematic situation. On motive and act we have much to learn from Kant. On the consequances we have much to learn from Dewey. But as always in matters philosophical, it is we ourselves finally who have to make the "wholistic" moral decision. This combines what absolutes we know, and hold, with the profoundly relativizing factors of our individual lives and circumstances. For my part, I know that it is a heavier burden to personalize one's moral decisions in this way and genuinely assume responsibilities for them, than to fob the entire matter off to some awesome and widely accepted "authority." It is a cop-out, as the saying goes these days, to refuse to think for one's self because somebody else, for *whatever* reason, has been appointed (or even annointed) to do precisely that sort of thinking for us. Even if one fully accepts such authoritative moral guidance, the relativizing of that guidance to one's own personal world should itself be left to no other authority than the individual involved. Salvation is nothing if it is not personal. Hence we stand alone (before the Alone, if we believe) ultimately in every moral decision we make. We should.

I would like to conclude by going back yet one more time to the idea of "wholing." It is an idea which probably can be related to Dewey's view of an organism as all the time a plenum of action which in the case of human beings lie open for re-directions and re-channelings in ever widening spheres of inter-subjective relationships. In the second chapter of my book, *The Self Beyond*[37], there is an explanation of principles common to followers of Aquinas, namely, *to exist is to tend toward* (*esse est tendere*) and *action follows being* (*agere sequitur esse*). It is safe to say that no classical or scholastic philosophies would have been possible without those two principles on which practically all their speculations revolved. Those philosophies held that the natures (essences) of things were beyond man's ken directly, and that the *only* way we could ever divine what things are in themselves was by watching how they act. Mr. Sadat and Mr. Begin, for instance, can look each other in the eye for heaven only knows how long, but in the end the only way each would ever find out what really is in the other's "heart" is through his actions, is this not so? And is this not somewhat reminiscent of Dewey's position on the continuity of the self with its ideals, of character with conduct, and the constant interplay between the two? Indeed it is hard to believe that Dewey himself did not know those "contemplative" principles when he launched forth on a lifelong career against their respective philosophies. No, his problem was rather that he saw very clearly that the mediaevals, while holding to an active metaphysics (in one form or another) also rendered it practically ineffectual by pointing it naturally and rigidly to an otherworldly End of Absolutely Perfect and First Being. That entailed a host of unpalatable (for him) consequences.

It would be absurd to propose some quick and easy reconciliation between the sticking points of disagreement here. What we can do, however, is show how some questions can be asked that may help clear out a usable path. For example, why cannot the great insights of Dewey be affirmed without necessarily going along with all of his negations? If the truth be told, there is no critical mind which does not function eclectically in this way, at least in the beginning. Why cannot a believer have the courage of his conviction enough to work through his affirmation of a supernatural reality vis-a-vis Dewey's critique on its practical ineffectiveness and fixed attachment to immutable goals? In a Kierke-gaardian way, he could then possibly point to his own life and self (cannot a Mother Teresa today do this?) as the existential critique of Dewey in turn. Why cannot the unity of the *is* with the *ought* be accepted without foreclosing of necessity the possibility of transcendent reality? Was this not in fact the grave and serious question English-speaking philosophers like William James and Alfred North Whitehead tried so hard to work through, namely, the idea of God in continual partnership with man in the struggle to increase goodness in the world? And so on.

To continue now with our reflections on tendential existence. Look at each being as pointed to action, as *actively* existing. To exist is, after all, to be *actual*. Hence the marvelous variety of activities all around us in the universe. Man sees all that variety, takes notes, reflects and then decides on his course of action. His own peculiarly human energies are then linked ever more to all these natural activities. The end point of all that linkage, the directing center of all these operations, is his *decision*, his free choice, is it not? Every choice, we heard Dewey say, is a making or re-making of the self along life's way with special emphasis, of course, on the decisions made at the crossroads. More, it is also a making and re-making of the "world" affected by and forged by our decisions, that is, the world of other human selves and nature. In brief, we can see both Being and Becoming, an individual as he *is* and as he *will be*, both centered on that all-important power in him, his *free choice*. We are walking structures of our past choices. We are also our own structure-makers able, usually with help from others, to rise from the immediacy of our situational limits to the "scheme of things entire" to see what needs doing in our ever-unfinished selves. In that moment of perceiving one's need or interest in order to become *whole* we also experience existentially the actual fusion of the *ought* with the *is*.

Call it "dominant inclination," "supreme value," "individual max-im," what you will---it seems that the countless little choices we make in the course of our day-to-day existence are in fact made on the basis of one dominant value which an individual holds for himself. Indeed the individual who would insist on having no such dominant value would also assert it by that very same act, namely, his condition is equivalently such a value. Not that we all know what our own dominant value is always explicitly. Freud has long since shown that powerful effects can well out of merely implicitly affirmed values. It is the task of philosophers, as Socrates, the father of them all, taught, to dig deep into themselves so as to bring forth into the daylight of explicit consciousness whatever value they cherish most. For only then would they be in a position to put that value through the searching examination of reason. Why all this? Because this is to love one's self truly and praiseworthily. We are not, after all, defined so much by our looks or our possessions, etc., as by our convictions, what we stand for. Both spontaneously and reflectively this is how we identify people: by what they *stand for*. Clearly, a man stands for what he freely chooses to stand for. And I am saying that his choice coincides with what he cherishes most, that one value which, consciously or otherwise, controls his choices big and small. There probably is a pattern to every human being discoverable the moment his dominant value is brought into explicit consciousness. It is my observation that this dominant value also constitutes the individual's own answer to that most human and humane of all questions: what is life all about?

In both thinkers we studied, we noticed a passion in the end for harmonizing everything that may possibly have seemed disparate as they went through their analyses. There is a lesson in that for us. It is good mental hygiene at the minimum to know one's self to the point, at any rate, where one has clarified to himself his own dominant value, and whether he ought to preserve, expand, or even destroy it in order to rebuild himself. His options are open. The one thing necessary is *growth*. And the norm finally for what growth is and what it is not is the ultimate (as we learned from Kant) tribunal of reflective reason examining our dominant value to see whether indeed it makes life (which is not easy for anyone) worth living. I propose then that our power of *free choice*, which stands as the controlling center of our various actions, and which thus is the core of ourselves, be viewed as the living point in which everything we are is centered dynamically: being, becoming, dominant value, personal meaning of life, all of them ultimately identically the self.

It only remains to quote Alexander Solzhenitsyn's words which I have treasured from the first time I came across them in the pages of *The Gulag Archipelago*. After recounting all the unimaginable inhumanities he and his Gulag fellows had undergone, and when beyond his own conceiving almost he realized he had survived it all and was free at last, Solzhenitsyn squeezes out of it all these words of wisdom. They are all the more moving and convincing because they are the final fruits of an awesome human experience shocked at how free men often blow up trivia into "tormenting" problems.

> *What about the main thing in life, all its riddles? If you want, I'll spell it out for you right now. Do not pursue what is illusory---property and position: Live with a steady superiority over life---don't be afraid of*

229

misfortune, and do not yearn after happiness; it is, after all, all the same: the bitter doesn't last forever, and the sweet never fills the cup to overflowing. It is enough if you don't freeze in the cold and if thirst and hunger don't claw at your insides. If your back isn't broken, and if your feet can walk, if both arms can bend, if both eyes see, and if both ears hear, then whom should you envy? And why? Our envy of others devours us most of all. Rub your eyes and purify your heart...[38]

"It is after all, all the same." Strange words those which call for reflection. Is Solzhenitsyn being numbed here by some sort of apathy (ataraxy, as the ancient Stoics termed it) because he happens to have survived it all? But then how explain him as a driven man today bent on stopping Mother Russia from devouring her very children who out of love for her, dare raise their voices in protest against everything symbolized by the Gulag Archipelago? If good must be fought for in the face of evil, how can it be "after all, all the same?" He explains in the next line. "The bitter does not last forever, and the sweet never fills the cup to overflowing." It is a theme fairly common, whether to great or merely crackerbarrel thinkers. Indeed we heard Dewey wax poetic on "the longest lane turns sometime," etc. Just as Dewey concluded by stressing our need for ratio, a sense of balance, so Solzhenitsyn seems to be saying the same thing, but of course in context of the horrors he experienced. Hence he reminds us of the most basic and important blessings of all which because of their nearness to us we all too readily overlook: our healthy life and limbs. What if we were disfigured, or partially dismembered, or had to leave and take our place among the terminally ill?

But there is something even deeper in that passage. After all, we do pass most of our days in relative health and freedom. Hence our problems really consist of the ups and downs of life. Yes, the ups too can be unbearable. As one journalist put it: "Being frustrated is unpleasant, but our real problems begin when we get what we want." I take Solzhenitsyn's words then as an exhortation to see everything in perspective, to have balance, to rise to the vision of the *whole*. We shall then see that he who is unhorsed today may be the victor tomorrow. And contrariwise. The fall of the first American President and all his men from power and property soon after being re-elected by the greatest landslide in history drives home the lesson that even in over-insured America everything can indeed be lost in one fell night. One keeps a sense of balance then by remembering the thought from another Spanish saying, perhaps a bit lowly, but quite perceptive for all that. Life, it is said, turns full circle many more times than a dog answering nature's call. What Solzhenitsyn says here about the final sameness of the bitter with the sweet; what Dewey said about life as an ongoing mixture of the secure with the perilous; what Kant taught us about our absolute worth, our dignity as rational beings---all these should go a long way toward rubbing our eyes and purifyng our hearts.

ACKNOWLEDGEMENTS

I want to give my thanks and acknowledgements to all publishers who kindly gave me permission to quote from their books, directly or indirectly. In particular I thank the following for the use of their respectively mentioned books:

Beacon Press, *Reconstruction in Philosophy.*
University of Chicago Press, *Theory of Valuation.*
Dover Publications, Inc., *Experience and Nature.*
G.P. Putnam's Sons, *The Quest For Certainty.*
Holt, Rinehart and Winston, *Theory of the Moral Life.*
Library of Liberal Arts, Bobbs-Merrill, *Fundamental Principles of the Metaphysic of Morals; Prolegomena To Any Future Metaphysics; Critique of Pure Practical Reason.*
Yale University Press, *Common Faith.*

As I said in the Preface, the desideratum would be the adoption of these paperbacks for class use *pari passu* with this book.

For convenience it may be good to repeat here the abbreviations for the main works of Kant and Dewey.

PAFM	= *Prolegomena to Any Future Metaphysics,* With an Introduction by L. W. Beck, Indianapolis, 1950.
FPMM	= *Fundamental Principles of the Metaphysic of Morals,* Translated by T. K. Abbott, Indianapolis, 1949.
CPR	= *Critique of Practical Reason,* Translated by L. W. Beck, Indianapolis, 1956.
MPV	= *The Metaphysical Principles of Virtue,* Translated by J. Ellington, Indianapolis, 1964.
MEJ	= *The Metaphysical Elements of Justice,* Translated by J. Ladd, Indianapolis, 1965.
RWLRA	= *Religion Within the Limits of Reason Alone,* Translated by T.M. Greene and H.H. Hudson, with "The Ethical Significance of Kant's Religion," by J. R. Silber, New York, 1960.
LoE	= *Lectures on Ethics,* Translated by L. Infield, New York, 1963.
CPPR	= *Critique of Pure Reason,* Translated by F.M. Müller, New York, 1961.

TML	= *Theory of the Moral Life,* New York, 1960.
RP	= *Reconstruction in Philosophy,* Boston, 1962.
QC	= *The Quest for Certainty,* New York, 1960.
EN	= *Experience and Nature,* New York, 1958.
TV	= *Theory of Valuation,* Chicago, 1966.
CF	= *Common Faith,* New Haven, 1972.

NOTES

I-1

1. Keith Ward, *The Development of Kant's View of Ethics,* Oxford, 1972, 3-4.
2. Robert P. Wolff, *The Autonomy of Reason, A Commentary on Kant's Groundwork of the Metaphysic of Morals,* New York, 1973, 160.
3. FPMM, xxi-ii.
4. K. Ward, *op.cit.,* 26.
5. H. J. Paton, *The Categorical Imperative, A Study in Kant's Moral Philosophy,* London, 1970, 198.
6. R. P. Wolff, *op.cit.,* 160.
7. PAFM, 24.
8. *An Enquiry Concerning Human Understanding,* Part I, Section iv.
9. K. Ward, *op.cit.,* 14.
10. *Ibid,* 28.
11. PAFM, 23, footnote.
12. *Ibid,* 16-18, 26.
13. *Ibid,* 43.
14. *Ibid,* 23, 25, 43.
15. *Ibid,* 26.
16. *Ibid,* 23, footnote.
17. *Ibid,* 14.
18. For a succint account of this distinction between *method* and *proposition* see James Collins, *A History of Modern European Philosophy,* Milwaukee, 1954, 477.
19. PAFM, 22.
20. *Ibid* Italics for these propositions will hence forth be omitted unless specially called for.
21. *Ibid,* 5.
22. K. Ward, *op. cit.,* 34.
23. PAFM, 80.
24. *Ibid,* 63, footnote.
25. PAFM, 61.
26. *Ibid,* 42, 46, 60, 62.
27. *Ibid,* 40; H. J. Paton, *op. cit.,* 227.
28. K. Ward, *op. cit.,* 38.
29. *Ibid*
30. PAFM, 62, 103, 109-10.
31. *Ibid,* 110.
32. J. Collins, *op. cit.,* 486.
33. H. J. Paton, *op. cit.,* 227, footnote.
34. PAFM, 28-41.
35. CPR, 39-53.
36. PAFM, 30.
37. *Ibid,* 30-1.
38. *Ibid,* 84-5.
39. *Ibid,* 31.
40. *Ibid,* 33.
41. *Ibid*
42. *Ibid,* 34.
43. K. Ward, *op. cit.,* 44-5.

44. PAFM, 42, 93.
45. *Ibid*
46. *Ibid,* 43.
47. *Ibid,* 48.
48. *Ibid,* 49, footnote.
49. On this key idea in Kant see J. Collins, *op. cit.,* 486.
50. PAFM, 113-14.
51. *Ibid,* 76-7, parenthesis inserted.
52. *Ibid,* 76, 100-02, 113; J. Collins, *op. cit.,* 491 footnote.
53. *Ibid,* 116.
54. *Ibid,* 76.
55. *Ibid,* 77.
56. J. Collins, *op. cit.,* 492.
57. *Ibid,* 498, footnote.
58. PAFM, 50-2; Lewis W. Beck, *A Commentary on Kant's Ctitique of Practical Reason,* Chicago, 1960,86-9; J. Collins, *op. cit.,* 497.
59. PAFM, 110, 113.

I-2

1. T.C. Williams, *The Concept of the Categorical Imperative,* Oxford, 1968, is good for a look at the major disagreements among Kant's commentors in English.
2. L. W. Beck, *Kant's Critique of Practical Reason,* Chicago, 1960, 9-18.
3. See CPR footnote, p.4 where morality is said to be our *ratio cognoscendi* (basis for awareness) of freedom, and freedom our *ratio essendi* (basis for being) of morality.
4. FPMM, 71-2.
5. *Ibid,* 7.
6. *Treatise on Human Nature,* Part I, Section 1.
7. FPMM, 5.
8. *Ibid*
9. *Ibid,* 24-7.
10. *Ibid,* 15.
11. *Ibid,* 18.
12. *Ibid,* 19.
13. *Ibid,* 38, footnote.
14. *Ibid,* 25.
15. H. J. Paton, *The Categorical Imperative,* London, 1970, 15; T. C. Williams, *op. cit.,* 15-17; 59-66; 74-7.
16. FPMM, 22; also, CPR, 159-65.
17. *Ibid*
18. FPMM, 21, 29.

19. *Ibid*, 22-3.
20. *Ibid*, 26.
21. *Ibid*
22. *Ibid*
23. *Ibid*, 28 footnote; CPR, 159-65.
24. L. W. Beck, *A Commentary on Kant's Critique of Practical Reason.* Chicago, 1960, 85.
25. FPMM, 34.
26. L. W. Beck. *op. cit.*, 86 footnote; FPMM, 34.
27. *Ibid*, 35.
28. There seems to be a textual inconsistency between earlier passages (p. 14) where Kant said happiness is not man's natural end since reason is the chief means nature gives him for the attainment of his end, and instinct better than reason would have achieved happiness more effectively, etc. Perhaps the solution lies in that natural desire and man's end or destiny are two quite different things. The fact that man has a natural desire to be happy does not make his natural destiny that of happiness. Eating, for instance, is a necessary and natural desire in man. But it clearly is not man's natural end or destiny.
29. *Ibid*, 35.
30. *Ibid*
31. CPR, 25.
32. FPMM, 37-8.
33. *Ibid*
34. *Ibid*
35. CPR, 27.
36. FPMM, 41.
37. R.P. Wolff, *The Autonomy of Reason,* New York, 1973, 171.
38. *Ibid*, 172.
39. FPMM, 41.
40. *Ibid*
41. *Ibid*, 42.
42. *Ibid*, 44.
43. *Ibid*, 44-5.
44. *Ibid*, 43.
45. *Ibid*, 45, parenthesis inserted.
46. *Ibid*, 46.
47. *Ibid*
48. *Ibid*, 47.
49. *Ibid*, 48.
50. *Ibid*
51. *Ibid*
52. *Ibid*, 49.
53. *Ibid*, 50.
54. See R. P. Wolff, *op. cit.,* 182 for an encomium on this section and for its relation to Rousseau's *Social Contract,* especially 183 on the unity of reason.
55. FPMM, 64.
56. H. J. Paton, *op. cit.,* 189.
57. *Ibid*

58. FPMM, 52.
59. *Ibid*
60. *Ibid*
61. H. J. Paton, *op. cit.,* 129-98.
62. FPMM, 54.
63. *Ibid*, 55.
64. H. J. Paton, *op. cit.,* 188.
65. *Ibid*, 187-92.
66. FPMM, 56.
67. *Ibid*, 57.
68. B.E.A. Liddell, *Kant on the Foundation of Morality,* Bloomington, 1970, 57-8.
69. *Ibid*, 193; FPMM, 58-9.
70. On how in Kant "everything gravitates ultimately toward the practical," see James C. Collins, "Kant's Logic as a Critical Aid, "*The Review of Metaphysics,* March, 1977, v. xxx, n. 3,440-61, especially 455 on.
71. FPMM, 69.
72. *Ibid*, 65.
73. *Ibid*, 65.
74. *Ibid*, 69.
74. See note 3 above.
76. FPMM, 66.
77. *Ibid*
78. *Ibid*
79. *Ibid*, 64.
80. *Ibid*, 71.
81. CPR, 18.
82. FPMM, 72.
83. *Ibid*
84. *Ibid*, 74: Cf. R. P. Wolff, *op. cit.,* 9-15 on the "four selves" in Kant.
85. FPMM, 77.

I-3

1. CPR, 124.
2. *Ibid*, 30.
3. *Ibid*
4. While every moral obligation is a "constraint," not every constraint is a moral obligation. Think, for instance, of a very unpalatable consequence someone powerful could offer you for your "choice" in the form of a hypothetical conditional statement. In the Abbot translation of the FPMM mainly used here, "obligation" is the word used instead of "constraint," while B.E.A. Liddell, v.g. *op. cit.,* 82-3 and passim, seems to prefer "constraint." L.W. Beck uses the two words interchangeably, v.g. *op. cit.,* 82-4: "For men and all rational creatures, the moral necessity is a constraint, an obligation."

5. CPR, 63.
6. FPMM, 12-14.
7. Kant, *The Metaphysical Principles of Virtue,* 58-9; CPR, 82.
8. LoE, 247.
9. FPMM, 15.
10. CPR, 63.
11. FPMM, 34; L. W. Beck. *op. cit.,* 86, footnote.
12. CPR, 61, 112.
13. *Ibid.,* 24-5.
14. CPR.96, FPMM,33. B.E.A. Liddell distinguishes between our *natural goal and our moral or rational goal: "Although it is highly unlikely (due to stepmotherly nature) that we will achieve fully our natural goal, we can surely achieve our moral or rational purpose, which is to be worthy of happiness. Thus the rational goal is in accord with man's natural goal, and not in opposition to it." Op. cit.,* 119. More on this complementary role of happiness and morality to each other towards the end of this chapter.
15. CPR, 37; FPMM, 35.
16. *Ibid.,* 35.
17. CPR, 25.
18. *Ibid.,* 17-39.
19. *Ibid.,* 22.
20. *Ibid.,* 24.
21. *Ibid.,* 24-5.
22. *Ibid.,* 36-7.
23. *Ibid.,* 37.
24. *Ibid.,* 38-9.
25. FPMM, 75.
26. CPR, 61-2.
27. FPMM, 12.
28. CPR, 62.
29. *Ibid.,* 40.
30. *Ibid.,* 18, 24, 32, passim; FPMM, 17.
31. CPR, 22-3.
32. FPMM, 33 footnote on "prudence."
33. *Ibid.,* 57-8; H. J. Paton. *op. cit.,* 212; L. W. Beck, *op. cit.,* 87-8.
34. FPMM, 58.
35. *Ibid.,* 25.
36. *Ibid.,* 15.
37. *Ibid.,* 15.
38. *Ibid.,* 20. "Is it better to produce good actions from bad motives or bad actions from good motives? The answer depends on the standard used for "better." If we want results, then good actions are better... If we want good character... then good motives are better. But in view of the general correspondence between motive and action, it is far better to have good motives, since they are the best guarantee of good results." B.E.A. Liddell, *op. cit.,* 63. We can ask further: Isn't man obliged to have a good character, while it is diffi-cult to show that he is obliged to have good results, so many things being beyond his control? His character, however, is by presupposition always in his control.
39. FPMM, 25.
40. CPR, 161.
41. FPMM, 18.
42. CPR, 156.
43. This motive to do one's duty as one sincerely sees it is "conscience." "...there is no such thing as an erring conscience. In the objective judgement of whether or not something is a duty, one can indeed sometimes be mistaken; but I cannot be mistaken in my subjective judgement as to whether I have compared something with my practical (here judicially acting) reason for the sake of such a judgement. For if I were mistaken in that, I would then not have exercised practical judgement at all, and in that case there is neither truth nor error. Unconscientiousness is not lack of conscience but the propensity not to heed its judgement. But when a man is aware of having acted according to his conscience, then as far as guilt or innocence is concerned, nothing more can be demanded." *The Metaphysical Elements of Virtue,* 59-60. On how this "intuitionist" element in Kant's doctrine (which at the same time seeks dynamic objectivity) comes close to contemporary intuitionists such as G.E. Moore and Sir David Ross, see T.C. Williams, *op. cit.,* 126-27; 134-35.
44. FPMM, 59-60.
45. *Ibid.,* 26.
46. *Ibid.,* 41.
47. B.E.A. Liddell, op. cit., 132-33; especially T.C. Williams, *op. cit.,* 41 where in dissent from C.D. Broad he writes: "It will be noted that Kant claims to have derived the categorical imperative, not from the concept of rationality, as Broad holds here, but from the notion of duty or categorical obligation." Footnote.
48. FPMM, 19.
49. *Ibid.,* 25.
50. J. H. Newman, *University Sermons,* London, S.P.C.K., 1970, 200.
51. T.C. Williams, *Op. cit.,* 22-3 where he lists the conclusions of Kant's commentators as to how many categorical imperatives there are. Thus Paton holds there are five, Duncan four, Caird three, Broad three, Ross five, while Williams himself quotes Kant to show that there is only one. See also J. R. Silber, "Proce-

dural Formalism in Kant's Ethics." *The Review of Metaphysics,* v. xxviii, .2, December 1974, 203 where he holds that the various formulations are one when seen from the thought procedure used in all of them. As regards those who would argue in the traditionalistic interpretation of Kant on the basis of his article, "The Supposed Right to Lie," J. R. Silber argues that we cannot throw out Kant's more open position in his major ethical writings based solely on that internally inconsistent article which Kant wrote in a rage and when he was well advanced in years. *Ibid.,* 223.

52. FPMM, 38.
53. *Ibid.,* 38.
54. *Ibid.,* 54.
55. *Ibid.,* 38.
56. *Ibid.,* 54.
57. *Ibid.,* 46.
58. *Ibid.,* 55.
59. *Ibid.,* 38.
60. *Ibid.,* 30.
61. CPR, 27.
62. *Ibid.,* 72.
63. H. J. Paton, *op. cit.,* 172. While giving his version of what perfect and imperfect duties mean, Paton observes that Kant "nowhere seems to define the distinction clearly." *Ibid.,* 147. For a summary of M. Singer's and Ross' interpretation of what Kant meant by perfect and imperfect duties, see T.C. Williams, *op. cit.,* 44; B.E.A. Liddell, *op. cit.,* 142 equates perfect and imperfect duties with negative (prohibition) and positive (commission) duties. As regards purposiveness and nature, Paton writes: "He is already supposing that nature --- at least human nature --- is teleological or what he calls later a kingdom of nature and not a mere mechanism." *The Moral Law,* 30.
64. FPMM, 39.
65. *Critique of Judgement,* 35 footnote.
66. FPMM, 39.
67. *Ibid.,* 40.
68. *Ibid.,* 41.
69. R.P. Wolff, *op. cit.,* 171.
70. FPMM, 45-6.
71. *Ibid.,* 44.
72. *Ibid.,* 45, footnote.
73. *Ibid.,* 73.
74. *Ibid.,* 11.
75. P. Weiss, *Man's Freedom,* New Haven, 1950, 56.
76. *Op. cit.,* 221-22.
77. CPR, 76.
78. *Ibid*
79. *Ibid.,* 79, 166.

80. FPMM, 11, CPR, 36-7.
81. *Ibid.,* 52-3; H.J. Paton, *The Categorical Imperative,* 171, 189; B.E.A. Liddell, *op. cit.,* 156: "The intrinsic worth of a rational being does not depend upon his *having* a good will, for few men, if any, have such a worth. Rather, it is because every man is a rational being and as such *could* have a good will, that we consider him a being of intrinsic value."
82. FPMM, 24-5.
83. *Ibid.,* 21.
84. CPR, 161.
85. *Ibid.,* 81.
86. FPMM, 59.
87. CPR, 79-80; H. J. Paton, op. cit., 63 and *The Moral Law,* 21 on his preference for translating Kant's word *achtung* used here to "reverence" rather than respect because of its kinship in Kant's mind to religious emotion.
88. CPR. 81.
89. FPMM, 46.
90. *Ibid*
91. *Ibid,* 47.
92. CPR, 47.
93. FPMM, 47.
94. *Ibid.,* 47.
95. CPR, 73.
96. *Ibid.,* 136.
97. LoE, 193-4.
98. Cambridge, Massachusetts, 1971, 3-4.
99. LoE, 221.

I-4

1. FPMM, 50.
2. ...we recognize that the law stands; but we say to ourselves, 'this is a very special occasion,' or 'I am a very special person' and so proceed to establish an exception to our own advantage. He (**Kant**) adds that although from the point of view of reason there is a contradiction in this, in action it is rather an *antagonism* in virtue of which we sophistically take the moral law to be general rather than truly universal. Paton, TCI, 139.
3. FPMM, 50.
4. CPR, note 1, 4.
5. FPMM, 50.
6. *Ibid*
7. *Ibid.,* 64-5.
8. *Ibid.,* 66.
9. CPR. 87.

10. LoE, 246.
11. FPMM, 57 on heteronomy as either from "inclinations or conception of reason."
12. CPR, 76.
13. *Ibid.*, 87.
14. *Ibid.*, 33.
15. *Ibid.*, 134.
16. *Ibid.*, 86, italics added.
17. *Ibid.*, 127.
18. *Ibid.*
19. *Ibid.*
20. Kant is not arguing here in the classical way: because there is no justice in this life, there must be another life where there *is* justice. Instead he goes the positive route basing immortality on the moral progress of man even though as he wrote in his *Critique of Judgement:* "Deceit, violence, and envy will always be rife around him, although he himself is honest. peaceable, and benevolent; and other righteous men that he meets in the world, no matter how deserving they be of happiness, will be subjected by nature, which takes no heed of such deserts, to all the evils of want, disease, and untimely death, just as are the other animals of the earth. And so it will continue to be until one wide grave engulfs them all --- just and unjust --- there is no distinction in the grave, and hurls them back into the absss of the aimless chaos of matter from which they were taken."
21. CPR, 128.
22. *Ibid.*, italics added.
23. *Ibid.*, 63-4.
24. FPMM, 13-14.
25. CPR, 151.
26. *Ibid.*, 113.
27. *Ibid.*, 148.
28. CPR, 126-27.
29. *Ibid.*, 133, also 96.
30. *Ibid.*, 134.
31. *Ibid.*, 135.
32. FPMM, 11.
33. *Ibid.*, 51-2.
34. *Ibid.*, 66.
35. CPR, 122.
36. *Ibid.*, 120.
37. *Ibid.*, 133.
38. *Ibid.*, 135.
39. *Ibid.*
40. *Ibid.*, 117.
41. *Ibid.*, 141. Cf. also Paton, TCI, 44, 109; Liddell. OFM, 48-49, 161.
42. CPR, 117.
43. *Ibid.*, 114.
44. *Ibid.*
45. *Ibid.*, 27-8.
46. *Ibid.*, 122.
47. *Ibid.*, 96.
48. *Ibid.*, 115.
49. *Ibid.*
50. *Ibid.*, 114.
51. *Ibid.*, 119.
52. The reason I have used the word *complete* goodness instead of *perfect* goodness is simply that this seems more consistent with Kant's insistence that the most human effort can ever achieve is virtue, even though he does talk confusingly at times of *holiness* also in this regard. For more on this see, Beck, CCPR, 268-69.
53. CPR, 130.
54. *Ibid.*
55. *Ibid.*, 149.
56. *Ibid.*, 89.
57. *Ibid.*, 166.
58. Ibid., 134. "The whole of Kant's moral philosophy might almost be described under the title of one of his last books as *Religion Within the Limits of Reason Alone.* For him religion is primarily the Christian religion purified, not only from the dogmas of an authoritarian church, but also from the miracles and mysteries and from what he regards as the substitution of historical beliefs for rational ones." Paton, TCI, 196. "*Enlightenment* meant the influences of American and French revolutions regarded as continuations of the Reformation 'though the French revolution was more bloody and more violent against religion, because there the Reformation had been defeated." *Ibid.*, 196.
59. CPR, 23.
60. D. W. Ross, *Kant's Ethical Theory,* Oxford, 1965, 32-3.

II-2

1. TV, 60-61.
2. RP, 24.
3. CF, 59.
4. RP, 7.
5. QC, 9-10; 292.
6. *Ibid.*, 8.
7. *Ibid.*, 11.
8. *Ibid.*, 27, 39-40.
9. RP, 7-10.
10. *Ibid.*, x.
11. *Ibid.*, 9.
12. *Ibid.*, 10.
13. *Ibid.*, 11.
14. Ibid., 10-14.
15. QC, 16.

16. EN, 215; RP, 17-19; QC, 15-16; 69, 90.
17. *Ibid.,* 13.
18. *Ibid.,* 19.
19. *Ibid.,* 17.
20. *Metaphysics,* Bk. XII, ch. 7, 1072b15-25; QC, 20.
21. *Ibid*
22. EN, 105.
23. QC, 21; RP, xii.
24. QC, 30.
25. *Ibid.,* 273.
26. RP, 20.
27. QC, 43.
28. *Ibid.,* 293.
29. RP, 26.
30. *Ibid.,* 30.
31. For a concise explanation of this quote from Francis Bacon's *Novum Organum,* see James Collins, *A History of Modern European Philosophy,* Milwaukee, 1954, 67.
32. RP, 31.
33. *Ibid.,* 32.
34. *Ibid.,* 34.
35. *Ibid.,* 36-7.
36. *Ibid*
37. *Ibid*
38. *Ibid.,* 40-41.
39. *Ibid.,* 43.
40. QC, 289.
41. RP, 47.
42. RP, 43.
43. TV, 62. Copernicus too was a "menace" but not, apparently, like Galileo.
44. "Letter to the Grand Duchess Christina," in *Discoveries and Opinions of Galileo,* Traslated by Stillman Drake, New York, 1957, 181-83.
45. RP, xxx-xxxii.
46. *Ibid.,* 51.
47. QC, 237.
48. EN, 132.
49. QC, 128.
50. CF, 38-9.
51. CF, 31,38-9,79; QC 289.
52. *Ibid.,* 123.
53. QC, 198.
54. CF, 31.
55. QC, 228.
56. *Ibid.,* 289.
57. CF, 62-3.

II-3

1. QC, 94, 100.
2. *Ibid.,* 114-15, 163-165.
3. RP, xvii.
4. *Ibid*

5. Cf. "Pragmatic America," by John Dewey in *Character and Events,* edited by J. Rather, New York, 1970, v. 2, 542-560. Also, R.B. Perry, The *Thought and Character of William James,* Cambridge, Massachusetts, 1948, 303, 311-312.
6. RP, 24.
7. QC, 114.
8. RP, 130
9. *Ibid.,* xxiv - xxv On Dewey's idea of outlawing war, cf. J. Rather, *op. cit.,* 551-703.
10. QC, 177.
11. "Of course I have repeated *an nauseam* that there are existences prior to and subsequent to cognitive states and purposes, and that the whole meaning of the latter is the way they intervene in the control and revalutation of the independent existences:" Letter of Dewey to W. James, in R.B. Perry, *op. cit.,* 311.
12. EN, 85-6, 296.
13. *Ibid.,* 156.
14. *Ibid.,* 67-9.
15. *Ibid.,* 182-83; RP, 90, TV, 54.
16. QC, 179, 189.
17. For the five steps in reflective inquiry, namely, (1) problem; (²) analytic clarification; (3) hypothetic solutions; (4) deductive elaboration of hypothetic solutions; (5) verification or disconfirmation, cf. *Guide to the Works of John Dewey,* edited by J.A. Boydston, Carbondale, Illinois, 1970, 34-5.
18. QC, 178.
19. EN, 182-83.
20. EN, 348, 350 and 409 where Dewey quotes James' description of the world at this preproblematic stage as a "buzzin' bloomin' confusion' and on the other hand, J. A. Boydston, *op. cit.,* 45, where says each thing has its own obdurate quality.
21. EN, 114.
22. J.A. Boydston, *op. cit.,* 42.
23. EN, 111, 276.
24. *The influence of Darwin on Philosophy and Other Essays in Contemporary Thought,* New York, 1910, 230.
25. EN, 338.
26. *Ibid.,* 396.
27. *Ibid*
28. For the contrast between the fixed ends in nature of classical metaphysics and Dewey's scientist end-in-view, cf. EN, 101, 104, 351-52.
29. QC, 236.
30. EN, 46.
31. *Ibid.,* 41.
32. CF, 55-6.
33. EN, 71.

34. QC, 130.
35. QC, 180.
36. *Ibid.,* 106.
37. EN, 185-86.
38. Cf. R. B. Perry, *op. cit.,* 302 for a "Pythagorean Table of Opposites" which is a way of summing up the pragmatic philosophical viewpont.

II-4

1. QC, 287.
2. *Ibid.,* 290.
3. TV, 58.
4. EN, 403.
5. Ibid., 8.
6. *Ibid.,* 9.
7. *Ibid.,* 16-17.
8. *Ibid.,* 24.
9. *Ibid.,* 25.
10. *Ibid.,* 27.
11. *Ibid.,* 29.
12. *Ibid.,* 30.
13. *Ibid.,* 36.
14. *Ibid.,* 396.
15. *Ibid.,* 101, 106.
16. TV, 45-9.
17. EN, 112.
18. TV, 46.
19. *Ibid.*
20. *Ibid.,* 18.
21. *Ibid.,* 33-4.
22. *Ibid.*
23. *Ibid.,* 32.
24. *Ibid.,* 31.
25. *Ibid.,* 32.
26. *Ibid.,* 30.
27. TV, 32.
28. QC, 268.
29. QC, 266.
30. TV, 37-8.
31. *Ibid.*
32. *Ibid.,* 19.
33. *Ibid.,* 40-1.
34. *Ibid.,* 24.
35. *Ibid.,* 43.
36. EN, 435.
37. *Ibid.,* 261.
38. *Ibid.,* 265.
39. *Ibid.,* 285.
40. *Ibid.,* 295.
41. CF, 41.
42. EN, 308.
43. TV, 23.
44. *Ibid.,* 49-50.
45. *Ibid.,* 26.
46. *Ibid.,* 25.

47. *Ibid.,* 27.
48. *Ibid.*
49. *Ibid.,* 29.
50. *Ibid.,* 53, 60.
51. EN, 278.
52. *Ibid.,* 282.
53. TV, 43.
54. *Ibid.*
55. *Ibid.,* 42.
56. EN, 63.
57. CF. 46.
58. This is not an idea peculiar to Dewey. One finds it understandably in materialistic philosophers who think man is all alone in the universe, and that he therefore wastes his time whenever he fancies another world and expends energy waiting for salvation from "beyond the eternal hills." Karl Marx's famous statement about the task of philosophy now being to *change* the world comes down to the same thing. Obviously, the methodologies for bettering the lot of man in Marx and Dewey differ.
59. CF, 78.
60. *Ibid.,* 8.
61. *Ibid.,* 50-1.
62. *Ibid.,* 42.
63. *Ibid.,* 43.
64. *Ibid.,* 39-48.
65. *Ibid.,* 84.
66. *Ibid.,* 48.
67. *Ibid.,* 34.
68. *Ibid.,* 73.
69. *Ibid.,* 72.
70. *Ibid.,* 74.
71. *Ibid.,* 46.
72. *Ibid.,* 47.
73. *Ibid.*
74. *Ibid.,* 50.
75. *Ibid.,* 81.
76. *Ibid.,* 50.
77. TV, 72.
78. CF, 79-80; EN, 32-3; 245.

II-5

1. TML, 70.
2. *Ibid.*
3. *Ibid.,* 71.
4. *Ibid.,* 32.
5. *Ibid.,* 72.
6. *Ibid.,* 16.
7. *Ibid.*
8. *Ibid.,* 72-3.
9. *Ibid.,* 75.
10. *Ibod.,* 18.

11. *Ibid.*
12. *Ibid.*, 77.
13. *Ibid.*, 12.
14. *Ibid.*, 4.
15. *Ibid.*, 5-6.
16. *Ibid.*, 6.
17. *Ibid.*, 6-7.
18. *Ibid.*, 7-8.
19. *Ibid.*, 7.
20. *Ibid.*, 25.
21. *Ibid.*, 26.
22. *Ibid.*
23. *Ibid.*, 37.
24. *Utilitarianism,* Indianapolis, 1957, 44-5.
25. TML, 38.
26. *Ibid.*, 80.
27. *Ibid.*, 79-80.
28. *Ibid.*, 32.
29. *Ibid.*, 37, on "goods of wisdom."
30. *Ibid.*, 62.
31. *Ibid.*
32. *Ibid.*, 38.
33. *Ibid.*, 42-3.
34. *Ibid.*, 39.
35. *The Rebel,* New York, 1956, 5.
36. *TML,* 41.
37. *Ibid.*, 46.
38. *Ibid.*
39. *Ibid.*, 48.
40. *Ibid.*, 48-9.
41. *Ibid.*, 49-50.
42. *Ibid.*, 51.
43. *Ibid.*, 60-1.
44. *Ibid.*, 50.
45. *Ibid.*, 53.
46. Utilitarianism, 18-19; TML, 57.
47. *Ibid.*, 57.
48. *Utilitarianism,* 14.
49. TML, 44.
50. *Ibid.*, 58.
51. *Ibid.*
52. *Ibid.*, 59.
53. *Ibid.*, 59.
54. *Ibid.*, 60.
55. *Ibid.*, 61.
56. *Ibid.*, 80.
57. *Ibid.*, 68.
58. *Ibid.*
59. *Ibid.*, 68.
60. *Ibid.*, 81.
61. *Ibid.*, 69-70.
62. *Ibid.*, 79.
63. *Ibid.*, 82.
64. *Ibid.*, 78.
65. *Ibid.*, 83.
66. *Ibid.*, 83-4.
67. *Ibid.*, 91.
68. *Ibid.*, 112.
69. *Ibid.*, 90.
70. *Ibid.*, 112.
71. *Ibid.*, 72.
72. *Ibid.*, 94.
73. *Ibid.*, 97-9.

74. *Ibid.*, 100.
75. *Ibid.*, 103.
76. *Ibid.*, 101.
77. *Ibid.*, 102, italics added.
78. *Ibid.*, 103.
79. *Ibid.*, 104.
80. *Ibid.*, 107.
81. *Ibid.*, 114.
82. *Ibid.*, 114-15.
83. *Ibid.*, 117.
84. *Ibid.*, 115.
85. St. Thomas, *S.T.,* I-II, q. 61, a. 2.
86. *Ibid.*, q. 65, articles, 2, 3, 4, 5.
87. *Nicomachean Ethics,* Bk. IX, ch, 8, 1169a, 18- 1169b,1.
88. *TML,* 121.
89. *Ibid.*, 122.
90. CPR, 157.
91. TML, 123. "To declare something *satisfactory* is to assert that it meets specifiable conditions. It is, in effect, a judgement that the thing "will do." It involves prediction; it contemplates a future in which the thing will continue to serve; it will do. It asserts a conse-quence the thing will actively institute; it will *do.* That it is satisfying is the content of a proposition of fact; that it is satisfactory is a judgement, an estimate, an appraisal. It denotes an attitude to be taken, that of striving to perpetuate and to make secure. QC, 260.

...expertness of taste is at once the result and the reward of constant exer-cise of thinking. Instead of there being no disputing about taste, they are the one thing worth disputing about, if by 'dispute' is signified discussion involving reflective inquiry. QC, 262.
92. TML, 126.
93. *Ibid.*
94. *Ibid.*, 128-29.
95. *Ibid.*, 130.
96. *Ibid.*
97. *Ibid.*, 133.
98. *Ibid.*, 134.
99. *Ibid.*, 135.
100. *Ibid.*, 141.
101. *Ibid.* "A moral law, like a law in physics, is not something to swear by and stick to at all hazards; it is a formula of the way to respond when specified conditions present themselves. Its soundness and pertinence are tested by what happens when it is acted upon. Its claim or authority rests finally upon the imperativeness of the situation that has to be dealt with, not upon its own intrinsic nature --- as any tool achieves dignity in the measure of needs served by it. QC, 278.
102. TML, 145.

103. "Where will regulation come from if we surrender familiar and traditionally prized values as our directive standards? Very largely from the findings of the natural sciences. QC, 273.

"For moralists usually draw a sharp line between the field of the natural sciences and the conduct that is regarded as moral. But a moral that frames its judgements of value on the basis of consequences must depend in a most intimate manner upon the conclusions of science." QC, 274.

104. TML, 145.
105. *Ibid.,* 149.
106. *Ibid.,* 150-51.
107. *Ibid.,* 150.
108. *Ibid.,* 148, parenthesis added.
109. *Ibid.*
110. *Ibid.,* 152.
111. *Ibid.,* 156.
112. *Ibid.,* 154.
113. *Ibid.,* 158.
114. *Ibid.,* 160-61.
115. *Ibid.,* 163.
116. *Ibid.,* 164.
117. RP, 194.
118. TML, 165.
119. *Ibid.,* 165.
120. *Ibid.,* 166, parenthesis added.
121. *Ibid.,* 167.
122. *Ibid.,* 168.
123. *Ibid.,* 170-71.
124. RP, 175.
125. TML, 172.
126. RP, 196.
127. TML, 172.
128. *Ibid.,* 174.
129. RP, 176.
130. *Ibid.,* 211.
131. QC, 275-76.
132. TML, 175-76, italics added.

Conclusion

1. See *Guide to the Works of John Dewey,* edited by Jo Ann Boydston, Carbondale, Illinois, 1970, 2; also, *The Early Works,* Jo Ann Boydston, general editor, Carbondale, 1969, v. 3,180-84, on "The Critical Philosophy of Immanuel Kant."
2. *Ibid.,* v. 1, 34-47.
3. *Ibid.,* 47.
4. FPMM, 40.
5. RP, 58-61.
6. See H. W. Schneider, "Dewey's Psychology." *Guide to the Works,* 1.
7. RP, 95-6.
8. EN, 10-11.
9. CF, 79.
10. RP, 87-99.
11. *Ibid.,* 99.
12. H. J. Paton. TCI, 148.
13. *Ibid.,* 172.
14. CF, 84.
15. *Religion Within the Limits of Reason Alone,* Bks. III & IV.
16. CF, 11.
17. *Ibid.,* 17-18.
18. *Ibid.,* 47.
19. *Ibid.,* 33.
20. *Ibid.,* 79.
21. F. Nietzsche, *The Gay Science,* translated by W. Kaufmann, New York, 1974, 205-06.
22. TML, iii.
23. FPMM, 21.
24. *Ibid.,* 24.
25. Passim in Dewey's writings.
26. Consider, for instance, the British scientist James Lovelock's "Gaia hypothesis" named after the earth goddess of the ancient Greeks. Conventional wisdom holds that the earth's environment conditions life, determining which species thrive and which die out. Lovelock stands this notion on its head: living things, he suggests, to a great extent control the environment in such a way as to ensure their survival; "the biosphere (all forms on life) was able to control at least the temperature of the earth's surface and the composition of the atmosphere;" hence "living matter, the air, the oceans, the land are parts of a gigantic system 'Gaia', which seems to exhibit the behavior of a single organism, even a living creature. From *Newsweek,* March 10, 1975, 49.
27. See next note.
28. "Logical Positivism, A Debate Between Copleston and Ayer," *A Modern Introduction to Philosophy,* edited by Paul Edwards and Arthur Pap, New York, 1965, 732.
29. *Ibid.,* 743.
30. *Ibid.,* 744.
31. *Ibid.,* 745.
32. B. Llamzon, *The Self Beyond,* Chicago, 1973.
33. See *The Existence of God,* edited by J. Hick, New York, 1964, 114-120.
34. *Chicago Sun-Times,* April 11, 1976, Section 2, 2.
35. *Ibid.*
36. *The Metaphysical Elements of Justice,* translated by J. Ladd, Indianapolis, 1965, 102.
37. Chicago 1974.
38. *The Gulag Archipelago,* London 1974, 591-592.

Index

Abbott, T.K., 17, 233
Abhorrence, inward, 67
Abilities,
    development, 75
Abortion, 78
Absolutism,
    moral, 205, 224
Abstraction, 8
Achievement, 175-76
Achtung, 235
Action, 134, 152, 234
Act, itself, 222, 227
Activity, 148
    intellectual, 60
    subhuman, 60
Admiration, 81
Adultery, 23-4
Affiliation religious, 156
Ages, Middle, 117
Alpha, 103
Altruism, 198, 199, 201
Amelioration, 153
Amputation, 83
Analysis, 124
Anatemka, 170, 171
Animism, 115
Antinomies, 161
Apodosis, 53
Appearances, 11, 13
Appraisal, 153, 190, 239
Approbation, 201, 304
Aquinas, 188, 227
Arabs, 69, 70
Archetypes, 116
Argument, 16
Aristocrats, 111, 113
Aristotle, 3, 8, 12, 19, 38, 56, 113, 114, 117, 188, 189, 192, 204
Arithmetic, 10
Arrogance, 79
Assessment, 146
Athos, Mt., 133
Attitude, religious, 156, 212
Augustine, St., 89
Author, nature, 90, 97, 215

Authority, 111
Awareness,
    reflective, 217
Ayer, A.J., 218-20, 240

Bacon, F., 120, 121, 237
Bad, 226
    Dewey in, 139, 147, 159, 203
Ball, 2, 5
Battering, 223-25
Beans, 78
Beauty, 192
Beck, L.W., 1, 17, 232, 233, 234
Becoming, 118-19
Being, 193, 197
    antecedent, 151, 217
    changeable, 172, 221
    ideal, 157, 159
    immutable, 151
    perfect, 151, 156
    postproblematic, 218, 220
    preproblematic, 218, 220
Belief, 90, 113, 142
Benevolence, 200
Bentham, J., 164, 184, 185
Bias, classical, 120
Blackmail, 64
Blessings, 135
Boydston, J.A., 237, 246
Brando, M., 134
Broad, C.D., 234
Brothers, 211
Burbank, L., 207

Camus, A., 174
Catechism, 168
Categories, 12, 13, 15, 16, 44, 117
Cause,
    absolute, 43
    succession, 5-6
Causality, 16
    efficient, 36, 267
    final, 206-07
    formal, 67, 206-07
Certainty, 124
Certitude, 117

Change, 113, 118-19, 143, 152, 171, 191
Character, 166, 185, 234
Chardin, P.T., 221
Charity, 108, 188, 201
Charles V, 95
Cheating, 58
Choice,
  self, 196-97, 199
Christ, 25
Christianity, 211
Claim, 107, 179, 209-10
  relationship, 179-82, 204
Class, 123
  privileged, 112
Clergymen, 159, 212
Codes, 180
Coercion, 80-2
Collins, J., 232, 233, 237
Command, 20, 22, 51, 54
  divine, 98
  moral, 22, 33, 35, 37
Commandments, 167
Commendation, 184
Community, 211
Compulsion,
  self, 89
Conceit, 79, 82
Concepts, 7, 13, 15, 25, 113, 208
  use, 209
Condemnation, self, 51, 92
Conduct, 166
  ignoble, 174
  moral, 195
  noble, 174
Conflict, moral, 171, 191
Conformity, 214
Connection, 173
Conscience, 189, 191, 234
Conscientiousness, 188, 192
Consiousness, 44
  rational, 44, 113
Consequences, 24, 138, 154, 155, 164, 167, 184, 197, 214, 218, 227
  infinite, 223
Conservatism, 191
Constraint, 45-52, 233
Consummation, 155
Contemplation, 105, 132

Contempt, self, 67
Contentment, self, 54, 92, 95
Contradiction,
  internal, 73
  will, 73
Control,
  technical, 124, 132, 138
  self, 188, 192
Controversies,
  de facto, 70
  de jure, 70
Conventionality, 203
Conversion, 160
Copernicus, 122, 127, 237
Copleston, F., 218-20, 240
Courage, 188-89
Creativity, 214
Creed, Dewey's, 212
Crisis, 227
Critique, Second, 79, 91, 98
Crusius, C., 2
Cults, 154
Custom, 102, 113

Darwin, C., 127
Dealer, 24
Death, 128, 135
Debate, moral, 190
Decision, wholistic, 224-26
Dedication, 140, 157
Deduction, 124
Deliberation, moral, 172, 193
Demand, 179
Demons, 156
Dependence, interpersonal, 79
Descartes, R., 3, 12, 15, 99, 120, 143, 166, 190
Desire, 49-50, 55, 148, 149, 154, 169, 174, 178
  natural, 233
Desirability, 149, 150, 169
Destiny, natural, 233
Determination,
  self, 75
Determinism, 39
Dialectic, natural, 25
Dignity, 34, 35, 37, 95
Discipline,
  self, 68, 176
Discovery, 124, 128, 132

Disinterestedness, 175, 199
Displeasure, 57
Dissatisfaction, 178
Dixitism, ipse, 191
Doer, 111-12
Dogmatism, 218
Doing, 112
Duration, endless, 98
Duty, 21, 25, 27, 43, 48, 55, 57, 62, 64, 67, 70, 168
  conflict, 167, 171, 210
  exclamation, 171, 210
  idea, 154
  imperfect, 29, 73, 209-10, 235
  Law, 67
  perfect, 29, 73, 209-10, 235

Earth, 216
Ecumenism, 161
Ego, transcendental, 13
Elan, 119
Elite, 111, 123
Elitism, 210
Ellington, J., 17
Emotion, religious, 235
Emphasis, selective, 143, 145
Empiricist, 2, 9, 121
End,
  absolute, 77, 151
  comprehensive, 151
  consummatory, 139, 148, 155
  desirable, 146
  experimental, 137, 146
  fixed, 151, 237
  higher, 155
  ideal, 159, 212
  justified by means, 155
  life, of, 91, 105
  man, of, 32, 68, 91
  nature, of, 83
  natural, 32, 68
  social, 194
End-in-himself, 31, 36, 76-8, 81, 86, 92
End-in-itself, 34, 75, 76, 155, 227
  classic, 147, 148.
End-in-view, 146, 151, 154, 155, 224
Enjoyment, 63, 150, 177
Enlightenment, 236

Environment, homogeneous, 132, 134
Epicureans, 48, 175, 178
Equator, 10
Equity, 187-89, 199
Essence, 221
Esteem, 79, 190
Estimation, 190
Eternity, 90
Ethics,
  deontological, 178, 182
  teleological, 178, 182
Euthanasia, 78
Evaluation, 153
Evil, 47-8, 49, 52, 105, 137, 150, 158-59, 216, 223
  physical, 226
  moral, 163, 226
Exaction, 179
Existence, 221
Execution, 225
Experience, 11, 15, 31, 45, 56, 58-9, 143-45, 208
  funded, 107, 137, 142, 160, 191, 214
  method, 208
  mystical, 158
Experimentation, rehearsal, 108, 193

Fact, 53
Factors, moral, 225
Faith, common, 158
Fame, 60
Fear, 37
Feeling, 38, 50, 81, 133, 134, 160
  respect, 79
  sensitive, 191
Finality, 217
Fire, crematory, 174
Folly, 178
Fool, 177
Force, 51
Ford, G., 33
Forms, 121
  Aristotelian, 8, 114-15
  Platonic, 8, 114-15, 131
Francis I, 95
Freedom, 18, 39, 42, 44, 87, 92, 214

vertical, 72
horizontal, 72
Freud, S., 127, 149, 216, 230
Friendship, 69
Fulfillment, self, 201

Gaia, 240
Galileo, G., 2, 120, 122, 127, 237
Gallows, 47
Generality, 31
Generosity, 85
Genetics, 78
Geometry, 10
Germans, 136, 208, 209, 224
Goal,
   natural, 234
   shared, 107
   ultimate, 75
God, 26, 44, 66, 92, 218, 222, 227
   Aristotle, in, 116
   Author, world, nature, 90, 97
   cause, 117
   Dewey, in, 157
   Ens Realissimum, 16
   existence, of, 91, 94
   Form, 116
   Geometer, 123
   will, of, 38, 98
Good, 47-8, 49, 52, 105, 158-59, 223, 226
   absolute, 20, 78, 89
   apparent, 172
   common, 194
   compensatory, 139
   comprehensive, 139, 176
   conflict, 107
   consummated, 96
   Dewey, in, 137, 147, 150, 158, 163, 203, 216
   enduring, 139, 176, 200
   highest, 91-9
   in-itself, 31, 55, 60-1, 76
   perfect, 96, 236
   real, 169, 172
   shareable, 106, 188, 200
   social, 178
   specious, 169
   supreme, 94, 96
   unconditional, 35
Gouinlock, J., 126

Gratification, postponement, 149
Greece, 112, 113, 114, 117
Greene, T.M., 17
Grenzbegriffe, 7
Growth, 137, 139, 149, 161, 172, 190, 203, 204, 205

Habit, 102, 135, 148, 191
Happiness, 19, 28, 36, 38, 55-8, 63, 173-74, 201, 215
   harmonized, 91-6, 186, 216
   law, and, 91-2
   morals, 91-2
   obligation, 95
   social, 186
Having, 193, 197
Heart, 49
Heavens, 98
Hedonism, 38, 173-74
Hegel, G., 69, 86
Heracliteanism, 31, 205
Hero-worship, 26
Heteronomy, 18, 37-8, 40, 43, 63-4, 84
Hick, J., 240
Holocaust, atomic, 142
Hopkins, G.M., 12
Hudson, H.H., 17
Humanity, advancement, 83
Hume, D., 2, 5, 6, 8, 11, 19, 52, 99, 184
Hunting, 10, 11
Hussein, 70
Husserl, E., 130
Hylomorphism, 12
Hypothesis, 124

"I", 15
Idea
   innate, 9
   Platonic, 119
   Protestant, 122
   Reason, 15
   Roman, 122
Ideals, 215
   aesthetic, 176, 192
   being, 153, 160, 195
   common, 162
   democratic, 158, 211
   self, 198

Idealism, melioristic, 149, 193
Imagination, 13, 153, 157
Immorality, 30, 88
  Dewey, in, 139, 147, 159, 203
  Kant, in, 23, 25, 87, 235
Immortality, 88, 215
Impact, 8
Impartiality, 187-89
Imperative, 68
  categorical, 22-4, 27-8, 31-2, 35, 42, 51, 58, 63, 67, 87
  first, 29, 71-2
  second, 29, 71-2
  third, 31-2, 71-2, 75
  fourth, 34, 71-2
  Dewey, in, 203
  Hypothetical, 27, 29, 31, 54, 58, 63
  moral, 31
  number of, 54, 58, 68, 71, 235
Impression, 8
Incentive, 79, 98
Inclination, 22, 25, 31, 34, 37, 41-2, 44-5, 48-9, 53, 95
  mob, 68, 88
  natural, 32
  pathological, 28, 42, 62, 66, 88
  reason, and, 50, 92
Individual, 100
  socialized, 142, 150, 170-71, 200
Individualism, 122
Individualistic, 56
Infield, L., 17
Injustice, 85
Inquiry, 124, 128, 132, 172, 237
Insensitivity, 206
Institution, 200
Instrumentalism, 128-29, 138
Integration, 143
Intellectual, 112
Intelligence, 59, 154, 156, 159, 192, 207, 209
  passionate, 160, 208
Intentionality, 8
Interest, 43, 132, 134, 154, 192
  individual, 41, 185
  moral, 85-6, 187, 199, 200
Intuition, 9, 10, 13, 15, 35, 191, 193

Intuitionism,
  Kant, in, 234
Israelis, 69, 70

James, W., 49, 72, 121, 143, 218, 224, 237
Judaea, 112
Judgement, 12, 13
  fact, 190
  twofold, 183
  value, 142, 190, 195
Judgement, Critique of, 236
Justice, 60, 189

Kalokagathia, 192
Kant, turning point, 206
Kennedy, J.F., 136
Kepler, J., 120
Kierkegaard, S., 72, 100
Kingdom, of ends, 34-6, 71, 76, 86-8
Knowledge, 112
  consequential, 146
  constitutive, 7, 14-5, 18, 40
  consummatory, 124
  democratized, 122, 161
  experimental, 123
  Greek, 119
  higher, 109, 113, 118, 122, 127, 210
  interested, 130-31
  lower, 109, 122, 127, 210
  new, 123
  open, 161
  power, 120
  regulative, 7, 14-5, 45
  romanticized, 109

Laboratory, 137
Ladd, J., 17, 240
Language, 138
Law, 23, 180, 185
  autonomous, 84
  duty, 67
  happiness, 91-2
  moral, 43, 76-7, 79, 87, 89, 239
  particular, 180
  system, 33
Laziness, 29, 32, 74, 83, 206
Leadership, scientific, 102

Legalism, 193
Legislation, 40
Leibniz, W., 3
Lepers, 174
Liddel, B.E.A., 37, 233-34-35-36
Life,
  good, 55, 59, 68, 171
  simple, 175
Lilienthal, A., 70
Locke, J., 176
Logic, 12-3, 15, 45, 121
Lovelock, J., 340
Luther, M., 224
Lying, 73, 83

Map, 145, 209
Man,
  autonomous, 78
  bad, in Dewey, 203
  common, 213
  definition, 44
  end-in-himself, 31, 76-7, 86
  good, in Dewey, 203
  good-in-himself, 76, 78, 84
  self-made, 29
Manipulation, 32, 82, 105, 127,
132
Marcel, G., 47
Marcos, F., 59
Marx, K., 115, 196, 238
Materialism, 176
Mathematics, 9
Matter, 8, 12, 114, 132, 152
  mind, 132, 152
Maturity, 149, 150
Maxims, 71
McDermott, J.J., 125
Meaning,
  Dewey, in, 131, 220
  prospective, 138
  retrospective, 138
Means, 77-8, 147, 150
  -ends, 54-5, 59, 60, 63, 76, 150,
155, 153-54, 197
  only-, 76, 78
Meliorism, 128-29, 137, 154
Member, 87
Memory, 110
Mental, 152
Metaphysics, 14, 113, 117

Aristotelian, 114
Method,
  Cartesian, 120
  empirical, 144, 145
  expansive, 4
  explicative, 4
  inductive, 121
  meliorating, 146
  new, 123
  progressive, 3, 4
  regressive, 4
  verifiable, 155
  wrong, 202
Mexico, 173-74
Might, 179
Mill, J.S., 5, 38, 169, 173, 176-77,
184-85, 197
Mind,
  cultivated, 176-77
  matter, 153, 207, 153
Moore, G.E., 234
Morality, 34, 55, 57, 61-2, 65
  absolute, 192
  conformistic, 193-94
  conventional, 183, 186
  customary, 167, 183, 187, 191-
93, 204
  de facto, 185
  de jure, 185
  English theories, 184
  incomprehensible, 43
  norm, 26
  reflective, 168, 198, 202
Motion, 118
Motivation, 64-6, 70
Motive, 64, 227, 234
  Dewey, in, 165, 198
Muller, F.M., 17
Mutilation, 83
Mystical, experience, 158
Myth, 125

Natural, 177
Nature, 15, 18, 29, 36, 39, 41-2, 44,
48, 72, 75-6
  before thought, 132, 133
  fixed, 151
  homogeneous, 138, 154, 216
  human, 205
  ineffable, 130

power, 124
Revelation, 123
rule-determined, 11
stepmotherly, 21, 61
Necessity, 52-3
absolute, 19
Newman, J.H., 70
Newton, I., 2, 3, 4
Nietzsche, F., 213, 240
Nixon, R., 33, 230
Nobility, 189
Norm,
Dewey, in, 186, 191
Nuomena, 6, 7, 15, 19, 36, 40, 41-2, 44, 52, 55, 59

Objects, 84
metaphysical, 117
Obligation, 49, 180, 233
universal, 19
Observer, cool, 24, 214
Omega, 103
Omen, 111
Opposites, table of, 238
Optimism, 160
Option,
momentous, 72
immoral, 82
Organism,
nature, 132, 153, 168
Ought, 46, 51
is, 19, 21, 58-9, 69, 142, 150, 160, 162, 194, 207
can, 90

Pain, 38, 50, 62, 139, 172-74, 185
Parmenideanism, 305
Pascal, B., 49
Passion, 47, 88, 160
Paton, H.J., 1, 2, 210, 232, 233, 234, 235, 236
Paul VI, 196
Pedagogy, moral, 65-6
Percept, 7
Perception, 10, 13, 25, 40
Perfection,
human, 38
idea, 26
Permanence, 143
Perry, R.B., 237-38

Person, 76
authority, 181
end-in-himself, 76, 81
Phenomena, 6, 7, '10, 16, 18, 40, 44, 52
Philippines, 59, 171
Philosophy, 221
aristocratic, 213
Christian, 117
classic, 129
critical, 7, 214
democratic, 213
naive, 7
new, 129
participator, 139
spectator, 132, 136, 138, 139, 206, 221, 224
Physical, 152
Physics, Newtonian, 2, 3, 4
Pietist, 1, 211
Pighouse, 151
Plato, 8, 51, 114, 116, 118, 119, 188
Pleasure, 38, 48, 57, 62-3, 173-75, 185, 189
higher, 176-77, 185
lower, 176-77, 185
Poetizing, 111
Pollution, 103
Popularity, 60
Positivism, 219
Postulate,
first, 87
second, 89
third, 91
Potency, 114
Potentiality,
pure, 118
Poverty, 174
Prayers, 56, 160, 173
Pretension, professorial, 213
Price, 34, 80, 84, 92, 95
Principle,
moral, 193-94-95
Prizing, 149, 150, 153, 190
Problem, 131-32, 134, 152, 166
Profane, 160
Progress, infinite, 90, 122, 127, 172

Prognostication, 111
Promise, 24, 29, 32
Prosperity, 83
Proposition,
  Analytic a priori, 4
  meaningful, 219-20
  metaphysical, 219-20
  synthetic a posteriori, 4
  synthetic a priori, 4, 13, 41, 45,
  52-3, 72
Protasis, 53
Protestantism, 1
Proverbs, 149
Prudence, 57-8, 82, 178, 204
Purpose, rational, 148, 234

Quality, 127, 144, 152, 161, 174,
177, 184, 187, 190, 193, 198, 202
Quantity, 127-28, 161, 184, 187,
193
Question, 130, 166
Quintessence, 127

Rand, A., 29
Ratio,
  cognoscendi, 87
  essendi, 87
Rationalism, 2, 9, 148
Rationalists, 121, 143
Rationality, 26, 42
Ratner, J., 237
Rawls, J., 85
Realism,
  transcendental, 7
Reality,
  changeable, 172, 221
  classic, 109, 116, 137, 139, 142
  'first class", 151
  metaphysical, 216, 217, 218
  objective, 45
  "second class", 151
Realization, 144
Reason, 14-16, 40, 43, 44-5, 48-51,
53, 106, 134, 143, 178
  autonomy, 26
  circular, 37
  fictitious, 164, 16
  higher, 132
  inclination, 92
  living, 108

lower, 132
pure, 34, 69, 76, 166, 207-08
relativization, 26
seduced, 25, 82
self-legislating, 33, 67
self-transparent, 34, 86
speculative, 97
Reasonableness, 173
Rebel, The, 239
Reconstruction, 102, 105, 107
Reduction, 124
Reductionism, 216, 221
Reflection,
  self, 161, 172, 177, 217
  philosophical, 135, 144, 146,
  166, 172
Reflexes, 133
Relationship,
  claims, 179, 182
  social, 100, 150
Relativism,
  moral (Dewey), 195, 205
Relief, 134
Religion, Kant, 93, 98, 236
Religious, 108, 156, 160, 212
Religiousness, 157, 159, 211-13
Remission, 90
Repeatability,
  public, 132
Republic, 51
Respect, 22, 33, 35, 37, 67, 79, 82,
92
Responsibility, 168, 180, 201-02
Rest, 119
Restoration, 103-04
Reverence, 235
Revelation, 31, 66
  nature, 123
Revolution,
  American, 236
  Copernican, I, 9, 120, 131, 141
  Dewey's, 129, 131, 141
  French, 236
  Kant's, 131, 144
  scientific, 129
  start, of, 191
Riches, 60, 174
Right, 83, 167-68, 178-79, 181,
194, 204

inviolable, 84
norm *(Dewey)*, 181-82
Righteousness, 92
Rome, 112
Ross, D.W., 99, 236
Rousseau, J.-J., 725, 233
Routine, 135, 171
Rule,
   golden, 32, 84
   moral, 193-94
Russell, B., 223

Sacredness, 85
Saints, 202
Santayana, G., 212
Satisfaction, 215-16, 239
   casual, 146-47
   higher, 177, 185
   immediate, 146, 178
   lower, 177, 185
   reflective, 146
   stable, 134
   value, 150
Schemata, 13
Schneider, H.W., 240
Science, 124
   advent, 119, 125
   applied, 129
   intervening, 212
   new, 109, 142
   not destructive, 129
   supervening, 212
Secular, 160
Seduction, 25, 82
Seer, 111
Self,
   another, 40
   dear, 24, 38, 66, 72
   Dewey, in, 195, 199, 201-03
   fulfillment, 201
   ideal, 197-98
   Kant, in, 42, 197
   love, 74
   moral, 195-96
   real, 42
Selfhood, 200
Selfishness, 22, 43, 64, 106, 198, 200, 210
Sense, common, 80
Shaftesbury, A., 184

Shock, 131, 134, 167, 208, 210
Shoplifting, 23-4
Silber, J.R., 17, 235
Sincerity, 69
Singer, M., 235
Sinner, 48, 202
Situation, problematic, 107
Slumber, dogmatic, 18
Socialization, 216
Smith, A., 184
Socrates, 25, 113-14, 177
Solution, 135, 138, 148
Solzhenitsyn, A., 223, 230
Sophists, 113
Soul, immortality, 15
Sovereign, 33-4-5, 37, 87
Space, 9, 11
Spencer, H., 198
Spectator, impartial, 178, 185-86, 192, 218
Spinoza, B., 3, 99, 143, 218
Spirit, scientific, 128
Spiritual, 160
Standard,
   de facto, 184-86
   de jure, 184-86
   idea, 184-86
   moral, 184-86
Stealing, 73
Stone, tablets, 176
Story-telling, 110-11
Subject, 87
Sublimity, 37, 79
Success, 177
Suicide, 29, 32, 55, 73-4, 83, 206
Superior, moral, 80
Supernatural, 161-62
Superstition, 125
Swedenborg, E., 6
Symbolization, 110-11
Sympathy, 188, 192, 200

Taste, 239
Taxes, 135
Tears, 56, 173
Technique,
   new, 122
   steps, 124
Teleology, 75, 116, 206-07
Tendency, natural, 75-6, 83-4, 148

Teresa, M., 174, 196, 218
Theist, 227
Theologians, 158
Theories, moral, 38, 167
Things-in-themselves, 11, 15-6
Thought, 130, 132, 134, 152, 171
  anticipatory, 139
  classic, 156
  Deweyite, 130, 137, 139
  impartial, 169
  moral, 166
  nature, 138
  participatory, 139
  philosophical, 139
  pure, 133
  reflective, 146-47, 174, 190
  scientific, 146, 221
Time, 9, 11
Tools, 138, 151
Tradition, 111-12, 123, 142, 170-71, 183, 191, 204
  traditionalist, 113
  orthodox, 117
Transformism, 221
Tribes, Germanic, 136
Typic, 84, 164

Uncertainty,
Understanding, 11, 13, 42, 44, 56
Unity, 154
Universality, 31, 53
Universalizability, 23, 30, 72, 76, 81, 84, 99, 222
  consequences, 72-3, 165
  de jure, 23
  internal, 30
  non-contradiction, 30, 72
  will, 30
Utilitarianism, 22, 24, 169, 184-85, 192, 197

Value,
  casual, 169
  familiar, 240
  ideal, 176, 178
  intrinsic, 235
  list, 34-5
  material, 178
  reflective, 169
  religious, 159
  sacred, 35, 85
  satisfaction, 150
  social, 113

traditional, 240
  ultimate, 103
Verification, public, 125, 161
Vice, 62, 168
  social, 183
View,
  old-world, 135, 137-38
  spectator, 218
Virtue, 62, 81, 88-9, 93-6, 168, 183, 186-87-88-89, 201, 236

Ward, K., 232
Weiss, P., 235
Whitehead, A. N., III
Will,
  absolute, 78
  aspects (two), 33, 36
  autonomous, 37-8, 40, 63, 67, 75, 88
  bad, 41-2
  God, of, 38
  good, 31, 41-2, 61, 78
  holy, 28, 37, 40, 88-9, 98, 236
  legislating, 32, 41
  moral, 20, 30, 37, 43, 62
  natural, 74-5
  omnipotent, 98
  perfect, 98
  physical, 30
  self-determining, 77
  subject, 33-4
  unconditional, 33, 35
  unqualified,
  virtuous, 37
Wille, 42, 63
Williams, T.C., 232, 234
Willküre, 42, 68, 84, 214
Wolff, R.P., 29, 75, 232-33, 235
World, 16, 39, 42
  classical, 112, 115
  data, 130, 132, 134
  familiar, 135
  fixed, 109
  ideal, 156
  invisible, 6
  mixed, 135
  separate, 115
  visible, 6
Worth, 35, 37, 51
  absolute, 35, 37, 76-7, 84
  relative, 35
Worthiness, 20-1, 92-3, 215
Wrong, 167, 181-82, 194, 199

ISBN: 0-8191-0534-1